GLOBAL PERSPECTIVES ON DESISTANCE

In recent years attention has switched from how adolescents are attracted into crime, to how adults reduce their offending and then stop – the process of desistance. There are now around a dozen major longitudinal and in-depth studies around the world, which have followed or are following offenders over their life course, charting their offending history and their social and economic circumstances.

The book is the first to offer a global perspective on desistance and brings together international leading experts in the field from countries including the UK, the Netherlands, Scandinavia, Spain, the US and Australia to set out what we know about desistance and to advance our theoretical understanding. Drawing on leading studies, this book sets the academic agenda for future work on desistance and examines the implications and potential positive effects of this research on desistance processes among current offenders.

Global Perspectives on Desistance is divided into three sections:

- Agency, structure and desistance from crime.
- Life phases and desistance.
- Criminal justice and state interventions.

Comprehensive and forward-thinking, this book is ideal for students studying criminology, probation and social work, social policy, sociology and psychology. It is also essential reading for academic criminologists, sociologists and policymakers and practitioners working in corrections and reform.

Joanna Shapland is the Edward Bramley Professor of Criminal Justice at the University of Sheffield and Director of the Centre for Criminological Research. She was awarded the Outstanding Achievement Award by the British Society of Criminology in 2013 and is Executive Editor of the *International Review of Victimology*.

Stephen Farrall is Professor of Criminology in the Centre for Criminological Research at the University of Sheffield. Stephen also edits the International Series on Desistance and Rehabilitation (published by Routledge).

Anthony Bottoms is Emeritus Wolfson Professor of Criminology at the University of Cambridge and also a Fellow of Desistance Study the University of Sheffield. He is pland, he co-directs the Sheffield

The study of desistance from crime has truly come of age with this impressive, international collection of some of the best research on the topic to date. Far from being the last word on desistance, the volume raises crucial, new questions for the next generation of studies in this fast-growing area.

Shadd Maruna, *Dean of the School of Criminal Justice,*
Rutgers University – Newark, USA

Over the last 25 years, research on desistance from crime has burst on the criminological scene. Unfortunately, much of that research has focused solely on the US. This volume adds a much needed global perspective to the ongoing discussion. Drawing on empirical research from a wide range of countries, our knowledge of desistance from crime is expanded and enhanced. The section on criminal justice and state interventions in particular adds an important dimension to the desistance debate. While contentious issues remain unresolved, this book is a must read for researchers and policymakers interested in what it takes to move offenders away from crime.

John H. Laub, *Distinguished University Professor,*
University of Maryland, USA

This volume offers an impressive array of divergent perspectives on the process of desistance from crime, and successfully integrates these diverse outlooks into a coherent story. Drawing on an assortment of varied research methodologies and cultural settings, the authors take stock of the state of knowledge on desistance and provide a useful roadmap for future desistance research.

Lila Kazemian, *Associate Professor, John Jay*
College of Criminal Justice, CUNY, USA

In this very rich and truly international collection, classical desistance discussions are updated and extended both theoretically, and in terms of research subjects. Importantly, this exciting edited book reveals how desistance theory now appears ready to start developing alternative treatment methods, and to move beyond a mere desistance paradigm. This integrated volume reveals how mature desistance research has become.

Martine Herzog-Evans, *University of Rheims, France*

GLOBAL PERSPECTIVES ON DESISTANCE

Reviewing what we know and looking to the future

Edited by Joanna Shapland, Stephen Farrall and Anthony Bottoms

LONDON AND NEW YORK

First published 2016
by Routledge
2 Park Square, Milton Park, Abingdon, Oxon OX14 4RN

and by Routledge
711 Third Avenue, New York, NY 10017

Routledge is an imprint of the Taylor & Francis Group, an informa business

British Library Cataloguing-in-Publication Data
A catalogue record for this book is available from the British Library

Library of Congress Cataloging-in-Publication Data
Names: Shapland, Joanna, 1950- editor. | Farrall, Stephen, editor. | Bottoms, A. E., editor.
Title: Global perspectives on desistance : reviewing what we know and looking to the future / edited by Joanna Shapland, Stephen Farrall and Anthony Bottoms.
Description: Abingdon, Oxon ; New York, NY : Routledge, 2016. | Includes bibliographical references and index.
Identifiers: LCCN 2015041198 | ISBN 9781138850996 (hardback) | ISBN 9781138851009 (pbk.) | ISBN 9781315724423 (ebook)
Subjects: LCSH: Juvenile Delinquency. | Juvenile delinquents—Rehabilitation. | Criminal behavior. | Crime—Sociological aspects. | Crime prevention.
Classification: LCC HV9069. G525 2016 | DDC 364.36—dc23
LC record available at http://lccn.loc.gov/2015041198

ISBN: 978-1-138-85099-6 (hbk)
ISBN: 978-1-138-85100-9 (pbk)
ISBN: 978-1-315-72442-3 (ebk)

Typeset in Bembo
by Swales & Willis Ltd, Exeter, Devon, UK

CONTENTS

List of figures   *viii*
List of tables   *x*
List of contributors   *xi*

Introduction   1
Joanna Shapland, Stephen Farrall and Anthony Bottoms

SECTION I
Agency, structure and desistance from crime   9

1 Mechanisms underlying the desistance process: reflections
   on 'A theory of cognitive transformation'   11
   Peggy C. Giordano

2 Human agency, criminal careers and desistance   28
   Christoffer Carlsson

3 'I've always tried but I hadn't got the willpower':
   understanding pathways to desistance in the Republic
   of Ireland   50
   Deirdre Healy

4 Structural context and pathways to desistance: research in Spain   66
   José Cid and Joel Martí

SECTION II
Life phases and desistance   83

5 Key behavioral aspects of desistance from conduct problems
 and delinquency   85
 Rolf Loeber, Magda Stouthamer-Loeber and Lia Ahonen

6 Learning to desist in early adulthood: the Sheffield
 Desistance Study   99
 Anthony Bottoms and Joanna Shapland

7 Issues to consider in future work on desistance from adolescence
 to early adulthood: observations from the Pathways to
 Desistance study   126
 Edward P. Mulvey and Carol A. Schubert

8 How important are life-course transitions in explaining
 desistance? Examining the extent to which marriage,
 divorce and parenthood account for the age–crime relationship
 in former juvenile delinquents   144
 Arjan Blokland and Niek De Schipper

9 Timing of change: are life course transitions causes or
 consequences of desistance?   170
 Torbjørn Skardhamar and Jukka Savolainen

SECTION III
Criminal justice and state interventions   185

10 Understanding desistance in an assisted context: key findings
 from tracking progress on probation   187
 Stephen Farrall

11 In search of desistance: notes from an Australian study   204
 Mark Halsey

12 The increasing stickiness of public labels   222
 Christopher Uggen and Lindsay Blahnik

13 Understanding and identifying desistance: an example
 exploring the utility of sealing criminal records   244
 Megan C. Kurlychek, Shawn D. Bushway and Megan Denver

14 The fuel in the tank or the hole in the boat? Can sanctions
    support desistance?   265
    Fergus McNeill

    Diversity or congruence? Sketching the future:
    an afterword   282
    Joanna Shapland, Stephen Farrall and Anthony Bottoms

Index   *294*

FIGURES

1.1	The change process	16
6.1	A heuristic and interactive model of the early stages of desistance	112
7.1	Global psychosocial change by age for each offending trajectory	135
7.2	Temperance scores by age for each offending trajectory	136
8.1	Percentage decline in the likelihood of conviction by age (any conviction)	155
8.2	Effects of life-course transitions on the likelihood of conviction (any conviction)	156
8.3	Life-course transitions by age	158
8.4	Unconditional and adjusted desistance curve (any conviction)	159
8.5	Unconditional and adjusted desistance curve (violence, property, traffic)	161
9.1	Three ideal typical trajectories derived from theory	172
9.2	Logistic regression parameters for the probability of offending each year before and after the year of marriage	175
9.3a	Predicted probabilities of offending in each month in the 36 months leading up to and following job entry: average results	177
9.3b	Predicted probabilities of offending in each month in the 36 months leading up to and following job entry: results by latent trajectory groups	178
10.1	Model of impact of probation supervision	191
10.2	Emotional trajectory of desistance (sweep 4)	194
10.3	Victimisation rates (percentages) by desistance status	196
10.4	Structural and individual level processes and criminal careers	200
12.1	U.S. age distribution of arrest	223
12.2	Year 1 array of legal and illegal activities	225
12.3	Year 2 array of legal and illegal activities	226

12.4	Year 3 array of legal and illegal activities	227
12.5	The offense distribution of U.S. arrests, 2007	230
12.6	Minnesota arrest and imprisonment rates, 2007	231
12.7	Employer "callbacks" by race and arrest record	232
12.8	U.S. correctional populations, 1980–2011	233
12.9	Number of U.S. citizens with a current or past felony conviction, 1980–2010	233
12.10	Spatial distribution of U.S. felon population as percentage of voting age population	234
12.11	Spatial distribution of African American felons as percentage of voting age population	235
12.12	Secondary or tertiary spillovers on health care	235
12.13	Time to arrest among drug treatment group	236
12.14	Time to robbery/burglary arrest	237
12.15	Time to cocaine or heroin use	237
12.16	Female arrest rates by welfare ban implementation	239
12.17	Female violent arrest rates by welfare ban status	239
12.18	Estimated incarceration rates in the US and Rwanda	240

TABLES

4.1	Population and sample characteristics	70
4.2	Differences between desisters and persisters in the sample	72
6.1	Summary of SDS ordinal regression analyses relating to the prediction of final levels of criminality	104
8.1	Descriptives for the current sample of juvenile offenders	154
8.2	Multilevel logistic models explaining the likelihood of conviction from ages 21–48	155
8.3	Reduction (in %) in magnitudes in the age coefficients and crime drop between ages 21–48	158
8.4	Multilevel logistic models explaining the likelihood of conviction from ages 21–48 for violence, property and traffic convictions	160
10.1	t-tests of citizenship statements	193
10.2	Variables associated with absence	197
10.3	Modelling absence	198
12.1	Predictors of subjective desistance	228
13.1	The proposed impact of the youthful offender seal on desistance	253
13.2	The proposed impact of the time mandated seal on desistance	255
13.3	The proposed impact of successfully contesting the decision	258
14.1	Ideal-type contrasts – offence-focused and desistance-focused practice	271
14.2	Probation practice paradigms	273

CONTRIBUTORS

Lia Ahonen, PhD, is Assistant Professor of Criminology, Örebro University, Sweden, and a visiting scholar at the Life History Studies Program, Department of Psychiatry, University of Pittsburgh, Pennsylvania. She has published on juvenile institutional care and corrections, organisational and policy issues in the justice system, juvenile delinquency and mental health problems.

Lindsay Blahnik completed her Bachelor of Arts degree at the University of Minnesota in 2015, majoring in sociology and political science. Her research examines how the transitional justice mechanisms implemented after the 1994 genocide have affected social cohesion in contemporary Rwanda.

Arjan Blokland is a senior researcher at the NSCR, Amsterdam and a professor of criminology and criminal justice at Leiden University, Leiden, the Netherlands. His research focuses on the way criminal careers develop over the life span, the interdependencies between criminal careers and transitions and events in other life-course domains, and the (collateral) effects of criminal justice sanctions on offenders' life courses. His research has been published in various international journals, including: *Criminology*, *Journal of Research in Crime and Delinquency*, *Journal of Quantitative Criminology* and *Journal of Abnormal Child Psychology*. He recently edited – together with Patrick Lussier – the book *Sex Offenders: A Criminal Career Approach* published by Wiley Publishers.

Anthony Bottoms is Emeritus Wolfson Professor of Criminology at the University of Cambridge and Honorary Professor of Criminology at the University of Sheffield. He is also a Fellow of the British Academy. With Joanna Shapland, he co-directs the Sheffield Desistance Study.

Shawn D. Bushway is a Professor of Public Administration and Policy at the Rockefeller College of Public Affairs and Policy at the University at Albany, SUNY. His research interests include employment and crime, sentencing policy, desistance and criminal background checks by employers.

Christoffer Carlsson has a PhD in criminology from the Department of Criminology, Stockholm University. He was the 2012 recipient of the European Society of Criminology's Young Criminologist Award for his qualitative research on turning points, life-course changes and desistance from crime. He is currently working as a researcher at the Institute for Future Studies, Stockholm, studying violent extremism from a life-course perspective. His work in life-course criminology has been published in various international journals, including *Criminology, Criminal Justice and Behavior* and the *British Journal of Criminology*.

José Cid is Associate Professor of Criminology and Criminal law at Universitat Autònoma de Barcelona. He has mainly undertaken research on the use of discretion by judges, the use of imprisonment, the comparative effectiveness of prison and alternatives and the use of back-end sentencing. Some of his research has been published in *Punishment and Society, European Journal of Criminology, Probation Journal* and *European Journal of Probation*. At present, he is mainly concerned with research on desistance in Spain, with adult and young participants.

Megan Denver is a PhD student in the School of Criminal Justice at the University at Albany, SUNY. Her research interests include prisoner reentry and desistance. She was previously a research associate at the Urban Institute and received her BA and MA from the University of Delaware.

Niek de Schipper studied sociology at Utrecht University and is currently a Masters student in methodology and statistics for the behavioural, biomedical and social sciences at Utrecht University. At the time of writing his chapter he was working as a junior researcher at the NSCR, Amsterdam.

Stephen Farrall is Professor of Criminology in the Centre for Criminological Research at the University of Sheffield. As well as exploring desistance from crime, he has also studied the fear of crime and is currently exploring the impact of 1980s 'New Right' politics on crime rates in the UK. His most recent book is *The Legacy of Thatcherism: Assessing and Exploring Thatcherite Social and Economic Policies* (British Academy Original Paperbacks) published by Oxford University Press in 2014 and co-edited with Colin Hay. Stephen also edits the International Series on Desistance and Rehabilitation (published by Routledge).

Peggy C. Giordano is a Distinguished Research Professor in the Department of Sociology at Bowling Green State University, Ohio. A Fellow of the American Society of Criminology, her research areas include gender and crime, social network influences on delinquency and adult criminal behaviour, long-term patterns of criminal continuity and change, and intergenerational transmission. Her research on desistance is based primarily on a 20-year follow-up of a sample of delinquent female and male youths, and papers exploring these data have twice been awarded the American Sociological Association's Crime, Law and Deviance Section Award for outstanding article. Current work extends this long-term interest in desistance to a longitudinal project that examines the cessation of intimate partner violence.

Mark Halsey holds a four-year Australian Research Council Future Fellowship for the study of intergenerational incarceration and is a Professor of Criminology at the Centre for Crime Policy and Research, Law School, Flinders University. He is the co-author (with Simone Deegan) of *Young Offenders: Crime, Prison and Struggles for Desistance* (Palgrave) and (with Andrew Goldsmith and Andrew Groves) of the forthcoming book *Tackling Correctional Corruption: An integrity Promoting Approach* (Palgrave).

Deirdre Healy, BA, PhD, is a lecturer at the UCD Sutherland School of Law, Dublin. Her research interests include desistance, reintegration, community sanctions and victimisation. She has a track record of high-quality publications in peer-reviewed international and Irish journals and her work has attracted interest from policymakers and practitioners as well as academics. She has published two books *The Dynamics of Desistance: Charting Pathways Through Change* (Routledge 2012) and *Rape and Justice in Ireland* (with Conor Hanly and Stacey Scriver; Liffey Press 2009) and edited the *Routledge Handbook of Irish Criminology* with Claire Hamilton, Yvonne Daly and Michelle Butler (Routledge 2015).

Megan C. Kurlychek is an Associate Professor at the University at Albany School of Criminal Justice, SUNY, and a Bureau of Justice Statistics Visiting Fellow. Before receiving her PhD in crime, law and justice from Penn State in 2004, Dr Kurlychek worked for the Pennsylvania State Senate, the Pennsylvania Commission on Sentencing and the National Center for Juvenile Justice. Her research maintains a policy focus exploring ways in which criminal justice policies either promote, or inadvertently prevent, desistance. In addition to being published in top journals in the field, her work has been heavily cited by the United States Equal Employment Opportunity Commission regarding the use of criminal records in employment background screenings.

Rolf Loeber, PhD, is Distinguished University Professor of Psychiatry and Professor of Psychology and Epidemiology at the University of Pittsburgh, Pennsylvania. He is Director of the Life History Program and is principal investigator of two longitudinal studies, the Pittsburgh Youth Study and the Pittsburgh Girls Study. He has published widely in the fields of juvenile antisocial behaviour and delinquency, substance use and mental health problems. He is an elected member of the

Koninklijke Academie van Wetenschappen (Royal Academy of Sciences) in the Netherlands and the Royal Irish Academy in Ireland.

Joel Martí is Associate Professor at the Department of Sociology of Universitat Autònoma de Barcelona. He is interested in methodological topics, such as social network analysis, qualitative analysis, mixed methods and action research. His current research is focused on personal networks, labour markets and desistance.

Fergus McNeill is Professor of Criminology and Social Work at the University of Glasgow, where he works in the Scottish Centre for Crime and Justice Research and in the sociology subject area. His academic work and practical engagements in the penal field explore and seek to reform institutions, cultures and practices of punishment and alternatives to punishment.

Edward P. Mulvey, PhD, is a Professor of Psychiatry at the University of Pittsburgh School of Medicine. His research focuses on the relationship of mental illness to violence and serious adolescent offenders. He was the principal investigator for the Pathways to Desistance study.

Jukka Savolainen is a Research Scientist at the Institute for Social Research, University of Michigan, where he serves as the Director of National Archive of Criminal Justice Data (NACJD). His research is focused on life-course criminology, cross-national studies of delinquency and situational aspects of violence.

Carol A. Schubert, MPH, is a researcher with the Law and Psychiatry Program, Department of Psychiatry, University of Pittsburgh, Pennsylvania. She has directed several large-scale research studies, including the Pathways to Desistance study. Her research focus has been on the experiences of youth in the juvenile justice system.

Joanna Shapland is Edward Bramley Professor of Criminal Justice at the University of Sheffield and Director of the Centre for Criminological Research. Her research interests include desistance, restorative justice (and the interaction between desistance and restorative justice), the informal economy, victimology and researching what is quality in probation supervision. She was awarded the Outstanding Achievement Award by the British Society of Criminology in 2013 and is Executive Editor of the *International Review of Victimology*.

Torbjørn Skardhamar is an Associate Professor of Sociology at the University of Oslo and a senior researcher at the research department of Statistics Norway. His work focuses on life-course criminology, statistical methods, spatial analysis and the use of registry data in social research.

Magda Stouthamer-Loeber, PhD, is retired Associate Professor of Psychiatry and Psychology, University of Pittsburgh, Pennsylvania. Her career has been devoted to the study of the development of antisocial and prosocial behaviour in children. She has focused on covert as well as aggressive antisocial behaviours and has studied desistance from delinquent behaviour. An important part of her work has been the running of longitudinal studies and the management of large data sets.

Christopher Uggen is Distinguished McKnight Professor of Sociology and Law at the University of Minnesota. He studies crime, law and deviance, firm in the belief that good science can light the way to a more just and peaceful world. Current projects involve a comparative study of re-entry from different types of institutions, employment discrimination and criminal records, crime and justice in genocide and the health effects of incarceration. Outreach and engagement projects include editing *Contexts Magazine* (from 2007–2011) and TheSocietyPages.Org (both with Doug Hartmann), a book series and multimedia social science hub drawing over one million readers per month.

INTRODUCTION

Joanna Shapland, Stephen Farrall and Anthony Bottoms

What is desistance, why is it important to research it and what relevance does it potentially have for criminal justice policy? Desistance is the name given to the process (or event) whereby someone who has been engaged in some act (or series of acts) ceases to undertake these acts. In criminology, 'desistance' has become the shorthand term to describe the process by which someone who was committing crimes on a frequent basis ceases to offend. Accordingly, criminologists do not normally speak of people 'desisting' after a single offence.

To achieve full desistance in the context of criminal careers research implies that the individual has ceased all offending. It is very hard, of course, to know exactly when someone has entirely desisted, because, during their lifetime, there is always the possibility that they might commit another offence, even after many years of not committing offences. What has become clear, however, over the last 20–25 years, is that most offenders do desist, even those who have been offending at a considerable rate and for some time. For many years, most attention was focused by criminologists on how individuals start to offend, or how offending may accelerate in adolescence. More recently, there has been much more interest in desistance. Part of this comes from the realisation that the processes of desistance are not necessarily the reverse of the processes behind becoming embroiled in crime – so there is a real need to study what is related to desistance. Part is driven by the policy-related consideration that if one could intervene positively to promote desistance (or at least not impede it), then it could have a considerable effect on preventing crime and reducing victimisation, given that a relatively small number of more persistent offenders commit a disproportionate amount of crime.

Some of the drivers of the current research into desistance are also to be found in the development of what has been called 'life-course criminology'. A significant number of longitudinal studies of crime over the life course were begun in the 1950s and 1960s, interviewing children or young people from that point onwards. As the studies progressed, many respondents started to slow their engagement in crime and, eventually, to cease it altogether. Thus, by the 1980s, a cohort of criminologists realised that they possessed large data sets in which many of those relatively heavily engaged in offending were no longer as active. One of the most well-known studies showing this is that of Laub and Sampson (2003), who continued to follow up into their sixties a juvenile offender cohort originally recruited in the 1950s by Sheldon and Eleanor Glueck (1974). In this way, the study of desistance 'forced' its way onto the criminological research agenda in the late 1980s and early 1990s. The studies were few and far between initially, but over time started to become more and more common as criminologists rose to the theoretical challenges and policy makers started to spot the potential of the research findings.

Given that desistance is about *stopping* committing crime, it follows that the population of interest is those who have been committing criminal offences (and, potentially, for the much younger age group who are below the age of criminal responsibility, those who commit acts which would be criminal offences if they were older). If we consider officially recorded convictions or arrests, then it is only a small proportion of the general population who are ever convicted (and a slightly larger proportion who are arrested). In relation to desistance, those who are of particular interest are those who have committed many offences, or could be said to be persistent offenders. Desistance research, therefore, is research into that often very small minority of the population who have committed several offences.

It is therefore difficult to study desistance using a general population sample, because the sample has to be very large to contain multiple offenders in any numbers. Given that desistance from crime typically occurs from late adolescence onwards – but can occur into one's forties, fifties or sixties – it is also important to follow those who have committed offences for a number of years. Though research, which has asked desisters and persisters to look back at their lives, has produced a number of valuable insights into the desistance process, one can never be completely sure whether retrospective accounts have been influenced by individuals' selective memory or from being narrated from a later vantage point when people have acquired different self-identities. These difficulties are lessened in longitudinal studies. A number of major longitudinal studies have now been in progress for some time in various parts of the world (for example, in the US, the Netherlands, Scandinavia and the UK), so these are now allowing us to consider desistance in some depth and to compare the results of different studies.

This book celebrates this 'coming of age' of research on desistance in many countries in the world. It also highlights some of the potential implications of the findings from desistance research for policy, particularly criminal justice policy. There is the possibility that policy on criminal justice and social welfare could build on insights from desistance to help to promote or 'speed up' desistance processes among persistent offenders. There is also the likelihood that some current policies may be creating obstacles to desistance, or slowing it down.

Policy implications of desistance research

In September 2014 in England, through an unintended juxtaposition of events, there occurred both the conference, which sparked this book, and the publication of some reflections on where the policy response to desistance is at in relation to England and Wales. In Sheffield, some of the world's leading researchers on desistance gathered to share and debate their respective findings in a conference organised by the Centre for Criminological Research at the University of Sheffield. Meanwhile, in London, the Criminal Justice Alliance for England and Wales[1] published a short report entitled *Prospects for a Desistance Agenda*. That report summarised the views of some 20 interviewees, mostly from the worlds of politics and criminal justice management,[2] in order to consider, from the point of view of policy and practice, 'where desistance stands at present, the barriers that may limit its further progress, and the opportunities and risks afforded by current developments'. It concluded that there were indeed some, 'barriers to the development of a desistance agenda, but also importantly causes for cautious optimism' (Annison and Moffatt 2014: 3).

Closer inspection reveals, however, that 'desistance' is still a relatively unfamiliar concept for policy makers and practitioners, and, 'some respondents admitted to not fully understanding [its] parameters' (Annison and Moffatt 2014: 8). Respondents were much more familiar with the term 'rehabilitation' and some tended to elide the two. It is important to recognise, though, that the two words have subtly different connotations. 'Rehabilitation' normally refers to a reduction or cessation of offending arising from some official intervention by or at the behest of a criminal justice agency, whereas 'desistance' is a more general term for the cessation of offending. Desistance therefore includes steps towards a law-abiding life taken by offenders themselves (through their own agency), as well as changes brought about through the influence of non-criminal justice actors such as romantic partners or sympathetic employers. Indeed, the evidence from desistance research is that desistance is often achieved to a considerable extent with only limited help from criminal justice professionals. Because of the nature of many evaluations of rehabilitation initiatives, which focus on the often short-term outcomes of that particular initiative and are not able to consider concurrent change in offenders' own perspectives or lifestyles, the long-term life course of offending and how it is influenced by offenders' individual decisions have not been much studied in rehabilitation research.

What then can desistance research add to rehabilitation research for policy makers and practitioners? The Criminal Justice Alliance (CJA) research, 'found that desistance theories' greatest strength was seen to be their common sense appeal. Developing relationships between practitioners and offenders and involving offenders in their rehabilitative plans seems entirely logical' (Annison and Moffatt 2014: 3). However, we would argue that the potential effect of desistance research is more radical: that many offenders attempt to develop their own paths towards desistance, and the primary task of the criminal justice system might therefore sometimes simply be to assist these self-generated plans. Second, it was clear that the CJA interviewees were not sure how robust the available evidence was. We do not know whether policy makers and practitioners from other countries feel the same, but we suspect that one difficulty has been that few books or documents have brought together the findings and lessons from different studies from different countries, to see whether those findings are concordant or discordant. That is one of the tasks of this book. There is now a significant number of both large-scale quantitative longitudinal studies and qualitative studies, conducted in several different countries, which have conclusively demonstrated the extent of desistance, even among persistent offenders. Arising from these large-scale studies, attempts are starting to be made to develop criminal justice interventions based on the concept of 'assisted desistance' (Porporino 2010). While it is right to say that the evidence for the added value of assisted desistance programmes is not yet robust, it is not at all the same thing as saying that the evidence for the existence of widespread desistance is not robust.

Although desistance, therefore, certainly exists, our understanding of exactly how desistance processes develop remains a work in progress. There is now much more evidence about these processes than there was at the turn of the millennium, but many important matters relating to desistance are still subject to debate and refinement. Up to September 2014, there had been few attempts to draw together the authors of these various studies on desistance into creative dialogue. This brings us to that other event of September 2014, the Sheffield conference, which has led directly to the chapters of this book.

The genesis of this book

All three of the editors of this book have been involved with research on desistance for a number of years. The book arose from a dream and some wish lists. Each of us, separately, had been thinking about how wonderful it would be if we were able to bring those who are leading major studies on desistance together in one place, to allow them to discuss each other's results and what are the current puzzles to be tackled in future research on desistance. We had each started to develop a wish list of which studies and scholars we would like to include and, in fact, those wish lists turned out to be very similar. The particular need for such a meeting arose, because each desistance study has been very good at publishing its own results as the study has developed – but naturally it has not always been able to consider its own results in the light of those of others. Meeting together, we started talking about how, by bringing these scholars together, we would be able to discuss the desistance process comparatively between those working in different countries and across age ranges and genders.

With funding from the Faculty of Social Sciences at the University of Sheffield, we were able to realise our dream. We held an international desistance conference at the School of Law at the University of Sheffield on 15–17 September 2014.[3] Almost all of those on our combined wish list readily accepted our invitation to come to Sheffield and, further, to write a paper in advance, detailing the results of their study over the years and considering the challenges for desistance research for the future. We also invited attendees to tell us about doctoral students and postdoctoral researchers who were studying desistance and invited them as well. The result was a very productive conference lasting 3 days and attended by some 50 desistance researchers, in which almost all the time was spent discussing the prepared papers. Subsequently, the presenters agreed to revise and have peer reviewed their chapters for this book.[4] In addition, some of the discussions were 'ideas sessions' in which particular questions about desistance were thrown open to the whole group. The results of these ideas sessions have been combined together as an Afterword to the main chapters in this volume.

The book itself is divided into three sections. The first section consists of chapters whose authors are primarily concerned with the **interplay between the agency of the offender** himself or herself in making a change towards desistance **and the societal conditions** which structure and shape lifestyles, neighbourhoods and opportunities. Empirical research has shown that desistance is only rarely a sudden change from committing crime to leading an entirely law-abiding life. More commonly, desistance seems to be a process in which progress may be slow or uneven, with some crime-free periods and some relapses. Initial desires to change one's lifestyle (in what may be called 'early desistance') may or may not be reinforced or rebutted by developing circumstances. Initial steps towards leading a less criminal life may run up against obstacles, such as finding legitimate employment, or desistance may be maintained by supportive partners, families or peers. Those possibilities or obstacles will be affected both by cultural factors within that society and also its economic and social possibilities at that point in time.

Whereas the chapters in the first section relate primarily to general theories of desistance, chapters in the second section concentrate upon **particular ages of offenders or stages of desistance**. We are reminded by Loeber and his co-authors that desistance should not be thought of as entirely for adults – that young people, including young children, may desist from aggressive or other antisocial behaviour, which they display at one point in their lives, but which may not reoccur. The following two chapters both consider specifically desistance in late adolescence and early adulthood, both in terms of the early stage of desistance for persistent offenders and also in relation to psychosocial and developmental maturation at this time. The final two chapters in this section look in some detail at so-called 'turning points' – that is, the idea that certain status changes (being married, becoming a parent, getting a stable job, etc.) may link to desistance, and whether these status changes are really causal (for example, which comes first: the change or the desistance?).

Contemporary interest in desistance also stems very much from the possibilities for the criminal justice system to 'piggy-back' on desistance processes to speed its progress, or at least maintain it, rather than set it back. The third section of the book therefore looks at the **relation between desistance and criminal justice**. Does supervision by the probation service have any effect on desistance, from the desister's own perspective, or is desistance all their own work? How can aftercare from prison and conditions on licence potentially set back intentions to desist, or cement them? Distinguishing between offences and legitimate conduct is an important purpose of the criminal law, but do the labels that the criminal justice system applies to those who offend, subsequently become obstacles when people try to desist? Depending upon how desistance may be occurring, will different proposed policy mechanisms be likely to have any effect on it? How might we reconceive penal policy to support desistance and build on would-be desisters' strengths?

Finally, in the **Afterword**, we pull together the discussions sparked by the chapters to consider whether a general theory of desistance is possible or desirable – and what the research has shown about the congruence or disparity between desistance processes. Is there one process of desistance? Or are there different processes, depending upon the age and maturation of offenders, their gender, their contacts and supporters, and the countries and societies in which they live? Where are the gaps in what we know about desistance and where are the similarities, even between studies conducted in different countries and decades? What are the key priorities for desistance research now as we take stock of the significant progress made since the turn of the century through the existing longitudinal and qualitative studies?

Our ambition for this collection was to bring together accounts, reflection and ideas for the future from those involved in some of the best studies of desistance from crime. Littered among the pages are, we think, some important hints about where research in this field might best develop in the future: sub-populations to study; processes to unpack further; theories to refine and explore; and research designs to reconsider. The task of research is never complete. As Robert Pirsig (1974) once commented, the sign of truly great research is that it raises more questions than answers. The contributors to this collection have, in our view, both neatly summarised their own studies and also provided much in the way of informed thinking as regards appropriate directions for the future – for research and indeed for policy making.

Notes

1 The CJA, 'is a coalition of 74 organisations – including campaigning charities, voluntary sector service providers, research institutions, staff associations and trade unions – involved in policy and practice across the criminal justice system' (Annison and Moffatt 2014: 2).
2 More specifically, the interviewees were 'civil servants, politicians, academics and senior public and voluntary sector representatives from across the country' (Annison and Moffatt 2014: 2).
3 We are very grateful to Lisa Burns, Paul Rosen and Keir Irwin Rogers for all their help in organising the conference and to the Faculty of Social Sciences of the University of Sheffield for their generous financial support.
4 A few leading scholars attended the conference, but were unable to contribute a chapter for this volume.

References

Annison, H. and Moffatt, S. (2014) *Prospects for a Desistance Agenda*. London: Criminal Justice Alliance.

Glueck, S. and Glueck, E. (1974) *Of Delinquency and Crime: A Panorama of Years of Search and Research*. Springfield, IL: Charles C. Thomas.

Laub, J. H. and Sampson, R. J. (2003) *Shared Beginnings, Divergent Lives: Delinquent Boys to Age 70*. Cambridge, MA: Harvard University Press.

Pirsig, R. (1974) *Zen and the Art of Motorcycle Maintenance: An Inquiry into Values*. New York: William Morrow and Company.

Porporino, F. (2010) 'Bringing sense and sensitivity to corrections: From programmes to "fix" offenders to services to support desistance', in Brayford, J., Cowe, F. B. and Deering, J. (eds) *What Else Works? Creative Work with Offenders*. Cullompton, UK: Willan.

SECTION I

Agency, structure and desistance from crime

This opening section consists of chapters whose authors are primarily concerned with what might be thought of as the interplay between the agency of the offender himself or herself in making a change towards desistance, and the wider societal, economic and cultural conditions, which structure and shape lifestyles, neighbourhoods and opportunities. The empirical research undertaken thus far, almost regardless of research site, methodology or theoretical stance adopted, has shown that desistance is only very rarely an abrupt change from committing crime to leading an entirely law-abiding life. Even when sudden changes have been documented, these often come after some period of reflection about desisting has already started, for example, the 'shock' of a near-death experience or of almost being caught, and may reinforce uncertainties, which already existed. More commonly, desistance seems to be a process, in which progress may be slow or uneven, with some crime-free periods and some relapses. Initial desires to change one's lifestyle (in what may be called 'early desistance') may or may not be reinforced or rebutted by circumstances. Initial steps towards leading a life in which engagement in crime was less prominent may run up against obstacles such as the difficulty in finding legitimate employment. Similarly, desistance may be maintained by supportive partners, families or peers. These possibilities or obstacles will be affected both by cultural factors within that society and also its economic and social possibilities at that point in time.

1

MECHANISMS UNDERLYING THE DESISTANCE PROCESS

Reflections on 'A theory of cognitive transformation'

Peggy C. Giordano

> *What is important to initiation of violence may be irrelevant to its cessation.*
> *(Fagan 1989: 414)*

Jeffrey Fagan's (1989) early observation pointed to the potential importance of distinguishing onset and desistance processes. Yet Sampson and Laub's theorizing and empirical research (Sampson and Laub 1993; Laub and Sampson 2003) have served as especially important catalysts for developing further this area of study—and the life course perspective on crime more generally. Sampson and Laub's analyses of data from follow-ups of a sample of delinquent youths (Glueck and Glueck 1950) documented that traditional risk factors, such as coming from a "broken home," were not especially useful as predictors of variability in the adult men's success in moving away from their earlier patterns of involvement in criminal behavior. Instead, these researchers focused attention on features of the men's adult lives—notably movement into a "good marriage" and a stable job—as transition events that were significantly related to crime cessation. However, in articulating their theoretical perspective, a conceptual thread nevertheless connects the early experiences and later circumstances: Sampson and Laub's theorizing included the idea that the lack of social control associated with inadequate parenting could in effect be overcome by the acquisition of informal social control that was later provided by a caring spouse. Thus, ideas about factors associated with onset may continue to figure into perspectives on specific mechanisms underlying the desistance process.

With this line of research as a general backdrop, in 1995 we conducted our own follow-up of a sample of delinquent girls (and a comparison sample of boys) we had originally interviewed in 1982 (see e.g., Cernkovich *et al.* 1985). The original data collection effort was a kind of add-on to a neighborhood-based study of 942 youths that was focused primarily on female delinquency. The impetus for collecting data

from a sample of incarcerated girls related to the difficulties inherent in investigating a phenomenon that has a low base rate of occurrence within the general
population. After completing a ten-year follow-up of the related sample of neighborhood youth, we wondered if it would be possible to locate a sufficient number
of the young women and men who had been interviewed during the time in which
they were incarcerated in state-level juvenile correctional institutions. Although
this meant casting a wider net and working with very poor locating information,
we were eventually able to find and interview 78 percent of these respondents,
who were at the time approximately 30 years of age. A third set of interviews was
completed when the respondents averaged 39 years of age, as part of an additional
follow-up that focused heavily on intergenerational transmission and the well-being
of children born to these respondents (Giordano 2010). These follow-ups (the
Ohio Longitudinal Study—OLS), although designed around somewhat more basic
research objectives (how did those girls turn out? how did their children turn out?),
nevertheless provided a window on variability in offending patterns over a relatively
long period of time. This allowed us to explore in more detail the respondents' patterns of persistence and desistance (Giordano *et al.* 2002, 2003, 2007, 2008).

Complications: gender, historical era, theoretical predilections, and insights from the data

The simplest way to position our findings based on the OLS study would have
been to concentrate on the uniquely gendered nature of these dynamics (i.e., the
notion that men accomplish desistance in this way, while women go about it that
way). But we had also completed follow-ups of similarly situated male delinquents
incarcerated during the same time period, and their responses and circumstances
also lacked an easy fit with some basic emphases of Sampson and Laub's age-
graded theory of informal social control. First, at the initial follow-up, a majority
of those in the sample were not married and stable jobs were in short supply for
a majority of these women and men. This likely reflected the confluence of societal-level social and economic changes, and personal biographies that frequently
included extensive drug use and periods of adult incarceration. Marriage and
employment operated for some as an important set of stabilizing influences, but at
the time of the first follow-up only 16 percent of these respondents had attained
what we called the "complete respectability package" that included marriage and
a full-time job. As Sampson and Laub's initial theorizing also included attention
to the quality of these bonds, we noted that the percentage who reported average or higher levels of marital happiness and wages above the 1995 poverty line
(8 percent) presented a portrait of even greater marginality and disadvantage. And
in this, gender similarities were more notable than differences (i.e., 7.7 percent of
women and 8.6 percent of men had attained what could be called the high-quality
respectability package) (Giordano *et al.* 2002). Given these base rates, it was not surprising that neither marital attachment nor job stability were significant predictors
of desistance in basic models relying on the OLS structured interview data.

The qualitative data nevertheless highlighted variability in the criminal involvement of these respondents, and our analyses of these in-depth life histories pointed to considerable complexity in the dynamics associated with desistance for this contemporary cohort of women and men.

The theory of cognitive transformation

Control theories—including those focusing on onset as well as those designed to illuminate the desistance process—are generally associated with factors external to the individual (i.e., the idea of constraints or controls over the individual's conduct). Traditional social learning theories, while differing in emphasis, also tend toward exteriority (i.e., the notion of peer groups influencing delinquency involvement). As a fan of the latter line of theorizing, the qualitative interviews we completed with these adult respondents provided a challenge not only to some aspects of Sampson and Laub's theory of informal social control but also to more traditional social learning perspectives. It seemed clear that individual-level cognitive changes were integral to desistance processes, and this was not just an artifact of our reliance on a narrative approach (i.e., the idea that respondents themselves would inevitably cast themselves as the stars of their own stories). A focus on cognitive processes or "transformations" helps us to understand: (a) why individuals exposed to potentially important catalysts for change, such as a loving spouse (or a romantic partner who could become a loving spouse), fail to benefit from this exposure; (b) why the same individual gains traction from, e.g., a job opportunity at time x when this was not an effective 'hook' for change at time y (Uggen 2000); and/or (c) why others generally lacking such traditional sources of social capital and informal control are sometimes able to make moves in the direction of a more prosocial lifestyle.

Our conditional-on-cognitive-transformations view of desistance is most consistent with the basic tenets of symbolic interaction (SI) theories. As suggested above, control-based treatments of desistance, and indeed many sociological treatments of the life course more generally, in our view, place too much conceptual weight on a few key transition events. The focus is on the actions of the change agent, while, "the actor is depicted as moving from adolescence to adulthood virtually unchanged, but for the good fortune of experiencing one or more of these events" (Giordano *et al.* 2007). The symbolic interactionist perspective provides a contrast to this viewpoint, and may best be described as a more egocentric version of social learning theory. As Mead (1934) noted, all but the most habitual of actions engage cognitive processes. Thus it is intuitive to expect that cognitive shifts and the individual's related agentic moves are implicated in desistance, particularly when this requires significant changes in life direction. It is noteworthy that several researchers involved in research on desistance during this time period developed perspectives that contributed uniquely to the field, but that nevertheless coalesced around the need to push the individual into the foreground of the change process (Farrall and Bowling 1999; Maruna 2001; see also Shover 1985).

Based on our analyses of the OLS interview data, we outlined four types of cognitive transformations that appeared to be associated with successful patterns of desistance. In addition to a general "readiness" or *openness to change* (a phenomenon that had been discussed extensively in connection with recovery from addictions), individuals also vary in their exposure and *receptivity to particular catalysts*. We referred to these as "hooks" for change, in order to highlight the actor's own role in latching onto potentially favorable influences, as well as to stress that while specific hooks may be considered especially "key" from the individual's own perspective, other elements may also be present that buttress the new direction. A further complication is that hooks for change must be objectively *and subjectively* available. For example, some respondents described increased receptivity to religion or spirituality at a particular point in their lives, even though they had previously been indifferent to it. For others, this particular path—while widely available—was not a comfortable fit.

A third type of cognitive transformation occurs when individuals can envision and begin to fashion a *replacement self* that can supplant the old one that must be left behind. The focus on identity change accords with the idea that human behavior involves complex processes that inevitably connect to self-conceptions (Mead 1934; Maruna 2001). This emphasis extends prior theorizing about identity and crime that had focused on the dynamics of onset and persistence (i.e., the notion that delinquent/criminal acts have meaning as they support one's developing identity (see e.g., Matsueda and Heimer 1997), or that stigma processes marginalize ex-offenders, solidifying criminal identities and extending their careers). Recently, Bushway and Paternoster (2013) argued that identity change is "the most promising theoretical direction for criminologists interested in desistance," and suggested that their identity theory properly places changes in self-conceptions *first* in the sequence of transformations that come to be associated with successful desistance. Our own view is that identity development and change is ongoing; thus it may be relatively difficult and potentially not feasible to establish with precision such a temporal order. Nevertheless, we agree with Bushway and Paternoster's basic premise that identity (and identity change) is important as it "motivates and provides a direction for behavior" (Bushway and Paternoster 2013: 222). For example, in describing the various cognitive transformations, we noted:

> [t]o the degree that cognitions serve as an organizing process, then identity provides a higher level of organization and coherence to one's cognitions. This involves more than a mental tidying up, because the new or refashioned identity can act as a cognitive filter for decision making. This filtering process is particularly critical as one moves into the future and inevitably encounters novel situations.
>
> *(Giordano et al. 2002: 1001)*

It is likely that most social psychological treatments of crime and desistance accord with the notion that issues of identity are important to an understanding of both life course continuity and change. Thus, the devil is in the detail, and there remains more room for debate about where identity shifts occur in the change process—as well as about the whys and hows of these changes. In our original formulation, we described a hypothetical sequence (openness to change → openness to particular "hooks" → identity transformations → changes in the meaning/desirability of the behavior itself (discussed in more detail below)). This seems at first glance to contrast with Paternoster and Bushway's (2009) view that identity change is the initial element of the change process. Yet, Mead's original discussion and our treatment of his ideas dealt explicitly with issues of timing. As we suggested at the time (Giordano *et al.* 2002):

> Mead (1913) . . . argued that as changes begin to occur, a new self is not likely to emerge at the outset. Problems in the environment appear first: "When, however, an essential problem appears, there is some disintegration in this organization, and different tendencies appear in reflective thought as different voices in conflict with each other. In a sense the old self has disintegrated, and out of the moral process a new self arises. There is of course a reciprocal relation between the self and its object . . . On the other hand, the consciousness of the new objective, its values and meanings, seems to come earlier to consciousness than the new self that answers to the new object." The problem in the present context is not the respondent's difficulties with the law, for these have appeared as a regular pattern across the life course. Mead (1913) argued that: "as a mere organization of habit, the self is not self-conscious." The problem occurs when the environment comes to include a catalyst for change and the actor recognizes it as such. This has the potential to further heighten an actor's "reflective thoughts" and to provide a framework for a new kind of lifestyle, and [in time] a new kind of self. We are in agreement with Mead's ideas about sequencing but would add that even in the early stages (in order to get things moving) an alternative view of self must at least be in awareness as a worthy hypothetical (extending Mead's notion about the human capacity to fix on objects that are "relatively faint" [or "at a distance"] (Mead 1964: 138).
>
> *(Giordano* et al. *2002: 1002–1003)*

As we have completed additional analyses of the OLS data and conducted other studies of desistance, we have revised our ideas about sequencing. We would not wish to argue that identity change is the initial "step," as suggested by Paternoster and Bushway (2009), but that the idea of a series of steps is itself not all that helpful or accurate as a description of what occurs (see e.g., Giordano *et al.* 2015b). It may in the long run prove more useful to consider these elements as unfolding simultaneously, and as mutually reinforcing facets of the change process (see Figure 1.1).

The limits of our sequencing notion are particularly apparent when we consider the fourth type of cognitive transformation we had outlined. In our initial discussion, we suggested not only that *changes in the meaning and desirability of the criminal behavior itself* were important but that they often constituted the final step

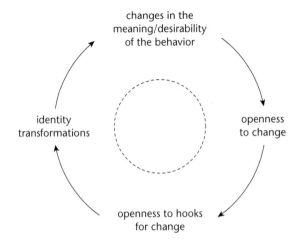

FIGURE 1.1 The change process.

in this sequence ("the capstone"). The general idea of changes in the individual's attitudes about or orientation toward crime is consistent with the SI view that individuals act on the basis of meaning(s). Conversely, this focus on changes in definitions and meanings contrasts with the basic tenets of control perspectives. Within the framework of the latter line of theorizing, a general proclivity to deviate is posited, while it is the degree of control or constraint that is subject to variability (whether as a way to explain differences across individuals or observed changes over the life course).

While we continue to believe that these changes in meaning are a central aspect of the change process, recent analyses (our own and that of other researchers) have sensitized us to the idea that shifts in attitudes toward crime, violence, and drug use, for example, are integral to all phases of the change process (see e.g., Shapland and Bottoms 2011). Furthermore, in effect, these cognitive shifts provide insight on the "why of increased openness to change, receptivity to specific 'hooks'," and so on (as suggested in Figure 1.1). Undoubtedly, our initial discussions reflected the heavy drug involvement of many of the OLS respondents. Thus, while these respondents often lamented that they were "tired of being tired" (suggesting a redefinition process), even those who had moved away from the drug scene often continued to experience a desire for drugs, or a pull of the old lifestyle for a considerable period of time (Giordano *et al.* 2002). Yet clearly, respondents who had started down a desistance path had centered on *other* features of the behavior or more general lifestyle that no longer worked for them or that had lost their former luster. In a subsequent analysis, we focused attention on emotional changes that foster desistance, suggesting that these changes are occurring in tandem with cognitive shifts, and also figure heavily into the desistance process. In this work, we argued that, "the diminution of positive emotions connected to crime" is also an important aspect of the redefinition process. Over time, the phenomenon itself and all that connects to it will not be experienced in the same way (either cognitively or emotionally) as earlier in the life course. Almost by definition, an adult *chronic* offender is one who has exposure to numerous crime scenes, fights, and/or drug-fueled parties, as well as the fallout from these experiences (see Shover 1985: 90). As one 30-year-old respondent, Paul, noted, reflecting on his teen years, "[back then] it excited me to do different things . . . to see what I could and what I couldn't get away with." Kristen sounded a remarkably similar theme, "It was like a rush, you know, let's see what we can do today and get away with." Developing more thoroughly the idea that "the thrill is gone," and the party is increasingly "over," Bushway and Paternoster (2013) recently focused attention on the overtly negative features of continued criminal involvement (i.e., it is not just a decline of positive meanings, but an increase in the perception of negative ones). These researchers drew on Baumeister's (1994) idea of "the crystallization of discontent" and Markus and Nurius's (1987) notion of the "feared" self to stress the role of such negatives in the change process:

> Before one is willing to give up his or her working identity as a law breaker, then, he or she must begin to perceive it as unsatisfying, thus weakening his or her commitment to it. This weakening of one's commitment to a criminal identity does not come about quickly, nor does it come about in response to one or two failures, but only gradually and to the linking of many failures and the attribution of those linked failures to one's identity and life as a criminal . . . [and later] the projection into the future of continued life dissatisfaction leads the person to begin to seek changes.
>
> *(Bushway and Paternoster 2013: 223)*

A social view of development and desistance

Paternoster and Bushway's (2009) discussion introduces a needed dose of vinegar to theorizing about the desistance process, and highlights the utility of conducting additional research on these negative dimensions as constituting, in effect, their own "hooks" for change. However, in positing that individuals simply tire of the old way of life and begin to activate new "positive selves" (e.g., as a, "working person, a person with a good spouse, a giving father, and a law abider"), these researchers have suggested that desistance is ultimately an "individualistic mental process." Certainly theoretical perspectives that emphasize cognitive transformations, the process of "making good," and the role of agency tend to thrust the actor into the foreground of change, as suggested at the outset. And in a very real sense, individuals are the "deciders," and the ones who must craft their own paths to change, and a specific path at that. Yet our analyses relying on the OLS sample and subsequently are in line with social theories of human development and, accordingly, suggest limitations to an overly atomistic view of this entire process.

Social influences on crime onset are well-established (neighborhood variations, early parental abuse as a robust predictor, effect of delinquent peers). By extension, then, social experiences should figure into redefinition and change processes as well. The latter view is less straightforward, because cognitive shifts and associated agentic moves seem to be located squarely on the shoulders of the individual (I changed my mind; I did what I had to do). Yet Mead (1934) argued convincingly that while cognitions (and emotions) are located within the individual, particular thoughts and emotional reactions arise *through continual processes of interaction and communication with others*. The adult life course expands one's social contacts and opportunities, and this accumulation of social experiences is deeply implicated in the individual's evolving perspective on the drawbacks of the old lifestyle and the possibilities for a new one.

"Developmental" changes that foster desistance

There are many ways in which adults are not children. In several prior analyses relying on the OLS data (and more recently the Toledo Adolescent Relationships Study—TARS), we have foregrounded what we termed secondary desistance processes to suggest that these dynamics play support if not starring roles in the shift away from criminal behavior. These changes may occur independent of exposure to specific hooks or catalysts (which appear more outsized in their appar-ent effects—and more obviously social), but these more subtle changes may also increase receptivity to particular catalysts. In turn, exposure to one or more cata-lysts may foster/amplify further such changes in world views and perspectives. For example, across the transition to adulthood, individuals may not only change their peer affiliations but over time become less susceptible in general to peer influ-ence (Giordano *et al.* 2003). Thus, the OLS respondents quoted below theorized a strong role for peer relationships as integral to their troubles with the law. In contrast, as adult narrators, they detailed cognitive transformations consistent with changes in this aspect of their lives:

> Come on Nancy, you know you want to do this . . . come on you want to go out and eat some soapers . . . come on let's go smoke some dope. Well being a teenager . . . off I went, you know, I thought right then, my friends were more important than my family. I was there. And I look back now God I could kick myself in the rear cause I'd do it so much different.

> Nobody told me, well Andy . . . or influenced me to break into this, this building, you know . . . But it was just wanting to fit in. Just with some of the . . . especially like Chester and Shawn . . . cause they were more, more wild and doing things . . . and they were cool.

We suggested that while these changes in the nature and impact of peer relation-ships may be more subtle, gradual, and less easily measured than a clear-cut event (i.e., timing of the transition to marriage), they should not be overlooked as fac-tors that pave the way for desistance to occur. Women and men alike sounded themes highlighting that as adults they are not likely to be as easily swayed—high influence from peers is a dynamic that respondents associated with being a "teenager," "younger," "a kid," or "little." We noted that while these changes can well be fostered by a clear transition event (as suggested by Warr's (1998) analysis linking marriage and reduced time with peers), they do not inevitably trace back to a visible catalyst (see also Shapland and Bottoms' (2011) depiction of ways in which desisters actively managed their environments to avoid peer-based temptations). In the OLS study, the low percentage of married individuals is something of a plus. Shifts that occur in the absence of a strong marriage bond draw attention to the full complement of social experiences that may foster a different set of attitudes— ones that connect directly to a traditional offending context (it has taken me 11 years; I've had a lot of different experiences, and I think of them as learning experiences; "being a follower ain't gonna get you nowhere but in trouble"). Consistent with these narrative accounts, analyses of responses to items comprising a peer influence scale administered during the adolescent and adult follow-up interview conducted some 13 years later documented a significant decline in perceived susceptibility ($p<0.001$). Reflecting that peer influence involves reciprocal processes, we noted also that delinquent youth generally score higher on items tapping attempts to influence or apply pressure to one's friends, and analyses revealed a significant decline in scores on this corollary scale as well (Giordano *et al.* 2003).

This decline in perceived susceptibility to peers corresponds to an acceleration of interest in romantic relationships, which become an increasing preoccupation from adolescence on through the adult transition (Sullivan 1953). Thus, more is happening than a drop in peer pressure; the *hierarchy of salience* in one's intimate relationships also undergoes significant changes. This change in basic emphasis is likely to occur even among those who have not acquired the benefits of the "good marriage," as the adult offender nevertheless has access to and is potentially influenced by these broader cultural frames and their own related changing expectations. This is another type of cognitive transformation associated with increased receptivity to previously identified hooks for change, including a larger role for romantic partner involvement.

Another potentially beneficial change that falls into this "secondary desistance processes" category involves transformations in the nature of relationships with parents/family of origin, as respondents have matured into adulthood. Prior research has shown that family problems, parental coercion, and the like are robust predictors of delinquency. Even though Sampson and Laub (1993) showed that variations in these family factors did not distinguish later criminal trajectories, it is potentially limiting to bracket off consideration of the role of bonds with parents and others in the family of origin. In many studies, "family" remains frozen in time as a set of adolescent risk factors; yet parents do not disappear from the scene in most instances. And within the contemporary context, parents and other members of the nuclear family represent a relatively enduring source of (potential) support and influence. Thus, changes in the character of parent–child relationships represent another type of transformation with implications for desistance. Respondents who participated in the OLS study sometimes described an "emotional mellowing"

(I realize now that she was doing the best she could with what she had) as they matured into adulthood. Although these qualitative data were suggestive of the benefits of such cognitive shifts, in a recent analysis relying on the TARS data, we examined the impact of changing parent–child ties more systematically. Results indicated that time varying measures of the quality of relationship with parents across the transition from adolescence to adulthood were significantly associated with within-individual changes in delinquency involvement over this period (Johnson *et al.* 2011), net of traditional covariates, including adult relationships and employment circumstances. This finding is consistent with the idea that such changes may occasion transformations in the meaning of the delinquent behavior itself (as a form of rebellion against perceived family difficulties), as well as the idea that improved relationships can provide tangible and moral support that facilitates the individual's forays into more prosocial territory. Even where parents remained involved in antisocial lifestyles or the relationship continued to be rocky, some OLS respondents described changes in perspective and associated agentic moves that allowed them to move forward ("I just decided I have to love her from a distance").

The above discussion offers a critique of the idea that offenders move forward in the life course essentially unchanged, but for their good fortune in experiencing one of a small handful of transition events. Certainly, this brief discussion does not provide a comprehensive roster or treatment of such changes, or fully explicate ways in which/conditions under which these factors influence desistance. As an example of research extending this general notion in useful ways, Carlsson (2013), in an analysis relying on interviews connected to the Stockholm Life-Course Project, recently developed a complex portrait of the age-specific nature of masculinity norms, and how these shifts in expectations may link up to movement away from criminal lifestyles. In particular, Carlsson (2013) highlights that previous discussions of masculinity–crime connections have remained somewhat static (i.e., in stressing themes such as aggression, independence, and sexual conquests that are essentially youth oriented conceptions of masculinity). This contrasts with narratives of adult respondents interviewed that reflected, e.g., perceived pressure to provide for oneself and loved ones as a more adult conception of what it means to "be a man." It is also potentially useful to consider that these and other shifts in perspective tend to be interrelated: reduced susceptibility to peer influence occurs in tandem with changes in views of self and others about what constitutes success (as a man, as a woman), and basic shifts in the salience of particular relationships.

The role of hooks for change

While we have suggested that these changing normative climates and the individual's own shifts in attitudes (and emotions!) play a significant role in desistance, Sampson and Laub's (1993) initial conceptual focus on the various transition events—notably marriage and employment—is well-motivated: clearly these are critical life course developments that can anchor a successful pattern of desistance. Given societal-level transformations within the contemporary context, however (e.g., marriage less likely/less stable, decline in availability of stable manufacturing jobs), our own analyses focused on a somewhat expanded list of hooks for change (e.g., religion, prison, but especially treatment experiences, parenthood). These catalysts may not always constitute clear watershed turning points, but can be foundations around which individuals build significant changes in life direction. Beyond adding to the basic roster of catalysts, what does a focus on cognitive transformations add to our understanding of their role in the change process? What does an SI/social view of these hooks for change offer, and how does this differ from a more individualistic treatment of the mechanisms involved?

Focusing on the "good marriage effect" itself provides a potentially useful illustration of our perspective, and specifically our emphasis on the reciprocal relationship between the actor and such environmental catalysts. Sampson and Laub (1993) outlined important advantages and sequelae of attachment to a spouse (build-up of investment/stake in conformity, changes in routine activities, spouse's control over the individual's conduct). Yet the why—other than chance or luck—of this new life development is not well explicated by the age-graded theory of informal social control. This omission is particularly notable when we consider that by and large these are the same offenders who have previously embraced non-conformity, avoided routine, and rebelled against a range of control attempts from any number of institutions and significant others. Thus, in our view, the individual's own openness to change and receptivity to specific hooks are critical features of the change process. Yet we resist in equal measure individualistic portraits of the change process (the idea that the offender simply tires of the old lifestyle, decides to craft a new identity, and goes about putting together the elements of a more respectable set of affiliations and routine activities). This depiction does not give sufficient weight to the array of social experiences and cultural expectations that fostered the changes in perspective, nor to the potentially key role of environmental factors in the redefinition and maintenance process.

What do "hooks" for change do? Hooks for change vary in their transformative potential, but effective ones and the worlds they open up not only act as a source of control over conduct but provide a specific blueprint for how to proceed as a changed individual. Thus, we argued that when it comes to partner effects, attachment (the cornerstone of control theories), while a generally positive development, is not nearly enough. Prosocial romantic partners *in particular* provide a strong contrast and their own behavior represents a roadmap for "doing" conformity or the "straight life," refining and reinforcing the new repertoire on a daily basis. This emphasis on "how to" (new attitudes, new conduct) is more consistent with social learning theories, but moves beyond the traditional terrain of this perspective (i.e., which has come to be linked primarily to the variable "delinquent peers"). Second, effective hooks for change contain a *projective* element that connects to *positive themes* as well as a more favorable *identity* that will supplant the one that must be left behind. Some hooks for change and associated identities (becoming a family man) virtually require the cooperation of others—this is a role that cannot be enacted without the spouse's buy-in and support. Finally, ideal hooks for change provide a *gateway to conforming others*. Again, the prosocial spouse is an excellent exemplar, as these individuals often have built-in ties to family and friends who provide ongoing support and reinforcement of the new direction. Yet our analyses showed that even though this particular "hook for change" has much to recommend it, the individual's own up-front motivation and continued invest-ment are required to make it work. Further, a motivated prosocial spouse ready to act as change agent, may be in short supply.

Our analyses of other specific hooks for change similarly demonstrated that an effect of exposure to a catalyst is far from automatic, and is inevitably influenced by the individual's own predilections and personal receptivity. An irony/complication following from this basic point is that the more personal and private a cognitive transformation, the more subject the new perspective is to further change. Thus, a number of individuals who participated in the OLS study indicated that they had benefited from spiritual transformations; yet the personal nature of their spiritual turn was at times implicated in the fragile quality of behavioral changes (e.g., when a relapse was theorized as the work of the devil). Thus, social reinforcement and support—even where the hook for change and the initial transformation trace to individual-level processes—often appeared to be critical features associated with sus-taining the new lifestyle. For example, Jane suggested that her friends from church helped her to benefit from the new spiritual direction, "even when I don't feel it."

Recent research on desistance from intimate partner violence and avenues for future research

Although most of our work on desistance has drawn on the OLS data, we recently completed a study of desistance from intimate partner violence (IPV) that relies on structured and in-depth qualitative data collected in connection with the TARS. The age distribution of the 5-wave TARS study (Giordano et al. 2015b) is useful for examining IPV desistance, as self-report and official statistics indicate peaks in prev-alence during adolescence and young adulthood, followed by significant declines (somewhat analogous to the age–crime curve, but not exactly—see Johnson et al. 2014). Although a full review of this research is beyond the scope of this chapter, we believe these analyses lend additional support for our social perspective on cog-nitive transformations, but suggest new considerations and suggestions for future research (Giordano et al. 2015b).

First, our analyses highlight the need to attend more systematically to the phe-nomenological aspects of specific crimes or other antisocial behaviors, a point that complicates the widely accepted "generality of deviance" notion. Certainly, a basic cache of risk factors operate whether the focus is on violence or drug use, and the same can be said for the basics of desistance. Nevertheless, the lived reality of specific offenses/offense patterns varies and may connect to distinct features of ces-sation processes. Thus, for example, the Glueck (1950) men who as teens had been involved primarily in acts of theft/burglary may well have experienced "desistance by default" as they had matured into adulthood (Laub and Sampson 2003). This situation contrasts with the life circumstances of many of the drug-involved offenders we interviewed in connection with OLS: discarding a significant addiction is very unlikely to occur outside the individual's own awareness and heightened resolve to change direction. The seductive, entrenched qualities of the latter and connections to an entire lifestyle (and attendant set of affiliations) reflect a different project that can influence whether, how and why change happens.

IPV provides another point of contrast in this regard. First, while theoretical treatments of IPV and applied efforts have focused on attitudes and relationship processes (e.g., power dynamics) that foster IPV, within the contemporary Western context hitting an intimate partner is not generally considered a source of status enhancement or overtly positive meanings. Research shows that these experiences are reliably associated with declines in mental health (even among perpetrators—see e.g., Johnson et al. 2014), relationship instability, and in studies tapping the acceptability of this behavior, receive low rates of endorsement (see e.g., Price et al. 1999). Garnering some experience with the realities or "lived experience" of IPV can heighten awareness of its negative features and sequelae, including the strong reactions of others to this conduct. These existential features of the experience may result in what we have labeled a "relationship learning curve" that is associated with the conscious intent to move away from the earlier pattern of behavior. This idea of positioning against negatives is congruent with Paternoster and Bushway's (2009) emphasis on "the crystallization of discontent," and highlights the need for more research on the relative salience of negatives and positives in understanding behavior change. This general notion of positioning against negatives is also consistent with (and indeed influenced our) revised perspective (see Figure 1.1) on sequencing, i.e., the idea that heightened appreciation of these negatives (a redefinition process) may foster other types of cognitive transformations—rather than occurring later in the sequence. Less clear is support (within our data and based on other studies) for Paternoster and Bushway's (2009) suggestion that this crystallization process does not tend to occur on the heels of one or two "failures," but only gradually and through a linking of many failures. This may not be a universally accurate description of IPV desistance processes, or even the process of desisting from crime. Instead, longitudinal studies indicate that many individuals desist from IPV and other antisocial patterns across a range of different levels of experience/chronicity. This is illustrated by, for example, Mulvey et al.'s (2010) research on adolescent desistance and our observation of substantial IPV cessation within and across relationships examined within the context of the TARS study (Giordano et al. 2015b).

Desistance from IPV can involve a range of specific mechanisms (routes to change) that are also somewhat unique: desistance and cognitive transformations are generally studied at the individual level, but the dyadic nature of some IPV experiences presents the possibilities for dyadic paths to desistance. The dyadic character of the phenomenon can also present fundamental roadblocks to lasting change, e.g., when one's partner has not experienced a similar cognitive transformation.

Alternatively, this feature of the experience presents more clear-cut opportunities (changing partners) relative to other forms of behavior change. We also noted that movement away from this unhealthy pattern did not necessarily connect to wholesale changes in lifestyle/affiliations, as has been theorized in many discussions of desistance and has figured so prominently in offenders' post-release requirements.

Gender and desistance

This research on continuity and change in IPV patterns also suggests avenues for additional research on gender and desistance. Our research has focused attention on girls and women for almost 40 years, and results across multiple analyses suggest limits to the bifurcation-of-theory approach (women get in/out of crime this way, men through a distinct set of processes). There is nevertheless a need to consider base rates and distinctive meanings as well as the effect of x factor on y outcome. For example, young men are more likely to affiliate with delinquent peers, but the effect of delinquent peers across gender tends to be quite similar in quantitative assessments. In examinations of romantic partner effects on desistance, we observe a generally similar impact of partner deviance across gender (Lonardo et al. 2009). Yet given the known base rates of crime according to gender, it is nevertheless important to highlight that men, on average, are more likely to marry up (that is, in the direction of a prosocial romantic partner). Conversely, women who have been stigmatized and often marginalized by drug involvement and periods of incarceration may have particular difficulty in locating a partner who operates as a prosocial influence.

Extending this line of research, we explored effects of gender on self-reports of IPV and again have found that predictors of IPV perpetration and victimization are remarkably similar across gender. However, a comprehensive understanding of the experience necessarily requires attention to distinctive base rates and meanings (examples of the latter: differences in fear, likelihood of injury). Focusing specifically on the issue of change in these patterns, we observe that, for example, women's narratives of change are more likely to include references to their children and their roles as mothers. Yet in an analysis of the effects of the transition to parenthood, we do not observe a significant within-individual effect for either women or men who participated in the TARS study. Conversely, our studies of relationship dynamics associated with IPV show that infidelity/infidelity concerns are strong risk factors (Giordano et al. 2015a) linked to within-individual variations in IPV reports. Again, interactions of gender and a scale indexing infidelity/infidelity concerns are not significant. Yet our examination of base rates provides a more complex portrait, as our data (and others, including analyses based on national samples) document that men are more likely to report infidelity or concurrent relationships (Ford et al. 2002). Thus, gendered relationship dynamics need to be taken into account as factors that influence conflict escalation as well as declines or desistance from this form of behavior. However, it is critical to conduct systematic research in these areas, as findings do not always conform to conventional wisdom. For example, across five waves of interviews, male respondents who participated in the TARS study on average score lower on perceived power within their relationships and higher on reports of partner control attempts (Giordano *et al.* 2012).

Cognitive transformations relating to IPV change often included increased recognition of the destructive qualities of infidelity (and male infidelity loomed large as a source of discord) as well as the need to avoid the use of negative forms of communication that individuals had begun to recognize were associated with conflict escalation (Giordano *et al.* 2015b). Our general point here is that the IPV learning curve encompassed specific areas of attitudinal and behavior change that may not be fully addressed by generic approaches.

The continuing impact of structural disadvantage

Finally, this study of IPV desistance highlights the need for more research on derailments (intermittent offending, the zig-zag pattern), and (relatedly) the considerable difficulties that trace directly to broader sources of structural disadvantage (see e.g., Farrall *et al.* 2011; Carlsson 2013). For example, while some prior IPV research has focused on the differences in male and female partners' earnings as a source of interpersonal conflicts, our results showed significantly higher odds of IPV among couples in which neither partner was "gainfully active" (defined as enrolled in school or employed full-time (Alvira-Hammond *et al.* 2014)). Social psychological approaches (and society) can ill afford to conceptualize persistence or derailments from a pattern of forward progress as simple functions of cognitive distortions (stinkin' thinkin') or inability to control or manage one's emotions. Sustained IPV desistance (and criminal desistance more generally) are for many not easy accomplishments. Unemployment, housing instabilities, mental health issues, and a full complement of other disadvantages are daily realities influencing more localized stress processes, access to prosocial networks, and the dynamics within intimate relationships. Research is needed that continues to forge direct links between the social psychological mechanisms involved in desistance (and derailments) and these broader sources of disadvantage (Bottoms *et al.* 2004).

References

Alvira-Hammond, M., Longmore, M. A., Manning, W. D. and Giordano, P. C. (2014), "Gainful activity and intimate partner aggression in emerging adulthood," *Emerging Adulthood* 2: 116–127.

Baumeister, R. (1994), "The crystallization of discontent in the process of major life change," in Heatherton, T. F. and Weinberger, J. L. (eds) *Can Personality Change?* Washington, DC: American Psychological Association, pp. 281–297.

Bottoms, A., Shapland, J., Costello, A., Holmes, D. and Muir, G. (2004), "Towards desistance: Theoretical underpinnings for an empirical study," *The Howard Journal of Criminal Justice* 43: 368–389.

Bushway, S. and Paternoster, R. (2013), "Desistance from crime: A review and ideas for moving forward," in Gibson, C. and Krohn, M. (eds) *Handbook of Life-Course Criminology*. New York: Springer, pp. 213–231.

Carlsson, C. (2013), "Processes of intermittency in criminal careers: Notes from a Swedish study on life courses and crime," *International Journal of Offender Therapy and Comparative Criminology* 57: 913–938.

Cernkovich, S., Giordano, P. and Pugh, M. (1985), "Chronic offenders: The missing cases in self-report delinquency research," *The Journal of Criminal Law and Criminology* 76: 705–732.

Fagan, J. (1989), "The social organization of drug use and drug dealing among urban gangs," *Criminology* 27: 633–670.

Farrall, S. and Bowling, B. (1999), "Structuration, human development and desistance from crime," *British Journal of Criminology* 39: 253–268.

Farrall, S., Sharpe, G., Hunter, B. and Calverley, A. (2011), "Theorizing structural and individual-level processes in desistance and persistence: Outlining an integrated perspective," *Australian and New Zealand Journal of Criminology* 44: 218–234.

Ford, K., Sohn, W. and Lepkowski, J. (2002), "American adolescents: Sexual mixing patterns, bridge partners, and concurrency," *Journal of the American Sexually Transmitted Diseases Association* 29: 13–19.

Giordano, P. (2010), *Legacies of Crime: A Follow-Up of the Children of Highly Delinquent Girls and Boys*. New York: Cambridge University Press.

Giordano, P., Cernkovich, S. and Rudolph, J. (2002), "Gender, crime, and desistance: Toward a theory of cognitive transformation," *American Journal of Sociology* 107: 990–1064.

Giordano, P., Cernkovich, S. and Holland, D. (2003), "Changes in friendship relations over the life course: Implications for desistance from crime," *Criminology* 41: 293–327.

Giordano, P., Schroeder, R. and Cernkovich, S. (2007), "Emotions and crime over the life course: A neo-Meadian perspective on criminal continuity and change," *American Journal of Sociology* 112: 1603–1661.

Giordano, P., Longmore, M., Schroeder, R. and Seffrin, P. (2008), "A life course perspective on spirituality and desistance from crime," *Criminology* 46: 99–131.

Giordano, P., Manning, W., Longmore, M. and Flanigan, C. (2012), "Developmental shifts in the character of romantic and sexual relationships from adolescence to young adulthood," in Booth, A., Brown, S., Landale, N., Manning, W. and McHale, S. (eds) *National Symposium on Family Issues, Vol. 2: Early Adulthood in a Family Context*. New York: Springer, pp. 133–164.

Giordano, P., Copp, J., Longmore, M. and Manning, W. (2015a), "Contested domains, verbal 'amplifiers,' and intimate partner violence in young adulthood," *Social Forces* 94(2): 923–951.

Giordano, P., Johnson, W., Manning, W., Longmore, M. and Minter, M. (2015b), "Intimate partner violence in young adulthood: Narratives of persistence and desistance," *Criminology* 53(3): 330–365.

Glueck, S. and Glueck, E. (1950), *Unraveling Juvenile Delinquency*. Cambridge, MA: Harvard University Press.

Johnson, W., Giordano, P., Manning, W. and Longmore, M. (2011), "Parent–child relations and offending during young adulthood," *Journal of Youth and Adolescence* 40: 786–799.

Johnson, W., Giordano, P., Manning, W. and Longmore, M. (2014), "The age-IPV curve: Changes in intimate partner violence perpetration during adolescence and young adulthood," Working Paper 2014–07, Bowling Green, OH: Bowling Green State University, Center for Family and Demographic Research.

Laub, J. and Sampson, R. (2003), *Shared Beginnings, Divergent Lives. Delinquent Boys to Age 70*. Cambridge, MA: Harvard University Press.

Lonardo, R., Giordano, P., Longmore, M. and Manning, W. (2009), "Parents, friends, and romantic partners: Enmeshment in deviant networks and adolescent delinquency involvement," *Journal of Youth and Adolescence* 38: 367–383.

Markus, H. and Nurius, P. (1987), "Possible selves: The interface between motivation and the self-concept," in Yardley, K. and Honess, T. (eds) *Self and Identity: Psychosocial Perspectives*. Oxford, UK: Wiley, pp. 157–175.

Maruna, S. (2001), *Making Good: How Ex-Offenders Reform and Reclaim Their Lives*. Washington, DC: American Psychological Association.

Matsueda, R. L. and Heimer, K. (1997), "A symbolic interactionist theory of role-transitions, role commitments, and delinquency," in Thornberry, T. (ed.) *Developmental Theories of Crime and Delinquency*. New Brunswick, NJ: Transaction, pp. 163–213.

Mead, G. (1913), "The social self," *The Journal of Philosophy, Psychology and Scientific Methods* 10: 374–380.

Mead, G. (1934), *Mind, Self, and Society from the Standpoint of a Social Behaviorist*. Chicago, IL: University of Chicago Press.

Mead, G. H. (1964), *On Social Psychology*. Chicago, IL: University of Chicago Press.

Mulvey, E. P., Steinberg, L., Piquero, A. R., Besana, M., Fagan, J., Schubert, C. and Cauffman, E. (2010), "Trajectories of desistance and continuity in antisocial behavior following court adjudication among serious adolescent offenders," *Development and Psychopathology* 22: 453–475.

Paternoster, R. and Bushway, S. (2009), "Desistance and the feared self: Toward an identity theory of criminal desistance," *Journal of Criminal Law and Criminology* 99: 1103–1156.

Price, E. L., Byers, E. S. and the Dating Violence Research Team. (1999), "The attitudes towards dating violence scales: Development and initial validation," *Journal of Family Violence* 14: 351–375.

Sampson, R. and Laub, J. (1993), *Crime in the Making: Pathways and Turning Points through Life*. Cambridge, MA: Harvard University Press.

Shapland, J. and Bottoms, A. (2011), "Reflections on social values, offending and desistance among young adult recidivists," *Punishment and Society* 13: 256–282.

Shover, N. (1985), *Aging Criminals*. New York: Sage.

Sullivan, H. (1953), *The Interpersonal Theory of Psychiatry*. New York: Norton.

Uggen, C. (2000), "Work as a turning point in the life course of criminals: A duration model of age, employment, and recidivism," *American Sociological Review* 65: 529–546.

Warr, M. (1998), "Life-course transitions and desistance from crime," *Criminology* 36: 183–216.

2

HUMAN AGENCY, CRIMINAL CAREERS AND DESISTANCE

Christoffer Carlsson

Introduction

More than ten years ago, Laub and Sampson described human agency as the 'missing link' in our understanding of both persistence and desistance (Laub and Sampson 2003: 141). Offenders, they noted, are 'active participants in constructing their lives' within the constraints of structure and context (Laub and Sampson 2003: 281). Human agency, conceived of in one way or another, has been deeply influential to life-course criminology and studies on desistance from crime (to mention just a few recent examples, see Carlsson 2013a; Healy 2013; King 2014). Developing a human agency committed to change, it is said, is perhaps even *the* most important predictor for desistance (LeBel *et al.* 2008). I return to definition(s) of human agency later in this chapter, but for the sake of clarity, in a very general sense, agency entails 'attempts to exert influence to shape one's life trajectory' (Hitlin and Elder 2007: 183). That is, we act with intent, based on our past experiences and striving towards the future and, in short, if an offender is to successfully desist from crime, it is crucial that s/he *wants* to and consciously *attempts* to do so.

Despite this development, King recently (2014), and rightly, noted that human agency is still a vague and elusive concept. Not that we do not have definitions: on the contrary, the definitions and conceptions of agency are numerous (e.g. Bottoms 2006). The purpose of this chapter is thus not to try and synthesize various conceptualizations of human agency, neither is it to provide empirical evidence for or against its importance for understanding and explaining criminal careers. Rather, my aim is to discuss and reflect upon human agency in a way that connects life-course theory to life-course methodology, and methodology to empirical findings.

Based on data from the Stockholm Life-Course Project (SLCP) – a life-course study of criminal careers that I have been involved in for a couple of years – I begin by presenting the study and reviewing empirical findings of the human agency–desistance connection. Having done so, I move on to discuss briefly what human agency is, arguing that perhaps a defining element of human agency may be that of intentionality. The following section constitutes the central part of the chapter, where I highlight a number of methodological underpinnings of studying human agency. I end the chapter with a number of tentative suggestions for future research.

The SLCP, human agency and desistance

The main purpose of the SLCP was to study and explain the different dimensions of the criminal career, e.g. the onset of crime, why offenders persist and why they desist. Thus far, the research findings of the SLCP have been reported in a number of papers and reports, among them Carlsson (2012, 2013a, 2013b, 2014), Sarnecki and Sivertsson (2013), Pettersson and Carlsson (2014) and Sivertsson and Carlsson (2014). It mainly consists of two research populations: the Clientele Boys and the §12 Youth.

The 1956 Clientele Study of Juvenile Delinquents was suggested by the Swedish Parliament in the mid-1950s, due to the then increasing rate of juvenile delinquency in Sweden (see SOU 1971: 49 for further details). In total 287 boys born in Stockholm during 1943–51 were enrolled in the study. The boys were divided into two groups, a crime group (n=192) and a matched control group (n=95).[1] The crime group was drawn from a random sample of boys who were: (1) at least 11 years old; and (2) registered for the first time for a non-trivial offence by the police department in Stockholm. The matched control group was drawn from the Swedish population records. In the 1980s, a follow-up was conducted (Sarnecki 1985) and the crime group was then divided into two groups, D1 (n=131) and D2 (n=61). In the D1 group, every boy was known by the police to have committed a crime prior to age 15. In the D2 group, the boys were known by the police to have committed 2 or more crimes prior to age 15. During the 1980s follow-up, 199 of the Clientele men were interviewed and of these, 157 were alive as we launched a new follow-up in 2010.

In 2010 we collected new, extensive register data on all 287 men, including criminal records, health and medical records, employment history, relationship history, and many other items. We also conducted new, long, life history interviews with a subset of the 199 men, aiming for depth rather than breadth, setting our goal at 30 interviews, that is, slightly more than 10 per cent of the total original sample.

The original D2 group – those with 2 or more registered offences prior to age 15 – consisted of 61 individuals. In the 1980s follow-up, 54 were still alive and of those, 36 were interviewed. In the 2010 follow-up, 26 of those 36 men were still alive, but even after extensive searches we were unable to locate 7 of the men. Letters were sent out to all remaining 19 men, and 15 of them were interviewed (the others declined, or were in such bad health that they could not be interviewed). The 15 persons interviewed in 2010 thus constitute a subset of the 36 D2 individuals interviewed in the 1980s.

In my own research on the Clientele boys, I have to date primarily made use of the interviews with these offenders, whose criminal careers were characterized by frequent and serious criminal offending. This follows the logic of Laub and Sampson (2001: 10) who argue that we should study the criminal career 'among those who reach some reasonable threshold of frequent and serious offending'. We know that low-rate offending in adolescence is normative, and the SLCP offender population is no exception here: they had all committed crimes, but the vast majority of them desisted in the transition to adulthood (see Sarnecki 1985).

The §12 Youth study was originally based on a Stockholm sample of 122 women and 298 men (n=420), born during 1969–74. During 1990–94 they were subject to interventions by the Swedish Social Services under the Care of Young Persons (Special Provisions Act), for residential treatment in so-called 'youth homes', or '§12 homes', then operated by the Stockholm County Council. Under this law, the state has the right to detain and treat young people involved in serious juvenile delinquency, substance misuse and/or 'other socially destructive behavior'. In a follow-up study made during 1998–99, when the sample was 24- to 29-year-olds, 132 of the 420 (31 per cent) were interviewed. Due to practical reasons, no official publications were produced, and thus closer documentation of this follow-up is missing. In 2010 we launched a second follow-up study on the original 420. Aside from collecting the same register data on all 420 as we did on the Clientele men, we also contacted 118 of the 132 who were interviewed in the previous follow-up. The remaining 14 had either died, or could not be located even after extensive searches. In total, life history interviews were conducted with 45 of the 118 (37 per cent). The structure of these interviews was similar to those with the Clientele men. In total 25 men and 20 women were interviewed, some only once but we interviewed several people multiple times.[2]

Human agency and desistance in the SLCP

In this section I summarize the work on human agency and desistance, using two publications as the main sources (Carlsson 2012; Sivertsson and Carlsson 2014).

The context of change and life-course processes

Carlsson (2012) shows how life-course processes, including the dynamics of human agency and the well-known concept of 'turning points' within them are often interdependent on each other, emerging in context-specific circumstances, and need to be understood as such. Even in a rather generous reading of research on turning points, the importance of context-specific transition processes is seldom explicitly stated. Life-course theories, Ulmer and Spencer note, often 'assume, or infer, these . . . processes' (Ulmer and Spencer 1999: 116), with explicit illustrations of the context and interconnectedness of processes of change in offending being even rarer (Laub and Sampson 2003, one could argue, is an exception, but even they tend to focus on processes of employment, family formation or military service as *separate* from, rather than *contingent* on each other).

With this basic outline in mind, the chapter conducts a close study of two life histories, one from our interviews with the Clientele boys ('David') and one with a §12 youth male ('Tomas'). In line with Gadd and Farrall (2004), who draw upon Hollway and Jefferson (2000), the two cases were selected on the basis that they were theoretically interesting with regards to processes of change in offending. Both cases included a similar background in social status and childhood experiences; early onset of offending; drug-use as an important part, but only a part, of the offending history; and salient changes in offending over time (including intermittency). The changes appear to have been brought about by a web of several processes, within which human agency is embedded and occupies an important position – but only in relation to the other processes.

Some of those processes may be structurally induced; others emerge at the interactional level. For example, in the account of David, several events and processes seem to indicate a turning point or a process of change in offending, including spiritualism, falling in love and engaging in a relationship, 'knifing off' the past by moving abroad, gaining a new sense of identity and getting diagnosed with HIV, and the development of human agency with the desire to quit. But none of these alone were salient enough for David to desist.

To understand the context of behavioural change and the possible impact of human agency in that process and how the offender's change towards desistance eventually unfolds, it is necessary to pay close attention to the *surrounding* processes, seeing how the changes become possible through past experiences, processes and events, and how human agency, in turn, makes future processes of change possible within that context. Thus, the chapter concludes, it is rare that processes of change in offending are dependent on only individual agency. Rather, they emerge in an interplay between the individual and the wider social community and society.

The meanings of human agency in high-risk individuals' life-course processes

Sivertsson and Carlsson's (2014) point of departure was the debate over the ability to make prospective, long-term predictions of criminal offending based on childhood risk factors. Using the 192 delinquent Clientele boys and the large amount of psychological and sociological variables collected in the original study, we began by constructing groups based on cumulative childhood risk, and then measured their subsequent criminal career outcomes. The results showed clear differences in adult offending. Around 80 per cent of the individuals in the high-risk group had been recorded for at least one non-trivial crime after adolescence, compared to around 40 per cent of those with the lowest risk. For both prevalence and incidence, a comparison between the four risk groups revealed an almost linear relationship.

However, while we found a pattern that followed the assumption of a cumulative risk effect, almost 20 per cent of the high-risk group were *not* recorded for a crime after age 15, whereas 40 per cent of the low-risk group *were* recorded for a crime. We therefore identified individuals in the low- and high-risk groups who did not develop the criminal careers that could be expected from their risk scores and analysed their life histories in detail; on the one hand, individuals who had a high childhood risk of future offending, but had desisted from crime in adulthood (we termed these *high-risk desisters*) and on the other, individuals with low childhood risk who had persisted in crime into adulthood (*low-risk persisters*). In this chapter, I limit my discussion to the high-risk desisters.

In adolescence, these men had engaged in serious juvenile delinquency and were thus well on their way to developing a persistent criminal career – but they did not. In the transition to adulthood, subjective changes occurred in their lives. This change was not always so explicitly described by our interview participants. Sven, for example, did not interpret himself as having been a 'criminal' who turned into a law-abiding citizen. Instead of a change in criminal activity or lifestyle, he talked about wanting to turn a 'hectic' life into a calmer and more responsible way of living, a 'turning' initiated by Sven himself. He used to be 'out [in pubs, clubs and on the street] all the time, seven days a week, for many years'. Then, approaching the transition to adulthood, he 'began to mature' and to 'value things differently'; he desired to 'settle down'. Such subjective changes 'may precede life-changing structural events and, to that extent, individuals can act as agents of their own change' (LeBel *et al.* 2008: 155). This process of change was described as an achievement, made possible through their capacity to act in the face of a difficult life situation. This way of responding to their life situation in an 'active manner' (Case and Haines 2009: 317) was further described as something they must manage on their own.

I: Yes, that [changing one's life] is difficult, I can imagine.

Ulf: Yes, that's depending on what kind of will you have, and how deep in trouble you are. You know, some people, they can't handle the loneliness, they have to go out and stuff like that. And that, it's damn easy to fall into, you know. But I have the view that, and I had that already when I was doing it [crime], how shitty it is. But there was like no . . . I couldn't keep it together. I had no job, no permanent place of living, I didn't have any stuff like that. I had nothing safe to hold on to. But then, when I managed to get that, everything started to shape up, and I did it all on my own. I won't, I can't say that anybody has helped me or anything, it was . . . It has worked out, I've had to fight a lot for it, on my own, but that's just good because I've made it.

Human agency is thus a necessary but insufficient condition for desistance to occur, as we see in Ulf's account. Structural opportunities (such as work and a stable place to live) are crucial. It was not until Ulf managed to 'get that' that 'everything started to shape up'. In that sense, the high-risk desisters' ways out of crime should not be understood as exceptional or as needing to be explained by other factors than those commonly used to explain desistance from crime in general: a change in one's self-image, coupled with social factors such as work and family life, can lead even high-risk individuals out of crime (Laub and Sampson 2003).

Human agency and desistance in the SLCP: two conclusions

In the SLCP our study of human agency generated two sets of conclusions, both of them being a possible subject for debate. The first one concerns the time- and context-contingent quality of human agency and how it may be connected to crime and desistance. The second conclusion follows from the first.

Time and context, crime and desistance

As people age and move along the life course and its various social institutions, their motivations change and this is reflected in the content of their human agency. But, conversely, people's human agency can influence their movement between social institutions and places in a social structure (which can, in turn, be reproduced and/or changed through individuals' agency; social structures are thus not static or constant). Following King (2014: 178), as individuals move through social contexts, they 'continually assess' these 'in relation to their goals and this may lead to a re-evaluation of these'. Contexts and life-course stages come with different social roles and resources, and these actively contribute to producing different forms of agency from individuals.

It is not surprising that young people often express no wish to cease their criminal offending, because it can be a fun, exhilarating and status-generating practice, leading to power and social inclusion in important peer groups. As people move along the life course, however, their agency tends to change; as offenders come of age, approach and enter the transition to adulthood – although that transition is less fixed in today's Western society than it used to be – they begin to develop a 'will to change' and to desist from crime.

In line with Shover (1996: 138), 'aging makes offenders more interested in the rewards of conventional lifestyles', as the temporal process of cumulative disadvantage makes the vulnerability and marginalization of the offender's life situation more perceptible. Similarly, the meaning of criminal behaviour tends to change. Having been a source of power, status and excitement in adolescence, it has now become a stigma, generating social exclusion. The risk-taking that was rewarding and exhilarating in adolescence has now become something negative: the revelation of one's own mortality and time as 'a diminishing, exhaustible resource' (Shover 1985: 83) is mirrored in the offender's changed self-perception. A similar theme is found in Paternoster and Bushway's (2009: 1116) theoretical development of a 'feared possible self' as a catalyst for change, where the offenders are faced with an 'image of what kind of future they now realize they do not want'. Whether or not this change in agency is enough for desistance to occur is the topic of the second conclusion.

Exploring the agency/desistance dynamics

It is, of course, possible for something like a process of 'desistance by default' to occur as the offender encounters structural or institutional turning points (Sampson and Laub 2005), but it is much more common for desistance from crime to be informed by a change in human agency.

Thus, in line with Giordano *et al.* (2002), in the SLCP we found that at different stages of the life course, offenders tended to vary in their 'openness' and capacity to respond to potential hooks for change. In the case of more serious offenders, this mechanism is especially important, since they often belong to segments of the social structure where the likelihood of exposure to institutional turning points is low. Consider, as an example of this, the following brief extract from our interview with Oliver, a long-time drug user who persisted in crime for a long time (from Carlsson 2013a):

Oliver: [When you consciously attempt to desist,] you resist temptations, you don't answer the phone, you go looking for work . . . you try to keep yourself busy and the day only has 24 hours, you know. So it [offending] got much less intense, until it became something I only rarely did.

Here, the catalyst of the desistance process is quite evident; it is Oliver's own will to change.

In accounts such as Oliver's, and Ulf's narrative of change above, we see two things: first, the way agency can make even high-risk individuals desist from crime. Second, we also see the intricate interplay between 'subjective' factors, such as cognitive changes, and 'objective' factors, such as work or family life (LeBel *et al.* 2008). Here is where the SLCP may provide a more in-depth analysis of the dynamics of agency, structure and desistance.

A person may take advantage of various hooks for change when they are presented to them, but they may also try and navigate themselves into a position where they are more likely to be presented to them. Individuals' human agency can also condition the very experience of the various social problems they tend to encounter as they attempt to desist; that is, it can make individuals 'better able to weather disappointments or setbacks' (LeBel *et al.* 2008: 154). This balancing act, where hope is weighed against realism, is difficult for many offenders to achieve (Paternoster and Bushway 2009), and in the SLCP we found that many of the serious offenders' desistance processes tended to be informed by this mechanism throughout their way out of crime.

Having managed to enter the process of desistance through exercising their human agency, attaching themselves to 'hooks for change', they also made strategic moves and choices to make sure they managed to continue on their new path. At the time of the interview, for example, Ulf (in Sivertsson and Carlsson 2014) was a blue-collar worker who said that he would 'probably change his job', had he been able to pursue higher education. He was not satisfied with his employment, but he still considered getting it as one of the most important events in his life. This change – initiated by himself through his human agency – was central for him to be able to leave crime behind, and it continued to be so because if he lost it, he would probably 'fall back again'. To stay with his job he adopted small, conscious strategies, trying to 'make the best out of it', such as trying to only socialize with colleagues whose company he enjoyed and not thinking about his job other than during working hours.

When people do something, they sometimes experience doubt and regret. In fact, Matza (1969: 106) claims that doubt and regret 'are implicit in human engagement'. There is thus an inherent uncertainty in agency, having clear implications for any discussion of desistance: false starts, incomplete attempts at desistance and the way criminal behaviour may wax and wane over time are simply aspects of human and thus social life.

Accordingly, our studies of desistance in the SLCP support the argument made by Giordano *et al.* (2002: 992) that 'agentic movies' are often the most influential factors that drive the desistance process. But having said that, the SLCP also highlights the fact that 'any account of human action ... also needs to account for the role of structure in enabling or constraining that action' (King 2013: 318). It is, in other words, important to resist the current tendency – which Healy (2013: 565) suggests is a consequence of the forces of late modernity – to regard structural problems as personal shortcomings, and instead recognize the interconnectedness of the social and personal world of the offender.

Understanding human agency

Human agency is a contested concept, for many reasons. First, its meaning is rather unclear and in the instances where it appears to be less so, it is still a problematic concept. Returning to Hitlin and Elder's general outline, agency entails 'attempts to exert influence to shape one's life trajectory' (Hitlin and Elder 2007: 183). This is, however, a very broad statement, and so I go straight to one of the most influential, well-known and intricate definitions that tries to cover the complexities of agency. In their seminal paper, Emirbayer and Mische (1998: 970) adopt a symbolic interactionist perspective and define agency as:

> [t]he temporally constructed engagement by actors of different structural environments – the temporal-relational contexts of action – which, through the interplay of habit, imagination and judgment, both reproduces and transforms those structures in interactive response to the problems posed by changing historical situations.

Definitions such as this one are great theoretical achievements and at the same time lead to great difficulties. For, on the one hand, although theorists such as Emirbayer and Mische provide us with definitions that try to capture the very complexity that surrounds the concept and phenomenon of agency, such definitions often do not lend themselves very well to empirical research. On the other hand, when empirical research tries to understand the role that agency plays (or does not play) in the desistance process, the operationalized version of agency tends to be relatively simplistic (Hitlin and Elder 2007). This tension naturally leads to contention. Can agency be captured in empirical reality? Can it perhaps even be measured in numbers (a question I will return to at the end of this chapter)? If so, it seems reasonable to break down the concept into dimensions – but what dimensions? In empirical research, the attempts range widely – from 'the ability to initiate self-change' (Thoits 2003), 'self-efficacy' (Gecas 2003) 'or planful competence' Clausen (1991), to Alexander's (1992) 'moments of freedom' and 'effort', and beyond.

In general, it seems to me that most attempts at breaking down agency into dimensions include notions of intentionality and transformation (see Lindegaard and Jacques 2014). In the case of desistance from crime, the transformative dimension of agency may be a useful point of departure for understanding the beginning of the desistance process. However, since Maruna (2001) showed us that desistance, more than anything, is a process of maintenance, it seems reasonable to assume that some element of continuity (once change has been initiated) is also involved. Does such continuity, no matter how conscious and deliberate it is on the part of the offender, *not* consist of 'agentic moves'? That seems unlikely.[3]

Intentionality, on the other hand, seems closer to what we actually mean and refer to when we discuss agency: we may have a certain intention in (not) acting in a given way, but whether or not things work out the way we intend them to is contingent upon the social world within which we live and the position(s) we occupy in that world – that is, social structure and stratification (Matsueda 2006). I do not suggest that human agency is equal to intentionality; clearly, it is not. However, it does seem to me that intentionality may be the one element of human agency that we can agree on is close to its core. Intentionality (not to be confused with *intensionality*), of course, is a contested philosophical concept and I do not intend to move into such deep waters here. I will just offer one suggestive view of intentionality, namely, a Heideggerian one: in this view, intentionality is primarily practical and can be understood as a kind of skilful coping, undertaken by a social, norm-bound, engaged and context-dependent, embodied being. To break it down a bit, to 'skilfully cope' with something is – or, since Heidegger is notoriously difficult to read, could at least be understood – to be practically and consciously engaged in an intentional project (such as wanting to change one or several parts of one's life, e.g. from being unemployed to being employed, from using drugs to stopping using drugs, etc.).

What causes an individual to intend one thing rather than another, and what makes this intention shift over time (i.e. in the short or long term)? Here, life-course criminology offers different answers: some (including me) suggest a thoroughly social mechanism, where social experiences, 'foster new definitions of the situation . . . and a blueprint for how to succeed as a changed individual' (Giordano *et al.* 2002: 1607). Others argue that 'intentional self-change is understood to be more cognitive, internal, and individual' (Paternoster and Bushway 2009: 1106).

At any rate, it seems to me that a closer examination of the various elements or dimensions of human agency should be a priority for us in the future. When we say that an individual exercises their human agency – what do we mean by that? In fact, one common critique of human agency (as a concept) may be closely connected to our inability to pin down what we mean: thus, agency can become a kind of residual category, which the researcher uses when a behaviour cannot be explained by the common, sociological determinants (see Matsueda 2006). In clarifying our thinking about agency – and thus our way of working with the concept – the dimension of intentionality could be one such useful and basic starting point.

Human agency and empirical desistance studies

For the remainder of this discussion, I focus on a question that, in one way, is much more interesting. Regardless of how we define human agency – what it is, what it is not and what causes within-individual changes in agency over time – we, as empirical researchers, are confronted with a very practical task: to study its relationship to the criminal career. As I have emphasized above, studies which explore the connection between human agency and desistance tend to find that a human agency committed to change is one of the most – if not *the* most – important predictor of desistance. Almost all such studies are qualitative in nature and predominantly use life history interviews as their method.

In one way, this is self-evident and in no need of discussion. After all, if we are studying the importance agency has (if any) for an individual's process of change – rather than studying, say, relations between variables – we are forced to turn to the actual individual. In another way, however, we should carefully study the relation between method and empirical data in this regard. This, I think, is where we must improve significantly to move ahead.

Life history interviews

Qualitative studies of criminal careers have always been important: consider, for example, Meisenhelder's (1977) early interview study, which, based on interviews with a small number of property offenders, outlined the process of exiting a criminal career using social control theory. Still, it was not until Sampson and Laub's (1993) first book on the Gluecks' (1950) data that qualitative analyses of criminal careers really took off. In life-course criminology, the life history interview has become a particularly important method. Among other things, this interview form reveals, 'in the offenders' own words the personal–situational context of their behavior and their views of the larger social and historical circumstances in which their behavior is embedded' (Laub and Sampson 2003: 58). Consider the benefits Laub and Sampson (2003: 58f) see in life history interviews:

> First, the life-history method uniquely captures the process of both becoming involved in and disengaging from crime and other antisocial behavior . . . Second, life histories can uncover complex patterns of continuity and change in individual behavior over time. Life-history narratives focus on the whole of life, not just one dimension or a set of variables . . . A third advantage is that life histories reveal the complexity of criminal behavior . . . . A fourth advantage is that life histories are grounded in social and

historical context....A fifth advantage is that the life-history method shows the human side of offenders.

By interviewing (ex-)offenders in depth about their lives in and out of crime, going beyond the structured survey-like interview form, something like a story or *narrative* emerges. The idea underlying this perspective on the social world is the notion that we 'understand the occurrence of events by learning the steps in the process by which they came to happen' (Becker 1998: 61). This doesn't necessarily imply linearity or continuity, but rather that, as Shaw (1930: 13) notes, 'any specific act of the individual becomes comprehensible only in the light of its relation to . . . past experiences' and the individual projecting themselves into the future.

This, I believe, is a relatively common conception of the value of life history interviews. There are two interconnected issues here, which are crucial to consider. For simplicity, I refer to them as *the issue of exaggerated order* and *the issue of self-representation*.

The issues of exaggerated order and self-representation

Given the stage that any person has reached in a career, one typically finds that he constructs an image of his life course – past, present, and future – which selects, abstracts and distorts in such a way as to provide him with a view of himself that he can usefully expound in current situations.

(Goffman 1961: 150)

Goffman presents the life-course criminologist with a problem that – while a feature of social life in general – can make interviews difficult to use and interpret, given that the researcher has a specific goal in mind. The potential problem can be defined in terms of self-presentation (Järvinen 2001). Interview situations are sites of knowledge production and interview participants construct stories and narratives according to more or less distinct frameworks grounded in and contingent upon a specific social and historical context:

A life history is a social construction, created by the narrator in interaction with his environment. A biography is a story put together with the help of culturally available instruments and ingredients . . . When interview subjects talk about their lives, they do so with the help of explanatory models that are legitimate in their culture . . . To give meaning to the narrator himself and to the listener, the story must be structured, and this structuring process thus follows a socially fixed pattern.

(Järvinen 2000: 372f)

We recognize this from recent developments in narrative criminology (Presser 2009; Sandberg 2013). When an individual tells their story by looking into the past, what tends to emerge through the narrator is a story that is logical and ordered. Human life, however, consists of contradictions, indetermination, confusion, reversion and indecisiveness (Blumer 1969; Järvinen 2000). Consider the fact that processes of desistance often seem to be contingent on a variety of factors, events and experiences (e.g. Carlsson 2012). It is easy to retrospectively construct and order these factors, events and experiences into a smooth and ordered path through time and place. From the perspective of the present, it provides an explanation that is meaningful, both to us as researchers and to the interview participant. However, such an explanation may exaggerate the amount of logic and order that is inherent in human social life.

Life history narratives, in other words, are fragmented, and 'analysing them as unified will always be a simplification' (Sandberg 2013: 80). As researchers, we can easily bring forth a unified narrative, depending on the questions we ask: if we only ask about the individual's criminal history, the interview participant will tell a relatively coherent story of crime. Adding to this tendency, of course, is the common use of various versions of the life history calendar (e.g. Freedman *et al.* 1988) where the complexity and contradictions inherent in human life can be structured in a seemingly logical, ordered manner.[4] Life histories, moreover, are contingent on the factor of time:

> A biography is a narrative told by a person no longer the same as the person the story concerns. The function of the story, however, is to create a meaningful relationship between 'the present of the past, the present of the present, and the present of the future'.
>
> *(Järvinen 2004: 63)*

A relatively logical question derives from this: what kind of sense does a life history narrative make (Bradbury and Sclater 2000)? Is it psychological, social, cultural – or merely linguistic? But, Järvinen continues, and this is important for understanding the dynamics of life histories, during the interview the past that emerges through the lens of the narrator's present situation is not an 'anything goes' past. '*Life* does not disappear out of the *life histories*, leaving us with mere *histories*, comprehended as textual structures' (Järvinen 2004: 64).

If we take this perspective – as I do here, although it is not by any means the only one to take – life histories are thus personal creations, but not exclusively so, and at the same time products of social life, but not determined by it. In other words, in the interview situation the interview participant constructs a narrative that is meaningful and acceptable to them, not only in a personal sense but also in a social one (Holstein and Gubrium 1995).

In sum, then, while life-course criminologists have valuably utilized the life history interview approach, we have at the same time tended to side-step the very old and equally controversial issue of 'life as lived' versus 'life as told' (Bradbury and Sclater 2000). This is a problematic state of affairs when we turn to the concept and phenomenon of human agency.

Human agency in life history interviews

Consider, once again, this interview extract with Ulf (from Sivertsson and Carlsson 2014):

I: Yes, that [changing one's life] is difficult, I can imagine.

Ulf: Yes, that's depending on what kind of will you have, and how deep in trouble you are. You know, some people, they can't handle the loneliness, they have to go out and stuff like that. And that, it's damn easy to fall into, you know. But I have the view that, and I had that already when I was doing it [crime], how shitty it is. But there was like no . . . I couldn't keep it together. I had no job, no permanent place of living, I didn't have any stuff like that. I had nothing safe to hold on to. But then, when I managed to get that, everything started to shape up, and I did it all on my own. I won't, I can't say that anybody has helped me or anything, it was . . . It has worked out, I've had to fight a lot for it, on my own, but that's just good because, I've made it.

Many life-course criminologists (including me) would analyse this narrative along these lines: human agency constitutes a central explanatory mechanism, not only in Ulf's initial change towards desistance but also in the maintaining of desistance – but it is not enough. On the contrary, Ulf initially 'had nothing safe to hold on to'. In that sense, human agency must align with the social and material resources (a job, a permanent place of living) in order for desistance to actually occur, but agency is still the catalyst and driving force of desistance.

One of my main points with this chapter is to consider the methodological underpinnings at work here. We know from studies of narrative inquiry, interview techniques and other related methodological issues that when people narrate their lives they tend to do so in ways that highlight themselves as active agents, not least when narrating important life-course changes such as desisting from crime (see Holstein and Gubrium 1995; Atkinson 1998; Hollway and Jefferson 2000; Kvale and Brinkmann 2008). This does not mean that individuals narrate their lives in ways that are 'untrue' or 'wrong'. Rather, it means that the life history interview tends to generate the kind of life story that a person lives by (Maruna 2001), and the story that they live by tends to be a story in which they have had something to say and do to affect its outcome – in other words, the life history interview tends to generate narratives where human agency becomes a central, explanatory mechanism.

Similarly, the life history interview often generates a narrative grounded in the interview participant's attempt to present themselves in a specific way during the interview. Here, I take the example of masculinity and its importance for male criminal careers (Carlsson 2013b). Interviewing 25 Swedish males born in the early 1970s, I studied the dynamics of masculinities, persistence and desistance using qualitative life history interviews. In the discussion section of the chapter, I noted that, 'their self-presentations during the interviews were part of their masculinity projects' (Carlsson 2013b: 685). One of the ways in which the interview participants did this is illustrated by the interview participant 'Sam' (Carlsson 2013b: 673):

Sam: You know, nobody can tell me what to do. That's always been, because I do what I want. If I don't want to do something, then I won't do it. I just won't, because I don't feel like going by anybody else's rules. I kept going [persisted in crime] as long as I wanted to.

In this extract, Sam simultaneously connects the way he 'is' to his past, but also, crucially, he demonstrates a certain masculinity project *within* the interview situation. This does not mean that human agency does not matter when it comes to why Sam and others act the way they do: in the case of a masculinity project, it impacts on action as well as the way actions are retrospectively narrated (Connell 2005). The point is that the reasons behind why interview participants present themselves in the ways that they do are contingent on various dimensions of identity, including age, gender, class, ethnicity and so on. In the case of men's masculinity projects, we would be wise to consider the fact that stressing one's human agency may be an important constitutive dimension of that very project. However, the point I want to make is not restricted to gender, but is more general: in the interview situation, what is ultimately at stake is the interview participant's self and the interviewer's impression of it.

Once again, then, life as told may be an important facet of life as lived, but we must be careful not to equate them, and particularly when we study human agency. To a greater extent than we have thus far, the least we should do is acknowledge these potentially very important methodological dilemmas that underpin our analyses.

The social and political narrative context

Adding another layer to human agency, we must also consider the socio-historical, political context within which the interview participants of various longitudinal research projects tell their stories today. Given the proposition that narratives reflect both the personal and social world of the narrator, we should expect that a changing political climate impacts on the narratives that are told. When it comes to the narratives of offenders, it may be particularly relevant to map the changes in criminal policy that have taken place in Western society during the last 30 to 40 years; changes which numerous times have been documented extensively and eloquently in the literature (e.g. Garland 2002; Hagan 2010; Pratt and Eriksson 2013). The more rational choice-oriented criminal policy models may have been less distinct in Sweden and Scandinavia than in the US or UK, due to the stronger, traditional frame of the welfare state (Garland 2002). Even in Scandinavia, however, it has meant distinct changes in the way people who commit crimes are conceived of and dealt with by the criminal justice system and its associated agencies. Consider Tham's (2012) description of the political change in Sweden:

During the 1960s and 1970s, the offender was a victim. He was a victim of his upbringing and an unjust society. He did not really want to commit crimes but felt forced to do so by his circumstances . . . Today the offender is unambiguously a villain. He chooses to commit crimes himself, and he is fully aware that he is violating other people's rights. This is in line with a neo-liberal outlook and where one also has to accept the consequences of one's own actions: Make crime, do time.

(Tham 2012: 20)

Many of the recently initiated criminal justice policies are driven by what King (2013: 324) terms the 'individualization thesis'. That is, King continues on the same page, these policies neglect the structural constraints that 'inhibit identity construction and . . . the importance of access to economic resources and cultural spaces that make self-realization a possibility'. Our era is one of increased individualization under the cloak of neoliberal politics, where the individual (at least to a greater extent than in the past) is responsible for their successes and failures:

[w]hen structural problems are regarded as personal shortcomings that must be resolved through individual action, young people feel responsible for their inevitable failure to achieve life success . . . most young people endorse the late-modern principle that personal effort is the primary route to success.

(Healy 2013: 565)

What does this mean for the qualitative study of human agency? Narratives where human agency – where the individual's own choices, will, intentions and so on are emphasized – fit very well with this general political climate and its consequent perspective on the human subject. Stories where agency is a driving force and a central explanation for the waxing and waning of the criminal career, are just the kind of account that people are expected to produce within such a context. Our time and place is one 'where agency has been pushed to the forefront in social life' (Healy 2013: 571) and, as such, we must consider its potentially important impact on the narratives (ex-)offenders tell us about their lives.

'Yes. We know. And?' – concluding and looking forward

In sum, then, human agency is not only a concept that is difficult to pin down and study empirically; no matter how we choose to conceive of and use it, we also run into additional methodological dilemmas in practical, empirical data collection.

I do not believe that this methodological discussion includes anything new; on the contrary, my remarks are similar to dilemmas and problems that are often found in textbooks on qualitative interview methodology. Since this is the case, it is quite remarkable that they (to my knowledge, I should add) are rarely mentioned when we report qualitative research findings, both in books and journal articles. Thus, I suggest that in the near future we should devote more attention to these elements of human agency, its connection to the criminal career and to desistance in particular.

Despite my cautionary remarks in this chapter, human agency is *not* a mere artifact of the method. After all, a basic principle of the life-course approach is that humans are, 'fundamentally active beings' (Hitlin and Elder 2007: 185). Not to consider agency in criminal career research would indeed not be to consider an important explanatory mechanism. In fact, while most evidence of this does come from qualitative studies, a number of quantitative studies also suggest that indicators of agency very much impel and facilitate desistance (Maruna 2004; LeBel *et al.* 2008).

That being said, if I have touched upon issues that indeed are important, we have a lot of work to do. Below are a number of implications, which follow from the arguments of this chapter.

1.   The need for continued labour on developing agency as a concept

It is crucial to continue to devote theoretical labour on developing and clarifying the concept of human agency. Importantly, it may be useful to strive towards clarifying and breaking down agency, to the extent that it is possible, in order to make it more accessible to empirical study. In fact, the distinction between theoretical development and empirical exploration is likely to be counterproductive here: I am inclined to agree with Becker (1998), whose approach to the development of concepts and theory is to do so in constant dialogue with empirical data.

At the same time, those involved in empirical research should be more careful and precise when utilizing the concept of human agency (one such example is King 2014). I do not suggest that we should all unite under one definition when we use the concept; only that we make clear what we mean when we do. Otherwise, we do risk exposing ourselves to the perhaps somewhat just criticism that agency is what remains of the variation in our data, when the other concepts we use have done their job.

2.   Human agency and the criminal career: is there a connection? How does it look?

The second implication follows from the first. The main life-course criminological work on agency has been done on change and desistance. That is, it is common to equate agency with change; agentic moves are moves an actor makes in order to change their current state, situation or trajectory. In a similar vein, Matsueda (2006: 91) describes human agency as a mechanism for 'creativity' and 'innovation' – in other words, change.

We may want to pay equal attention to the connection between agency and other features of the criminal career as well, such as escalation or continuity (i.e. persistence). It is a mistake, Bottoms (2006) argues, to assume that 'true action' cannot be habitual or continuous. In a study on intermittency (Carlsson 2013b), I suggested that one form of intermittency could be characterized by continuity rather than change; the interview participants described their lulls and drifts in offending in terms of 'things rumbling on' and 'staying in the game'. In line with this, another paper (Carlsson 2013a) argued that persistence can be a way of demonstrating one's power, will and control over one's own everyday life at a certain stage in the life course. To persist in crime can thus be an agentic move, a way of handling a difficult situation within a process of interpersonal and structural cumulative disadvantage, where what is at stake is one's own perception of self.

We know that agency in several ways may be connected to desistance, but what about the other part(s) of the criminal career? To give just one example, a recent study by Lindegaard and Jacques (2014: 85) argues that agency has 'a dark side as well' and that some people engage in crime to 'transform their life'. When this happens, they suggest, agency is a cause of crime. In a brief analysis, they also argue that agency can be a 'crucial factor' in the continuation of crime (Lindegaard and Jacques 2014: 96). In line with my own research (Carlsson 2013a), they find that criminal offending 'allowed them to redefine themselves in a manner that gave them self-esteem and power' (Lindegaard and Jacques 2014: 96). In order for us to understand more fully the ways in which agency works, moving beyond the study of desistance can be meaningful and promising.

3.   Expand studies of human agency beyond qualitative research

As noted before, life-course criminological research on human agency has been predominantly qualitative. This is hardly surprising, considering the strengths of qualitative methodology when it comes to understanding the social reality of the individual actor and their life-world. However, just as qualitative life-course criminological inquiries have greatly contributed to a research field dominated by quantitative methods (e.g. Blumstein *et al.* 1986), quantitative attempts at studying and understanding dimensions of human agency could greatly increase and deepen our knowledge here. Indeed, as I noted above, some exploratory quantitative attempts have already been made (e.g. Maruna 2004; LeBel *et al.* 2008; Paternoster and Bushway 2009) and we need to follow their example.

I understand that exactly how this can and should be done is not an easy problem to solve, but my contention is that it will be worth the work. If we do this, due to the benefits of quantitative analysis, we may begin to uncover broader patterns of human agency – what may obstruct or enable it and what it needs to work in tandem with in order for desistance to occur and be maintained – within a given population of (ex-)offenders.

4.   Devote methodological attention to the study of human agency

Finally, it is time to examine empirically the methodological dimensions of studying human agency. Although I touched upon this in the previous implication above, I would like to end with a somewhat different methodological focus: a qualitative one.

We have made lots of ground since we began our empirical studies of agency, criminal careers and desistance. However, it seems to me that our research field could benefit from empirically examining the impact our methodological choices have on our findings and analysis in any given case. To give just one example, how do the questions we ask our interview participants (and the way in which we ask them) impact upon the narratives they tell us, with regard to human agency? For example, imagine that we split a sample of ex-offenders into two groups that, on a group level, are identical when it comes to, say, composition of age, gender, class, ethnicity and criminal histories. We then try and break down the concept of human agency into concrete interview questions and, as we interview the ex-offenders in Group 1, we explicitly ask about its possible importance in the desistance process. If we then interview Group 2 about the desistance process, but *without* asking explicitly about the possible importance of human agency – do their narratives of desistance differ from those collected in Group 1, or does human agency still emerge as a central, explanatory mechanism? Even such a relatively simple methodological study could generate substantial knowledge and help to answer one of the oldest scientific questions, namely, how the concept and phenomenon are connected to the method.

Another suggestion is to use the life history method as it was originally conceived. While the life history interview was considered a crucial element of the life history method, it was not the only one, and partly due to the very reasons I have outlined in this chapter. As Shaw (1930: 2) sharply observes:

> The value of [the life history interview document], however, is greatly diminished because of the absence of supplementary case material which might serve as a check on the authenticity of the story and afford a basis for a more reliable interpretation of the experiences and situations described . . . Thus each case study should include, along with the life-history document, the usual family history, the medical, psychiatric, and psychological findings, the official record of arrest, offenses, and commitments, the description of the play-group relationships, and any other verifiable material which may throw light upon the personality and actual experiences of the delinquent in question.

Shaw, of course, uses words that I would not, such as *authenticity*, *verifiable*, *reliable* and *actual experiences*. The general value of using several data sources to get a deeper and clearer understanding of something, however, has been illustrated in a few life-course criminological works, such as Steffensmeier and Ulmer's (2005) study. In this version, the life history method is extremely demanding and time-consuming – but for empirical purposes and the development of theory, it is also a highly valuable tool (Becker 1966).

For methodological purposes, and in order to develop our understanding of human agency, I suggest that analyses of this kind may be equally useful. Consider, for example, the possibility of 'triangulating' our interview with the (ex-)offender with data such as the (ex-)offender's journal (if they keep one), interviews with their friends, interviews with treatment officials, reading and analysing the individual's treatment journals (in Sweden, the behaviour and in-treatment progress of juvenile delinquents and young adult offenders who serve time in special youth reformatories is carefully monitored and documented in individual journal-like documents), interviews with probation officers and official probation data and so on. Each of these data sources comes with its own possibilities and problems, of course, and must be used accordingly.

Such an analysis, while potentially very rewarding, still entails a largely qualitative enterprise. However, in conjunction with my previous point – which suggested that we broaden our methodological tool box even more and encourage researchers to think of ways to operationalize, measure and analyse human agency *quantitatively* – I believe we will move towards a state within life-course criminology where the desistance process is not only more clearly and deeply understood but also methodologically rigorous.

Notes

1 Initially, a pre-study was conducted with 50 boys in the crime group and 50 in the control group. For the main study, due to resources, they revised the design and took a larger sample of 'crime boys' (n=150), but matched only *every third* boy with a 'control boy' (n=50). The initial size of the total sample (including both the pre-study and the main study) was thus 300, but due to attrition and sampling errors the total size was reduced to 287. The boys were matched on four variables: age, social group, family type and neighbourhood.
2 It is important to acknowledge a number of limitations to the SLCP. The size and character of the samples make any inferences difficult: our findings are based on a relatively small number of delinquent boys who are, predominantly, white, working-class and living in metropolitan areas. The way we approached our interviews and what we gained in depth and context, we lost in breadth; a perennial compromise of social science research.
3 While on the topic of continuity: note that although human agency, at least in life-course criminology, is often used to understand processes of change, there is nothing, it seems to me, that excludes processes of continuity (e.g. agency may be a useful concept to understand persistence in crime, as well as desistance, see Carlsson 2014; Lindegaard and Jacques 2014).
4 While the life history calendar inevitably structures a human life on a path consisting of various trajectories, this is also its main purpose and one of its strengths. I should note that it can also be used to *highlight* complexity and contradiction. The number of life-course criminological studies where this is done, however, seems to be very low.

References

Alexander, J. C. (1992), 'Some remarks on "agency" in recent sociological theory', *Perspectives* 15: 1–4.
Atkinson, R. (1998), *The Life Story Interview*. London: Sage.
Becker, H. S. (1966), 'Introduction', in Shaw, C. R. (ed.) *The Jack-Roller. A Delinquent Boy's Own Story*. Chicago, IL: University of Chicago Press.
Becker, H. S. (1998), *Tricks of the Trade*. Chicago, IL: University of Chicago Press.
Blumer, H. (1969), *Symbolic Interactionism. Perspective and Method*. Berkeley, CA: University of California Press.
Blumstein, A., Cohen, J., Roth, J. A. and Visher, C. A. (eds) (1986), *Criminal Careers and Career Criminals*. Washington, DC: National Academy Press.

Bottoms, A. H. (2006), 'Desistance, social bonds, and human agency: A theoretical exploration', in Wikström, P.-O. H. and Sampson, R. J. (eds) *The Explanation of Crime. Context, Mechanisms, and Development.* Cambridge, UK: Cambridge University Press.

Bradbury, P. and Day Sclater, S. (2000), 'Conclusion', in Andrews, M., Day Sclater, S., Squire, C. and Treacher, A. (eds) *The Uses of Narrative. Explorations in Sociology, Psychology, and Cultural Studies.* New Brunswick, NJ: Transaction Publishers.

Carlsson, C. (2012), 'Using "turning points" to understand processes of change in offending. Notes from a Swedish study on life-courses and crime', *British Journal of Criminology* 52: 1–16.

Carlsson, C. (2013a), 'Processes of intermittency in criminal careers: Notes from a Swedish study on life-courses and crime', *International Journal of Offender Therapy and Comparative Criminology* 57: 913–938.

Carlsson, C. (2013b), 'Masculinities, persistence, and desistance', *Criminology* 51: 661–693.

Carlsson, C. (2014), *Continuities and Changes in Criminal Careers.* Dissertation. Stockholm, Sweden: University of Sweden, Department of Criminology.

Case, S. and Haines, K. (2009), *Understanding Youth Offending: Risk Factor Research, Policy and Practice.* Portland, OR: Willan Publishing.

Clausen, J. S. (1991), 'Adolescent competence and the shaping of the life course', *American Journal of Sociology* 96: 805–842.

Connell, R. W. (2005), *Masculinities.* Cambridge, UK: Polity Press.

Emirbayer, M. and Mische, A. (1998), 'What is agency?', *American Journal of Sociology* 103: 962–1023.

Freedman, D., Thornton, A., Camburn, D., Alwin, D. and Young-DeMarco, L. (1988), 'The life history calendar: A technique for collecting retrospective data', *Sociological Methodology* 18: 37–68.

Gadd, D. and Farrall, S. (2004), 'Criminal careers, desistance, and subjectivity. Interpreting men's narratives of change', *Theoretical Criminology* 8: 123–156.

Garland, D. (2002), *The Culture of Control. Crime and Social Order in Contemporary Society.* Chicago, IL: University of Chicago Press.

Gecas, V. (2003), 'Self-agency and the life course', in Mortimer, J. T. and Shanahan, M. (eds) *Handbook of the Life Course.* New York: Kluwer.

Giordano, P. C., Cernkovich, S. A. and Rudolph, J. L. (2002), 'Gender, crime, and desistance: Toward a theory of cognitive transformation', *American Journal of Sociology* 107: 990–1064.

Goffman, E. (1961), *Asylums.* London: Penguin.

Hagan, J. (2010), *Who Are The Criminals? The Politics of Crime Policy from the Age of Roosevelt to the Age of Reagan.* Princeton, NJ: Princeton University Press.

Healy, D. (2013), 'Changing fate? Agency and the desistance process', *Theoretical Criminology* 17: 557–574.

Hitlin, S. and Elder, G. H. Jr. (2007), 'Time, self, and the curiously abstract concept of agency', *Sociological Theory* 25: 170–191.

Hollway, W. and Jefferson, A. (2000), *Doing Qualitative Research Differently.* London: Sage.

Holstein, J. A. and Gubrium, J. F. (1995), *The Active Interview.* London: Sage.

Järvinen, M. (2000), 'The biographical illusion: Constructing meaning in qualitative interviews', *Qualitative Inquiry* 6: 370–391.

Järvinen, M. (2001), 'Accounting for trouble: Identity negotiations in qualitative interviews', *Symbolic Interaction* 24: 263–284.

Järvinen, M. (2004), 'Life histories and the perspective of the present', *Narrative Inquiry* 14: 45–68.

King, S. (2013), 'Transformative agency and desistance from crime', *Criminology and Criminal Justice* 13: 317–335.

King, S. (2014), *Desistance Transitions and the Impact of Probation*. London: Routledge.

Kvale, S. and Brinkmann, S. (2008), *Interviews. Learning the Craft of Qualitative Research Interviewing*. London: Sage.

Laub, J. H. and Sampson, R. J. (2001), 'Understanding desistance from crime', *Crime and Justice: A Review of Research* 28: 1–69.

Laub, J. H. and Sampson, R. J. (2003), *Shared Beginnings, Divergent Lives. Delinquent Boys to Age 70*. Cambridge, MA: Harvard University Press.

LeBel, T. P., Burnett, R., Maruna, S. and Bushway, S. (2008), 'The "chicken and egg" of subjective and social factors in desistance from crime', *European Journal of Criminology* 5: 131–159.

Lindegaard, M. R. and Jacques, S. (2014), 'Agency as a cause of crime', *Deviant Behavior* 35(2): 85–100.

Maruna, S. (2001), *Making Good. How Ex-Convicts Reform and Rebuild Their Lives*. Washington, DC: American Psychological Association.

Maruna, S. (2004), 'Desistance from crime and explanatory style: A new direction in the psychology of reform', *Journal of Contemporary Criminal Justice* 20: 184–200.

Matsueda, R. (2006), 'Criminological implications of the thought of George Herbert Mead', in Deflem, M. (ed.) *Sociological Theory and Criminological Research: Views From Europe and The United States*. Oxford, UK: Elsevier.

Matza, D. (1969), *Becoming Deviant*. New Brunswick, NJ: Transaction Publishers.

Meisenhelder, T. (1977), 'An exploratory study of exiting from criminal careers', *Criminology* 15: 319–334.

Paternoster, R. and Bushway, S. (2009), 'Desistance and the "feared self": Toward an identity theory of criminal desistance', *Journal of Criminal Law & Criminology* 99: 1103–1156.

Pettersson, L. and Carlsson, C. (2014), 'Sex, drugs, and masculinities: A life-course perspective', in Jon, N., Lander, I. and Ravn, S. (eds) *Masculinities in the Criminological Field*. London: Ashgate.

Pratt, J. and Eriksson, A. (2013), *Contrasts in Punishment: An Explanation of Anglophone Excess and Nordic Exceptionalism*. London: Routledge.

Presser, L. (2009), 'The narratives of offenders', *Theoretical Criminology* 13: 177–200.

Sampson, R. J. and Laub, J. H. (1993), *Crime in the Making: Pathways and Turning Points through Life*. Boston, MA: Harvard University Press.

Sampson, R. J. and Laub, J. H. (2005), 'A general age-graded theory of crime: Lessons learned and the future of life-course criminology', in Farrington, D. P. (ed.) *Integrated Developmental and Life-Course Theories of Offending. Advances in Criminological Theory*, volume 14. London: Transaction Publishers.

Sandberg, S. (2013), 'Are self-narratives strategic or determined, unified, or fragmented? Reading Breivik's manifesto in light of narrative criminology', *Acta Sociologica* 56: 69–83.

Sarnecki, J. (1985), *Predicting Social Maladjustment. Stockholm Boys Grown Up*. Stockholm, Sweden: Esselte Tryck.

Sarnecki, J. and Sivertsson, F. (2013), *Att bryta en kriminell livsstil* (Leaving a criminal lifestyle). Stockholm, Sweden: Kriminalvården.

Shaw, C. R. (1930), *The Jack-Roller. A Delinquent Boy's Own Story*. Chicago, IL: University of Chicago Press.

Shover, N. (1985), *Aging Criminals*. New York: Sage.

Shover, N. (1996), *Great Pretenders. Pursuits and Careers of Persistent Thieves*. Boulder, CO: Westview Press.

Sivertsson, F. and Carlsson, C. (2014), 'Continuity, change, and contradictions: Risk and agency in criminal careers to age 59', *Criminal Justice and Behavior*, available via OnlineFirst, doi:10.1177/009385 4814552100.

SOU 1971. *Unga Lagöverträdare I. Undersökningsmetodik. Brottsdebut och återfall. 1956 års klientelundersökning rörande ungdomsbrottslingar* (Juvenile Delinquents I. Research method. Onset of crime and recidivism. The Clientele Study of 1956). Stockholm, Sweden: Esselte Tryck (in Swedish), p. 49.

Steffensmeier, D. J. and Ulmer, J. T. (2005), *Confessions of a Dying Thief: Understanding Criminal Careers and Illegal Enterprise.* New Brunswick, NJ: Transaction Publishers.

Tham, H. (2012), 'The influence of the drug issue on criminal policy', *Journal of Scandinavian Studies in Criminology and Crime Prevention* 13: 12–30.

Thoits, P. A. (2003), 'Personal agency and multiple role-identities', in Burke, P. J., Owens, T. J., Serpe, R. T. and Thoits, P. A. (eds) *Advances in Identity Theory and Research.* New York: Kluwer.

Ulmer, J. T. and William Spencer, J. (1999), 'The contributions of an interactionist approach to research and theory on criminal careers', *Theoretical Criminology* 3: 95–124.

3

'I'VE ALWAYS TRIED BUT I HADN'T GOT THE WILLPOWER'

Understanding pathways to desistance in the Republic of Ireland

Deirdre Healy

Introduction

Early explanations of the desistance process focused on sociological processes and concepts such as maturation, but recently scholars have turned their attention to the study of agency. Although many theorists agree that agency is involved in behavioural change, there is a lack of consensus regarding some of its key attributes including its content and structure (the 'what'), the timing and reasons for its emergence at particular points in the life-course (the 'why'), the ends to which it is directed (the 'wherefore') and the mechanisms that operate at the intersection between the individual and the social world (the 'how').

The term 'agency' has been used to describe a variety of subjective resources, including amongst others decision-making skills (Paternoster and Pogarsky 2009), the capacity to respond creatively to environmental opportunities and constraints (Giordano *et al*. 2002, 2007) and self-mastery (Maruna 2001). Moreover, some definitions emphasise 'upfront' agentic work (e.g. Giordano *et al*. 2002: 992), whereas others (e.g. Maruna 2001) are arguably more relevant to the later stages of change. Yet other usages incorporate the notion of agency within an analysis of wider social processes (e.g. Farrall *et al*. 2011). This conceptual confusion has produced disparate findings regarding the role of agency in desistance.

Furthermore, it is widely contended that the goal of the desistance process is the formation of a new conventional self, built around adult roles in work and family life (e.g. Laub and Sampson 2003). However, structural barriers may prevent putative ex-offenders from fully realising adult identities by impeding access to pro-social relationships, employment, financial independence and civic participation (Farrall *et al*. 2010). Studies of the general population reveal that individuals who report higher levels of agency tend to experience better adult outcomes (Côté 1997). Yet, it is not clear how people – particularly marginalised groups such as ex-offenders – navigate structural obstacles and opportunities to achieve valued goals. In addition, the impact of contact with the criminal justice system on desistance has not been widely researched (although see, e.g. McAra and McVie 2007; Farrall *et al.* 2014).

This chapter aims to investigate these issues further in an Irish context. Its purpose is not to develop a new theoretical framework but to test and consolidate existing knowledge about key constructs. Specifically, it: (a) examines the extent to which social opportunities and constraints shape the construction of a conventional adult self; (b) explores the psychology of desistance with a particular emphasis on the roles of agency, coping and identity; and (c) investigates the impact of probation supervision on the change process.

Methods

A prospective design was used to capture the shifts that occurred in participants' offending, cognitions and social circumstances as they negotiated the transition to desistance (see Healy 2012a for a detailed overview of methods, procedures and measures). During the first phase of the research (which was conducted in 2003–04), in-depth qualitative interviews were conducted with 73 repeat offenders on probation in Dublin, Ireland. All participants were male, aged 18 to 35 and had at least two previous convictions. Participants' police and probation records were also consulted. During the second phase (which was conducted from 2008–10), all participants' criminal justice records were re-examined and a sub-set of the original sample (n=14)[1] were re-interviewed.

Three psychometric instruments were used at both measurement points, namely: (a) the Psychological Inventory of Criminal Thinking Styles (PICTS: Walters 1995), which measures, 'the attitudes, beliefs, and rationalizations offenders use to justify and support their criminal behaviour' (Walters 2012: 272); (b) CRIME PICS II (Frude *et al.* 1994), which measures criminal attitudes, likelihood of re-offending and victim empathy and also contains a problem inventory, which can be used to explore the impact of self-reported social problems on criminality; and (c) the Level of Service Inventory-Revised (LSI-R: Andrews and Bonta 1995), which provides an external evaluation of offenders' social circumstances, because it is completed by criminal justice professionals.

During the first phase of the study, 62 per cent (n=45) of participants reported that they had not offended for at least a month prior to the interview and 24 stated that they had been crime-free for at least a year. In total, 66 per cent were reconvicted during the 4-year follow-up period, although there was a significant reduction in the frequency and severity of offending, which suggests that participants were moving towards desistance. This was evidenced by an overall shift in participants' reconviction profiles. For example, the most common re-offences were motoring and property offences, which compares favourably to participants' offence profiles at the first sweep, when robbery and drugs offences were the most common types. One of the most striking findings to emerge from the reconviction analysis was the length of time it took for participants to acquire their first reconviction. On average, the sample remained conviction-free for 1,113 days (SD=575), or over 3 years after their first interview. The gaps in their criminal records are unlikely to be attributable to delays between the commission of the offence and the conviction for that offence since the average number of days to re-arrest was also quite lengthy at 961 days (SD=680).[2] Interestingly, those who reported that they were desisting at the first interview were significantly less likely to be re-imprisoned, indicating that participants' early intentions endured over time.

Socio-cultural context

Desistance is intricately linked with the process of 'becoming a more fully integrated member of civil society', but its outcomes are shaped by the structural opportunities and constraints that exist within a given society (Farrall *et al.* 2010: 554). One of the central aims of this study was to explore the impact of the Irish socio-economic context on pathways to desistance among repeat offenders. The study focused on two key markers of adulthood that are known to be associated with desistance, namely employment and family formation (more generally, see Laub and Sampson 2003). Ireland constitutes an interesting case study in this regard, because the country has experienced a series of turbulent transformations since the 1990s, which have shaped and re-shaped its economic, social and political landscape.

Ireland has traditionally been viewed as a homogenous, insular and impoverished nation with strong religious and community values (Ferriter 2004). However, the emergence of the Celtic Tiger economy in 1994 meant that the country experienced a period of affluence, modernisation, ethnic diversification and urbanisation. The 2008 recession engendered another dramatic reversal in Ireland's fortunes and resulted in the return of emigration and unemployment along with high levels of personal and national indebtedness. Although there is some disagreement about the impact of austerity measures on vulnerable groups, official figures show that rates of poverty and deprivation have risen since 2008 (CSO 2013). The crisis and its aftermath have also eroded public faith in political institutions (European Commission 2013). To a certain extent, the current study formed a natural experiment since the first phase was conducted during the height of the Celtic Tiger economy, while the second phase was conducted during the depths of the recession.

The transition to adulthood should have been relatively easy for ex-offenders during the Celtic Tiger years (see Fahy *et al.* 2007) for a detailed socio-economic review of this period). The labour market underwent significant expansion, particularly in the low-skilled – but relatively well-paid – construction and services industries. This, along with labour shortages, meant that even individuals with minimal skills were able to obtain high-quality employment. Furthermore, the Irish people displayed a strong cultural commitment to family formation during this time, evidenced by significant increases in marriage and birthrates from the 1990s onwards and a comparatively low divorce rate. It is also likely that the generous welfare supports introduced by the government to assist families and the unemployed helped to ease the transition to adulthood and cushioned vulnerable groups against the full effects of poverty and social exclusion.

Conversely, it is likely that the onset of the recession in 2008 created significant structural barriers to adulthood. Although marriage and birthrates were largely unaffected, the collapse of the labour market meant that even well-educated groups found it difficult to gain employment.[3] The unemployment rate peaked at 14.7 per cent in 2012 with low- and semi-skilled occupational sectors suffering the most severe job losses. Furthermore, the government's decision to reduce welfare support and increase taxation as part of a package of austerity measures exacerbated the financial difficulties faced by low-income families and the unemployed.

The first phase of the study provided an opportunity to examine the impact of the Celtic Tiger years on desistance. The analysis revealed significant disparities between offenders' experiences and general population trends. Despite favourable macro-economic circumstances, few participants had attained the developmental markers normally associated with adulthood. For example, just ten were in full-time employment and over a third reported that welfare payments constituted their primary source of income. In addition, 38 per cent stated that they had experienced difficulties paying for basic necessities like food and clothing. The findings in relation to family formation were more encouraging. The majority of participants with children reported that they had strong relationships with them. However, over half of all participants still lived in the parental home, indicating that they had not yet made the transition to independent living.

This raises an important question – why did these men not benefit from a benign socio-economic climate? It appeared that participants' pathways to desistance were shaped primarily by the opportunity structures within their immediate social environment rather than those within the broader macro-environment. The majority were residing in communities that were blighted by poverty, educational disadvantage, chronic unemployment and welfare dependence.[4] Participants also explained that they encountered drug use, violence and criminality in their neighbourhoods on a daily basis. The link between poverty and crime is evident in the following quote where Andy[5] describes how his childhood experience of deprivation encouraged him to commit crime in order to acquire material goods:

> My mother had five boys, me father didn't work at the time . . . So we were victims for the older kids in the flats who had the Nike and had the Levis . . . We didn't have any of them . . . When I was younger, growing up, I always said 'I can't wait 'til I get bigger' and I remember my brothers telling me that they heard me dreaming, 'I'm going to have ten pairs of Levis'.

Although gender issues were not explored in this study, because the sample consisted entirely of males, it is possible that female accounts would have emphasised other types of purchases, such as food (see e.g. Byrne and Trew 2008).

The second wave of interviews permitted an examination of the impact of the recession on desistance. The findings suggested that the adverse economic climate militated against desistance in two ways. First, several participants who became unemployed during the recession explained that they did not know how to access social support, training and education without the assistance of a probation officer. Consequently, they became trapped in a cycle of long-term unemployment and welfare dependence, which generated a sense of despondency and ultimately led to a relapse into criminality. This suggests that adverse structural conditions may undermine feelings of agency, at least among some ex-offenders. Second, a number of participants reported that unemployment had rendered them visible to the police once again, because they were spending more time in public places. Although Isaac occasionally committed shoplifting offences, he had significantly reduced his criminal behaviour by the second interview. In the following quote, he describes being stopped by police when out walking in his neighbourhood and elucidates the negative emotional impact of what could be described as a 're-labelling' experience:

> The post office up in [the] village was after being robbed ...The next moment, the police drove by. Obviously, the copper knew me, turned around ... Obviously we got stopped coz every time something had been robbed – 'stop [Isaac]'. I just feel like sometimes when police stop you, they only stop you coz they know you for your past. Like it's embarrassing when you're with someone.

In sum, the findings suggested that the opportunity structures within the wider socio-economic context played a limited role in shaping individual pathways to desistance. Their impact appeared to have been mediated by the opportunities and constraints within participants' immediate social environment. The results therefore support sociological theories of desistance that emphasise cultural and situational contexts (e.g. Bottoms *et al.* 2004; Farrall *et al.* 2010). Yet, despite their limited social prospects, the majority of participants reported that they were attempting to desist, which suggests that other, more subjective, factors were also at play.

Agency, coping and the search for a 'wherefore'

The second element of the study explored the psychology of desistance with a particular emphasis on the roles of agency, coping and identity formation. The findings supported De Unamuno's (1954 [1913]) contention that human beings are primarily concerned with understanding the 'wherefore', or *telos*, of their lives. A plausible 'wherefore' may encourage agentic action by providing actors with a sense of purpose and direction (Williams and Gantt 2013). Likewise, the ability to envision a valued future self may activate latent agentic potential among prospective desisters (see also Giordano *et al.* 2002; King 2013; Soyer 2014).

The analysis suggested that the ability to imagine a meaningful and credible new self may constitute an important mechanism underpinning agentic action and coping behaviour (Healy 2012a, 2013, 2014). All participants had envisaged valued alternative identities, but desisters were more confident than offenders that they could achieve these imagined selves.[6] Furthermore, prospective desisters who believed that their desired identity was unattainable found it difficult to exercise agency and coping behaviour and tended to experience regular relapses into drug use and crime. At the time of his second interview, Ronan was unemployed, resided with his parents and possessed few social bonds. Although he had significantly reduced his offending behaviour and drug use, he believed that a meaningful conventional life was beyond reach, because of the neuro-physiological problems he suffered as a result of a severe head injury. As he elucidated:

> Like in a way [crime] made me who I am so I can't really . . . but I still regret all of it. Still wish I never done it. [It] made me a disabled fuckin' person who can't even get a job, who's left without a job, lucky to have a house, on drugs, intertwined with drugs for the rest of me life, on methadone for the rest of me life, looking like I'll never have a job, never have a programme, never have anything to do with me life and just deserved it. A no-good waster. That's what I think it made me.

Ronan's failure to imagine a credible future self made it difficult for him to exercise agency or coping behaviour in his social interactions. Although he sometimes succeeded in resisting opportunities to use drugs or commit crime, he often yielded to temptation because, as he put it, he had 'nothing to do' in the present and 'nothing [to] see ahead' in the future. His agentic potential lay dormant in the absence of a credible desired self.

In contrast, prospective desisters who had transmuted an imagined identity into a meaningful crime-free self expressed higher levels of agency and tended to cope effectively with challenges. In addition, they no longer committed crime or engaged in substance misuse. Their achievements seemed to be facilitated by the presence of a plausible 'wherefore', which incentivised them to operate agentically within the social world. Connor's outlook at his second interview was extremely positive and he was confident that he would achieve his desired goals. In the following quote, he sets out his plans for the next five years:

> [I would like to be] still in college. I can go further than that to five years – qualified from that, get a good job. Looking further than that then, get my own place, me own family. Just still to be happy. Still drug-free. Which I know I will be. Just to be successful at life. To be a success at life. So yeah, that would be the plan. Just to do things right.

Connor successfully employed a range of coping strategies to achieve his desired ends. For example, he created a stringent daily schedule to ensure that his time was filled with meaningful activities, and monitored his thoughts and emotions on an ongoing basis to maintain a positive state of mind. During his interview, Connor provided an insightful analysis of the role played by the 'wherefore' in desistance, explaining, 'I'm enjoying life now. People who end up going back [to crime], they're obviously not happy in themselves'.

Consistent with Giordano *et al.*'s (2002, 2007) cognitive transformation theory, these findings suggest that agency may be best understood as a dynamic interaction between the person and their social world that is directed towards the achievement of a valued self and shaped by the actor's cognitive, emotional and social resources as well as environmental opportunities and constraints. This definition raises an important question: *how* do prospective desisters use agentic resources to achieve valued goals and identities? Further analysis of narrative accounts suggested that effective coping behaviour may constitute one key expression of agency, since highly agentic participants tended to use coping styles consistently and effectively to achieve their goals (although there are some etiological similarities between these concepts, it must be noted that coping and agency are different phenomena; see Lazarus and Folkman (1984) on coping theory). The men's coping strategies, which can be categorised into cognitive, emotional and social approaches, are described next.

Cognitive

The most important cognitive coping style employed by participants can be classified as decision-making, or problem-solving, strategies. During the first phase of the study, a third of the sample reported that they regularly experienced intrusive thoughts about crime. While the men used a variety of techniques to deal with these thoughts, the most common approach was to reflect on the negative consequences of re-offending. In his first interview, Dylan describes how he contemplated the potential loss of family ties whenever he was tempted by a criminal opportunity:

> Say, walking by a place, you look in, there's a bank. Jaysus, I wonder would you get anything out of there. Things like that. But then you have to stop and think of jail . . . I missed [my son's] birth, I missed his communion and I missed his confirmation. I don't want to miss his twenty-first and his wedding.

In other words, desisters carefully weighed their options when faced with difficult situations, whereas offenders tended to pursue quick-fix solutions. In fact, the PICTS thinking style, cognitive indolence, which concerns the capacity to identify, consider and evaluate choices, showed the strongest statistical relationship with measures of past, current and future offending (see Healy 2012a). Illustrating this tendency, Nick wanted to stop offending, but appeared to lack the wherewithal to follow through on good intentions. As he explained in his first interview, 'I've always tried but I hadn't got the willpower. I just want to make a go of things, put it all behind me'. In the following extract, he expresses frustration at his inability to resist the temptation to use drugs when bored (for further discussion of crime and the emotions, see Ferrell 2004):

> It's the way I deal with boredom sometimes. Just the buzz of doing it, kind of. What'll I do, crime like. Everything goes through your head from drugs

to crime to now going to the pictures. Sometimes you make the wrong decision . . . Sometimes you're just so bored and you get so sick, stuck in a rut doing the same thing. Just trying to do something different. Could be drugs or crime or whatever, stealing something.

Desisters were also more likely than offenders to engage in approach coping activities. That is, they attempted to resolve problems and achieve their goals through active engagement with the social world. For example, when Ian got out of prison, his probation officer told him about job opportunities in the field of addiction counselling. At the time of his first interview, he was participating in unpaid volunteer work in order to gain the experience he needed to pursue further training in the field. The following quote demonstrates his willingness to capitalise on the desistance opportunities that were offered to him:

> I just got a bit of information . . . that maybe I could do a bit better than doing security. Like there were opportunities, places out there that would take people with experience of using drugs and they needed these people with the experience to come in and show other people and to work with people like that. So that started to open me up a bit to whole new possibilities.

In contrast, people who were still involved in crime tended to drift with circumstances and felt unable to take active control of their lives. At his first interview, Max was employed in a job that he believed could lead to a rewarding career. Despite his desire to stop offending, he found himself drawn back into crime through his friendship with a criminal peer group. As he put it, 'if I hadn't been with [my friend], I probably wouldn't have been doing [robberies]'. His inner conflict is highlighted in the following extract where he explains, 'I've done a few robberies since. Now I wish I didn't do them. I've got a lot of money out of it but afterwards "Jeez, what the hell did I do that for? Will I be caught?"'.

Emotional

Effective coping also encompasses inward-focused solutions that are designed to manage negative emotions. Research suggests that emotion-oriented approaches are particularly relevant for individuals dealing with intractable problems (e.g. Fang *et al.* 2006). Interestingly, desisters were more likely than offenders to describe their affective states in positive terms, which suggests that the transition to desistance is associated with enhanced wellbeing.

Similar to Maruna's (2001) findings, an important emotion management strategy concerned the ability to re-frame negative experiences in more favourable terms. Although the majority of participants expressed feelings of regret when discussing the past, desisters were somewhat more likely to engage in a positive re-appraisal of their criminal lives. In particular, they claimed that their adverse experiences had elicited a more profound understanding of themselves, others and the social world. In the following extract from his first interview, Ken describes how his experience of addiction encouraged a non-judgemental attitude towards others:

> Well I don't regret [my criminal past]. It was an experience, do you know what I mean. Like if I have kids now, at least I'll be able to tell them coz I went through it, do you understand. It's just like . . . you can't help it. It was just the way it turned out so I wouldn't be quick to judge others. Some people wouldn't know anything about that. I'd have more of an understanding coz I've done it. I understand about addictions and all now. You know the way some people walk down and see somebody stoned out of their head. They'd automatically walk across to the other side of the road.

In contrast, offenders were more likely to experience a deep-rooted sense of shame and to believe that their mistakes had left permanent and indelible scars on their lives. A sense of lost opportunities permeates Scott's quote from his first interview where he speaks about his desire for a second chance:

> If I could change it I would. I'd change it back to when I was a baby. I'd start all over again . . . I'd change . . . not going on drugs. I'd change . . . I'd have a job. I'd probably still have my daughter with my girlfriend . . . So it would just be that I'd be working and I wouldn't be near drugs. I know I wouldn't.

A second key strategy related to expectation management. In general, desisters adopted an optimistic demeanour when questioned about their likelihood of desistance.[7] However, their narratives suggested that optimism may be an acquired skill rather than an innate disposition. The hard work and determination required to sustain a positive outlook is clearly highlighted in Donal's story. As he explained in his second interview:

> Everyone finds [desistance] hard. It's a hard process. It's a slow process as well. It doesn't happen overnight. You have to work at it. Because I notice if I stop doing what I'm supposed to be doing, you start thinking the way you used to think. So it's a constant battle to try and stay positive and keep away from what you used to do.

Conversely, offenders held ambivalent attitudes about their future prospects and believed that they would be vulnerable if presented with a low-risk criminal opportunity. Intriguingly, a number of established desisters also expressed uncertainty about their likelihood of remaining crime-free. Tim was reluctant to acknowledge his status as a desister even though he had not offended for some time and had never encountered the imaginary scenario he describes in the following extract from his second interview:

> Being honest, I could be walking on the streets tomorrow and I could have
> to defend myself in a fight. And I'd probably end up hurting him or [get-
> ting] beaten up. It could go either way. So I don't know really what I could
> predict. I wish I could!

Such sentiments do not necessarily reflect residual doubts about the decision to stop offending. Rather, they could be an expression of a phenomenon known as defensive pessimism, which occurs when people set low expectations in order to motivate themselves to work harder to avoid negative outcomes (Norem and Cantor 1986).

Social

As discussed earlier, the majority of participants lived in disadvantaged communities and possessed low social capital. It is perhaps unsurprising then that four-fifths expected to encounter barriers to desistance, particularly in relation to education, employment, accommodation and addiction. Both offenders and desisters were equally likely to anticipate obstacles to change, which indicates that social exclusion was a universal experience among the men. Indeed, the psychometric analyses found that the relationship between measures of social circumstances and offending behaviour was relatively weak (see Healy 2010, 2012a). The difficulties experienced by ex-offenders when seeking work are clearly illustrated in Lee's first interview where he describes his disappointment at being unable to find employment:

> I'm very articulate, I can speak and I'm confident in speaking and stuff like
> that, like I've great interview skills. And the job would more or less be mine
> but as soon as I mention 'yeah well I do have a criminal record' – okay we'll
> get back to you. And you never hear from them.

Despite similar backgrounds and expectations, desisters and offenders employed different social coping strategies when faced with challenging circumstances. Specifically, desisters were more likely to seek practical and emotional support from others rather than attempt to solve a problem themselves. Participants preferred to approach informal sources of support, such as family and friends, rather than formal sources, such as probation officers or treatment providers (see Farrall (2002) for similar findings in an English probation sample). It may be that people embrace the notion that change occurs not solely through inner processes but also through the active use of social and contextual processes the further they progress towards desistance. If so, rehabilitation models that focus exclusively on addressing cognitive distortions and promoting responsibilisation may be insufficient as an active means to foster lasting change (see also McNeill (2012)). Nathan's case illustrates the important role played by support networks in eliciting effective coping behaviour. In his second interview, he described how he began to lose hope after his attempts to find a drug treatment programme proved unsuccessful. His father then contacted a local politician who immediately arranged a place for Nathan on a methadone maintenance programme. Nathan described the impact of this intervention as follows:

> I kept getting told there's no doctors there. You're not in the area code to go on that list. So I'd given up then. I'd tried . . . So then the aul lad [dad] kicked the ball going. . . . The only hope I had or anyone else had was [names local politician]. He stood up . . . I never met the man before in my life and [after] talking to me da for a couple of minutes – the next morning I got a phonecall – be here at half five.

In sum, the findings suggested that offenders and desisters differed primarily in terms of their strengths, namely their ability to reflect on their lives, manage difficult emotions and utilise social supports, rather than in terms of their deficits or 'criminogenic needs'. This indicates that strengths-based approaches, which aim to build on offenders' existing qualities, talents and resources, may be beneficial for desistance (see also Laws and Ward 2011). In addition, the findings corroborate theoretical perspectives, which emphasise the roles played by reflection (Paternoster and Pogarsky 2009), meaning-making (Maruna 2001), social support (King 2013) and emotional wellbeing (Giordano *et al.* 2007) in agentic action.

A note on the early stages of change

The study also aimed to shed light on the mechanisms and contexts that shaped the transition to desistance. Participants' narrative accounts suggested that critical life events, both positive and negative, prompted them to reflect on and re-consider their life choices. Key events included the birth of children, long prison sentences and participation in rehabilitation programmes. Interestingly, quantitative analyses suggested that the early stages of change were accompanied by immediate and substantial psychosocial shifts, which then stabilised and became embedded over time (for a detailed discussion of the psychometric results, see Healy 2010, 2012a). This contrasts with the prevailing view of desistance as a tentative and gradual process, but is consistent with many other theoretical traditions, such as the theory of quantum change, which proposes that change can be rapid and dramatic (e.g. Miller and C'de Baca 2001). Despite these dramatic shifts, the experience of the self as an agentic being seemed to emerge gradually over time as actors accumulated successes in the conventional world (Healy and O'Donnell 2008). It is possible that the initial movement towards desistance generated a long-term momentum towards lasting change even though prospective desisters often experienced uncertainty and setbacks in the short term. Although this study was among the first to explore the early stages of change, subsequent studies have provided further insights into the transition to desistance (e.g. Bottoms and Shapland 2011; King 2013).

Probation policy and practice

The third element focused on the impact of probation supervision. Unlike other Anglophone jurisdictions, the history of probation in Ireland is characterised by continuity rather than change (for a detailed discussion of the origins and development of probation practice, see Healy 2009, 2012a, 2012b). Probation officers continue to embrace penal welfare ideals and employ a social casework approach in their day-to-day work with offenders. Although the Irish Probation Service has recently begun to adopt some aspects of the 'new penology', including risk assessment tools and offending behaviour programmes, these practices have not yet made substantial inroads.

During the first phase of the research, probation officers were asked to provide information about participants' supervision plans and to assess their needs, level of engagement and likelihood of desistance. The analysis revealed that probation officers intended to focus on welfare issues, including addiction, employment, education and relationships. Moreover, they planned to use social casework techniques to deal with these matters, including one-to-one counselling, home visits and referrals to rehabilitation agencies. The majority of probationers also perceived probation as welfare-centred and identified a range of benefits associated with this model, including practical assistance, emotional support and relationship building. The impact of a strong working relationship on motivation is clearly illustrated in Dermot's comments during his first interview:

> [My probation officer is] a nice kind of guy and I wouldn't want to let him down. I'd feel bad 'cause he wouldn't give out really. He'd just say 'ah what have you done?' or 'This is not good', you know. But he would be strict enough as well. He'd put his foot down, do his job. I wouldn't want to let him down out of respect.

Although many participants felt that probation supervision supported their personal efforts at change, only one cited it as the primary factor in his decision to desist. Overall, people who were involved in crime were more likely than desisters to perceive supervision in negative terms and to emphasise its surveillance function. In his first interview, Leonard described his resentment over the constant monitoring of his actions:

> It used to annoy me, the way they keep interfering. I'd tell me ma I was doing well, and she'd [probation officer] come up to the house and tell her I wasn't and get me into trouble with me ma. It would wreck your head. I've always had something hanging over my head since I was 13.

The second sweep of interviews provided additional insights into the long-term impact of probation and allowed participants to retrospectively reflect on their experiences. While participants' memories were framed in largely positive or neutral terms, probation supervision did not always produce long-term improvements in their life chances, and a significant minority reported that they were still experiencing problems with employment, education, addiction and housing. These difficulties were exacerbated by the fact that adult criminal convictions are never expunged in Ireland.[8] Evan was employed during his time on probation, but lost his job during the recession. The next quote illustrates his belief that his employment prospects were severely constrained by his criminal record:

> When I got out of prison, I had a bit of luck with me sister's boyfriend. He had started working for a company and he got me in. So that was kind of handy. But I don't think I'd have actually got a job now if I got out and put it down on my record that I was in [prison]. And especially if you divulge what you're actually convicted of – drugs. For somebody in this country, it's considered one of the worst charges you can have.

For the most part, the Irish Probation Service does not deliver rehabilitation programmes directly but funds external agencies to provide services on its behalf. Participants spoke in positive terms about these programmes, citing in particular the strong working relationships they formed with staff, the addition of structure and routine to their days and the possibility that they would achieve meaningful outcomes, including educational qualifications. However, many held ambivalent attitudes towards methadone maintenance programmes. Lorcan, who characterised himself as a 'government junkie', believed that methadone maintenance helped him to desist from crime but also prevented him from escaping the 'addict' identity. In his words:

> As far as I'm concerned when I'm on methadone, I'm still an active user . . . The drug is methadone, it's the same thing. It's a synthetic heroin. He's [the doctor] over there telling me that I'm a lifer on it, and I'm strongly telling him I'm not and I got so frustrated over it . . . Your life is more manageable but you're still on a string, you're a puppet, that's how I look at it.

In sum, the findings revealed that probationers respond positively to a model which operates according to penal welfare ideals. Probation supervision is therefore best conceptualised as a catalyst for – rather than a cause of – change. Probation officers should therefore strive to find a balance between facilitating personal autonomy and providing appropriate levels of assistance both during the supervision period and after it ends. However, the practice of using methadone maintenance as a long-term solution to heroin addiction may need to be reconsidered. These findings are consistent with the tenets of desistance-focused practice paradigms which emphasise the role of both personal motivation and social capital (e.g. Farrall 2002; Farrall *et al.* 2014).

Conclusion

This chapter has presented the results of a study which explored the dynamics of desistance in the Republic of Ireland. The findings revealed that even highly favourable socio-economic conditions do not necessarily aid desistance among the socially excluded. Instead, cognitive shifts appeared to operate at the forefront of change, while social factors played a critical, secondary role.[9] In addition, the study found that probation supervision exerted a relatively limited impact on desistance although it did support participants' personal efforts at change.

Moreover, the significance of psychosocial maturational processes, particularly those involved in the transition to adulthood, must not be under-estimated since participants had aged several years between the first and second interviews.

Future research priorities should include comparative studies to investigate similarities and differences in the experience of desistance across a variety of structural contexts. These studies should explore the nexus between structure and agency and examine the social, political and cultural factors that facilitate or constrain desistance. Key variables should include inter alia poverty, inequality, political economy and punitiveness.

In addition, the growing theoretical interest in agency means that researchers should concentrate on formulating and empirically testing a clear and agreed definition of the concept. Mixed-methods approaches are best suited to studies of nebulous, multi-dimensional variables like agency, because they incorporate the strengths of both qualitative and quantitative designs.

Finally, efforts should be made to test, consolidate and modify existing perspectives. Researchers have produced an abundance of theories, which are, in many cases, supported by limited empirical evidence. Theoretically driven investigations could isolate and test key constructs, such as 'agency', 'redemption' and 'identity'.

In conclusion, research on desistance has produced a rich, varied and multi-faceted literature. It is hoped that the results of the study described in this chapter will add to knowledge about critical aspects of the change process, including the role of socio-cultural contexts, agency, coping and probation supervision.

Notes

1 It was initially anticipated that the majority of participants would be re-contactable, but this proved not to be the case for several reasons, some of which may be unique to this study. First, 32 individuals could not be contacted at all either because they moved house and left no forwarding address, were homeless, on the run or had died. The unusually high levels of drug addiction and homelessness among the sample may account for their mobility and morbidity. Efforts were made to contact all of the remaining 41 participants; however, the ethical protocols set by the UCD Human Research Ethics Committee permitted only one contact per address. Nevertheless, the qualitative methodology, along with the diverse outcomes and experiences of the sample, ensured that the findings were theoretically interesting, despite the small sample size.

2 Compared to convictions, arrests tend to occur closer in time to the commission of the crime.

3 These facts are taken from the Central Statistics Office website: www.cso.ie.

4 The socio-economic profile was created using the Pobal Deprivation Index developed by Haase, T. and Pratschke, J. (2008).

5 All names used in this chapter are pseudonyms.

6 The term 'imagined desistance' was coined by Soyer (2014: 97) to capture the gap between actual and desired realities in offenders' sense of self.

7 Optimism was measured using a scale devised by Burnett (1992) and adapted by Farrall (2002).

8 Since 2007, two Spent Convictions Bills have appeared before the Dáil (Irish parliament), but neither had been enacted into law at the time of writing.

9 This is not to suggest that social capital does not influence desistance. In fact, the weak relationship between social indicators and criminality may be explained by the fact that both offenders and desisters possessed limited social capital.

References

Andrews, D. and Bonta, J. (1995), *Level of Service Inventory – Revised*. Toronto, Canada: Multi-Health Systems.

Bottoms, A. and Shapland, J. (2011), 'Steps towards desistance among male young adult recidivists', in Farrall, S., Hough, M., Maruna, S. and Sparks, R. (eds) *Escape Routes: Contemporary Perspectives on Life After Punishment*. Abingdon, UK: Routledge.

Bottoms, A., Shapland, J., Costello, A., Holmes, D. and Muir, G. (2004), 'Towards desistance: Theoretical underpinnings for an empirical study', *The Howard Journal of Criminal Justice* 43(4): 368–389.

Burnett, R. (1992), *The Dynamics of Recidivism*. Oxford, UK: Oxford University Centre for Criminological Research.

Byrne, C. and Trew, K. (2008), 'Pathways through crime: The development of crime and desistance in the accounts of men and women offenders', *The Howard Journal of Criminal Justice* 47(3): 238–258.

Côté, J. (1997), 'An empirical test of the identity capital model', *Journal of Adolescence* 20(5): 577–597.

CSO (2013), *Survey on Income and Living Conditions 2011 and Revised 2010 Results*. Dublin: CSO. Available at: www.cso.ie (accessed 4 January 2016).

De Unamuno, M. (1954 [1913]), *The Tragic Sense of Life*. New York: Dover Publications.

European Commission (2013), *Standard Eurobarometer 80: Public Opinion in the European Union – Autumn 2013*. Available at http://ec.europa.eu/COMMFrontOffice/PublicOpinion/index.cfm/General/index#p=1&instruments=STANDARD (accessed 4 January 2016).

Fahy, T., Russell, H. and Whelan, C. (2007), *Best of Times? The Social Impact of the Celtic Tiger*. Dublin, Ireland: IPA.

Fang, C., Daly, M., Miller, S. *et al.* (2006), 'Coping with ovarian cancer risk: The moderating effects of perceived control on coping and adjustment', *British Journal of Health Psychology* 11(Part 4): 561–580.

Farrall, S. (2002), *Rethinking What Works with Offenders*. Cullompton, UK: Willan Publishing.

Farrall, S., Bottoms, A. and Shapland, J. (2010), 'Social structures and desistance from crime', *European Journal of Criminology* 7(6): 546–570.

Farrall, S., Sharpe, G., Hunter, B. and Calverley, A. (2011), 'Theorising structural and individual-level processes in desistance and persistence: Outlining an integrated perspective', *Australian and New Zealand Journal of Criminology* 44(2): 218–234.

Farrall, S., Hunter, B., Sharpe, G. and Calverley, A. (2014), *Criminal Careers in Transition: The Social Context of Desistance From Crime*. Oxford, UK: Oxford University Press.

Ferrell, J. (2004), 'Boredom, crime and criminology', *Theoretical Criminology* 8(3): 287–302.

Ferriter, D. (2004), *The Transformation of Ireland 1900–2000*. London: Profile Books.

Frude, N., Honess, T. and Maguire, M. (1994), *CRIME PICS II*. Cardiff, UK: Michael and Associates.

Giordano, P., Cernkovich, S. and Rudolph, J. (2002), 'Gender, crime and desistance: Toward a theory of cognitive transformation', *American Journal of Sociology* 107(4): 990–1064.

Giordano, P., Schroeder, R. and Cernkovich, S. (2007), 'Emotions and crime over the life-course: A neo-Meadian perspective on criminal continuity and change', *American Journal of Sociology* 112(6): 1603–1661.

Haase, T. and Pratschke, J. (2008), *New Measures of Deprivation for the Republic of Ireland*. Dublin, Ireland: Pobal.

Healy, D. (2009), 'Probation matters', *Irish Jurist* XLIV: 239–257.

Healy, D. (2010), 'Betwixt and between: The role of psychosocial factors in the early stages of desistance', *Journal of Research in Crime and Delinquency* 47(4): 419–438.

Healy, D. (2012a), *The Dynamics of Desistance: Charting Pathways Through Change*. Abingdon, UK: Routledge.

Healy, D. (2012b), 'Advise, assist and befriend: Can probation supervision support desistance?', *Journal of Social Policy and Administration* 46(4): 377–394.

Healy, D. (2013), 'Changing fate? Agency and the desistance process', *Theoretical Criminology* 17(4): 557–574.

Healy, D. (2014), 'Becoming a desister: Exploring the role of agency, coping and imagination in the construction of a new self', *British Journal of Criminology* 54(5): 873–891.

Healy, D. and O'Donnell, I. (2008), 'Calling time on crime: Motivation, generativity and agency in Irish probationers', *Probation Journal* 55(1): 25–38.

King, S. (2013), 'Early desistance narratives: A qualitative analysis of probationers' transitions towards desistance', *Punishment and Society* 15(2): 147–165.

Laub, J. and Sampson, R. (2003), *Shared Beginnings, Divergent Lives: Delinquent Boys to Age 70*. Cambridge, MA: Harvard University Press.

Laws, R. and Ward, R. (2011), *Desistance from Sex Offending: Alternatives to Throwing Away the Keys*. New York: Guilford Press.

Lazarus, R. and Folkman, S. (1984), *Stress, Appraisal and Coping*. New York: Springer.

Maruna, S. (2001), *Making Good: How Ex-Convicts Reform and Rebuild Their Lives*. Washington, DC: APA.

McAra, L. and McVie, S. (2007), 'Youth justice? The impact of system contact on patterns of desistance from offending', *European Journal of Criminology* 4(3): 315–345.

McNeill, F. (2012), 'Four forms of offender rehabilitation: Towards an inter-disciplinary perspective', *Legal and Criminological Psychology* 17(1): 18–36.

Miller, W. and C'de Baca, J. (2001), *Quantum Change: When Epiphanies and Sudden Insights Transform Ordinary Lives*. New York: Guilford Press.

Norem, J. and Cantor, N. (1986), 'Defensive pessimism: Harnessing anxiety as motivation', *Journal of Personality and Social Psychology* 51(6): 1208–1217.

Paternoster, R. and Pogarsky, G. (2009), 'Rational choice, agency and thoughtfully reflective decision making: The short and long-term consequences of making good choices', *Journal of Quantitative Criminology* 25(2): 103–127.

Soyer, M. (2014), 'The imagination of desistance: A juxtaposition of the construction of incarceration as a turning point and the reality of recidivism', *British Journal of Criminology* 54(1): 91–108.

Walters, G. (1995), 'The psychological inventory of criminal thinking styles, part I: Reliability and preliminary validity', *Criminal Justice and Behaviour* 22(3): 307–325.

Walters, G. (2012), 'Criminal thinking and recidivism: Meta-analytic evidence on the predictive and incremental validity of the psychological inventory of criminal thinking styles (PICTS)', *Aggression and Violent Behaviour* 17(3): 272–278.

Williams, R. and Gantt, E. (2013), 'Psychology and the death of aspiration', *Theory and Psychology* 23(2): 184–204.

4

STRUCTURAL CONTEXT AND PATHWAYS TO DESISTANCE

Research in Spain[1]

José Cid and Joel Martí

Introduction

The overview of desistance studies elaborated by Laub and Sampson (2001) sets a challenge for future researchers: do the factors they highlighted as relevant to understanding desistance (attachment to a spouse, job stability and successful experience in the military) continue to be pathways to desistance in contemporary societies? Some authors have answered that the socio-economic context of the post-Second World War era was very different – with respect to opportunities for stable jobs and family formation – from the reality of post-industrial societies (Giordano *et al.* 2002). Other scholars have considered that the relevance of some institutions as turning points may depend on the social meaning and social policies related to them in each country. For example, in Scandinavian countries some institutions that have not generally been considered as turning points may assume this function. This may happen with cohabitation, given that in these societies cohabitation is seen as an institution similar to marriage, or with paternity, given that policies devoted to sustain parents with children may increase the positive influence on men of having children (Savolainen 2009). Extending this line of research, Farrall *et al.* (2010) explored the structural changes in the modern UK that might have affected the possibilities of desistance: employment (fewer opportunities for non-qualified people), families and housing (delaying the age for achieving one's own house and reducing the possibilities of independence) and criminal policy (labelling offenders as risky persons and weakening the focus on reintegration).

Following Farrall *et al.* (2010), this chapter aims to locate and understand pathways to desistance within a specific structural context (namely Spain). We first explain some features of contemporary Spain relevant to desistance. Then we describe the research we have carried out in Barcelona from 2010 to 2012 with formerly imprisoned men. Third, we convey some results of this research focusing on the relationship between structural context and pathways to desistance. Finally, we discuss some practical and theoretical implications of the research.

Structural context

There are four areas that may be considered as underpinning pathways to persistence and desistance in the context of our research in Spain: the labour market, the role of the family in welfare, recent migration trends and policies, and the rehabilitation model of the Spanish penitentiary system. We take each in turn.

The labour market

Spain is characterized by high levels of precariousness in its labour market. Major segments of the labour force are working in temporary employment and the informal economy. During economic crises, this part of the population has a higher probability of being unemployed: according to Eurostat the rate of unemployment in Spain, historically higher than in the other EU countries, reached 26 per cent in 2013 (35 per cent for persons with lower levels of education).[2] The job crisis has especially damaged traditional male occupations such as the construction sector, one of the main sources of occupation for unqualified male workers. The population at risk of poverty has also reached one of the highest levels among the EU countries.[3] Thus, previously imprisoned people who managed to re-enter society during these years not only had to deal with their low skills and prison stigma but also encountered a scarce and precarious employment market. Ex-prisoners receive a monthly unemployment benefit for 18 months after release (irregular immigrants are excluded), but this payment (426€ in 2014) is not a living wage.

The chances of finding a stable job, associated with desistance (Sampson and Laub 1993; Uggen 2000), may be very limited for former prisoners in a scenario of high unemployment and precarious jobs aggravated due to the economic crisis.

Family and welfare

Esping-Andersen (1999) proposed a typology of three models of welfare state in industrial capitalist countries: the liberal, the social-democratic and the conservative-corporatist. Although there is disagreement with respect to the inclusion of Southern European countries among the corporatist model of welfare or the existence of a fourth, Mediterranean, model (Ferrera 1996; Moreno 2001; Valiente 2010), there is no dispute about the relevance of the family for the welfare of individuals in Spain and in other Southern European countries. While the state has assumed some universalistic benefits – education, health and pensions – the development of other social policies is very limited in comparison with those countries with a social-democratic model. Therefore, the transfer of material and emotional resources by other members of the family is very relevant in the provision of welfare to individuals (Moreno 2001). In this context, family is an important source of informal support that may promote a process of desistance (Calverley 2011;

Schroeder *et al.* 2010; Bottoms and Shapland 2011). Particularly in a scenario of economic crisis with many people losing their jobs and homes, the provision of accommodation and money by the family can be very relevant for the resettlement of ex-prisoners.

On the other hand, although the participation of women in the labour market has increased strongly in the last 50 years, the culture of men as main breadwinners has not disappeared, as may be evidenced by the low female employment rate (54 per cent in 2013) in comparison with the EU average (63 per cent in 2013)[4] and by their more relevant role caring for the rest of the family members.[5] In the context of a male breadwinner culture, this welfare model may strain those former prisoners with families who lack resources to meet material needs.

Immigration trends and policies

During the first decade of the twenty-first century, Spain experienced a considerable increase in its immigrant population from non-EU countries, especially from Latin America and North Africa. According to the 2011 Census of Population, non-EU nationals represent 9 per cent of the total population in Spain. This proportion grows to 11 per cent in more economically active regions such as Catalonia. Most of this population has been occupied mainly in low-qualified and precarious jobs in sectors such as construction, agriculture, food service activities and domestic work. The economic crisis has mainly affected the precarious employment occupied by immigrants and, as a consequence, the gap in the rate of employment between foreigners and nationals has increased: 46 per cent v. 56 per cent in 2013.[6] The vulnerability of the immigrant population is remarkable among those with non-legal status, given their chances for income are reduced to unemployment or working in the informal economy. In this context, it has been claimed that Spanish immigration policy does not promote the regular settlement of immigrants with equal conditions to those of nationals, and it has contributed to the discrimination and exclusion of this population (Cachón 2009). The disadvantages of the non-EU immigrant population may also be seen in their overrepresentation in prisons: in 2013 the proportion of non-EU prisoners in Catalan prisons was 38 per cent.[7]

Therefore, any research on desistance in Spain should take into account some specific issues that affect the foreign population that has been convicted and imprisoned. The commitment of the first generation of immigrants to settlement in the new country (Tonry 1997) may be related to a working identity that could facilitate the desistance process. The importance of ethnic identity has also been underlined to understand processes of desistance of ethnic minorities in other countries (Calverley 2013).[8] However, other factors related to immigration may operate in the opposite direction. On the one hand, having a criminal record bars someone from obtaining a residence permit (which is a condition of obtaining a regular job) and this reduces the possibilities of desistance based on job settlement. On the other, some part of the imprisoned migrant population lacks the strong social bonds that may foster desistance.

Rehabilitation model

The rate of imprisonment in Spain has increased by 252 per cent between 1980 and 2010[9] and this change is partially due to punitive policies adopted after the reintroduction of democracy in Spain in 1978,[10] with criminal law reforms that have extended the length of prison sentences (Cid and Larrauri 2009). In spite of this punitiveness, Spain has maintained a penitentiary system that is formally based on a rehabilitation model (García-España and Díez-Ripollés 2012). This model is grounded on the idea that every person serving a prison sentence may have at some point in their sentence support for re-entry. According to this model, rehabilitation starts in prison providing treatment for criminogenic needs. Once the prisoner is deemed to have completed treatment, a process of a transitional release into society is started with home leaves, followed by an open regime – ideally working outside the prison and returning to prison at night – and finishing with parole (Cid 2005). This model of rehabilitation offers possibilities for cognitive transformation, one aspect that some authors have considered a crucial dimension in the desistance process (Maruna 2001; Giordano *et al.* 2002). Not only might the provision of treatment inside prison be relevant as a hook to provide narratives of change among prisoners (Giordano *et al.* 2002) but also the stimulation for change can increase a feeling of self-efficacy that has been associated with successful desistance (Maruna 2001). Furthermore, the interventions during the period of transitional release include elements – such as provision of work, involvement of the family and an adequate level of supervision – that have been linked to a successful re-entry (Petersilia 2003; Travis 2005). However, the main problem with the Spanish rehabilitation model is that in practice not everyone benefits from it: in fact, only approximately 40 per cent of prisoners in Catalonia ended their sentences with a transitional release, with 60 per cent being released at the expiration of the sentence (Cid and Tébar 2010). Prisoners excluded from the transitional release process are mainly those with longer criminal records, a part of the sentence served on remand, a larger record of disciplinary infractions and few chances of benefiting from home leave while serving their sentence (Tébar 2006).

This lack of universality in the implementation of the rehabilitation model leads to a prison system that concentrates its efforts on promoting desistance only on a part of the prison population while discarding the rest. The implementation of the rehabilitation model is a positive factor for desistance, but it may produce negative contributions, even criminogenic effects, for those prisoners that this model is prone to exclude.

The research

As far as we know, no research on desistance has been conducted in Spain, or in other Southern European countries. In 2010 we began a research project, funded by the Spanish Government, focusing on identifying factors that lead to desistance after imprisonment.

The research population consists of men who were imprisoned for property offences and drug dealing in the province of Barcelona (Catalonia) whose sentences were set to expire between April and July 2010. From this population, a purposive sample was selected to include participants of different ages (because desistance pathways may differ between youths and adults). To ensure the presence of desisters and persisters in these diverse situations, the sample included men who were ending their sentences in both open and closed regimes, which is an effective predictor of recidivism in Catalonia (Capdevila and Ferrer 2009). In the first wave, we interviewed 67 men,[11] 36 (54 per cent) of whom we followed up and re-interviewed during the period between one year and two years after the expiration of the prison sentence (Table 4.1).

The main instrument used in the research was the narrative interview. The first interview was intended to identify the biography and narrative of the participants at the final stage of their sentence. The interview had three sections: the person's background (neighbourhood, family, education, job, delinquency, drugs

TABLE 4.1 Population and sample characteristics

		Population[1]	Sample (T1)	Sample (T2)
Age at the expiration of the sentence	Up to 26	17%	22%	25%
	27–34	33%	31%	33%
	35–44	30%	33%	31%
	Over 44	21%	13%	11%
	Mean age	36	35	35
Nationality	Spanish	58%	60%	72%
	Foreigner	42%	40%	28%
Offence	Property	60%	69%	83%
	Drug dealing	31%	25%	17%
	Property and drug dealing	9%	6%	0%
Type of release	Expiration of the sentence	46%	40%	44%
	Early release (open prison or parole)	51%	60%	56%
Imprisonment during adult life[2]		n/a	0.49	0.53
Time employed during adult life[3]		n/a	0.36	0.36
Recidivism rate		n/a	27%	42%
N		330	67	36

Notes

1 Males convicted for violent and non-violent property offences and drug-dealing offences in the province of Barcelona, with sentences expiring between April and July 2010.

2 Proportion of calendar years in the adult life (since 18 years old) in which the participants have spent some time in prison.

3 Proportion of calendar years in adult life (since 16 years old) in which the participants were working at least 6 months during the year.

and imprisonment); the experience of the current prison sentence; and future perspectives after the expiry of the prison sentence. The second interview was aimed at exploring the trajectory of the participants after ending their prison sentences. Apart from the interviews, data on social background were obtained using a life-history calendar, and data on re-incarceration during the two years after the expiration of the sentences have been provided by the Catalan prison service.

The analysis of the data obtained in the field work has been carried out, until now, with three different aims. The first study (Cid and Martí 2012) was based on a qualitative analysis of the interviews at the first follow-up of the sample and was aimed at exploring the origin of the narratives of desistance and persistence that the individuals had in the final period of the expiration of the prison sentence. The second study (Martí and Cid 2015) consisted of a mixed methodology – qualitative and quantitative. The quantitative data were obtained from life-history calendars and from a quantitative analysis of the interviews of the 67 participants in the first wave. The aim of the analysis was to explore the relationship between family visits, the desistance narrative and recidivism. The latest study (Cid and Martí 2015) consisted of a qualitative analysis of the narratives of the 36 participants that have been followed up and was oriented towards exploring which of the theories considered – social control, cognitive transformation and social support – might be more apt to explain the pathways of desistance and persistence found in our sample. In this chapter we try to link the pathways of desistance and persistence described in our research with the structural features of contemporary Spain.

Table 4.2 shows a quantitative description of the differences between participants who had finished the second wave, classified as desisters and persisters. On the one hand, the background of persisters (measured by the time imprisoned and time employed during adult life) is more problematic than that of desisters, although in both groups (persisters and desisters) there are persons with similar backgrounds who have followed different paths in relation to desistance. On the other, the circumstances during imprisonment and at release of desisters and persisters have been very different. Desisters were more prone to have espoused a desistance narrative at the end of the prison sentence, to have been on early release and to have counted on some social bond in the re-entry to society. As explained in the following section, our research indicates that although there are different pathways that bring someone to desistance, the more prevalent one starts with the support that the person has received from relatives during imprisonment and at release. The support of the family, combined with support from the prison and parole system, has influenced the emergence of narratives of change that have brought the participants to desistance.

Pathways to desistance and persistence: key points

In this section we discuss some of the results of our research, trying to underline how the pathways of desistance and persistence found in our study are related to the structural context we have previously described. Detailed results that support our discussion can be found in Cid and Martí (2012, 2015) and Martí and Cid (2015).

Turning points and returning points

The concept of a 'turning point' is central in explaining desistance in the 'Age-graded theory of informal social control' developed by Laub and Sampson (Sampson and Laub 1993; Laub and Sampson 2003). Turning points means, in this theoretical

TABLE 4.2 Differences between desisters and persisters in the sample

	Desisters (N = 21)[1]		Persisters (N = 15)[1]	
	N	Per cent	N	Per cent
Age at expiration of sentence: median (min-max)	34 (24–70)		31 (24–43)	
Imprisonment during adult life: median (min-max)[2]	0.32 (0.17–1)		0.69 (0.29–1)	
Time employed during adult life: median (min-max)[3]	0.51 (0–1)		0.14 (0–0.64)	
Desistance narrative at first interview[4]	17	81%	2	13%
Early release[5]	16	76%	4	27%
Conventional family support (post-sentence)[6]	16	76%	3	20%
Conventional partner (post-sentence)[7]	10	48%	3	20%
Work/pension (post-sentence)[8]	6	29%	1	7%
At least one social bond in the post-sentence period (conventional family support/conventional partner/work or pension)	18	86%	4	27%

Notes

1 Persisters: new offence that leads to reincarnation committed within two years of the expiry of the sentence. Using reincarceration as a measure of desistance may be problematic if some of the non-reincarcerated participants were offending and able to avoid incarceration. In two cases, this was the case at the time of the second interview, but these two participants who reported reoffending were later incarcerated. With respect to the group of desisters, we found two situations: most of them did not report any criminal offence since the expiration of the sentence; other participants reported some criminal offences (or other kinds of illegal behaviour) but, compared to their previous criminal careers, these offences were less serious and, in principle, not imprisonable offences.

2 See definition in Table 4.1.

3 See definition in Table 4.1.

4 Breaking with offender identity and expressing self-efficacy in achieving conventional plans.

5 Expiring sentence in open regime (day parole) or on parole.

6 Instrumental and emotional support from parents or siblings, taking into account that the emotional support should include support for change.

7 Stable relationship with a partner that has supported change in the participant.

8 Being employed most of the time after the expiration of the sentence (more than 50%) or receiving a life pension for being unable to work.

★ Data on 20 participants (one missing case).

perspective, the participation of the person in new adult roles (such as a good partner or stable job) that produces a stake in conformity and life routines that become
incompatible with an offending lifestyle. In our sample, some desisters had started
their change as the result of a commitment to a new conventional partner and had
been imprisoned afterwards. But, for most of them, the change started in prison
without the emergence of any turning point devised by Laub and Sampson. In
these cases, parents and partners were very supportive during imprisonment, they
gave emotional and material support in their visits and participants developed the
feeling of a moral duty to compensate their family for all the suffering caused and
all the support received. The causal mechanism of these 'returning points' (Cid and
Martí 2012) may be well understood within the framework of social support theory
(Cullen 1994), which makes it understandable that 'returning' points are processes
that maintain change (Carlsson 2012). Receiving support generates feelings of reciprocity in the participants to fulfil the desire of the family and partners to see the
participant earning early release and living a conventional life. The emergence of
returning points required not only a supporting family during imprisonment[12] but
also a concern for the change of the participant.[13]

The results of our research with respect to turning points and 'returning' points –
the fact that returning points consisted of change as compensation for the support
received and were more prevalent than turning points in which change is based on
the acquisition of adult roles – should be read in the context of the study. First, the
limited relevance of turning points in this research may be related to the fact that
our participants spent a relevant part of their adult life in prison (see Table 4.1).
This is, in part, due to a penal system with long sentences in the EU context that
makes the transition to adult roles difficult. A second point relates to the salience
of returning points in our study. This result is in line with the finding that family
support – both from original families and from formed families – during imprisonment favours the formation of narratives of change (Visher and O'Connell 2012)
and may reduce the chances of recidivism (Bales and Mears 2008; Cobbina et al.
2012). The idea that the high level of familial bonds in Spanish society is a factor
that favours processes of desistance also has its limitations. In this sense we have
observed not only that the emergence of narratives of change is difficult when the
family does not play a conventional supportive role or is not able to meet the evident needs of the former imprisoned person but also that the process of desistance
may fail when the person feels frustrated by the lack of family resources (Martí and
Cid 2015). The idea that emerges from these findings is that social bonds are only
able to promote change when they are able to promote support and are prosocial
(Giordano et al. 2002).[14]

Masculinity and desistance

In a recent paper, Carlsson (2013) argued that the idea of masculinity tends to
favour delinquency during adolescence, but also can promote desistance during
the transition to adulthood. Offender behaviour that is explained as an expression

of the idea of 'being a man' during adolescence (Matza and Sykes 1961; Moffit 1993; Agnew 2006) is socially perceived as incompatible with the idea of 'being a man' in adulthood (Massoglia and Uggen 2010). As Gadd and Farrall (2004) showed, there are different social discourses about the role of masculinity in which men may invest. The start of the desistance process is linked to a change in the perception of masculinity, in the sense of being capable of succeeding in carrying out tasks oriented to a conventional life. This new role can favour desistance not only for the reasons stated by the age-grade theory of informal social control (Sampson and Laub 1993; Laub and Sampson 2003) but also because it is a way to express masculinity. Accordingly, pathways of persistence would be related to obstacles that former imprisoned males encountered to acquire masculine adult roles (Carlsson 2013).

The results of our research are partially coherent with this perspective. The distance of the participants from their offending lifestyle, usually labelled as a child-like behaviour, was one element of the desistance narratives. Some of these participants were successful in acquiring a full adult status (economic independence and family formation) and did desist in the follow-up. Then there were the participants that did not develop this identity change and persisted at release.[15] However, there was also an intermediate category of participants that developed an identity change, but who were not able to achieve the adult status to which they were aspiring. They had been unemployed since release or had lost the job they had during early release. Given this lack of economic independence, their emancipation projects were delayed and they mostly lived with their parents. Nevertheless, most of these participants desisted in the follow-up period and their desistance is not fully accountable within the frameworks of the theories that are focused in the acquisition of an adult status – such as the age-graded theory of informal social control (Sampson and Laub 1993; Laub and Sampson 2003) or the gendered approach developed by Carlsson (2013). The reasons given by these participants for their desistance emphasized their own morality, the attachment to family and partners and the help received to overcome the strain of unemployment and lack of money.[16]

Our research confirms the value of the transition to adult roles (economic independence and family formation) and the new commitments produced as relevant factors and processes to understand desistance (Laub and Sampson 2003; Massoglia and Uggen 2010; Carlsson 2013), but it suggests that the maintenance of social support may explain the stability of the desistance trajectories, despite adverse social circumstances that impede achieving masculine adult roles. This finding should be seen as a further evidence of the point made by other researchers (Giordano *et al.* 2002; Farrall *et al.* 2010; Schroeder *et al.* 2010; Bottoms and Shapland 2011), suggesting that in societies where stable work and family formation are hard to achieve for people that have accumulated social disadvantage, other sources of desistance, like support from the family, may be more relevant. The strong family ties of Spanish society in the context of an economic crisis that has had a special impact on the more disadvantaged part of the population, seems relevant in understanding these pathways to desistance.[17]

Immigration and desistance

Due to the high rates of immigrant populations in Spanish prisons, the initial sample of the research (see Table 4.1) had 40 per cent of foreign participants. Although in the follow-up we have been much less successful with these participants, the follow-up sample of the present research contains some immigrants.

In the immigrant sub-population, there are two profiles (Cid and Martí 2012). The first one has an offending trajectory similar to most of the national participants: they were habitual offenders during adolescence in their country of origin, or they had travelled alone to Spain as children and had been socialized in a criminogenic context. The second profile of immigrants came to Spain in adulthood, did not report either offending or abuse of drugs during childhood and adolescence, reported having been working in Spain after their arrival and had started to offend afterwards. The narratives of this second group of immigrant participants had a common element in denying an offender identity. In some cases they considered themselves 'innocents', they considered the offence as 'one mistake in life', or they justified the offences in terms of the exploitation to which they were submitted or the necessity to survive when they became unemployed. The differences between desisters and persisters in this profile were not based on a change of identity but in self-efficacy, particularly in their confidence in getting a job at the end of the prison sentence.

What we found in the follow-up of the late-starter immigrant participants who had initiated a process of desistance, was that they had experienced a very stressful situation of unemployment and lack of support at release, both situations in which desistance projects can fail or have many chances to fail. These participants had built their desistance narratives on their confidence in getting a job after release that might be able to sustain their families. Their inability to achieve masculine roles seemed to play a relevant role in accounting for the failure of their desistance projects.[18]

The paradox of the imprisoned adult immigrant population of this research is that although they may have a better background than the native population – late onset of offending, less criminogenic needs, a working identity – they experienced greater obstacles to resettlement. Not only did former imprisoned immigrants have weaker family networks than the native population but they also suffered legal and social barriers to entry into the labour market. The discriminative context for this population in Spain should also be considered in understanding the limited role that the transition to adult roles as a pathway to desistance has in this research.

Imprisonment and desistance

There is no theoretical agreement on the effect of imprisonment on desistance. According to the rational choice theory, imprisonment is a negative event in the life of offenders that may produce a reflection on the 'feared self' (Paternoster and Bushway 2009) and is associated with the 'openness to change' that other researchers have outlined as the initial moment of the desistance process (Giordano et al. 2002).

Other theories argue that imprisonment is associated with persistence, because the labelling produced by imprisonment affects social bonds negatively and reduces the stake in conformity (Sampson and Laub 1993, 1997). Furthermore, social learning argues that the effects of imprisonment depend on whether the sentence was punitive or was aimed at challenging criminogenic needs (Andrews and Bonta 2003). Blumstein (2004) reasons that the null effect found in some research on the effects of imprisonment on recidivism was probably because these theories have a different effect on each individual. However, a recent overview of the research on this issue reveals that the balance seems moderately in favour of the criminogenic effects of imprisonment (Nagin *et al.* 2009; see also Jolliffe and Hedderman 2012).

What we have found in our research seems to give credit to the idea of Blumstein about different effects of imprisonment according to the circumstances in which imprisonment is experienced. On the one hand, we have the desisters. Most of them developed a process of a change of identity as a result of the support given by family during imprisonment. Imprisonment was not the catalyst for change, but some experiences during imprisonment played a role in the process of change, contributing to the feeling of self-efficacy in most desisters. These participants tried to profit from the opportunities given by the prison system in areas such as education, work and treatment. At some moment in their sentence, they earned early release and were able to maintain their desistance project and comply with the supervision requirements of open regime and parole. It seems that the progressive model or transition to society had some impact on the development of a feeling of self-efficacy with respect to the achievement of conventional plans. In contrast, we have the experience of imprisonment of the persistent participants. For most of them, imprisonment was not meaningful, only a punitive and probably criminogenic experience. Most of them did not engage in education or treatment and did not initiate any re-entry programme.[19]

The interaction between the familism of the Spanish society and the progressive character of the penitentiary system seems to have promoted pathways of desistance among one group of our participants. As mentioned before, participation in rehabilitation during imprisonment was one way to reciprocate for the family support received from partners. As one of the interviewees said when explaining his process of change, 'I'll do it for me and for them [my parents]'. But at the same time this interaction may explain pathways of persistence among the participants that lacked this external support and did not take part in rehabilitation programmes.[20]

We may conclude that we have a dual penitentiary policy: it supports processes of change in those prisoners that have external support for change, but inhibits change in those that lack external support that backs the desistance process.

Conclusions

As Farrall *et al.* (2014) state in their recent overview of their longitudinal research, one structural factor that affects desistance is the availability of legitimate identities in every context. One of the main results of our research is that the transition to adult roles of job stability and family – that it is one of the pathways of desistance most favoured by international research – is not very prevalent in our sample. This result should be related to a job market in which stability in low-skilled jobs is disappearing. The recent economic crisis has worsened the situation, transforming precarious work into unemployment and poverty. In this context, the chances of achieving a stable job are very limited for people who have spent time in prison. Moreover, finding a stable job can be even more difficult for the immigrant population since they suffer legal and social barriers to re-entry and this may also affect their possibilities of emancipation.

The pathway to desistance that was more prevalent in our research – the family support that interacts with the penitentiary system to promote a process of change while serving a prison sentence and successful re-entry afterwards – also seems to be linked to the role of familism in Spanish society. The fact that Spanish families share a cultural duty to support other members of the family means that for relevant prisoners a pathway to desistance may be available based on receiving support and given change as a compensation. However, this model of welfare has important limitations. Particularly it should be noted that it leads to discrimination against people who lack family support and the burden that it can set on more disadvantaged families (Codd 2007). In these cases, males, influenced by the 'male as a breadwinner' culture, may feel frustrated at not having the resources to sustain their families.

With respect to the policy implications of this research, there are two imprisoned minorities that should be given special attention in order to favour processes of desistance: people who lack a family able to provide conventional support (emotional and instrumental), and immigrants. The first group may receive less support during imprisonment and may be less motivated or given less consideration to take advantage of the resources offered by the prison system. This group could benefit from policies oriented to provide alternative sources of support. The second group suffer from the legal barriers to citizenship of having a criminal record and could benefit from policies aimed at reducing the obstacles to work after the expiration of their sentences (Larrauri 2011).

Moving to the theoretical implications of the research, it should be said that, similar to the results of other longitudinal studies (Farrall et al. 2014), no single theory may be enough to understand the pathways of desistance and persistence in our sample. Some cases are well explained within the framework of the age-grade theory of informal social control (Sampson and Laub 1993; Laub and Sampson 2003); in others the cognitive transformation seems to precede the process of desistance (Giordano et al. 2002), but probably in most cases the conventional support has been the catalyst for a process of change (Cullen 1994). Our research is aimed at adding knowledge about desistance by emphasizing that a main causal process – the provision of conventional support that motivates the person to endeavour to undertake a process of change as compensation for the support received – seems to lead to desistance. Other researchers have found similar processes (Schroeder et al. 2010; Calverley 2011), which may enhance the importance of social support theory in the explanation of desistance.

Our final conclusion relates to what we think should be relevant areas for future research. Our first point concerns the importance of extending the research on the relation between social support and desistance. We think that most of the research in this area is based on family support, but we need to know whether other forms of support – such as formal support from the state or support from the community and in particular from the voluntary sector – may produce the same mechanisms as family support to foster desistance. This research is very relevant in order to inform re-entry policies. Our second point relates to the relationship between imprisonment and desistance. On the basis of our research, we suggested that the different effects of imprisonment on the process of desistance of our participants may be due to an interaction between the familism of the Spanish society and the progressive character of the penitentiary system. Although we are aware of some research oriented to reveal other mechanisms that link imprisonment with desistance and persistence, we think this is an area in need of more research and that it would be beneficial to do comparative research among different penitentiary systems. Finally, we think there is little research on the relationship between immigration and desistance. As a result of it being a more difficult population to study, we know little about the processes of desistance among immigrant populations. Further studies in this area may reveal more about the identity of some ethnic minorities as a factor that foster desistance and also about the way in which the immigrant population is able to desist in a context in which they suffer discrimination compared to the national population.

Notes

1 The research on which this chapter is based was supported by the Spanish Ministry of Science and Technology (Grant number DER 2008-0541/JURI); the Catalan Agency for Management of University and Research Grants (Grant number 2009 SGR-01117); and by the Catalan Centre of Law Studies and Specialized Training (Grant number: JUS/4110/2010). We would like to thank the editors of the book and the anonymous reviewers for their insightful comments to previous drafts of this chapter.
2 Source: Eurostat, Labour Force Survey.
3 Source: Eurostat, Statistics on Income and Living Conditions.
4 Source: Eurostat, Labour Force Survey.
5 Source: Sweden Statistics, Harmonized European Time Use Survey. Across 15 European countries, Spain is the second highest country in which men devote less time to domestic work and is the fourth highest country in which women devote more time to it.
6 Source: Eurostat, Labour Force Survey.
7 Source: Catalan Statistical Institute, *Direcció General de Règim Penitenciari i Recursos*. The rate of foreign people in prison in the rest of Spain was 33 per cent in 2012 (Secretaría General de Servicios Penitenciarios – data from the rest of Spain include all foreigners, EU and non-EU).
8 Calverley (2013: 189) explains how some Asian minorities within the UK share some values – such as the support of other members of the family, the value of forgiveness and the importance of religion that favours the processes of desistance of members of these minorities. These values may not be present in other minorities and therefore, 'some communities may be better at fostering desistance than others'.
9 Source: Secretaría General de Instituciones Penitenciarias, *Numero de Internos en los Centros penitenciarios. Evolución semanal; Secretaria de Servicios Penitenciarios, Rehabilitación y*

Secretaría General de Instituciones Penitenciarias and Secretaria de Serveis Penitenciaris, Rehabilitació i Justicia Juvenil.

10 The military dictatorship established by Franco after the Spanish Civil War (1936–1939), lasted until the death of Franco (1975). The transition to democracy, based on a deal between the successors of the Franco regime and the democratic opposition, brought a general election in 1977 and the approval of a new Constitution in 1978. The prison population at the end of the Dictatorship was really low by European standards and it changed dramatically afterwards. Some reasons may be suggested for this new trend: the concentration of the Franco regime on political offences, the economic crisis of 1973, the increase of crime in the 1970s and 1980s, related also to the explosion of drug consumption, and the lack of a reductionist policy in the dominant legal culture (some of these reasons are explored in Cid and Larrauri (1998, 2009)).

11 The sample was obtained in two stages. In the first one all offenders in the province of Barcelona whose sentences were ending between April and May 2010 were asked by the penitentiary administration to participate in the research. In this stage 47 qualitative interviews were done. In the second stage, which targeted offenders being released between June and October 2010, 20 additional interviews were undertaken, focusing on those profiles and narratives less present in the first stage, in order to obtain a sufficient variety of narratives (desistance and persistence). In the second stage, only offenders up to 35 years old who were in an open regime and on parole (that probably had a desistance narrative) were invited to participate in the research. Taking into consideration the two stages, the consent rate reached 61 per cent.

12 In Martí and Cid (2015) we show how family visits are one of the factors that account for there being a desistance narrative in the first round of interviews.

13 Some participants received visits during imprisonment, but did not develop a desistance narrative. In some cases, the visits were from a partner not committed to the change in the participant; in other cases the participants regretted that the family bond was weakened after a long period of imprisonment and they felt visits were not meaningful anymore.

14 This idea was suggested by one of the anonymous reviewers of our chapter. Finestone (1967), in his pioneer work on desistance of members of the Polish and Italian communities in the US, showed that Italian families were more reintegrative than Polish families to returned prisoners, but were less able to exercise control over their members. He suggested that rehabilitation policies for Italians should be based on cooperation with families by trying to isolate the person from their peer group.

15 The narratives of these persistent participants varied. In some cases, the idea of masculinity is present – men have to bring money into the home – but in most cases the justification of persistence was based on the perception that offending was the only option they had in life (Cid and Martí 2015).

16 Healy (2014), in her research on Irish probationers, describes a typology of what she calls 'liminal desisters', characterized by assuming a conventional identity, but without having reached enough social capital – family, job – to sustain the new identity. The typology presented by Healy presents similarities with the desisters in our sample who had not reached adult status. However, this class of desisters in our sample seemed more confident in avoiding a new offence than the liminal desisters of Healy's research.

17 One anonymous reviewer of our chapter considered that the concept of 'returning' points extends rather than contradicts the theory of Sampson and Laub. The reviewer indicates that, according to those authors, social bonds that are strong and of good quality facilitate desistance. We agree with the reviewer that child–parent bonds in adult life present similarities to social bonds defined as turning points, such as good cohabitations and stable jobs. Attachment is one aspect that is present in both turning points and returning points as a mechanism that maintains change. However, we think that while in turning points it is the structural position in which the person lives, which generates the transformation of the person, in returning points the change is due to the individual, who needs to build their own pathway to desistance (see Cid and Martí (2015) for a wider development of this idea).

18 We have been able to follow three late-starting immigrants who had a desistance narrative at first interview. Two of them had a family and felt frustrated at not being able to support their children. In both cases, the idea (approached in the previous section) of masculinity – that may persist when the person is unable to fulfil the conventional male role of the breadwinner – was confirmed. The third case was a single participant who had made an effort to avoid offences that might cause him to be re-incarcerated and survived working in the informal economy and committing some small offences to obtain money.

19 We have indirect confirmation of the role of the progressive system in promoting desistance. From the qualitative analysis, we have evidence that participation in rehabilitation and early release contributed to the feeling of self-efficacy that is one element of the desistance narratives. A quantitative analysis of recidivism (based on incarceration) of the original sample (done in Martí and Cid 2015) confirms that the desistance narrative at the end of prison is associated with recidivism.

20 Our research does not sustain the idea of imprisonment as a 'turning point'. Imprisonment was not a turning point in itself for most of the individuals of the sample. Most narratives of desistance emerged in response to the support that the participants received from the family during imprisonment. The way in which they experienced imprisonment – the support received from prison and parole officers, the participation in rehabilitation programmes, the manner of release – made a contribution to the development of narratives of change. Probably the progressive character of the Spanish prison system made the maintenance of change easier after release that was seen as a critical point in other research (Soyer 2014).

References

Agnew, R. (2006), *Pressured into Crime. An Overview of General Strain Theory*. Los Angeles, CA: Roxbury.

Andrews, D. and Bonta, J. (2003), *The Psychology of Criminal Conduct*, third edition. Cincinnati, OH: Anderson.

Bales, W. and Mears, D. (2008), 'Inmate social ties and the transition to society: Does visitation reduce recidivism?', *Journal of Research in Crime and Delinquency* 45: 287–321.

Blumstein, A. (2004), 'Prisons: A policy challenge', in Wilson, J. Q. and Petersilia, J. (eds) *Crime*. Oakland, MI: ICS Press.

Bottoms, A. and Shapland, J. (2011), 'Steps towards desistance among male young adult recidivists', in Farrall, S., Sparks, R., Maruna, S. and Hough, M (eds) *Escape Routes: Contemporary Perspectives on Life after Punishment*. London: Routledge.

Cachón, L. (2009), *La España Inmigrante: Marco Discriminatorio, Mercado De Trabajo Y Políticas De Integración (The Immigrant Spain: Discriminatoy Framework, Labour Market and Integration Policies)*. Barcelona, Spain: Anthropos.

Calverley, A. (2011), 'All in the family. The importance of support, tolerance and forgiveness in the desistance of male Bangladeshi offenders', in Farrall, S., Sparks, R., Maruna, S. and Hough, M. (eds) *Escape Routes: Contemporary Perspectives on Life after Punishment*. London: Routledge.

Calverley, A. (2013), *Cultures of Desistance. Rehabilitation, Reintegration and Ethnic Minorities*. London: Routledge.

Capdevila, M. and Ferrer, M. (2009), *Tasa de Reincidencia Penitenciaria 2008 (Rate of Reincarceration 2008)*. Barcelona, Spain: Centre d'Estudis Jurídics i Formació Especialitzada.

Carlsson, C. (2012), 'Using "turning points" to understand processes of change in offending. Notes from a Swedish study on life courses and crime', *British Journal of Criminology* 52: 1–16.

Carlsson, C. (2013), 'Masculinities, persistence and desistance', *Criminology* 51(3): 661–693.

Cid, J. (2005), 'The penitentiary system in Spain. The use of imprisonment, living conditions and rehabilitation', *Punishment & Society* 7(2): 147–166.

Cid, J. and Larrauri, E. (1998), 'Prisons and alternatives to prison in Spain', in Ruggiero, V., South, N. and Taylor, I. (eds) *The New European Criminology: Crime and Social Order in Europe*. London: Routledge, pp. 146–155.

Cid, J. and Larrauri, E. (2009), 'Development of crime, social change, mass media, crime policy, sanctioning practice and their impact on prison population rates', *Sistema Penal & Violência* 1(1): 1–21.

Cid, J. and Tébar, B. (2010), 'Spain', in Padfield, N., Van Zyl Smit, D. and Dünkel, F. (eds) *Release from Prison. European Policy and Practice*, Cullompton, UK: Willan.

Cid, J. and Martí, J. (2012), 'Turning points and returning points. Understanding the role of family ties in the process of desistance', *European Journal of Criminology* 9(6): 603–620.

Cid, J. and Martí, J. (2015), 'Imprisonment, social support and desistance: A theoretical approach to pathways of desistance and persistence for imprisoned men', *Journal of Offender Therapy and Comparative Criminology*, DOI 10.1177/0306624X15623988.

Cobbina, J., Huebner, B. and Berg. M. (2012), 'Men, women and post release offending: An examination of the nature of the link between relational ties and recidivism', *Crime and Delinquency* 58: 331–361.

Codd, H. (2007), 'Prisoners' families and resettlement: A critical analysis', *The Howard Journal of Criminal Justice* 46(3): 255–263.

Cullen, F. (1994), 'Social support as an organizing concept for criminology: Presidential address to the academy of Criminal Justice Sciences', *Justice Quarterly* 11: 527–559.

Esping-Andersen, C. (1999), *Social Foundations of Postindustrial Economies*. Oxford, UK: Oxford University Press.

Farrall, S., Bottoms, A. and Shapland, J. (2010), 'Social structures and desistance from crime', *European Journal of Criminology* 7(6): 546–570.

Farrall, S., Hunter, B., Sharpe, G. and Calverley, A. (2014), *Criminal Careers in Transition. The Social Context of Desistance from Crime*. Oxford, UK: Oxford University Press.

Ferrera, M. (1996), 'The "Southern model" of welfare in social Europe', *Journal of European Social Policy* 6(1): 17–37.

Finestone, H. (1967), 'Reform and recidivism among Italian and Polish criminal offenders', *American Journal of Sociology* 72(6): 575–588.

Gadd, D. and Farrall, S. (2004), 'Criminal careers, desistance and subjectivity. Interpreting men's narratives of change', *Theoretical Criminology* 8(2): 123–156.

García-España, E. and Díez-Ripollés, J. L. (eds) (2012), *Realidad Y Política Penitenciarias (Prison Policies and Prison Situation in Spain)*. Valencia, Spain: Tirant lo Blanch.

Giordano, P., Cernkovich, S. and Rudolph, J. (2002), 'Gender, crime, and desistance: Toward a theory of cognitive transformation', *American Journal of Sociology* 107: 990–1064.

Healy, D. (2014), 'Becoming a desister. Exploring the role of agency, coping and imagination in the construction of a new self', *British Journal of Criminology* 54: 873–891.

Jolliffe, D. and Hedderman, C. (2012), 'Investigating the impact of custody on reoffending using propensity score matching', *Crime and Delinquency* 20(10): 1–27.

Larrauri, E. (2011), 'Convictions records in Spain: Obstacles to reintegration of offenders?', *European Journal of Probation* 3(1): 50–62.

Laub, J. and Sampson, R. (2001), 'Understanding desistance from crime', *Crime and Justice. A Review of Research* 28: 1–69.

Laub, J. and Sampson, R. (2003), *Shared Beginnings, Different Lives. Delinquent Boys to Age 70*. Cambridge, MA: Harvard University Press.

82 José Cid and Joel Martí

Martí, J. and Cid, J. (2015), 'Encarcelamiento, lazos familiares y reincidencia: Explorando los límites del familismo' (Imprisonment, family bonds and recidivism: Exploring the limits of familism). *Revista Internacional de Sociología* 73(1), doi: http://dx.doi.org/10.3989/ris.2013.02.04 (accessed 24 December 2015).

Maruna, S. (2001), *Making Good. How Ex-Convicts Reform and Rebuild their Lives*. Washington, DC: American Psychological Association.

Massoglia, M. and Uggen, C. (2010), 'Settling down and aging out: Toward an interactionist theory of desistance and the transition to adulthood', *American Journal of Sociology* 116: 543–582.

Matza, D. and Sykes, G. (1961), 'Juvenile delinquency and subterranean values', *American Sociological Review* 26: 712–719.

Moffit, T. (1993), 'Adolescence-limited and life-course persistent antisocial behavior: A developmental taxonomy', *Psychological Review* 100(4): 674–701.

Moreno, L. (2001), 'La "vía media" española del modelo de bienestar mediterráneo' (The Spanish "middle way" in the Mediterranean model of welfare). Papers, *Revista de Sociología* 63/64: 67–82.

Nagin, D., Cullen, F. and Jonson, C. L. (2009) 'Imprisonment and reoffending', *Crime and Justice* 38: 115–200.

Paternoster, R. and Bushway, S. (2009), 'Desistance and the feared self: Toward an identity theory of criminal desistance', *Journal of Criminal Law and Criminology* 99: 1103–1156.

Petersilia, J. (2003), *When Prisoners Come Home. Parole and Prisoner Reentry*. Oxford, UK: Oxford University Press.

Sampson, R. and Laub, J. (1993), *Crime in the Making. Pathways and Turning Points through Life*. Cambridge, MA: Harvard University Press.

Sampson, R. and Laub, J. (1997), 'A life-course theory of cumulative disadvantage and the stability of delinquency', in Thornberry, T. (ed.) *Developmental Theories of Crime and Delinquency*. New Brunswick, NJ: Transaction Publishers.

Savolainen, J. (2009), 'Work, family and criminal desistance', *British Journal of Criminology* 49: 285–304.

Schroeder, R., Giordano, P. and Cernkovich, S. (2010), 'Adult child–parent bonds and life-course criminality', *Journal of Criminal Justice* 38: 562–571.

Soyer, M. (2014), 'The imagination of desistance. A juxtaposition of incarceration as a turning point and the reality of recidivism', *British Journal of Criminology* 54: 91–108.

Tébar, B. (2006), *El modelo de libertad condicional español* (*The Spanish Model of Parole*), Pamplona, Spain: Aranzadi.

Tonry, M. (1997), 'Ethnicity, crime and immigration', *Crime and Justice* 21: 1–29.

Travis, J. (2005), *But They All Come Back. Facing the Challenges of Prisoner Reentry*. Washington, DC: The Urban Institute Press.

Uggen, C. (2000), 'Work as a turning point in the life course of criminals: A duration model of age, employment, and recidivism', *American Sociological Review* 67: 529–546.

Valiente, C. (2010), 'The erosion of "familism" in the Spanish welfare state: Childcare policy since 1975', in Ajzenstadt, M. and Gal, J. (eds) *Children, Gender and Families in Mediterranean Welfare States*. London: Springer.

Visher, C. and O'Connell, D. (2012), 'Incarceration and inmates' self perceptions about returning home', *Journal of Criminal Justice* 40: 368–393.

SECTION II

Life phases and desistance

Whereas the chapters in the first section focused on the relationship between agency and wider structures, those in the second section concentrate upon particular ages of offenders or stages of desistance. Desistance, despite the concentration on the prolific and persistent offender (which usually implies some degree of adulthood), should not be thought of as entirely for adults – young people, including young children, may desist from aggressive or other anti-social behaviour, which they display at one point in their lives and which may not reoccur. Some of the chapters in this section deal with desistance in late adolescence and early adulthood – both in terms of the early stage of desistance for persistent offenders and also in relation to psychosocial and developmental maturation at this time. Other chapters in this section consider the notion of 'turning points' – that certain status changes (being married, becoming a parent, finding stable work or being injured) – may in some way be related to desistance. There has been much debate about the degree to which this concept helps or obfuscates matters (are such turning points simply retrospective reconstructions, for example?). Nevertheless, the concept is an important one and our contributors attempt to explore the ways in which such status changes occur – does the change or the desistance occur first?

5

KEY BEHAVIORAL ASPECTS OF DESISTANCE FROM CONDUCT PROBLEMS AND DELINQUENCY

Rolf Loeber, Magda Stouthamer-Loeber and Lia Ahonen[1]

Robins (1966), in her classical study on conduct disordered boys, observed that close to half of the boys initially registered in child guidance clinics because of conduct problems did not become sociopaths in adulthood. Since the publication of that study, many more studies have been published about continuities and discontinuities in delinquency and antisocial behavior (see below). However, compared to studies on the persistence of delinquent behavior (Robins 1966; West and Farrington 1973; McCord 1978; Wolfgang *et al.* 1987), studies on desistance from delinquent behavior are in the distinct minority (but see Laub and Sampson 2001; Farrington 2007; Kazemian and Farrington 2010). Even rarer are studies on desistance of conduct problems. Conduct problems are defined as acting out problems typical for childhood and adolescence and include, for example, minor forms of persistent aggression, chronic disobedience, and truancy. Typically, there are no justice ramifications to conduct problems. Delinquency is defined as the breaking of criminal laws, leaving the person open to processing in the (juvenile) justice system. The key reason to include desistance from conduct problems in a review of desistance from delinquency is that most of the eventual serious delinquents had conduct problems when young (Loeber and Dishion 1983), but do not necessarily continue to display all former forms of conduct problems during their delinquency career.

This chapter focuses on the behavioral aspects of desistance, such as observable behavioral expressions measured in self-reports and/or official records of delinquency. Thus, this chapter does not deal with associated cognitions accompanying desistance (decision making, curtailment of strategies to making use of opportunities), or motivational states that often co-occur with desistance (less urge to steal, lower level of impulsivity, lower need to get into a physical fight, etc.). In addition, this chapter does not focus on predictors, life events, or causal factors of desistance, which are the centerpiece of many other chapters in this volume.

The main reason for the focus on behavioral aspects of desistance is that these aspects constitute the end of deviancy processes. In most cases, behavioral desistance is observable, and it is relevant to naturally occurring improvements in behavior, and is of interest to all forms of remedial interventions. To illustrate the latter, Wilson and Kelling (1982) proposed the broken windows theory, which contains aspects of both escalation and desistance. Its main stance is that monitoring and maintaining the physical aspects of the man-made environment (including repairing broken windows) may discourage delinquent individuals from engaging in further vandalism (i.e., desist from vandalism) and discourage them from escalating to more serious forms of delinquency (i.e., desist from serious offenses).

As to the current chapter, the senior author's journey in desistance research started in 1988 when working with Richard Tremblay on analyses of a sample of over 1,100 kindergarten boys who had been followed up for four successive years in Montreal (Loeber *et al.* 1989). The study showed that half of the boys categorized as fighters fully desisted over time. A perplexing result, however, was that in some boys the cessation of fighting was associated with other later nonaggressive problem behavior (theft and truancy). Thus, for these boys, desistance in aggression was associated with the emergence of *other* antisocial acts; thus a form of displacement of behaviors rather than actual desistance. The finding is only one of the unanswered questions about desistance, which are the topic of the present chapter.

Most of the data reviewed in this chapter are drawn from the Pittsburgh Youth Study (PYS), which was started in 1989. In addition, this chapter will draw on data from the Cambridge Study on Delinquent Development. Because most criminological studies on desistance focus on official records only and mostly on late adolescence/early adulthood, we will also concentrate on desistance earlier in life, both in terms of offending and in terms of conduct problems. The inclusion of conduct problems in this review of desistance will allow a much broader sweep over a crucial period of juveniles' development of problem behaviors from childhood into early adulthood than can be usually found in most criminological studies.

The current chapter will first review some important aspects of behavioral desistance and the effects of using different methods of analysis:

1. definitions of behavioral desistance and different forms of desistance;
2. peak developmental periods of desistance;
3. typologies of desisters;
4. differential desistance from different types of offenses;
5. developmental pathways in distance from multiple types of delinquency;
6. the building down of delinquent acts;
7. false desistance in different data sources;
8. capacity to offend and the display of desistance;
9. desistance from conduct problems and delinquency and the replacement by prosocial behavior;
10. gender differences in desistance.

The chapter closes with a list of pressing research questions.

Defining behavioral desistance and different forms of desistance

The terminology of behavioral desistance is often misunderstood, and there is no consensus about its definition (Kazemian and Farrington 2010). For example, desistance is not necessarily the opposite of persistence or continuity, but can be much more multifaceted. Neither is desistance a dichotomy, being present or not; instead, desistance can be best conceptualized as a gradual process (Kazemian and Farrington 2010), occurring within individuals' development of delinquency and prosocial behavior over time. In the area of delinquency, Loeber and Le Blanc (1990) defined desistance in two ways. First, desistance occurs when delinquents decrease in their frequency, variety, and/or severity of offending. Second, desistance occurs when delinquent individuals never exceed a particular severity level (thus desisting from serious or specific forms of delinquency, or in the case of nondelinquents desist from any form of offending). In a later slight modification, Le Blanc and Loeber (1998) distinguished between four different forms of desistance in deviant behavior including deceleration in the frequency, variety and/or severity of delinquent behavior, specialization, and ceiling effects. These aspects of desistance from delinquency also apply to desistance from conduct problems. The following are several examples of different shades of desistance, which is partly based on Le Blanc and Loeber (1998).

Stable desistance

An individual desists from offending and the desistance completely persists over time; this process is not limited to an all or nothing phenomenon, but can also take place by means of deceleration, that is a decrease to the frequency of offending, which does not have to be zero. Stable desistance should be distinguished from different forms of partial desistance:

a.   *Temporary desistance* refers to a condition in which an individual ceases offending beyond the usual period of inter-offense time interval, but subsequently remits or relapses (e.g., Baicker-McKee 1990; Loeber *et al.* 1991).
b.   *De-escalation desistance*, which is a decrease in the severity of offending. Individuals who do so cease the more serious forms of offending, but continue to offend at the less serious level of delinquency, and have been called "de-escalators" (Loeber *et al.* 1991).
c.   *Substituting desistance* refers to the cessation of one offense type and the replacement by another offense type.
d.   *Specialization* refers to the narrowing down of individuals' offense types, for example, from different forms of violence and property offenses to property offenses only.
e.   *Ceiling effects*. Discussions about desistance should not be limited to instances where individuals display a particular offense type and then cease. Most

individuals never commit serious offenses such as rape, robbery, or homicide. We consider the absence of offense categories in an individual's repertoire of offenses as a form of ceiling effect. For example, Van Domburgh et al. (2009) documented that although some early-onset offenders escalated to serious offenses, a large proportion of early offenders only committed moderately serious forms of offenses, and thus permanently desisted from engaging in serious offenses (i.e., permanently as long as studied).

Peak developmental periods of desistance

Most studies on the prevalence of desistance have focused on late adolescence/early adulthood, co-occurring with the down-slope of the age–crime curve (Farrington 1986; Moffitt 1993) and have considered that particular time-window as the peak period of desistance in delinquency. Loeber and Farrington (2012), in reviewing desistance studies, concluded that most offenders desisted in their early twenties. For example, Stouthamer-Loeber et al. (2004) found that about one-third of boys in the oldest sample of the PYS became persistent serious delinquents between ages 13 and 19; out of that group, 39.5 percent desisted from serious offending between ages 20 and 25, and these desisters were about equally divided between those who desisted completely and those who still committed some delinquency, but at a lower level of seriousness. Studies also indicate that the highest concentration of desistance takes place during early adulthood *irrespective* of age of onset (Loeber and Farrington 2012), which corresponds with the down-slope of the age–crime curve.

However, research findings also show that desistance processes are not limited to the down-slope of the age–crime curve, but evolve and take place throughout the course of that curve. For example, Stouthamer-Loeber et al. (2010) found that in the youngest cohort of the PYS, 30.8 percent of those with an onset of moderate/serious delinquency in middle childhood desisted by early adolescence, and this was 19.1 percent for those with an onset in late childhood. Thus, not only do desistance processes also operate during childhood and early adolescence, they constitute the least studied forms of desistance in criminology.

It should be noted, however, that most of the knowledge about desistance from offending in late adolescence/early adulthood is based on prevalence studies. In contrast, for desistance as measured by frequency, variety, or severity of offending (and offense type), each may have a slightly different peak in both offending and the period of desistance. None of the studies that we reviewed used an index of frequency, variety, and severity.

Conduct problems might follow a slightly different pattern of desistance. There are probably two peak periods for desistance of conduct problems. The first peak was to a large extent identified through the pioneering work by Tremblay and colleagues (Tremblay et al. 1996; see also Loeber et al. 1989; Loeber and Hay 1994) who showed that toddlers' behavioral problems, including hitting, biting, and kicking decreased during the preschool period, that is between ages 2 and 5 for girls, and ages 2 and 6 for boys (with some decrease afterwards up to age 11). Thus, it is "natural" for many toddlers, and not only boys, to show some pattern of aggression, but most toddlers desist, or in modern parlance "grow out of it." In the process, children learn alternative ways of communicating with other children and adults in school and other settings outside of the family. We will later review the importance of desistance from conduct problems being accompanied by the adoption of prosocial behaviors, thus another form of "replacement."

The decrease in aggression during the preschool years can be contrasted with a contrary developmental movement in deviant behavior during elementary school. It is likely that for boys, the percentage of boys who are aggressive subsequently gradually (in the PYS) *in*creased between ages 7.5 and 10.5 (Broidy *et al.* 2003). Whether this is a relapse and temporary desistance followed by a renewed onset is not clear. Further, indirect forms of aggression tend to increase between ages 4 and 8 (Côté *et al.* 2007) and beyond, which complicates the patterns of desistance. This is a period in which peer relations can dramatically change as well, with two different processes often taking place: (a) rejection by peers displaying nondeviant behavior; and (b) youngsters' selection of deviant peers for joint activities (Loeber and Hay 1994).

We have found only one longitudinal study comparing desistance from conduct problems to desistance from delinquency at different time periods (Baicker-McKee 1990), a topic that is of interest for long-range development in the critical time periods taking place from infancy to early adulthood. In summary, relatively little is known about the waxing and waning of conduct problems, how this relates to delinquency development with age, and how this reflects on desistance processes and their timing from late childhood into early adulthood.

In summary, desistance from delinquency can best be conceptualized as a process that evolves between childhood and adulthood, and that is not solely taking place during late adolescence/early adulthood. The gradual progress of desistance at different ages requires very different explanations than the current traditionally used explanations for desistance in offending in early adulthood, such as marriage, employment, changes in peer relations, and joining the military (for review, see Loeber and Farrington 2012; Kazemian and Farrington 2010).

Typologies of desisters

Another important approach to desistance is to classify individuals according to the developmental pattern in desistance and persistence. Most well known is the distinction made by Moffitt (1993) between life-course persistent offenders and adolescent-limited offenders; thus a distinction between delinquents who persisted and those who desisted. The distinction was partly based on her observation that much desistance tends to take place during the down-slope of the age–crime curve. However, in later analyses (Moffitt *et al.* 2002), she refined this distinction between offenders and nonoffenders, and reported on five categories of offenders: life-course persisters (10 percent), adolescent-limited (26 percent), recovery (8 percent), abstainers (5 percent), and an unclassified category (51 percent).

Although better justified than the original classification, a key problem in the "improved" classification was that about half of the sample remained in a nonclassified category, which in all probability included different forms of desisters.

Another key issue is whether desistance patterns are comparable across gender. The vast majority of desistance research focuses on males, mostly because of the low base rate of delinquency and conduct problems in females compared to males, but also because most follow-up studies have focused on males. However, a recent report (Huizinga and Miller 2013) investigated different types of desistance in girls from the Denver Youth Survey and the Fast Track Project. The developmental patterns identified in girls were persisters (who continued to engage in delinquency), desisters (stopped offending), and intermittent (sporadically involved in delinquency over time). This typology is rather simple since it is based on prevalence and not necessarily changes in delinquency or displacement of non-adaptive behaviors.

Baicker-McKee (1990) studied antisocial and delinquent behavior in males between the ages of 8 and 18–19 over six assessments in the Cambridge Study on Delinquent Development, with ratings of troublesome behavior and conduct problems at ages 8–9, and 10–11, and convictions starting at age 10–11. She distinguished between persisters and desisters in conduct problems at the younger ages and delinquency at the older ages.[2] She identified the following groups: (a) innocents, i.e., nondeviant individuals; (b) experimenters, i.e., individuals who were deviant at one point, but who subsequently desisted; (c) desisters, i.e., individuals who after having been rated twice as deviant, subsequently desisted; (d) relapsed desisters, i.e., those who after apparent desisting were rated high again in their deviancy; and (e) persisters, i.e., those who were rated high on deviance on at least two time points and subsequently were not rated nondeviant at two consecutive time points. One of the main advantages of this classification is that it accounts for all possible combinations of developmental sequences, and therefore is exhaustive.

Stouthamer-Loeber et al. (2008) followed up boys over an extended period of over 12 years and focused on the duration of desistance, distinguishing between short-term and long-term desistance from moderate/serious delinquency. Finally, Van Domburgh et al. (2009), using data from the same study from ages 7 to 20 (youngest cohort), made a much simpler distinction between early-onset offenders (onset prior to age 12) who later became: (a) persisters (68.4 percent of the early-onset offenders); (b) desisters (20.3 percent); or (c) intermittent offenders (11.3 percent). Thus, for this early-onset sample of boys, the percentage of desisters was less than one-third of the percentage of persisters over a period of 13 years. In summary, definitions of the typologies of desisters and persisters often differ depending on whether prevalence, severity, or duration is the focus of study. Typologies may also vary depending on the length of the follow-up available, with longer follow-ups leading to clearer distinctions between persisters and desisters.

The formulation of categories of abstainers and offenders in the preceding study was accomplished by means of careful examination and counts of a priori developmental sequences of offenses and establishing typologies of offenders, including desisters. However, this method has been critiqued by Nagin (2005) on the basis that: (a) there was an assumption that homogeneous subpopulations exist without empirically verifying their existence; (b) the number of subpopulations may be incorrectly established; and (c) there may be a lack of verification that someone belongs to a certain subpopulation. To remedy this, Nagin (2005) proposed more statistically independent verification of developmentally distinct group memberships based on longitudinal data. Reviews of trajectory studies on externalizing problems ranging from oppositional behavior to aggression and delinquency (e.g., Van Dulmen *et al.* 2009), based on latent class analysis, semi-parametric group modeling/latent class growth curve analysis, or growth mixture modeling, have found one or more offender groups with a desisting pattern over time.

Trajectory analyses, although valuable, are less clear than a priori analyses of observed sequences in problem behaviors about assigning membership of individuals to distinct developmental groups. Particularly, individual group membership based on trajectory analyses "is an approximation and not a true entity." Even if an individual is assigned to a particular developmental trajectory, there always is a nonzero chance that the individual "belongs in a different group" (Van Dulmen *et al.* 2009: 292). In contrast, the a priori method of discovering group membership can clearly be mutually exclusive (Loeber *et al.* 1993).

The question can be asked how count categorization compares to computer-driven trajectory analyses that have become more common in the recent years (e.g., Nagin 2005; Van Dulmen *et al.* 2009). Lacourse (in Stouthamer-Loeber *et al.* 2008) computed the conditional probability of serious violence and serious theft trajectory groups with the observed typology of offenders. The results showed that "the translation of trajectory membership into the observed typology was better than the reverse," but that "intermediate trajectories corresponded far less than the extremes" (Stouthamer-Loeber *et al.* 2008: 285). These conclusions are not surprising, because extremes in distributions always have been easier to predict than intermediate values. What is clear is that most trajectories of violence show peaks at different ages, but all decline with age (albeit during different time windows), and this also applies to trajectories of theft (Lacourse *et al.* 2008, figures 8.2–8.4). But again, trajectories tend to be based on prevalence data, and are expressed in the probability of trajectory membership. Therefore, in their current use, trajectory analyses, compared to observed typologies of persisters and desisters, do not produce information pinning down which individuals will persist and become chronic offenders, for what duration and for what frequency of offending. Instead, what we are left with is information about a probability that someone belongs to a certain trajectory group.

Differential desistance from different types of offenses

In general, the peak of the age–crime curve for violence tends to be later than the peak of the age–crime curve for property offenses (Farrington 1986; Lacourse *et al.* 2008). Does this mean that in most delinquent cases, desistance from property offenses tends to precede desistance from violence acts? We have not been able to find studies addressing this. Other research, however, points to differential desistance for specific offense types, such as property offenses. For example, Le Blanc and Fréchette (1989) found that the median age of termination for vandalism was 13.3 years, compared to age 17 for petty theft, and age 21 for fraud. These results indicate the wide time-window needed for the study of these behaviors.

However, another issue is that persistence of different offense types will influence desistance rates. Some research shows that aggression and violence have higher stability over time than is the case for property offenses (Loeber and Hay 1994). Thus, one would expect desistance rates to be lower for violence compared to property offenses. Yet, this is not necessarily the case. Stouthamer-Loeber *et al.* (2008: table 9.2) found that desistance rates varied by offense types (2008: table 9.1) with desistance from serious theft in the oldest cohort being more common than desistance from serious violence over a three-year period (59.6 percent vs. 46.6 percent) and also over a shorter, two-age period (70.6 percent vs. 58.5 percent). However, these results were not replicated for the youngest cohort, which, compared to the oldest cohort, displayed less violence. Moreover, desistance from moderate/serious violence compared to desistance from moderate/serious theft during late adolescence was not strikingly different (51.4 percent vs. 48.6 percent in the youngest sample, and 36.2 percent vs. 27.8 percent in the oldest sample, respectively). Thus, results are not equivocal that desistance from theft is higher than desistance from violence.

What may matter more is the co-occurrence of different forms of delinquency than the occurrence of a single category of offenses. For example, Stouthamer-Loeber *et al.* (2008) found that those males "who had committed violence as well as theft were less likely to desist early than those who had committed only violence or theft" (Stouthamer Loeber *et al* 2008; 282), but this effect was not observed for desistance in early adulthood. This may indicate that the more complex and multifaceted the problem behaviors, the less likely it is that desistance takes place already in adolescence.

Another key category of offending with yet different developmental patterns is drug dealing. A comparison of drug dealing with other forms of delinquency shows that persistence is substantially higher for drug dealing than for other non-violent delinquency; and the same is true for gun carrying (Loeber and Farrington 2012). This means that desistance rates for drug dealing and gun carrying are much lower than for other offense types, and desistance takes place at later ages than for other types of crime. Along that vein, Saner *et al.* (1995) found a desistance peak for drug dealing at age 24, and argue that this type of crime is seen as very lucrative with relatively speaking low risks of getting caught compared to the financial benefits of engaging in such crimes. It may have to do with the fact that drug dealing is an economic crime with substantial monetary consequences.

The building down of delinquent acts

Suppose we have a young person who regularly stole from cars, for example at a rate of 30 times per year. How can we best conceptualize how such a person stops stealing from cars, and what can we learn in the process from studies examining changes in the frequency of offending? In a pioneering study, Barnett *et al.* (1989), using official records of offending, examined the probability of "termination" of offending and found that the probability of desistance increased when the inter-offense time interval decreased. Thus, increase in the inter-offense time interval is an important criterion for the study of desistance. Although inter-response time applies to many forms of frequent forms of offending, some offenses have a very low frequency (e.g., homicide), and, as a consequence, the building down processes as represented by the inter-offense time intervals are far less clear.

Developmental pathways in desistance from multiple types of delinquency

Most offenders commit not just a single offense type (e.g., shoplifting) but tend to commit a variety of offense types. The question is, "What is the process of desistance from multiple offense types?" To understand this better, we will briefly turn to developmental pathways to serious delinquency outcomes (an escalation model), because the conceptualization of such pathways can constitute a template for models representing desistance from multiple forms of delinquency.

Loeber *et al.*'s (1993) model of developmental pathways in offending documents the escalation from minor forms of delinquency and minor forms of conduct problems to more serious forms. Much less is known about de-escalation processes leading to complete or partial forms of desistance. Le Blanc and Fréchette (1989) postulated that less serious forms of delinquency are desisted earlier than serious forms of offending. In their earlier cited work, they found that vandalism and petty theft were desisted first and fraud later. Thus, the principle appears to be that those offense types that have an early onset tend to be desisted earlier, while offense types that have a later onset, tend to be desisted later (Loeber and Hay 1994).

However, it is quite possible that the reverse desistance process can take place as well, with more serious forms of delinquency being desisted first and the less serious forms later in the developmental process. For example, Stouthamer-Loeber *et al.* (2004) found that about half of those who desisted from serious delinquency between ages 20 and 25 still committed some delinquency, but at a lower seriousness level. The latter would accord with the notion that negative consequences of violence are often more pronounced than the negative consequences of less serious forms of aggression and perhaps the likelihood of getting caught is much higher for violence than property crimes. Clearly, these speculations need to be verified by means of empirical research on developmental sequences in desistance.

False desistance in different data sources

The accuracy of desistance measurements and the possibility of false desistance (Farrington 2007; Kazemian 2012) always remain an issue, because they may distort researchers' perception of what is actually going on and whether reported desisters are actually persisters, depending on what measurements and definitions are used. The most typical problem is when researchers infer desistance from short follow-up data, which is particularly a problem when: (a) the measurement of desistance is curtailed during a life period when typically desistance often takes place (Stouthamer-Loeber *et al.* 2004); and (b) patterns of intermittency are easily interpreted as mistaken "desistance" (Kazemian and Farrington 2010).

Probably the single cause of false desistance is the type of data selected. For example, self-reports of desistance from delinquency are not necessarily accurate over the adult life-course and best need independent verification, and underreporting by adults has been noted in the Cambridge Study in Delinquent Development (Farrington *et al.* 2014).

Similarly, official delinquency records data suggesting desistance from offending should be queried for their accuracy. First, periods of incarceration may be mistakenly interpreted in official delinquency records as stable desistance. Second, increasingly, studies have documented that official records of offending highly underestimate actual offending as evident from self-reports. Particularly, the following are important: (a) for every court petition there are many self-reported offenses (e.g., in the PYS in the US, Farrington (2007) found 33.8 self-reported offenses for each court petition per offender); (b) the duration of a self-reported delinquency career is much longer than for delinquency careers based on official records (Le Blanc and Fréchette 1989; Farrington *et al.* 2014), which means that on average the end of a criminal career is later in self-reports than in official records and that self-reported desistance will typically be later than officially recorded desistance; (c) the age of onset of self-reported criminal careers usually precedes the age of onset of officially recorded criminal careers by four to six years (Le Blanc and Fréchette 1989; Farrington *et al.* 2014), which means that only self-report studies can reveal early forms of desistance from offending; and (d) studies based on official records of delinquency produce a smaller number of trajectories compared to studies using other forms of assessment (Van Dulmen *et al.* 2009).

In conclusion, knowledge about desistance patterns overall is less reliable and valid when based on official records only, leading to more false positive errors (individuals desisted according to official records, but not according to self-reports). This may mean that the prevalence of desistance is over-estimated by an uncertain amount and that predictors of such desistance are weaker than may initially be thought. For that reason, Loeber *et al.* (2008) created an all-source measure of delinquency, which complemented official records with self-reports, and then calculated persistence and desistance on the basis of this combined and more comprehensive measure.

Capacity to offend and the display of desistance

It is sometimes thought that desistance from, for example, shoplifting, is simply the cessation of shoplifting. However, we argue that this is too simplistic and that the process of desistance actually is more complicated. Let's start with another area of behavior change. Many young people learn to ride a bike, but as they age, they find other means of locomotion and in the process cease riding a bike. From the outside, so to say, it appears that they have "desisted" from riding a bike. However, when after many years the same individuals are offered by someone the opportunity to ride a bike, they usually have no difficulties in riding the bike. In other words, they retained the capacity to ride a bike, and when challenged to ride again, they are able to perform again. Capacity refers here to the motoric and cognitive skills that make it possible for individuals to ride a bike without immediately crashing it.

We argue that many forms of delinquency, including for example shoplifting, are of the same kind in that the behavior they present consists of a set of complex actions and cognitions (such as casing places to steal, timing of theft to avoid detection, avoiding being recorded by security cameras, covering up the item to go through security gate(s), etc.). We argue that in the course of individuals' permanent desistance from shoplifting, there are many skills and cognitive strategic elements that actually remain in an individual's behavioral and cognitive repertoire rather than being eliminated as well in the course of desistance from shoplifting. This is of importance for the study of temporary forms of desistance and the "relapse" in offending.

Desistance from conduct problems and delinquency and the replacement by prosocial behavior

Desistance studies often share a limitation, because of the lack of conceptualization or measurement that can shed light on the degree to which desistance from conduct problems and delinquency is followed, if not greatly facilitated, by the acquisition or "turning-on" of prosocial behaviors. For example, Loeber et al. (1989), when studying the cessation of physical fighting in Montreal boys between kindergarten and the next four years, found that desisting fighters "showed the highest rate of prosocial behaviors" (Loeber et al. 1989: 46–47) compared to stable high fighters and variable high fighters. Although clearly not proof, the finding supports the notion that cessation from fighting is aided by the introduction into the boys' repertoire of alternative social problem-solving skills.

Gender differences in desistance

It is well known that girls compared to boys show less serious forms of delinquency, such as violence and homicide. More needs to be explained as to why such ceiling effects are differentially in place for each gender.

An indicator of gender differences in desistance is the fact that developmental curves—both in conduct problems and delinquency—tend to peak earlier for girls than boys and that such earlier peaking denotes the presence of earlier desistance processes in girls. For example, research shows that girls' aggression during the preschool period tends to peak earlier than for boys, and that girls tend to outgrow such behaviors at an earlier age than boys (Tremblay et al. 1996). A similar phenomenon has been observed for the age–crime curve (Farrington 1986) with the girls' age–crime curve peaking earlier than that for boys, indicating again earlier desistance processes taking place for girls than for boys.

Some unresolved issues to be addressed in future research

Studies have made different distinctions between different forms of desistance, and similarly the classification of offenders, including desisters, has produced different approaches. Currently, delinquency classifications are often directly the product of each longitudinal study and the time frame available, and there is no generally agreed upon classification scheme (such as recidivism) that can make results on desistance and desisters comparable across studies.

The following are some examples of possible research addressing current hiatuses in the behavioral aspects of desistance studies (left out here are key questions pertaining to predictors and explanations of desistance, for which see Kazemian and Farrington 2010):

- What is the sequence and possible interrelationship between desistance from conduct problems and desistance from delinquency?
- If delinquent acts are desisted from, how often are they replaced by specific prosocial behaviors, and does such replacement facilitate desistance or does such a sequence of behavior occur by chance and is not relevant for episodic desistance to become stable desistance?
- How can the measurement of desistance be improved so that there is a higher consensus about its definition, and a higher accumulation of research findings based on agreed criteria for desistance?
- What are the key features of desistance in terms of decreasing frequency, variety, and severity of offending?
- What are developmental pathways to desistance in multiple forms of delinquency in terms of the sequence and decreasing severity of different types of offenses?
- To what extent during the process of desistance are decreases in frequency, variety, and severity occurring simultaneously? And is this the same for different types of offenses?
- What are developmental pathways toward desistance from multiple types of delinquency?
- How can capacity to offend be better researched in relationship to desistance?
- What are the causes of gender differences in desistance from conduct problems and delinquency?

Notes

1 The authors are indebted to Marc Le Blanc, David P. Farrington, and Dustin Pardini for their inspiration, collaboration, and knowledge over many years, which has made the PYS the unusual study it is. We are grateful to Jennifer Wilson for checking the references.
2 For ease of exposition, nondelinquent antisocial behaviors and delinquents acts are denoted here as "deviant behavior."

References

Baicker-McKee, C. (1990), "Saints, sinners, and prodigal sons: An investigation of continuities and discontinuities in antisocial development." Unpublished PhD dissertation. Charlottesville, VA: University of Virginia.

Barnett, A., Blumstein, A. and Farrington, D. P. (1989), "A prospective test of a criminal career model," *Criminology* 27: 373–388.

Broidy, L. M., Nagin, D. S., Tremblay, R. E., Bates, J. E., Brame, B., Dodge, K. A., Fergusson, D., Horwood, J. L., Loeber, R., Laird, R., Lynam, D. R., Moffitt, T. E., Pettit, G. S. and Vitaro, F. (2003), "Developmental trajectories of childhood disruptive behaviors and adolescent delinquency: A six-site cross-national study," *Developmental Psychology* 39: 222–245.

Côté, S. M., Vaillancourt, T., Barker, E. D., Nagin, D. and Tremblay, R. E. (2007), "The joint development of physical and indirect aggression: Predictors of continuity and change during childhood," *Development and Psychopathology* 19: 37–55.

Farrington, D. P. (1986), "Age and crime," *Crime and Justice: An Annual Review of Research* 7: 29–90.

Farrington, D. P. (2007), "Advancing knowledge about desistance," *Journal of Contemporary Criminal Justice* 23: 125–134.

Farrington, D. P., Ttofi, M. M., Crago, R. V. and Coid, J. W. (2014), "Prevalence, frequency, onset, desistance and criminal career duration in self-reports compared with official records," *Criminal Behaviour and Mental Health* 24: 241–253.

Huizinga, D. and Miller, S. (2013), "The girls study group," in *Understanding and Responding to Girls' Delinquency*. ODP Bulletin. Washington, DC: US Department of Justice, Office of Justice Programs, Office of Juvenile Justice and Delinquency Prevention.

Kazemian, L. (2012), "Pushing back the frontiers of knowledge on desistance from crime," in Loeber, R. and Welsh, B. C. (eds) *The Future of Criminology*. Oxford, UK: Oxford University Press, pp. 134–140.

Kazemian, L. and Farrington, D. P. (2010), "The developmental evidence base of desistance," in Towl, G. and Crighton, D. (eds) *Forensic Psychology*, second edition. Oxford, UK: Blackwell, pp. 133–159.

Lacourse, E., Dupéré, V. and Loeber, R. (2008), "Developmental trajectories of violence and theft," in Loeber, R., Farrington, D. P., Stouthamer-Loeber, M. and White, H. R. (eds) *Violence and Serious Theft: Development and Prediction from Childhood to Adulthood*. New York: Routledge, pp. 231–268.

Laub, J. H. and Sampson, R. J. (2001), "Understanding desistance from crime," in Tonry, M. (ed.) *Crime and Justice*, volume 28. Chicago, IL: University of Chicago Press, pp. 1–69.

Le Blanc, M. and Fréchette, M. (1989), *Male Criminal Activity from Childhood through Youth: Multilevel and Developmental Perspectives*. New York: Springer.

Le Blanc, M. and Loeber, R. (1998), "Developmental criminology updated," in Tonry, M. (ed.) *Crime and Justice*, volume 23. Chicago, IL: Chicago University Press, pp. 115–197.

Loeber, R. and Dishion, T. (1983), "Early predictors of male delinquency: A review," *Psychological Bulletin* 94: 68–99.

Loeber, R. and Le Blanc, M. (1990), "Toward a developmental criminology," in Tonry, M. and Morris, N. (eds) *Crime and Justice*, volume 12. Chicago, IL: University of Chicago Press, pp. 375–473.

Loeber, R. and Hay, D. F. (1994), "Developmental approaches to aggression and conduct problems," in Rutter, M. and Hay, D. F. (eds) *Development through Life: A Handbook for Clinicians*. Oxford, UK: Blackwell Scientific, pp. 488–516.

Loeber, R. and Farrington, D. P. (2012), *From Juvenile Delinquency to Adult Crime: Criminal Careers, Justice Policy and Prevention*. New York: Oxford University Press.

Loeber, R., Tremblay, R. E., Gagnon, C. and Charlebois, P. (1989), "Continuity and desistance in disruptive boys' early fighting in school," *Development and Psychopathology* 1: 39–50.

Loeber, R., Stouthamer-Loeber, M., Van Kammen, W. B. and Farrington, D. P. (1991), "Initiation, escalation and desistance in juvenile offending and their correlates," *Journal of Criminal Law and Criminology* 82: 36–82.

Loeber, R., Farrington, D. P., Stouthamer-Loeber, M. and White, H. R. (2008), *Violence and Serious Theft: Development and Prediction from Childhood to Adulthood*. New York: Routledge.

Loeber, R., Wung, P., Keenan, K., Giroux, B., Stouthamer-Loeber, M., Van Kammen, W. B. and Maughan, B. (1993), "Developmental pathways in disruptive child behavior," *Developmental Psychopathology* 5: 103–133.

McCord, J. (1978), "A thirty-year follow-up of treatment effects," *American Psychologist* 33: 284–289.

Moffitt, T. E. (1993), "Adolescence-limited and life-course-persistent antisocial behavior: A developmental taxonomy," *Psychological Review* 100: 674–701.

Moffitt, T. E., Caspi, A., Harrington, H. and Milne, B. J. (2002), "Males on the life-course-persistent and adolescence-limited antisocial pathways: Follow-up at age 26 years," *Development and Psychopathology* 14: 179–207.

Nagin, D. S. (2005), *Group-Based Modeling of Development*. Cambridge, UK: Cambridge University Press.

Robins, L. N. (1966), *Deviant Children Grown Up*. Baltimore, MD: Williams and Wilkins.

Saner, H., MacCoun, R. and Reuter, P. (1995), "On the ubiquity of drug selling among youthful offenders in Washington, DC 1985–1991: Age, period or cohort effect?," *Journal of Quantitative Criminology* 11: 337–362.

Stouthamer-Loeber, M., Pardini, D. A. and Loeber, R. (2010), "Desistance and persistence of delinquency from middle childhood to early adulthood." Paper presented at the meeting of the American Society of Criminology, San Francisco, November.

Stouthamer-Loeber, M., Wei, E., Loeber, R. and Masten, A. S. (2004), "Desistance from persistent serious delinquency in the transition to adulthood," *Development and Psychopathology* 16: 897–918.

Stouthamer-Loeber, M., Loeber, R., Stallings, R. and Lacourse, E. (2008), "Desistance from and persistence in offending," in Loeber, R., Farrington, D. P., Stouthamer-Loeber, M. and White, H. R. (eds) *Violence and Serious Theft: Development and Prediction from Childhood to Adulthood*. New York: Routledge, pp. 269–398.

Tremblay, R. E., Masse, L. C., Pagani, L. and Vitaro, F. (1996), "From childhood physical aggression to adolescent maladjustment: The Montreal prevention experiment," in Peters, R. D. and McMahon, R. J. (eds) *Preventing Childhood Disorders, Substance Abuse, and Delinquency*. Thousand Oaks, CA: Sage, pp. 268–298.

Van Domburgh, L., Loeber, R., Bezemer, R., Stallings, R. and Stouthamer-Loeber, M. (2009), "Childhood predictors of desistance and level of persistence in offending in early onset offenders," *Journal of Abnormal Child Psychology* 37: 967–980.

Van Dulmen, M. H., Goncy, E. A., Vest, A. and Flannery, D. J. (2009), "Group-based trajectory modeling of externalizing behavior from childhood through adulthood: Exploring discrepancies in the empirical findings," in Savage, J. (ed.) *The Development of Persistent Criminality*. Oxford, UK: Oxford University Press, pp. 288–314.

West, D. J. and Farrington, D. P. (1973), *Who Becomes Delinquent?* London: Heinemann.

Wilson, J. Q. and Kelling, G. (1982), "The police and neighborhood safety: Broken windows," *Atlantic Monthly* 127: 29–38.

Wolfgang, M. E., Thornberry, T. P. and Figlio, R. M. (1987), *From Boy to Man: Delinquency to Crime*. Chicago, IL: Chicago University Press.

6

LEARNING TO DESIST IN EARLY ADULTHOOD

The Sheffield Desistance Study

Anthony Bottoms and Joanna Shapland

In this chapter we summarize some of the main features and findings of the Sheffield Desistance Study (SDS), for which the fieldwork was carried out between 2003 and 2007.[1] In light of experience in conducting this study, we also reflect briefly on some ways in which the understanding of desistance might be taken forward in the future.

Conceptually, the SDS owes its origins to attempts by one of us to develop a typology of modes of compliance with the law (Bottoms 2001, 2002). Compliance with the law is, of course, a very wide field of analysis, embracing topics as diverse as the long-term decline in homicide rates (Eisner 2003) and the success of situational constraints in reducing property crime (Clarke 2009). However, for anyone seriously interested in compliance, one striking and now well-established fact about criminal careers deserves the closest attention; namely that most offenders, even persistent offenders, eventually stop offending. Moreover, this greater compliance is not usually deferred to middle age: data from longitudinal research studies show that the age-range 20–25 is the modal half-decade for reductions in the frequency of offending among 'chronic' offenders (see, for example, Laub and Sampson 2003: chapter 5; Blokland *et al.* 2005; Ezell and Cohen 2005: 164; Piquero *et al.* 2007: 136). These considerations led us in the SDS to construct a short-term prospective research study of desistance in which we identified a population of repeat offenders aged 19–22. We followed them up for 3–4 years in the expectation that many would reduce their criminality during that period and that we could chart their journeys towards desistance or persistence. Given the focus on *mechanisms* in Bottoms' (2001, 2002) papers on compliance,[2] one main aim of the study was to cast additional light on the mechanisms through which some offenders would come to change their patterns of behaviour during this period. We also knew from earlier research that much desistance is gradual and sometimes fitful; accordingly, we recognized that we would be studying in particular the early stages of desistance.

Three aspects of this methodological strategy must be emphasized, because they speak to the strengths and limitations of the SDS. First, as noted above, we imposed a *deliberate restriction on the age-range* of the studied population. As we stated in an early paper, this required us to 'to confront, head-on' how the offenders in the study would cope with the transition away from adolescence 'towards their visions of adulthood' (Bottoms *et al.* 2004: 384). Taking steps towards desistance during the early twenties might well differ from attempted desistance at later stages of life,[3] and it seems reasonable to relate the study of desistance at particular life-stages to what is known more generally about psycho-social development in the relevant age-range.

Second, we chose to focus on desistance only among *repeat offenders*, believing (as others have done) that this is theoretically the most interesting, and in policy terms the most urgent, task for criminological understanding in this field. There is of course no precise definition of the term 'repeat offender', but we operationalized it in a minimalist way by requiring all members recruited to the study population to have been convicted on at least two separate occasions ('conviction occasions') for so-called 'standard list' offences.[4]

Third, we were particularly interested in the early stages of desistance (the initial process of 'turning towards compliance'), and for that reason we chose a *prospective methodology*, following recently active offenders for 3–4 years. As is well known, one strategy that has sometimes been adopted in research on desistance is to select samples of matched 'desisters' and 'persisters', and, looking back, attempt to specify how they reached their different destinations. Without question, such studies have made very important contributions to our understanding of desistance: see in particular Maruna's (2001) Liverpool Desistance Study, and the classic interview study by Laub and Sampson (2003) of 52 men in their sixties who had once been persistent juvenile offenders. Retrospective studies of this kind are particularly well placed to throw light on the later stages of individuals' journeys to desistance. Necessarily, however, such research designs have limitations when it comes to analysing the early stages of desistance, partly because of the time that has elapsed between early desistance and the retrospective research interview, and partly because of the well-known selectivity that all of us introduce into accounts of our past life histories, even when we are trying to be totally honest. The SDS, by opting for a prospective study of a sample of recently active offenders, had an obverse set of strengths and weaknesses: we were less able to study fully completed desistance, but we were able to consider early-stage desistance with a greater degree of detail and immediacy, particularly as the interval between successive interviews with sample members was relatively short – normally between 9 and 12 months.

In the first published paper from the SDS, written while fieldwork was still in progress (Bottoms *et al.* 2004), we sketched a tentative 'interactive theoretical framework' which, we hoped, would help us to address some of the explanatory challenges posed by the study of desistance. This framework included not only the offender's 'programmed potential' (the statistical probabilities arising from prior personal and social characteristics) but also the agentic decisions and the 'social context' (structures, culture, situations) that would occur in the 3–4 years during which research participants would be studied (Bottoms *et al.* 2004: 368; the relevance of 'situations' is more fully discussed later). This theoretical approach necessarily required us to adopt a research strategy that embraced both quantitative and qualitative research methods. In the period since that preliminary paper was written, we have become increasingly convinced that adequate explanations of desistance need to adopt an interactive theoretical approach of this kind (see the overview of desistance research in Bottoms 2014); and in what follows, we will attempt to summarize some of the most distinctive results to have emerged from the SDS in relation to these matters. To offer a preview of just a few highlights, we believe that the Sheffield study has demonstrated – at least for those in their twenties – the particular importance for desistance research of the concepts of *active maturation* and of *learning to live a non-criminal life*. Within this framework, the study also emphasizes the significance of the *obstacles* that would-be desisters frequently face, and the strategies of *diachronic and synchronic self-control* that they often adopt to help them avoid certain obstacles. More tentatively, we have also begun to explore some *ethical aspects* of journeys towards desistance – a topic of seemingly obvious relevance to the process of leaving crime behind, but one that has mostly been neglected in the desistance literature.

As a guide for those wishing to learn more about the SDS, it might be useful here to list the principal published papers emanating from the Study since the 2004 'framework paper'. They are: Bottoms and Shapland (2011) (the first statement of research results, primarily focusing on quantitative data); Shapland and Bottoms (2011) (on the social values of the sample); Shapland *et al.* (2012) (on the sample's perceptions of the criminal justice system); Bottoms (2013) (on diachronic self-control as an aid to desistance); Bottoms and Shapland (2014) (on the potential relevance of virtue ethics to the study of desistance); and Shapland and Bottoms (forthcoming) (on changes in offending and offence patterns during the research period).

Structural and methodological features of the SDS

In light of the research strategy outlined above, we identified the following eligibility requirements for recruitment to the study sample:

- born in 1982, 1983 or 1984 (accordingly, the age-range of the sample at first interview was 19–22, with a mean of 20 years 9 months);
- currently serving *either* a short- or medium-length custodial sentence, *or* a community sentence under the supervision of the probation service;[5]
- having a minimum of two conviction occasions for 'standard list' offences;
- having a current address in Sheffield at the time of the last conviction.

The locus of the SDS is Sheffield, which is one of the six largest cities in England outside London, although, unlike most of those cities, it is not part of a conurbation and so has a distinctive, 'stand alone' character. In 2001, just before the start of the

SDS, Sheffield had a resident population of 513,000. It used to be a world leader in the steel industry, but that industrial base suffered a rapid and catastrophic decline in the 1980s, from which the city has been gradually but successfully recovering. Economically and socially, Sheffield is a very divided city, with marked inequalities between different neighbourhoods and a generic contrast between the poorer East and the more affluent West. Thus, while the city's unemployment rate in 2000 was only a little above the national average (4.2 per cent as against 3.4 per cent), within Sheffield some eastern wards had more than 6 per cent unemployment, while the two most affluent wards in the West had rates below 2 per cent (Winkler 2008: 28). Unsurprisingly, most known offenders – including most participants in the SDS – live in the more deprived eastern parts of the city (Bottoms 2012b: 459).

Returning to the specifics of the SDS, the data sources used in the study were of two kinds. First, with the kind co-operation of the South Yorkshire Police, we were allowed access to the full criminal records of the sample, both historical (back to age 10) and during the period of the research fieldwork.[6] Second, we aimed to conduct four lengthy interviews (each lasting about 90 minutes) with each research participant; and, as previously noted, the intervals between these interviews were relatively short (9–12 months). Consistent with our mixed quantitative and qualitative methodological strategy, these interviews contained a variety of different kinds of question: some were highly structured (including some psychological scales); some were semi-structured; and some were open-ended, intended to elicit data of an 'appreciative' kind.[7] Examples of results from each of these types of question are included within the body of this chapter.

For legal reasons, invitations to offenders to participate in the study had to be issued by Sheffield based staff of the (then) National Probation Service; any consent to participate was then communicated to the research team.[8] In consultation with the research team, the probation service decided to use different invitation methods according to whether an offender was serving a community sentence or a custodial sentence: those in the former category were approached orally by their supervisors, while those in custody were sent letters inviting them to send post-paid reply slips to the University. The latter proved to be the more successful recruitment strategy, probably in part because an interview would help to alleviate the boredom of spending time in custody. As a consequence, 82 per cent of the initial interviews of the research sample took place in a prison or (for offenders under 21) a young offenders' institution.

This indirect recruitment framework had two main consequences. First, the final research sample was smaller than we had hoped (N=113), and – unfortunately – it included no women.[9] The modest size of the sample of course limits the conclusions that can be drawn from the research, but it does not preclude statistical analysis. Indeed, interestingly, the size of the SDS sample is closely comparable with the number of repeat offenders in the well-known Cambridge Study of Delinquent Development.[10] Second, the disproportionate recruitment of sample members from among those serving custodial sentences meant that, on average, the final sample had a significantly more extensive criminal history than the remainder of the population of 679 males from which it was drawn. (Thus, although the minimum eligibility requirement was two conviction occasions for standard list offences, the actual mean number of such occasions in the recruited sample was eight.[11]) However, for once the non-representative character of the sample is not really a disadvantage. It had always been our intention to focus the research especially on repeat offenders, and the recruitment process had the ultimate (although unintended) effect of selecting a very recidivistic study sample.

The retention rate in the sample was good, with 78 per cent completing the third interview, and a slightly different 78 per cent completing the fourth. Reassuringly, also, on four key variables there was no statistically significant difference between those who completed, and those who did not complete, the fourth interview (Bottoms and Shapland 2011: 50). As regards ethnicity, four-fifths of respondents self-reported that they were 'white British' (79 per cent), a proportion that is very similar to the Sheffield population as a whole at the time of the 2001 population census (81 per cent). Unfortunately, given the small overall size of the SDS sample, we have not been able to analyse differences between ethnic groups in journeys to desistance, though for an important UK study of this topic see Calverley (2013).

In order to facilitate the 'appreciative' dimension of the study, we aimed where possible to tape-record interviews, although not all prisons allowed us to do this, and there were also, unfortunately, technical problems with the quality of a significant proportion of the recordings. We transcribed the interviews of the one-sixth of the sample (18 cases) for whom a full set of tape-recordings was available, and this became our 'qualitative sub-sample'. Given the technical problems noted above, we were fortunate that this sub-sample was broadly representative of the sample as a whole.[12]

Some key results

During the 3–4-year follow-up period, some 80 per cent of sample members were reconvicted. However, as anticipated, there was a significant reduction in the *frequency* of formal reconviction during this time (from an average of 8.2 standard list offences per offender in the year before the first interview, to only 2.6 per year in the period after the third interview, approximately three years later).[13] As regards self-reported offending, a minority of sample members self-reported an increase in offending over the period of follow-up, but this was within a general pattern whereby self-reported offending was much more polarised at the end of the study than at the beginning. That is, at the end of the study some were reporting high levels of continuing offending, but more were reporting no or very little offending, and there were few cases in between (Bottoms and Shapland 2011: 54–55).

One of the main quantitative analyses of the SDS focused on the offending levels of the sample at the end of the research period, as measured both by official convictions and by self-reported offending. The analyses, using ordinal regression, modelled which of the variables relating to events prior to the final follow-up period (i.e. variables reporting data from interview 3 or earlier) would best predict final offending levels. The results are fully described in Bottoms and Shapland (2011) (including lists of all variables entered in the regressions and tests for multi-collinearity), and they are shown in summary form in Table 6.1.

The broad character of the results is similar for the separate analyses of official and self-reported criminality. In each case, the final level of offending was best statistically explained by a combination of:

1. measures of lifetime official criminality (the more prior crime, the higher the final level of offending);
2. variables measuring aspects of the actual or perceived recent circumstances of the respondent (i.e. employment; self-identity linked to criminal friends; and the perceived aggregate of obstacles to going straight).

We believe that these statistical findings, set in the wider context of the Sheffield results, are of considerable interest. In particular, they are consistent with three features of the evidence from desistance research more generally, which bear rehearsing in the present context.

First, since the ground-breaking study by Sampson and Laub (1993), it has become increasingly clear that explaining desistance from or persistence in offending requires an understanding of the social circumstances encountered or created, and the agentic choices made, by known offenders in their twenties. The 'employment' and 'friends' variables in the SDS regression equations are clearly consistent with this body of evidence, showing as they do that matters beyond previous history are relevant to the statistical prediction of reoffending or persistence.[14] One useful way of describing the significance of results of this kind is through the concept of

TABLE 6.1 Summary of SDS ordinal regression analyses relating to the prediction of final levels of criminality

(a) Official criminality (standard list offences)

Total lifetime official offending	P=.003
Self-reported obstacles to desistance[†]	P=.015
Whether self-identity linked to peers[†]	P=.004
Robbery pattern in official offending	P=.000
[Pseudo R^2 = 0.44]	

(b) Self-reported offending between interviews 3 and 4

OGRS2 prediction of reoffending score (largely based on official offending history)	P=.005
Self-reported obstacles to desistance[†]	P=.012
Employed/unemployed between interviews 2 and 3	P=.035
[Pseudo R^2 = 0.42]	

† = Measured at interview 3

Source: Bottoms and Shapland (2011: tables 2.5 and 2.6).

Note: Fuller details of the methodology and results are given in those tables and at pp. 79–80 of the paper.

asymmetric causation (Uggen and Piliavin 1998), which emphasizes that the factors that lead to desistance from a criminal career are not necessarily simply the reverse of the original criminogenic factors, but might involve a different set of processes, such as entering a new relationship or acquiring new interests or skills.[15]

Yet, second, research into criminal careers has shown that what are sometimes described as 'static' risk factors – aspects of an offender's past life that cannot be changed, such as his/her history of offending, or family dynamics in childhood – may often remain as powerful predictors of reoffending, even when later changes in life circumstances are taken fully into account (Caudy *et al.* 2013). In the SDS equations, factors of this kind are represented by the 'lifetime offending' and the 'OGRS' variables (respectively in the regressions relating to official convictions and self-reported offending). Moreover, these 'static risk factors' are not simply a statistical phenomenon; they arise out of the lived experience of the individual and his/her embedded memories, which – taken together with societal reactions to this history – can act as a significant limitation on the opportunities available to would-be desisters and their ability to maximise their potential. While rightly focusing on the dynamics of change, desistance researchers must never forget the difficulties of change for individuals who have extensive criminal records and, very often, disadvantaged life histories.[16]

The third feature of the research background has rightly been emphasized by Blokland and Nieuwbeerta (2005). As they point out, while much of the desistance literature has focused on the effects of specific changes in life circumstances, particularly marriage and employment, these matters – though certainly important – seem to account for only a limited proportion of the overall reduction in offending over the life span. Hence, 'much of the effect age has on crime remains unexplained' (Blokland and Nieuwbeerta 2005: 1233). In the SDS regression analyses, this point is exemplified in the pseudo-R-squared values in the two equations, which show that less than half of the statistical variance is explained by the identified variables, important as these are. It seems to be a reasonable inference from such findings that the reduction in frequency of offending in the early twenties might be related to a complex (but difficult to measure) range of personal and social experiences during these transitional years, including physiological changes and the development of general psycho-social maturity. It is therefore time to look at such issues more closely.

The transition to adulthood[17]

Terrie Moffitt (1993) has insightfully suggested that 'adolescence-limited offenders' (those whose offending begins in adolescence and terminates at or before early adulthood) desist from offending because, on the threshold of adulthood, they make a reappraisal of their lives and recognize that continuing to offend will be damaging to their futures in several respects. The evidence of the SDS is that, in the early twenties, this kind of appraisal of life-choices is also common among those with an earlier start to their criminal careers.[18]

In the first interview, we posed an open-ended question, with no prompts, that asked the respondent 'what kind of person would you like to become?' The answers showed that 'the great majority . . . seemed to be aiming at a conventional future', because they said things like 'go straight', 'live a normal/regular life' or 'be a good person' (Shapland and Bottoms 2011: 262). In the third interview, we also asked some more detailed questions about future housing, employment, etc., in each case with a focus on 'how would you *like* to see yourself living say in 10 years' time?'. As before 'the overall pattern of responses reflect[ed] preferences for a settled, conventional life, with relatively limited aspirations', although there was 'a small minority who had dreams of a big house and good money' (Shapland and Bottoms 2011: 263). Backing up these general aspirations, answers to a structured question (asked at each interview) about intentions to desist showed a majority in the first interview saying they had made a 'definite decision to try to stop', and increasing proportions over time reiterating this commitment, or saying that they had now stopped offending (Bottoms and Shapland 2011: 57). It was also interesting that statements of intention to desist were, in the first two interviews, strongly correlated with a measure of 'self-efficacy',[19] that is, 'a belief about what one can do under different sets of conditions with whatever skills one possesses' (Bandura 1997: 37). This result can be read as supporting the idea that, among recidivist offenders, serious attempts to achieve desistance will require self-belief and drive.

The above data show that most SDS respondents wanted a different and more conventional future for themselves – the kind of aspiration that, in the criminological literature on desistance, Paternoster and Bushway (2009) have referred to as a person's *desired self*. These authors suggest that persistent offenders might be motivated to begin a process of desistance by focusing on their 'desired self' in contrast to their current situation, and they further suggest that negative thoughts of a *feared self* might also be part of the overall motivation. (For a review of the wider psychological literature on 'possible selves', see Oyserman and James 2009.) In the SDS we asked no structured questions relating to the idea of a 'feared self', but aspects of that concept emerged in some of our qualitative data, referring to fears of spending much of one's future in prison, having no dependable partner or friends and so on (see the case studies reported in Bottoms and Shapland 2014).

But aspirations do not necessarily become realities, so what evidence do we have that respondents thought they had actually changed? In the fourth (final) interview, we asked two related questions: 'Do you see yourself as any different from three years ago?', and 'Do you think and behave in a different way now than three years ago?'. (These questions were again open-ended, with no prompts.) Responses to both questions were strongly positive, but the answers were subtly different. As regards the first question (perceptions of self), the majority of respondents self-reported that they felt themselves to be now 'more mature/more responsible/a nicer person/feel better about myself'. In response to the second question, the dominant comments concerned reductions in impulsive behaviour and better future planning ('I think before I act now/I'm more mature and calmer/I think more about the future') (for data, see Bottoms 2012a: 41).

In these unprompted responses, the concept of 'maturity' is prominent. This concept needs to be treated with some care, because in the history of criminology it has sometimes been used to explain desistance in an unhelpfully circular or tautological way.[20] However, circularity is not a necessary feature of its use, and two more defensible approaches can also be discerned in the literature, respectively focused on issues relating to 'responsibility' and 'temperance' (i.e. regulation of impulsivity). Interestingly, these two concepts are very closely related to the responses of SDS sample members to the two retrospective research questions, as noted above.

To take 'temperance' first, there is important recent physiological evidence that – contrary to the previously received view – the pre-frontal cortex, and therefore the capacity for full impulse control, does not complete its development until the mid-twenties (Johnson *et al.* 2009).[21] This is clearly of potential relevance to the decline in offending levels in the early twenties, especially when it is linked to cognate psychological evidence of improved temperance – as discussed, for example, by Prior *et al.* (2011) and by Mulvey and Schubert in Chapter 7 of this volume.

Turning then to the concept of 'responsibility', in a candid autobiographical note on the development of his work in the field of 'emerging adulthood', Jeffrey Arnett (2014) describes how, in an early study, he constructed a list of about 30 criteria for having reached adulthood, based on the extant literature. However, field testing quickly revealed that, 'although I thought I had covered everything, I had missed the criterion that was of the utmost importance to most [young] people', namely responsibility (Arnett 2014: 156). In Arnett's more recent and more systematic work, respondents in their twenties identified as primary criteria for reaching adulthood the two concepts of 'taking responsibility for yourself' and 'making independent decisions' (Arnett 2015: 313–314). These results should be considered alongside the very shrewd comment by the Danish criminologist Britta Kyvsgaard (2003: 241) that most of the literature on criminal careers 'has paid little attention to the subjective aspects of maturation in terms of personal philosophy or one's perception of one's place in the world and the potential connection that such changes might have to changes in offending'. The implication of this comment is that, when people seriously reappraise their life-directions and 'personal philosophy', we might expect them to take more responsibility for the direction of their lives, and this subjective process might therefore have a significant impact on some aspects of their behaviour, including offending. Since there is abundant evidence that, for offenders and non-offenders alike, this kind of self-appraisal is an important feature of the transition to adulthood, these matters need to be taken very seriously by desistance researchers.[22] Importantly, also, there is at least tentative evidence, both from the SDS and elsewhere, that offenders who seriously decide to try to desist have lower subsequent reoffending, despite the rocky paths that they sometimes encounter (LeBel *et al.* 2008; Shapland and Bottoms forthcoming).

But while there was indeed evidence of maturation in the SDS (in the sense of both 'temperance' and 'responsibility'), it must always be remembered that this was a group with, on average, extensive criminal histories and significant educational and social deficits. This meant that the process of maturation was, for them, not at all a straightforward or passive matter; rather, it required active and sustained effort, often against considerable obstacles:

> On the evidence of the Sheffield study . . . people strive to move towards their basic moral views about the person they think they should be . . . This can be portrayed as a maturational theory, *but it is an active maturation*, animated by the impetus of offenders themselves. It is also a *far more deliberate, more painful and more risky maturation* than for most of their age group.
>
> *(Shapland and Bottoms 2011: 276–277, emphasis added)*

We will discuss some implications of these conclusions in the next section. First, however, we need to consider more specifically some evidence from the SDS about perceptions of offending (that is, actually committing criminal acts) in the transition to adulthood. In a previous paper, we summarized the view of Matza (1964) that in adolescence 'juvenile delinquents hover, normatively speaking, between the worlds of criminality and of social convention, with the latter having significant purchase' (Shapland and Bottoms 2011: 259); and we went on to provide empirical evidence that the same was true in the (older) SDS sample, notwithstanding their significantly greater involvement in criminality. That is to say, these men have become accustomed to committing acts of crime on a regular basis, yet our data also show that they are clearly aware of the importance of law-abiding behaviour to a functioning society (Shapland and Bottoms 2011). As early adulthood developed, most of them increasingly demonstrated a wish to turn away from a life of crime, but – at least in the early stages of this process – they lived in a liminal state where, in certain situations, crime was seen as a possible solution to (for example) financial difficulties. They also received very different messages on these matters from those close to them:

> On the one hand, our sample trusted their mates – but their mates typically also had offending pasts and were potential influences towards continuing offending . . . On the other hand, most respondents . . . were in a steady relationship . . . or had recently been in one . . . with [most] partners disapproving of their offending. A majority were also living with their parents – and their parents normally also disapproved of their offending. So the influence of mates was tending to pull in one, pro-offending direction; the influence of parents and partners in the other, non-offending direction. Our respondents keenly felt these tugs on their lives in different directions.
>
> *(Shapland and Bottoms 2011: 271)*

Thus, the process of 'active maturation' is not simply an internal psychological matter; it is continually shaped, prompted and/or inhibited by relationships with significant others.

Learning to live a non-criminal life

Building on the above analyses, we can now state the central conclusion that we have derived from the SDS about early-stage desistance among repeat offenders: *desistance is the process of learning to live a non-criminal life when one has been leading a largely criminal life.* The point made by this sentence is simple: if one has been regularly committing crimes, and the great majority of one's friends are also regular offenders, then, even if and when one has decided to try to change one's lifestyle, it is not straightforward to do so – any more than it is straightforward for most people to lose weight or to stop smoking. What is involved is a deliberate change of lifestyle (mixing with different people, avoiding certain places, developing different routines), as well as a process of learning to react differently to certain potentially testing situations (for example, a shortage of money, or being 'dissed' in the pub). Against that background, it is not surprising that those intending to desist sometimes find themselves committing offences, even although their calm rational selves would tell them not to do so. Awareness that this is a possibility is widespread among would-be desisters, and is often referred to as the possibility of 'doing something stupid'.[23]

'Learning to live a non-criminal life' necessarily raises the complex question of how one should best theorize the 'agentic' dimensions of the desistance process, a topic that cannot be fully addressed in this chapter (but see Healy 2013 for a valuable recent review). Instead, we shall focus briefly here on perhaps the two most influential discussions of agency in the literature on desistance, namely those of Paternoster and Bushway (2009) and Giordano *et al.* (2002).

We have already drawn upon Paternoster and Bushway's (2009) helpful conceptualization of the 'desired self' and the 'feared self'. Their primary thesis, using these concepts, is that offenders 'are committed to their working [criminal] self until they determine that the cost of this commitment is greater than the benefits'. This 'initial motivation' is then seen as bringing with it 'a change in social networks that stabilize the newly-emerging self' (Paternoster and Bushway 2009: 1103). While there is value in this formulation, the authors' adoption of an explicitly cost–benefit-based motivational model renders their approach vulnerable to familiar criticisms of exclusively rational-choice-based theories, especially when utilized on an individual rather than an aggregate basis. The Sheffield data suggest a subtler picture: desistance in this sample seems to begin because of a felt (perhaps a vaguely felt) *dissonance* between the offender's desired self and his current life. It then often proceeds in complex ways that are not fully captured by a simple cost–benefit model – in particular, through the importance of developing normative bonds (Sampson and Laub 1993) and the fact that 'doing something stupid' while attempting to desist is by no means an uncommon experience.

The 'cognitive transformation theory' of Giordano *et al.* (2002) is closer to our own understanding of the desistance process (for a full account and appraisal of this theory, see Chapter 1 by Peggy Giordano in this volume). That being the case, it is necessary here to address Laub and Sampson's (2003) critique of Giordano and colleagues. Both these sets of authors acknowledge a degree of congruence between their respective theories (Giordano *et al.* 2002: 1056; Laub and Sampson 2003: 299, n. 4), yet there is one very important difference between them. Laub and Sampson (2003: 149) claim that cognitive transformation processes are found only among 'some' offenders, and that 'most . . . desist in response to *structurally induced* turning points' (emphasis added). The full meaning of this phrase becomes clearer at a later point, when Laub and Sampson (2003) say that:

> The image of '*desistance by default*' best fits the desistance process we found in our data . . . Many men *made a commitment to go straight without even realizing it.* Before they knew it, they had invested so much in a marriage or a job that they did not want to risk losing their investment . . . We agree that the offenders' own perspectives and words need to be brought into the understanding of desistance . . . however, offenders can and do desist without a 'cognitive transformation'.
>
> *(Laub and Sampson 2003: 278–279, emphasis added)*

Of course, no one doubts that there are some cases of 'desistance by default'. But whether this is the dominant mode of desistance, as Laub and Sampson explicitly suggest, is – on the evidence of the Sheffield study – much more doubtful. The best way of illustrating this is through our data on *diachronic self-control*, a concept that we derived from the work of the philosopher Jeanette Kennett (2001: chapter 5).

Within criminology, the dominant understanding of self-control is that of Gottfredson and Hirschi (1990), who define low self-control as a 'tendency to pursue short-term, immediate pleasure', rather than give consideration to the longer-term consequences of action (Gottfredson and Hirschi 1990: 93). Thus, for these authors, self-control, or the lack of it, is in effect a psychological trait, akin to temperance. They further claim that this trait is largely formed by age 8–10 years, and that the comparative level of an individual's self-control (vis-à-vis other people) remains largely unchanged throughout life. Thus, offenders are people with comparatively low self-control.[24] This conceptualization has been strongly challenged by Wikström and Treiber (2007), whose understanding of self-control is remarkably similar to Kennett's (2001: 133) independently-developed view that the 'central case' of self-control is to be found in situations where, for a given individual, 'there is a mismatch between an all-things-considered judgement of [long-term] desirability on the one hand, and the agent's actual strongest [current] desire on the other'. Thus, for Wikström and Treiber (2007), 'self-control is something we do, rather than something we are . . . [it] is the successful inhibition of perceived action alternatives, or interruption of a course of action' in order to bring actions into line with all-things-considered moral judgements. Wikström and Treiber (2007) acknowledge that different individuals may have differential capacities to exercise self-control, so defined, but they argue that 'capacity to exercise self-control' is not the same as Gottfredson and Hirschi's (1990) generalized trait of self-control, because it comes into play only in specific circumstances, namely where a given act seems desirable and tempting, yet the actor knows that it is not in his/her long-term interests, and/or it is against his/her ultimate values, to proceed with the act.[25] The evidence of the SDS is that would-be desisters frequently experienced temptations of this sort, for example, when they or their family hit a financial crisis ('the rent is due – shall I steal in order to be able to pay it?').

As Kennett (2001) points out, self-control can be exercised both *synchronically* (for example, by deliberately not eating the tempting cream cake on the plate) and *diachronically* (for example, by organising one's life so as to minimize the number of occasions when fatty foods will be within sight or reach). There is evidence in the Sheffield Study that both these forms of self-control were exercised by sample members (Shapland and Bottoms 2011: 272–275). Of particular interest is that many would-be desisters (14 out of the 18 in the qualitative sub-sample) used diachronic self-control tactics to help them to avoid potentially criminogenic situations, for example, by structuring their daily lives so as to avoid meeting former criminal associates, or deliberately not going to certain pubs or other places where they believed that violence might erupt (Bottoms 2013). The widespread use of such tactics is evidence that 'desistance by default' (which entails 'making a commitment to go straight without even realising it') was not the dominant mode of desistance in this sample. It is also important to note that the main way in which sample members exercised diachronic self-control was by avoiding potentially *criminogenic situations* – a point to which we shall return.

A model of the early stages of desistance

On the basis of our qualitative data, we developed a 'heuristic and interactive model of the early stages of desistance' (Bottoms and Shapland 2011: 70), which is reproduced here as Figure 6.1.

At the centre of this model are two circles, respectively representing: (i) the individual's earlier personal, social and criminal history; and (ii) the social context surrounding the individual, represented as potential 'social capital' (or the lack of it). The dark arrows surrounding the circles are intended to symbolize the fact that the individual's more dynamic day-to-day journey, represented by the white arrows around the edge of the diagram, always takes place in interaction both with his earlier history and with the broader social context. The 'journey' around the edge of the diagram is then presented as a gradual and fitful process, which frequently encounters obstacles. It will be noted also that, like Giordano *et al.* (2002), we postulate only a gradual change in identity during this process. The initial steps seem to be more cognitive, followed at a later time by the acquisition of different habits and greater empathy for others (we develop this second point later).

A case study will help to illustrate some of these points: the comments in parentheses relate to aspects of the heuristic model (Figure 6.1). When we first met him, 'Len' was aged 20 and was on probation. He had been convicted on eight occasions and had served one sentence in a young offenders' institution (YOI). Because of his offending, he was estranged from his mother, and he had been

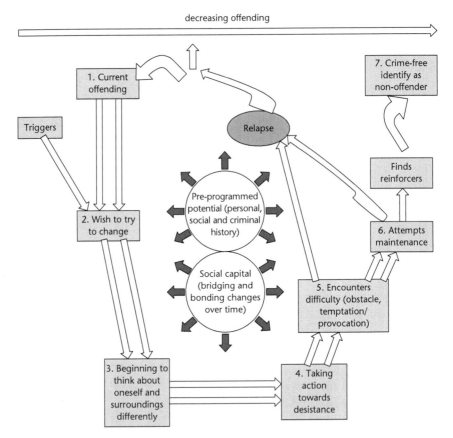

FIGURE 6.1   A heuristic and interactive model of the early stages of desistance.

Source: Bottoms and Shapland (2011: 70).

homeless and 'sleeping rough'; however, through the intervention of a probation officer, he had now been found a place in a small hostel near the city centre. He said he felt no shame or regret for his offences, because they were mostly drug-related and 'when you're on drugs you don't care'. But he claimed he now wanted to stop, because he was 'sick of . . . waking up, trying to find money, trying to find something to eat, stuff like that, day in, day out' (Step 2: *Wish to try to change*). He began to think differently about himself and reduced his offending (Steps 3 and 4), but then one night he met an old friend; they got drunk, stole a car and were caught while driving it (Step 5: *Encounters difficulty (obstacle/temptation/provocation)*). This conviction acted as a shock, and he was determined not to relapse again. (Step 2: *Wish to try to change*). During his time at the hostel, his relationship with his mother had been improving, so he moved back home with her to the out-skirts of the city. By the fourth interview, Len said he was completely off both drugs and alcohol, and he had stopped offending. He usually stayed at home seven nights a week, and he considered it important to think before he acted, and also to 'avoid my old group of friends', i.e. to exercise diachronic self-control (Step 6: *Attempts maintenance* [*of changed pattern of life*]). He said 'I'm more grown up about things, and I take more responsibility for the things I do' (Step 7: *Crime-free identity as non-offender* [*Improved maturity acts as reinforcer – expressed through both 'responsibility' and 'thinking first'; acquires fresh self-perceptions and identity*]).

We can usefully now return to the theoretical starting-point of the Sheffield study, namely Bottoms' (2002) typology of modes of compliance with the law. That paper postulated, in a nutshell, that there are four main mechanisms of compliance or potential compliance, namely the *instrumental*, the *normative*, the *situational* and the *habitual*. In Len's case, as in many other cases, we can see each of these mechanisms at work. Both Len's initial homelessness and his subsequent conviction acted as powerful instrumental motivators of change, along with a normative desire to be leading a different kind of life. Subsequently, his improved relationship with his mother was of great normative significance. Additionally, like many others, he adopted a situational self-control strategy (staying at home) to avoid his former mates; and, throughout, we see him gradually acquiring more law-abiding habits. Most importantly, perhaps, this case study illustrates the crucial point that the mechanisms of compliance within an individual's journey to desistance are usually *plural*, *interactive* and *cumulative*.

Len's case also illustrates an important cautionary point about the concept of a 'turning point' – a concept that has, following the analyses of Laub and Sampson (2003), become prominent in the literature on desistance. In his *Journal*, Sören Kierkegaard once commented that 'it is perfectly true, as philosophers say, that life must be understood backwards – but they forget the other proposition, that it must be lived forwards' (quoted in Wollheim 1984: 1). In retrospective research interviews, such as those conducted by Laub and Sampson (2003), desisters can indeed often identify crucial 'turning points' on their journeys away from crime, such as the beginning of a stable life partnership. But it is important to note that people can *only* identify such turning points retrospectively. Contemporaneously, neither the subject nor an outside observer can know whether a given circumstance (such as a new relationship) will be a 'turning point' or just another life event, or perhaps a 'false start', since as Shadd Maruna (2001: 25) put it, 'nothing inherent in a situation makes it a turning point'. For example, in Len's case, at the end of the follow-up period one could certainly look back and identify the drink-driving conviction and the consequent move back to his mother's house as turning points, but in other circumstances (for example, if there had been a rift in his relationship with his mother after his move home) the situation might have looked very different. That does not mean, of course, that there is no research value in trying to identify whether certain life developments – such as a romantic partnership or stable employment – can be reliably assessed retrospectively as regular 'turning points' in would-be desisters' lives. It does mean, however, that we cannot know prospectively whether, in an individual case, such a life event will or will not be a turning point. That outcome will depend also on what happens after the event in question, to strengthen or subvert the initial change, although this 'post-event' period has been neglected in the desistance literature. With that cautionary word, we can now turn to the topic of relationships.

Relationships

Within the international literature on desistance, the most frequently discussed specific topic is undoubtedly the social bond of marriage or partnership, originally highlighted in the work of Sampson and Laub (1993), and – in general – strongly supported by later empirical studies (see the review by Horney *et al.* 2012). In such social bonds, the primary mechanism aiding desistance/compliance is normative, though other mechanisms are also sometimes in play. In the SDS such relationship-based bonds did not appear as specific variables in the regression analyses on later criminality (see Table 6.1), but that is not to say that they were unimportant for this sample. In particular, when in the final interview we asked respondents to identify the best thing that had happened to them in the last three years,[26] the most frequently mentioned matters were a good relationship with a girlfriend, or the arrival of a child or children. Together, these were mentioned by almost half of those who felt able to say that something good had happened in their lives (Bottoms 2012a: 41).

More generally, it was notable that relationship-based items dominated the responses to this question about the best recent developments in respondents' lives. Thus, in addition to the data noted above, nearly one-fifth of those who mentioned any 'best thing' spoke of an event in their family of origin, including improved relationships with family members, especially parents (Bottoms 2012a: 41). This is supporting evidence for a notable aspect of our qualitative data, namely that the beginnings of desistance in early adulthood are not infrequently accompanied by a degree of rapprochement with the family of origin (following earlier tensions caused by the history of offending), and that such rapprochements can themselves provide valuable support to journeys towards desistance.[27]

Returning to the topic of romantic attachments, in light of the SDS data we need to revisit Mark Warr's (2002) famous challenge to Sampson and Laub's (1993) 'marriage and desistance' thesis, in which he argued that marriage might disrupt or dissolve male offenders' previous peer associations, and it might be this disruption, rather than marriage itself, that produces lower levels of crime in early adulthood. In both instances, the outcome is the same, but Warr argued that 'the social mechanism that produces the outcome is fundamentally different' (Warr 2002: 101).

Subsequent analyses of desistance have arguably paid insufficient attention to Warr's challenge. In the SDS we have not yet systematically reported our data on 'mates' (male friends), but the general picture is clear enough: as a wish to desist gathers strength (often aided by a romantic partnership), so the offender increasingly tries to disengage from previous criminal associates. However, we are inclined to think that rather than postulating alternative hypotheses in relation to these processes (as Warr did), it might be more valuable to embrace both marriage/partnership and male peers within a unified theory of normative influence. Social psychological work on social norms has shown that norms do not need to be fully internalized in order to affect action, because human subjects are often highly compliant with group norms, even when these conflict, or partially conflict, with their own norms or judgements (Turner 1991). Moreover, an individual's behaviour can alter relatively quickly to conform with group expectations, if he/she changes group allegiance (Bicchieri and Muldoon 2014). These observations make much sense of some of the transitions that are very evident in the SDS data, always interconnected with the subject's wish to change; and they help to explain the power of temptation within particular situational contexts, as on the night when Len and his friend got drunk and stole a car. As we shall shortly see, they also raise important questions about the role of ethical decision making in journeys towards desistance, but before we can tackle that matter we need to examine the important topic of the obstacles to desistance.

Obstacles to desistance

In each of the four interview schedules used sequentially in the SDS, we offered respondents a card that included a list (adapted from the work of Ros Burnett (1992)) of what we described as 'things others have said that have made it difficult to go straight or to stay straight'. We then asked each respondent to state 'which of these would apply to you?'. The results derived from this simple self-reported checklist were remarkably interesting, in several respects. A score obtained by simply counting the number of identified obstacles proved to be a robust statistical predictor of future offending, both official and self-reported, even when measures of prior lifetime offending had been taken into account (see Table 6.1 and Note 14). Reassuringly, also, most of the listed obstacles were checked by a declining proportion of respondents as they moved from interview 1 through to interview 4 (Bottoms and Shapland 2011: 61, table 2.4); and the rank order of the identified obstacles remained remarkably constant during this time (which spanned on average about three years per respondent).

A more unexpected result concerned the nature of the four most frequently identified obstacles in the checklist. In rank order, they were 'lack of money'; 'opportunity for easy money'; 'need for excitement or to relieve boredom'; and 'lack of work'. Two of these items explicitly refer to money, and we came to realize that they are prominent in the rank order for the simple reason that *'going straight' after chronic property offending frequently entails a loss of income*. Since there is research evidence that much offending by persistent offenders is triggered by a perceived need for immediate cash (Wright and Decker 1994), respondents who genuinely wish to desist face – and recognize that they face – significant tests of their resolve when their personal finances run into trouble and/or when someone offers them an opportunity to earn some easy money through crime. The mainstream desistance literature has, however, mostly bypassed these financial issues.

The other two obstacles high in the rank order also merit brief comment. One refers to the 'need for excitement or to relieve boredom', and is a vivid reminder of the emotional attractions of offending in adolescence and early adulthood (see Katz 1988). The other item – 'lack of work' – links the discussion of desistance to wider socio-structural issues, since the structural conditions of late-modern, information-focused economies do not make it easy for young men with very few formal qualifications, and poor work records, to obtain stable employment. With our colleague Stephen Farrall, we have written elsewhere about these socio-structural issues (Farrall *et al.* 2010), advocating that they be considered alongside Amartya Sen's (2009) 'capability approach'. These matters therefore remind us, first, that attempts to desist often take place within what we have called an 'obstacle-strewn society' (Shapland and Bottoms 2011: 275); and second, that a constant challenge for desistance researchers is to hold together the structural, the situational and the agentic dimensions of their analyses.

Attentive readers will have noticed, perhaps with surprise, that 'taking drugs' was not among the top four identified difficulties in the 'obstacles scale'; in fact it ranked sixth both at the beginning and the end of the study (Bottoms and Shapland 2011: 61). However, a main reason for this modest ranking was that (contrary to some popular conceptions) at the beginning of the study, only just under half of the sample (47 per cent) self-identified as having a significant drug problem.[28] For those who did have a drug problem, the temptation to continue with drug-taking was often the major obstacle to desistance: hence, whether an individual's self-reported offending had increased or decreased during the study was significantly related to both: (i) identifying drugs as an obstacle to desistance at interview 1; and (ii) admitting to a self-identified drug problem at interview 4 (Shapland and Bottoms forthcoming).

The importance of 'obstacles' within the empirical results of the SDS led us to give them a prominent place in our 'heuristic model' (Figure 6.1). That model by implication (and, we believe, correctly) suggests that encountering obstacles is a normal feature of desistance journeys for this sample (as indeed it often is in the changes of lifestyle attempted by non-offending 20–25 year-olds). But what are the consequences for desistance when an obstacle is encountered? It might be successfully overcome, but frequently it is not (and when it is not, that might further limit the would-be desister's future opportunities). However, we need to emphasize (and the details of Figure 6.1 try to reflect this) that succumbing to an obstacle does not necessarily lead to a complete relapse. Instead, it can be a partial (although often painful) setback, followed by further efforts to desist – as indeed happened in Len's case.

The everyday ethical aspects of desistance

The anthropologist James Laidlaw (2014: 1) has pointed out that:

> It is not only academic philosophers who ask questions such as 'How should one live?', 'What is a good life?', or 'What sort of person should one be?'. And it is not only religious preachers or political reformers either. Everywhere

human conduct is pervaded by an ethical dimension – by questions of the rightness and wrongness of actions, of what we owe to each other, of the kind of persons we think we are or aspire to be.

That being the case, one might expect social scientists to have produced many ground-breaking studies of what Michael Banner (2014) has memorably called, 'the ethics of everyday life'; that is, studies focused on the small, but important, ethical choices that we all regularly make. But for various reasons, too complex to go into here, social scientists have in the past often been distinctly uncomfortable about approaching such topics. Fortunately, in recent years, researchers in several social scientific disciplines have begun to try to rectify this situation. In criminology, the most notable attempt in this direction has been Per-Olof Wikström's 'situational action theory' (Wikström 2010), which places 'morality' at the heart of its explanation of crime. As yet, however, mainstream desistance theory has not seriously grappled with 'the ethics of everyday life', and it is one of the aims of the SDS to promote a discussion of this topic.[29]

An initial paper on these themes (Shapland and Bottoms 2011) considered the general social values of the SDS sample. The results of that analysis in some ways surprised us, because they revealed that most (not all) respondents 'reported . . . conformist values, for example with regard to future aspirations (employment, housing, etc.) and to the importance of staying within legal boundaries' (Shapland and Bottoms 2011: 256). We have discussed the first of these conclusions earlier in this chapter. Examples of the second conclusion include the findings: (i) that responses to two hypothetical offending scenarios revealed moral reasoning that was 'primarily other-directed and sympathetic to the victim' (Shapland and Bottoms 2011: 268); and (ii) that 60 per cent of respondents 'found the label of "offender", when applied to themselves, "upsetting, shaming or regrettable"' (Shapland and Bottoms 2011: 264). Additionally, there were some interesting empirical differences between those who expressed a definite wish to desist (or had already desisted) and others: the former group were, for example, more likely to give higher ratings when asked to assess the seriousness of various specified offences (Shapland and Bottoms 2011: 269).

These broadly conventional moral views were expressed from the outset of the SDS fieldwork, yet – as we have seen – 80 per cent of the sample were reconvicted during the period of the research. Accordingly, there was some obvious dissonance between expressed values and behaviour. However, and contrary to the suggestions of David Matza (1964), we found little evidence that SDS respondents used *neutralizations* to explain away this dissonance.[30] Instead, it seemed that the dissonance could best be explained: '(1) by complex processes of maturation, in which intentions to "go straight" co-exist with lapses into learned (habitual) criminal responses; and (2) by the spontaneous character of much offending, with for example invitations to offend by criminal friends being common' (Shapland and Bottoms 2011: 256). Thus, ethics and the practical living of everyday life became intimately interconnected; indeed, at each of the last three interviews, on average two-thirds of respondents said that, since the previous interview, they had *either* nearly committed an offence, but had pulled back, *or* had declined an invitation from a 'mate' to take part in a crime (Shapland and Bottoms 2011: 273). It was of special interest that those attempting to desist were more likely to give 'moral' rather than 'pragmatic' reasons for having declined invitations to offend.

In attempting to think further about these and related issues, we have, like a number of anthropologists interested in everyday ethics, 'found virtue ethics[31] [to be] more readily congenial than any other style or school in modern moral philosophy' (Laidlaw 2014: 47).[32] In the present context, however, we shall not attempt to develop that line of thinking. Instead, we shall conclude by exploring a broader issue relating to 'everyday ethics' and processes of desistance, which has, in our view, significant relevance for the future of desistance research; namely, the sequential development of desistance.

Both in social science and in ethics, precision in delineating the nature of the topic under discussion is always helpful. Thus, for example, Michael Banner (2014: 125–127) points out that one prominent mode of discourse about Alzheimer's disease tends to be somewhat apocalyptic, picturing it as 'death before death', 'the loss of the self' and so on. But he then cites empirical evidence that 'the path of this disease is not necessarily like the path of a tsunami that overwhelms everything in one almighty rush'; rather, there can be identifiably separate processes of 'death of autonomy, death of memory, death of self-consciousness' and so on. Accordingly, adequate reflection on the ethics of responding to Alzheimer's will require some 'patient anthropological fieldwork' on the 'character of human subjectivity in dementia'.

There are, we think, some parallel issues to be faced in the field of desistance. On the basis of the present research literature (which, on this point, is not very extensive), both Frank Porporino (2010) and Deidre Healy (2013) have suggested that 'the concerns and preoccupations of early desisters seem to be different from those of later desisters' (Porporino 2010: 73). The difference, perhaps, is that 'early-stage desisters [are] preoccupied with "becoming normal" and their goals [are] more likely to revolve around finding conventional roles in work and family life' (Healy 2013: 561). By contrast, later desisters often seem to move on to a 'deeper' and more 'other-centred' (empathetic) set of concerns (Porporino 2010: 73).[33] The SDS studied primarily the early stages of desistance, so we can provide only limited evidence on this issue. However, case studies within the qualitative sample did show an interesting progression over time: at the first interview, offenders rarely expressed much concern for the harm they had caused to victims, yet it was not uncommon for regrets about such harm to be expressed in later interviews, *after* the first steps towards desistance had been taken. (See for example the case of 'John', described in Bottoms and Shapland 2014: 326.) Interestingly, also, an ordinal regression on 'views about future offending' at the time of the fourth interview showed that 'empathy' was one of only two significant predictors of having stopped offending/having a definite intention to desist (Bottoms and Shapland 2011: 59–60). These data provide at least tentative evidence that, among those who are serious about stopping offending, the nature and character of moral understanding may change and deepen as desistance progresses; and they point to the need for a fuller and deeper ethical exploration of these apparent transitions.

Pointers to future research

In conclusion, and based on our study, we offer four suggestions for future research in the field of desistance:

1. Each empirical study of desistance reports within the limits of its sample, its location and its timing. The SDS studied mostly white male recidivists in early adulthood in a post-industrial city in Northern England, shortly before the worldwide financial crash. There is a clear need to pull together results from different starting ages, genders, ethnic groups and countries.
2. We have considered the 'transition to adulthood' as a key topic in the modal age-range for desistance, namely the early twenties. This has convinced us that desistance research needs to be more closely aligned with developmental research than it mostly has been in the past (see also Chapter 7 by Mulvey and Schubert in this volume).
3. There is now evidence that subjective decisions to desist are associated with later reductions in offending, but as yet we have an insufficiently detailed understanding of the complex processes of: (i) deciding that one wishes to desist; (ii) attempting to alter one's lifestyle to achieve this change; (iii) frequently encountering obstacles and setbacks; (iv) achieving reinforcement of initial change; and (v) self-reflections linked to these processes. This will perhaps require further development of the well-known issues relating to the relationship between agency and structure, which we partially addressed in Farrall *et al.* (2010). We have also found that a mechanism-based approach is helpful in analysing these change processes (notably in drawing attention to the importance of situational self-control), and we believe there is scope to develop such an approach more fully.
4. The SDS focuses very much on the early stages of desistance, whereas other research studies, especially retrospective analyses, focus on later stages. There is a clear need for more detailed research work on how and why the characteristic features of early desistance (in a nutshell, trying to 'become more normal') bridge into the apparently subtler processes of later desistance. That research will also necessarily require deeper scrutiny of the ethical issues involved in desistance processes, which the SDS has tried to highlight.[34]

Notes

1 The Sheffield Desistance Study was conducted at the University of Sheffield and funded by the UK Economic and Social Research Council as part of an inter-university Research Network on 'Social contexts of pathways in crime', led by Professor P-O. Wikström, University of Cambridge. The subsequent work of Anthony Bottoms on the Study was assisted by the award of a Leverhulme Emeritus Research Fellowship.
2 On the contrast between 'mechanism explanations', 'covering law explanations' and 'statistical explanations' in the social sciences, see Hedström (2005: chapter 2).
3 For example, F.-Dufour and Brassard (2014: 320) report that their small sample of nine 'transformed' Canadian desisters differed from the SDS sample in not holding largely 'conformist' ultimate values. However, they point out that the Canadian group – who had all

begun offending as juveniles – had a mean age at estimated desistance of 36 (median 35). Hence, they were 'entrenched in their pattern of prior criminality, which . . . would explain the very criminal set of attitudes found in this group prior to desistance' (E-Dufour and Brassard 2014: 330).

4 A 'conviction occasion' is a court appearance at which one or more convictions for specific offences is recorded. (It is common in England for an offender to be convicted for several offences at a single conviction occasion.) The 'standard list' of offences is, broadly speaking, a list of crimes that are *mala in se* rather than *mala prohibita*; thus, it includes crimes such as assaults, sex offences, thefts, burglaries, robberies, fraud, criminal damage and drug offences, but excludes the majority of motoring offences and administrative offences.

5 Because our access arrangements were, for reasons explained later, organized through the probation service, offenders who received non-custodial sentences not administered by that service (such as fines) could not be included in the sample. Offenders in receipt of custodial sentences were included unless the length of their sentence meant that they would probably not be released during the period of the research fieldwork.

6 The age of criminal responsibility in England is ten, and all court convictions and formal police cautions from that age are noted in an offender's full criminal record. In the SDS the cut-off date for recording fresh convictions or cautions was 31 August 2007.

7 On the importance of appreciative understanding within the methodology of the social sciences, see Runciman (1983).

8 The potential research population was identified by police staff, who applied the eligibility criteria for the study (see above) to the full set of criminal records within the care of South Yorkshire Police (SYP). Criminal records are 'personal data' for the purposes of the Data Protection Act 1998, and the Act places restrictions on the ways in which holders of personal data (in this instance, SYP) may utilize them. In light of this background, SYP decided that it was necessary for them, or an appropriate agency acting as their delegate, to contact potential interviewees requesting their consent to be interviewed by a University-based research team. Because it was thought that offenders would be more likely to respond positively to such an approach if it came from the probation service rather than the police, SYP delegated the task of approaching potential participants to the National Probation Service (South Yorkshire). We are most grateful to SYP and the probation service for assisting the research by establishing and implementing these procedures.

9 It had originally been hoped to recruit samples of both men and women, using the same eligibility criteria, but this plan had to be abandoned, because very few eligible women could be recruited within the relevant timeframe.

10 The CSDD sample consists of 411 males, but only 118 of these had 2 or more conviction occasions by the age of 40 (Farrington *et al.* 2006: 24).

11 A further comparison with the Cambridge Study is instructive: in that population, a total of 164 men had been convicted of a standard list offence by age 40, with an aggregate of 686 conviction occasions for such offences (Farrington *et al.* 2006: 17). At the beginning of the Sheffield study (when all members of the sample were below age 23), the SDS sample had already acquired an aggregate of 909 conviction occasions for standard list offences.

12 There were no significant differences between the qualitative sample and the remainder of the study sample on the key variables of age, lifetime official criminality and early social disadvantage. There was, however, only one ethnic minority participant in the qualitative sample. Where case studies have been reported in the publications of the SDS (e.g. Bottoms and Shapland 2011: 67–8; 2014), these are derived from the qualitative sub-sample.

13 These figures are standardized to exclude periods in custody.

14 That might also be true of the 'obstacles score', but interpretation of this variable is not completely straightforward, because (with the exception of a perceived drug problem) it was the total number of obstacles rather than specific types of problem that predicted later criminality: see Shapland and Bottoms forthcoming. It could therefore be argued that the aggregate score is more a general reflection of a respondent's optimism or pessimism about desistance, rather than a true indication of the current external circumstances in which he found himself.

15 For an empirical demonstration of this point, based on data from the Pittsburgh longitudinal study, see Stouthamer-Loeber *et al.* (2004); they report that they 'did not find much evidence that the same factors that predict onset also predict desistance' (Stouthamer-Loeber *et al.* 2004: 914).

16 For example, as we have reported elsewhere:

> about half the men [in the Sheffield sample] had been excluded from school for at least a month during their school career; 86 per cent had left school with no qualifications; and nearly 60 per cent had had no job of any kind (including casual jobs) during the year before the first interview.
>
> *(Bottoms and Shapland 2011: 51–52)*

Clearly, histories of this kind are not advantageous to would-be desisters when they are looking for stable employment.

17 There is no agreed terminology to describe the age period of the early twenties in contemporary Western societies. Jeffrey Arnett (2015: chapter 1) has influentially promoted the term 'emerging adulthood', which he regards as a 'separate life stage' (Arnett 2015: 24), a claim which is controversial (see the debates in Arnett *et al.* 2011). Additionally, Arnett (2015: 15) claims that emerging adulthood is 'the age of possibilities, when many different futures remain open', but this description has been strongly challenged by Jennifer Silva (2013: 35) in relation to the prospects of 'working class adult[s] in an age of austerity'. Given these debates, we have chosen to avoid the term 'emerging adulthood' and to use instead, and somewhat interchangeably, either 'early adulthood' (as in the title of this chapter) or 'the transition to adulthood' (as here). In Britain, the latter term has gained in stature through its adoption by the influential criminal justice pressure group the Transition to Adulthood Alliance (or T2A Alliance).

18 For example, across all the interviews in the SDS, respondents' views about likely future desistance or continued offending were shown to be not strongly related to the total amount of past criminality (Bottoms and Shapland 2011: 60), because some with long criminal histories expressed a clear wish to turn their lives around.

19 For more details, see Bottoms and Shapland (2011: 60). The self-efficacy measure was not included in the interview schedules for interviews 3 and 4.

20 That is, it has sometimes been claimed that 'maturation causes desistance', while simultaneously treating a reduction in offending as evidence of greater maturity.

21 This physiological evidence did not come to our attention until after the completion of the fieldwork for the SDS, so it played no part in our choice of questions for the interview schedules.

22 Of interest in this connection is Jennifer Tanner's (2006) work on 'recentering' in early adulthood, which shows that 'life-marker events' (events of particular significance in shaping the course of adults' lives) occur disproportionately in the twenties. Tanner suggests that a programme of empirical research, which focuses on the plans that those in the transition to adulthood make, revise and act upon 'should provide insight into more and less adaptive pathways through this critical age period' (Tanner 2006: 49–50).

23 This phenomenon is known to philosophers as 'weakness of will' (see Stroud 2014), and it incorporates some notoriously difficult analytic problems. The field of desistance offers many rich empirical examples for those interested in this topic.

24 Gottfredson and Hirschi are, of course, fully aware of the drop in offending levels in early adulthood, among both occasional and persistent offenders. However, they argue that this 'cannot be explained by change in the person or by his exposure to anticriminal institutions'; accordingly, 'we are left with the conclusion that it is due to the inexorable aging of the organism' (Gottfredson and Hirschi 1990: 141). Note however the evidence in this volume in Chapter 7 by Mulvey and Schubert that comparative temperance levels among different groups can vary over time.

25 In the Peterborough Adolescent Development Study, conducted by Wikström and colleagues, a measure of capacity to exercise self-control showed a remarkable stability by

age during the adolescent years (13–17) (Wikström *et al.* 2012: 137). However, one could expect this capacity to increase in the twenties, given the physiological evidence previously described.

26 Strictly, the question asked about 'good things' and the data described reports the first such 'good thing' mentioned by the respondent. One-sixth of respondents did not feel able to identify any 'good thing'.

27 Arnett (2015: chapter 3) shows that a changed relationship with parents is common among those in the transition to adulthood – he headlines it as a transition 'from conflict to companionship'. Of course, however, parent–adolescent conflicts are often significantly more severe when the adolescent is a repeat offender, so it is of great interest that rapprochements occur frequently even in such cases.

28 In the SDS, a self-identified 'drug problem offender' was one who, at a given interview, *either* admitted to being dependent on drugs (of any kind) *or* to taking hard drugs and regarding this as a problem.

29 There is much congruence between the main concepts utilized in Situational Action Theory and some of the principal findings of the SDS (for example, those relating to moral values, self-control and the importance of situations). We intend to discuss these issues on a future occasion.

30 A 'neutralization' is an attempt to deflect blame from oneself for an offence, for example, by saying things like 'the shop can afford it', 'he started it', 'everyone does it' and so on.

31 'Virtue ethics' is a technical term for one of the three major approaches within contemporary normative ethics (the others are consequentialism and deontology). Central topics considered within virtue ethics include 'motives and moral character, moral wisdom or discernment . . . and the fundamentally important questions of what sort of person I should be, and how we should live' (Hursthouse 2013). It is these 'fundamentally important questions' that potentially provide a special link between virtue ethics and discussions of desistance.

32 For discussions of virtue ethics in relation to the SDS, see Shapland and Bottoms (2011: 275–276); Bottoms and Shapland (2014).

33 For Porporino, these include Maruna's (2001) findings about 'generativity' and 'redemption scripts'; but as Healy (2013: 561) notes, in these respects 'Maruna's study has not been consistently replicated, despite its popularity'.

34 We are most grateful to Ed Mulvey for his constructively critical comments on an earlier version of this chapter.

References

Arnett, J. J. (2014), 'Presidential address. The emergence of emerging adulthood: A personal history', *Emerging Adulthood* 2: 155–162.

Arnett, J. J. (2015), *Emerging Adulthood: The Winding Road from the Late Teens through the Twenties*, second edition. New York: Oxford University Press.

Arnett, J. J., Kloep, M., Hendry, L. B. and Tanner, J. L. (2011), *Debating Emerging Adulthood: Stage or Process?* New York: Oxford University Press.

Bandura, A. (1997), *Self-Efficacy: The Exercise of Control*. New York: W. H. Freeman and Co.

Banner, M. (2014), *The Ethics of Everyday Life: Moral Theology, Social Anthropology and the Imagination of the Human*. Oxford, UK: Oxford University Press.

Bicchieri, C. and Muldoon, R. (2014), 'Social norms', in Zalta, E. N. (ed.) *The Stanford Encyclopedia of Philosophy* (Spring 2014 edition). Available at http://plato.stanford.edu/archives/spr2014/entries/social-norms/ (accessed 31 December 2015).

Blokland, A. and Nieuwbeerta, P. (2005), 'The effects of life circumstances on individual trajectories of offending', *Criminology* 43: 1203–1240.

Blokland, A., Nagin, D. and Nieuwbeerta, P. (2005), 'Life span offending trajectories of a Dutch conviction cohort', *Criminology* 43: 919–954.

Bottoms, A. E. (2001), 'Compliance and community penalties', in Bottoms, A. E., Gelsthorpe, L. R. and Rex, S. (eds) *Community Penalties: Change and Challenges.* Cullompton, UK: Willan Publishing.

Bottoms, A. E. (2002), 'Morality, crime, compliance and public policy', in Bottoms, A. E. and Tonry, M. (eds) *Ideology, Crime and Criminal Justice: A Symposium in Honour of Sir Leon Radzinowicz.* Cullompton, UK: Willan Publishing.

Bottoms, A. E. (2012a), 'Active maturation: Why crime falls in early adulthood', *Eurovista: Probation and Community Justice* 2: 39–42.

Bottoms, A. E. (2012b), 'Developing socio-spatial criminology', in Maguire, M., Morgan, R. and Reiner, R. (eds) *The Oxford Handbook of Criminology*, fifth edition. Oxford, UK: Oxford University Press.

Bottoms, A. E. (2013), 'Learning from Odysseus: Self-applied situational crime prevention as an aid to compliance', in Ugwudike, P. and Raynor, P. (eds) *What Works in Offender Compliance: International Perspectives and Evidence-Based Practice.* Basingstoke, UK: Palgrave Macmillan.

Bottoms, A. E. (2014), 'Desistance from crime', in Ashmore, Z. and Shuker, R. (eds) *Forensic Practice in the Community.* London: Routledge.

Bottoms, A. E. and Shapland, J. M. (2011), 'Steps towards desistance among male young adult recidivists', in Farrall, S., Hough, M., Maruna, S. and Sparks, R. (eds) *Escape Routes: Contemporary Perspectives on Life after Punishment.* London: Routledge.

Bottoms, A. E. and Shapland, J. M. (2014), 'Can persistent offenders acquire virtue?', *Studies in Christian Ethics* 27: 318–333.

Bottoms, A. E., Shapland, J. M., Costello, A., Holmes, D. and Muir, G. (2004), 'Towards desistance: Theoretical underpinnings for an empirical study', *The Howard Journal of Criminal Justice* 43: 368–389.

Burnett, R. (1992), *The Dynamics of Recidivism.* Oxford, UK: Centre for Criminological Research.

Calverley, A. (2013), *Cultures of Desistance: Rehabilitation, Reintegration and Ethnic Minorities.* London: Routledge.

Caudy, M. S., Durso, J. M. and Taxman, F. S. (2013), 'How well do dynamic needs predict recidivism?: Implications for risk assessment and risk reduction', *Journal of Criminal Justice* 41: 458–466.

Clarke, R. V. G. (2009), 'Situational crime prevention: Theoretical background and current practice,' in Krohn, M. D., Lizotte, A. J. and Hall, G. P. (eds) *Handbook on Crime and Deviance.* Dordrecht, The Netherlands: Springer.

Eisner, M. (2003), 'Long-term historical trends in violent crime', in Tonry, M. (ed.) *Crime and Justice: A Review of Research*, volume 30. Chicago, IL: University of Chicago Press.

Ezell, M. E. and Cohen, L. E. (2005), *Desisting from Crime: Continuity and Change in Long-Term Crime Patterns of Serious Chronic Offenders.* Oxford, UK: Oxford University Press.

Farrall, S., Bottoms, A. E. and Shapland, J. (2010), 'Social structures and desistance from crime', *European Journal of Criminology* 7: 546–570.

Farrington, D. P., Coid, J. W., Harnett, L., Jolliffe, D., Soteriou, N., Turner, R. and West, D. J. (2006), *Criminal Careers up to Age 50 and Life Success up to Age 48.* Home Office Research Study No. 299. London: Home Office.

F.-Dufour, I. and Brassard, R. (2014), 'The convert, the remorseful and the rescued: Three different processes of desistance from crime', *Australian and New Zealand Journal of Criminology* 47: 313–335.

Giordano, P. C., Cernovitch, S. A. and Rudolph, J. L. (2002), 'Gender, crime and desistance: Toward a theory of cognitive transformation', *American Journal of Sociology* 107: 990–1064.

Gottfredson, M. R. and Hirschi, T. (1990), *A General Theory of Crime*. Stanford, CA: Stanford University Press.

Healy, D. (2013), 'Changing fate?: Agency and the desistance process', *Theoretical Criminology* 17: 557–574.

Hedström, P. (2005), *Dissecting the Social: On the Principles of Analytic Sociology*. Cambridge, UK: Cambridge University Press.

Horney, J., Tolan, P. and Weisburd, D. (2012), 'Contextual influences', in Loeber, R. and Farrington, D. P. (eds) *From Juvenile Delinquency to Adult Crime: Criminal Careers, Justice Policy and Prevention*. New York: Oxford University Press.

Hursthouse, R. (2013), 'Virtue ethics', in Zalta, E. N. (ed.) *The Stanford Encyclopedia of Philosophy* (Fall 2013 edition). Available at http://plato.stanford.edu/archives/fall2013/entries/ethics-virtue/ (accessed 31 December 2015).

Johnson, S. B., Blum, R. W. and Giedd, J. N. (2009), 'Adolescent maturity and the brain: The promise and pitfalls of neuroscience research in adolescent health policy', *Journal of Adolescent Health* 45: 216–221.

Katz, J. (1988), *Seductions of Crime*. New York: Basic Books.

Kennett, J. (2001), *Agency and Responsibility: A Common-Sense Moral Psychology*. Oxford, UK: Clarendon Press.

Kyvsgaard, B. (2003), *The Criminal Career: The Danish Longitudinal Study*. Cambridge, UK: Cambridge University Press.

Laidlaw, J. (2014), *The Subject of Virtue: An Anthropology of Ethics and Freedom*. Cambridge, UK: Cambridge University Press.

Laub, J. H. and Sampson, R. J. (2003), *Shared Beginnings, Divergent Lives*. Cambridge, MA: Harvard University Press.

LeBel, T. P., Burnett, R., Maruna, S. and Bushway, S. (2008), 'The "chicken and egg" of subjective and social factors in desistance from crime', *European Journal of Criminology* 5: 131–159.

Maruna, S. (2001), *Making Good: How Ex-Convicts Reform and Rebuild their Lives*. Washington, DC: American Psychological Association.

Matza, D. (1964), *Delinquency and Drift*. New York: John Wiley & Sons.

Moffitt, T. E. (1993), 'Adolescence-limited and life-course-persistent antisocial behavior: A developmental taxonomy', *Psychological Review* 100: 674–701.

Oyserman, D. and James, L. (2009), 'Possible selves: From content to process', in Markman, K. D., Klein, W. M. P. and Suhr, J. A. (eds) *Handbook of Imagination and Mental Stimulation*. New York: Psychology Press.

Paternoster, R. and Bushway, S. (2009), 'Desistance and the "feared self": Toward an identity theory of criminal desistance', *Journal of Criminal Law and Criminology* 99: 1103–1156.

Piquero, A., Farrington, D. P. and Blumstein, A. (2007), *Key Issues in Criminal Career Research: New Analyses of the Cambridge Study in Delinquent Development*. Cambridge, UK: Cambridge University Press.

Porporino, F. J. (2010), 'Bringing sense and sensitivity to corrections: From programmes to "fix" offenders to services to support desistance', in Brayford, J., Cowe, F. and Deering, J. (eds) *What Else Works?: Creative Work with Offenders*. Cullompton, UK: Willan Publishing.

Prior, D., Farrow, K., Hughes, N., Kelly, G., Manders, G., White, S. and Wilkinson, B. (2011), *Maturity, Young Adults and Criminal Justice: A Literature Review*. Birmingham, UK: University of Birmingham.

Runciman, W. G. (1983), *A Treatise on Social Theory, Volume 1: The Methodology of Social Theory*. Cambridge, UK: Cambridge University Press.

Sampson, R. J. and Laub, J. H. (1993), *Crime in the Making*. Cambridge, MA: Harvard University Press.

Sen, A. (2009), *The Idea of Justice*. London: Allen Lane.

Shapland, J. M. and Bottoms, A. E. (2011), 'Reflections on social values, offending and desistance among young adult recidivists', *Punishment and Society* 13: 256–282.

Shapland, J. M. and Bottoms, A. E. (forthcoming), 'Offending and offence patterns in the early stages of desistance: A study of young men in England', in Blokland, A. and Van Der Geest, V. (eds) *The Routledge International Handbook of Life-Course Criminology*. London: Routledge.

Shapland, J. M., Bottoms, A. E. and Muir, G. (2012), 'Perceptions of the criminal justice system among young adult would-be desisters', in Lösel, F., Bottoms, A. and Farrington, D. (eds) *Young Adult Offenders*. London: Routledge.

Silva, J. M. (2013), *Coming Up Short: Working Class Adulthood in an Age of Uncertainty*. New York: Oxford University Press.

Stouthamer-Loeber, M., Wei, E., Loeber, R. and Master, A. S. (2004), 'Desistance from persistent serious delinquency in the transition to adulthood', *Development and Psychopathology* 16: 897–918.

Stroud, S. (2014), 'Weakness of will', in Zalta, E. N. (ed.) *The Stanford Encyclopedia of Philosophy* (Spring 2014 edition). Available at http://plato.stanford.edu/archives/spr2014/entries/weakness-will/ (accessed 31 December 2015).

Tanner, J. L. (2006), 'Recentering during emerging adulthood', in Arnett, J. J. and Tanner, J. L. (eds) *Emerging Adults in America: Coming of Age in the 21st Century*. Washington, DC: American Psychological Association.

Turner, J. C. (1991), *Social Influence*. Milton Keynes, UK: Open University Press.

Uggen, C. and Piliavin, I. (1998), 'Asymmetrical causation and criminal desistance', *Journal of Criminal Law and Criminology* 88: 1399–1422.

Warr, M. (2002), *Companions in Crime*. Cambridge, UK: Cambridge University Press.

Wikström, P-O. H. (2010), 'Explaining crime as moral action', in Hitlin, S. and Vaysey, S. (eds) *Handbook of the Sociology of Morality*. New York: Springer Verlag.

Wikström, P-O. and Treiber, K. (2007), 'The role of self-control in crime causation: Beyond Gottfredson and Hirschi's general theory of crime', *European Journal of Criminology* 4: 237–264.

Wikström, P-O. H., Oberwittler, D., Treiber, K. and Hardie, B. (2012), *Breaking Rules: The Social and Situational Dynamics of Young People's Urban Crime*. Oxford, UK: Oxford University Press.

Winkler, A. (2008), *Sheffield City Report*. Centre for Analysis of Social Exclusion (CASE), Report No 45, London: London School of Economics.

Wollheim, R. (1984), *The Thread of Life*. Cambridge, UK: Cambridge University Press.

Wright, R. T. and Decker, S. (1994), *Burglars on the Job: Streetlife and Residential Break-ins*. Boston, MA: Northeastern University Press.

7

ISSUES TO CONSIDER IN FUTURE WORK ON DESISTANCE FROM ADOLESCENCE TO EARLY ADULTHOOD

Observations from the Pathways to Desistance study

Edward P. Mulvey and Carol A. Schubert

Introduction

Longitudinal, survey, and qualitative research have repeatedly demonstrated that a large proportion of adolescents who commit illegal acts (and who might subsequently become involved with the juvenile justice system) curtail or stop offending as they enter adulthood (e.g., Glueck and Glueck 1950; Wolfgang *et al.* 1972; Loeber *et al.* 1991; Piquero *et al.* 2003; Thornberry *et al.* 2012). This straightforward observation has spawned an increasingly complex body of research on the dynamics of "desistance" from crime or antisocial behavior (Laub and Boonstoppel 2011) as well as novel methodological and analytical approaches to address this question (e.g., Nagin 2005). The energy behind these developments comes largely from the considerable potential of this line of investigation for expanding both the theoretical lens applied to antisocial behavior and the practical applications to reduce the harmful effects of these behaviors.

There are several theoretical frameworks that usually guide investigations of desistance during late adolescence, and the nuances of these are too involved to explore adequately here. It is simply worth noting that each of the extant theoretical frameworks usually emphasizes a particular factor or process as a critical feature of the overall picture. This is understandable. The desistance process in late adolescence results from a complex set of interactions among things, such as an adolescent's innate capacities, developmental stage, influential events, psychological processing of events, and opportunities for positive change (Farrall and Maruna 2004; Mulvey *et al.* 2004). Some theorists focus on the idea of possibly innate individual differences increasing the chances of an adolescent-limited criminal career (Moffitt 1993); others emphasize the importance of cumulative social and emotional bonds over time (Sampson and Laub 1993); and still others stress the centrality of adopting and integrating a new self-conception and sense of agency to maintain positive change (Maruna 2001; Giordano *et al.* 2002). It is an extremely complex undertaking to construct a singular theory that accommodates the many fluctuating influences, possible interactions, and multiple paths and intermittencies embedded in the desistance process. Any number of human behaviors cannot be covered adequately by a single theory.

Also, it is probably not essential that a single unifying theory emerges. There is considerable value in an enriched understanding of each of the central processes that propel an individual to stop doing crime or antisocial behavior. Such an understanding is the first step toward designing innovative and hopefully more effective programs and policies for people entangled in the personal and legal fallout that accompanies these behaviors. Most importantly, a focus on desistance opens a new door for thinking about interventions and policy. It provides an alternative to the predominant approach rooted in "fixing" the underlying causes that keep people involved in antisocial behavior. Desistance research offers the possibility of informing practitioners and policy makers about what might promote decreases in criminal or antisocial behavior, rather than what personal deficits have promoted or maintained this involvement. As Farrall and Maruna (2004: 361) note, "Being desistance-focused . . . implies a focus on the purpose and aspiration of the intervention rather than on the 'problem' that precipitates it." Knowing how desistance works opens up the possibility for new approaches to working with criminal offenders that push a recovery, rather than cure, process forward.

While an exciting possibility, we are really only at the beginning phases of this undertaking. Moving forward successfully will require considerably more integration of existing theories and the realities of practice as well as the accumulation of a sizable body of sound research. This will require grappling with numerous conceptual and operational research issues, many of which are not unique to studies of desistance but are often particularly thorny when addressing this question in particular. It is necessary to think through things like defining the construct cleanly (e.g., an end state versus a process, Laub and Sampson 2001), finding the right sample to demonstrate the processes of interest (e.g., low level or intermittent versus serious, chronic offenders, Massoglia and Uggen 2007), collecting data at the right granularity (e.g., extended periods or contextual influences in the short term, Horney *et al.* 1995), and designing sound data analysis strategies (e.g., testing for individual and event influences simultaneously, Curran *et al.* 2014). In addition, complex operational issues like obtaining funding, supervising staff, getting access to organizations and individual offenders, and protecting confidentiality have to be addressed.

In this chapter, we discuss three issues that deserve consideration in future research efforts on desistance to make them more productive and valuable to the field. We have identified these issues from our own experiences as part of the working group that conducted the Pathways to Desistance study (or "Pathways" study) in two United States' metropolitan areas. The Pathways study is a comprehensive, large-scale study that followed over 1,300 serious adolescent offenders regularly from adolescence into young adulthood, requiring about 10 years of data collection.

As often happens when an ongoing research project unfolds, we asked ourselves why we did not think through certain contours of the problem more carefully from the outset. We will draw on some of the study findings to date and our experiences in directing the study to illustrate the issues and as justification for why we consider each issue important in considering future work.

We focus on three issues. These are: (1) the difficulty of adequately capturing the most influential contextual factors and complexity of people's lives; (2) the necessity to integrate normal developmental processes into the conceptualization of desistance during late adolescence and early adulthood; and (3) the need to anticipate and explicitly test the sequencing and patterns of life events and behavioral changes. Consideration of these issues can help focus future work in this area and produce useful knowledge for innovations in practice and policy. Before we expand on these points, however, we will give you an overview of the study.

The Pathways to Desistance study

The Pathways study was initiated by the MacArthur Foundation Network on Adolescent Development and Juvenile Justice (https://www.macfound.org/networks/research-network-on-adolescent-development-juvenil/details) in collaboration with several federal agencies, foundations, and state agencies. The goal of the study is to provide information that could be useful for improving juvenile justice practice and policy in the United States. It was focused on trying to provide a richer picture of patterns of continued offending and desistance in serious juvenile offenders as a way to improve assessment and policy regarding risk and amenability determinations. It had a clear orientation toward generating translatable knowledge that could support informed juvenile justice reform efforts.

For practitioners and policy makers, the most pressing problems center on what to do with adolescents who have ongoing involvement in the juvenile justice system, often for serious crimes. They need more information about how to get and keep these adolescent offenders out of the system. Unfortunately, existing longitudinal research, by design, is often limited in its guidance to juvenile court professionals and service providers about what might be expected in the development of adolescent offenders involved with the court, or what might reasonably be expected from interventions and sanctions with these adolescents (Mulvey et al. 2004). Existing research is particularly deficient in characterizations of what happens to adolescent offenders from their involvement with the juvenile justice system, rarely providing detailed information about the type, intensity, or duration of interventions or sanctions (National Research Council/Institute of Medicine 2001).

It is thus not surprising that U.S. policy and practice with serious offenders in juvenile court often rely on fads, rather than facts, about the current crop of serious adolescent offenders and their amenability to treatment (e.g., "superpredators"; see Bennett et al. 1996, and then Zimring 1998; "budding psychopaths," see Edens et al. 2001) and/or the effectiveness of particular interventions (e.g., the impact of boot camps, see Styve et al. 2000). This lack of specific information about the adjustment of serious adolescent offenders over time has also promoted legal policies that rely on "wholesale" reforms; dealing with offenders uniformly based on the type of offense committed, rather than the relevant developmental or social factors presented by a particular adolescent (Zimring and Fagan 2000). Without more solid information about the lives of serious adolescent offenders, these trends are likely to continue. The Pathways study was oriented toward providing a substantial core of solid information about the characteristics and patterns of development in serious adolescent offenders to avoid the regular shifts in policy and practice based on the newest trend for framing juvenile offending in the United States.

It was noted at the outset that, although it is clear adolescent offenders do less crime as they age, there is very little known about *how* adolescents desist from antisocial activities. It would be valuable for courts and social service systems to know what pushes serious adolescent offenders toward productive lifestyles so that programs can support and promote such influences. Unfortunately, the information is sparser than would be desired about psychological or life changes among serious adolescent offenders that promote positive adjustment to early adulthood and a cessation of antisocial activity (Laub and Boonstoppel 2011). The Pathways study was designed to fill some of this gap in knowledge.

The Pathways study is a large-scale, two-site longitudinal examination of desistance from crime among serious adolescent offenders. The primary aim of the study is to examine how developmental processes, social context, and interventions and sanctioning experiences affect the process of stopping antisocial activities broadly, and crime in particular. The study employed a prospective design with a broad measurement focus and multiple sources of information (self-reports, collateral reports, and official records) to provide a picture of intra-individual change over time. This information permits an exploration of the effects of maturation, changes in social context, and sanctioning and intervention experiences on positive and negative changes in behavior, psychological functioning, and the transition into adult roles (see Mulvey *et al.* 2004 for a more detailed discussion of the theoretical background for the study).

The design of the Pathways study is deceptively simple. It followed a sizeable sample of serious adolescent offenders (n=1,354) from two metropolitan areas (Maricopa County, Arizona, n=654, and Philadelphia County, Pennsylvania, n=700) for seven years after their court involvement for a serious crime, documenting the changes in their lives over this period. Adolescents were enrolled into the study between November 2000 and January 2003. These youths were at least age 14 and below age 18 at the time of their committing offense and had been found guilty of a serious offense (almost exclusively felonies, with a few exceptions for some misdemeanor property offenses, sexual assault, or weapons offenses). The proportion of male youths found guilty of a drug charge was capped at 15 percent to avoid an over-representation of drug offenders. All females who met the age and crime criteria were approached for enrollment as were youths being considered for trial in the adult system. Twenty percent of the youths approached for participation declined.

Upon enrollment in the study, participants completed a baseline interview within 75 days after their adjudication (for those in the juvenile system) or 90 days after their decertification hearing in Philadelphia or an adult arraignment in Phoenix (if in the adult system). Follow-up interviews were conducted every six months thereafter for the first three years of the study and annually after that for seven years. In addition, interviews with collateral informants (mostly parents initially and peers thereafter) were conducted at baseline and annually for the first three years of data collection. Interviews were also conducted for a subgroup of adolescents when they left an institutional placement ("release" interviews). Data collection was completed in April 2010. Additional details regarding the enrollment process, study procedures, and sample characteristics can be found in Schubert *et al.* (2004).

A wide range of individual, social, and intervention-related variables were included in the interviews. These covered: (a) background characteristics (e.g., demographics, academic achievement, psychiatric diagnoses, offense history, neurological functioning, psychopathy, personality); (b) indicators of individual functioning (e.g., work and school status and performance, substance abuse, mental disorder, antisocial behavior); (c) psychosocial development and attitudes (e.g., impulse control, susceptibility to peer influence, perceptions of opportunity, perceptions of procedural justice, moral disengagement); (d) family context (e.g., household composition, quality of family relationships); (e) personal relationships (e.g., quality of romantic relationships and friendships, peer delinquency, contacts with caring adults); and (f) community context (e.g., neighborhood conditions, personal capital, social ties, and community involvement). Detailed information about the measures, the study design, and the investigators comprising the working group for the study can be found at www.pathwaysstudy.pitt.edu.

As noted above, data collection for the study was completed in April 2010. Efforts to retain adolescents across the study period were very successful, with approximately 90 percent of the sample interviewed at each follow-up point. Data for over 21,000 interviews and official records for each research participant (e.g., arrest data) are currently posted at the Inter-University Consortium on Political and Social Research at the University of Michigan. These data are currently available for researchers to use for their questions of interest. One of the major contributions of the study is a rich and readily accessible source of data regarding desistance in a highly policy relevant sample of adolescent offenders, with extensive information provided regarding measurement and previous findings provided on the study website (www.pathwaysstudy.pitt.edu).

A comprehensive study of this sort presents numerous opportunities to address specific questions related to the desistance process, and the working group of investigators and their collaborators have produced numerous papers on a variety of topics related to desistance and development in serious adolescent offenders. The group has produced findings related to: the relations among perceptions of procedural justice and subsequent offending; effects of changes in perceptions of risk/benefit of crime and subsequent offending; patterns of psychosocial maturity and criminal offending; the associations between substance use and offending; the outcomes of substance use treatment; the relations among acculturation and enculturation, substance use, and offending; family functioning in serious adolescent offenders; perceptions of opportunities and subsequent offending; neighborhood and gang effects on offending; and patterns of service provision/institutional care and offending. Some of the major findings so far have supported or sparked juvenile justice approaches that promote positive adolescent development, provide more community-based substance use treatment, limit the use of institutional placements, improve the overall climate of institutional settings, and implement ongoing risk/need assessments. The theoretically and policy relevant papers and issue briefs produced so far can be found on the study website given above.

Themes and issues

Despite the existing contributions that the Pathway study investigators and others have made toward enriching our view of how adolescents desist from antisocial behavior and extant policies that might promote this process, there is still much to be done. We do not yet have a totally clear view of how individual characteristics interact with contextual influences in the short run, or how developmental regularities set the stage for certain types of positive or negative outcomes. There are a range of issues yet to be addressed about the impact of system involvement or particular types of interventions.

How well this whole range of questions gets addressed (using the Pathways data and other studies) depends on the ability of future researchers to think clearly about their conceptualization of desistance, the mechanisms underpinning desistance, and how to carefully collect and analyze observations. As mentioned above, the investigators on the Pathways study certainly did their best (and continue to try) to master these tasks. In doing so, however, it has become apparent that there are several formidable issues that arise repeatedly and are difficult to address fully. Three of these are presented below. We believe they warrant consideration in future work if we really want to enrich our understanding of desistance and produce useful guidance for practice and policy.

Issue #1: accounting for the complicated nature of people's lives

Conceptualizing the process of reducing or quitting criminal activity or antisocial behavior can become complicated rather quickly. Questions of how to define desistance and how to test for its occurrence in an observed pattern of observations can be answered in numerous ways (Moffitt 1993; Bushway *et al.* 2001, 2003; Laub and Sampson 2001; Ezell and Cohen 2005). Characterizing and analyzing a single stream of repeated observations (like arrests) can present challenges in terms of assumptions about the processes behind observed declines in the values of the observations and the likely form of the distributions characterizing those observations. A considerable amount of intellectual effort has gone into methods for characterizing patterns of offending over time and detecting alterations from the expected patterns. While clearly a necessary first step, it is also clearly necessary to move past this line of work. Unfortunately, the field of desistance research runs the risk of greatly enriching the accuracy of describing a very limited slice of behavioral observations (self-reports or arrests), while missing the bigger picture of where these behaviors fit in the larger drama of a person's life (Mulvey 2014).

When interviewing individuals and listening to their stories, the complicated quality of their accounts is usually more striking than their patterns of offending. In a comprehensive review of an individual's life over a particular recall period, it is often stunning how many intersecting events can co-occur and how the occurrence of certain events affects the possibilities for other things to occur. Young people who are active in antisocial lifestyles are often not on regular schedules, with routinized and goal-directed activities. Work schedules can shift week-to-week, people can move in and out of residences with little notice or a clear plan of how long they are going to be there, close romantic relationships can erupt into public incidents with little notice, and all of these things can occur in close time to each other. Disagreements can produce immediate changes in living arrangements; a spending spree can result in the electricity being shut off and a subsequent visit from the child welfare officials; or a traffic ticket for an expired vehicle registration can make it difficult to get to work regularly, producing a job termination.

Being a marginal individual with few resources means that every day is spent living with the possibility of dramatic negative outcomes from some shift in resources. Small things are often difficult to accomplish, and particular events can have rippling effects. There is often little "play" in the balance between resources and needs, and unanticipated shifts can strain the overall system. The sense of people's lives, when you hear their stories, is that they live in a system best characterized by chaos theory; one ruled mostly by the initial conditions of their everyday world and one in which small perturbations in the system can have far-reaching impacts.

Modeling this kind of complex interconnectedness as a feature of the desistance process would be a massive task. Moreover, the effort would probably be misplaced. Building a complex model of social interactions or events in the same way that one might map out neural circuits in the brain is not within the grasp of social scientists. Recognizing the complexity and interconnectedness of events in people's lives, however, does have implications for how we structure more limited inquiries into desistance.

First, the undeniably complicated quality of life events makes it seem somewhat artificial to be looking for consistent effects of certain "turning points" in people's lives. It may be that limited financial resources (produced by some strain on spending, like an illness, or the loss of income from losing a job) could increase the overall likelihood of involvement in criminal activity. However, a number of other changes could also occur from such shifts in income, and having a fuller picture of the relations among these possible shifts and offending would also be valuable. For example, a drop in income could produce a change of residence and this shift could be related to crime opportunity.

Developing clearer mediated paths of factors related to desistance would seem to be more productive. Such studies at least take an initial step toward capturing some of the domino effect often seen in people's lives as they move into or out of criminal involvement. Given the fact that many of the paths into or out of periods of crime are probably the result of chained events, development of mediated models would provide the opportunity to assess the impact of multiple events in a sequence as well as comparisons of indirect and direct effects. This approach would more fully approximate the complex dynamics of desistance and would move beyond an accumulation of comparable estimates of the power of direct effects. Conceptualizing and testing multiple step models is often difficult analytically, but usually possible. Effort in this area could have considerable payoff for our understanding of desistance.

Qualitative studies of desistance have grappled with the complexity issue for some time. One merely has to look at some of the landmark studies in the field to realize how elucidating this approach can be for identifying the social factors that contribute to movements into and out of crime and antisocial behavior (e.g., Shaw 1930; Sutherland 1937; Matza 1964; Hagan and McCarthy 1998; Maruna 2001). These and other qualitative studies provide the bases for focused quantitative examinations of the effects of life context changes. The starting points for testing specific models are already there.

A recent study by Wright and his colleagues (2014) using the Pathways data illustrates this approach, i.e., starting with a commonsensical model of how moderation and mediation should work and then testing it. These researchers examined the direct and indirect effects of concentrated neighborhood disadvantage on youth reoffending from ages 18–22, when adolescents exert more choice on their living arrangements. They determined the direct effects of concentrated disadvantage on youth reoffending and indirect effects of individual-level mechanisms (e.g., unsupervised activities, exposure to violence). They also looked at the effect of a change in neighborhood conditions when a move occurred. They found that concentrated disadvantage is indirectly associated with youth reoffending primarily through its association with exposure to deviant peers. Such conceptualizations and analyses offer a richer picture of some of the types of dynamics that one observes when talking to people about their lives and the importance of how events "unfold" rather than if they "happened."

Issue #2: integrating developmental processes into the study of desistance

It is now generally accepted that adolescents are qualitatively different from adults (both neuropsychologically and psychosocially: Casey 2013; Scott and Steinberg 2008). Recent reviews have underscored the consistency of research findings indicating that adolescents follow a clear path of development (into their twenties) toward more reasoned decision making when emotionally aroused, less reliance on situational influences and peer influence, and increased future orientation (National Research Council 2012). It is reasonable to think that these changes are related to the process of desisting from crime during the period from adolescence into young adulthood.

This idea of psychological maturation is implied in one of the most widely cited psychological theories regarding the factors related to desistance (Moffitt 1993, 2003, 2006; Moffitt *et al.* 2002). In Moffitt's formulation of the patterns of involvement in antisocial behavior, she distinguishes between the vast majority of individuals, "adolescence-limited offenders," and the smaller proportion of adolescents who go on to adult crime, "life-course persistent offenders." Adolescent-limited offenders' are posited to become involved in antisocial behavior as a result of a desire to feel and appear more mature, yielding to peer pressure of imitating respected older adolescents and young adults. Those offenders who persist into adulthood are thought to have enduring neurological and cognitive deficits that, combined with environmental risk, lead to continued, and potentially lifelong, involvement in antisocial behavior.

This theoretical framework implies that psychosocial maturity plays a major role in persistence in antisocial activity. The actual development of maturity should reduce an individual's perceived need to engage in antisocial behavior to achieve this end, thereby contributing to desistance from crime and delinquency. Moreover, juvenile offenders who are relatively more psychosocially mature for their age, or who mature faster than their peers, should "age out" of offending sooner than others.

Psychosocial maturity is also a central feature of Gottfredson and Hirschi's (1990) general theory of crime. This approach proposes that deficits in self-control are the major factors behind criminal involvement. Self-control encompasses orientation toward the future (rather than immediate gratification), planning ahead (rather than impulsive decision making), physical restraint (rather than the use of aggression when frustrated), and concern for others (rather than self-centered or indifferent behavior) (Gottfredson and Hirschi 1990: 89). This theoretical orientation thus also predicts that, at any one point in time, individuals who are less mature than their peers should be more likely to engage in antisocial behavior.

Investigators from the Pathways study have shown a relationship between the development of psychosocial maturity and rate of criminal offending. The study used a framework from developmental psychology for conceptualizing and measuring maturity (Steinberg and Cauffman 1996; Cauffman and Steinberg 2000) that included three components: "temperance" (the ability to control impulses, including aggressive impulses); "perspective" (the ability to consider other points of view, including those that take into account longer-term consequences, or that take the vantage point of others); and "responsibility" (the ability to take personal responsibility for one's behavior and resist the coercive influences of others). These three components of psychosocial maturity were assessed at each of the follow-up interviews in the Pathways study, allowing for an examination of how changes in the measures of psychosocial maturity corresponded to those seen in criminal offending.

The researchers examining these aspects of development (Monahan *et al.* 2014) found a consistent pattern across each of the six individual indicators of psychosocial maturity (impulse control, suppression of aggression, consideration of others, future orientation, personal responsibility, resistance to peer influence) and a global index of psychosocial maturity. Individuals showed increases in all aspects of psychosocial maturity over time, but the rate of increase slowed in early adulthood. There is steady psychosocial maturation from age 14 to around age 22, after which point maturation begins to slow. The investigators then looked at how these patterns of psychosocial maturity looked in five identified trajectory groups characterizing patterns of self-reported offending over different ages. The question here was whether these groups with different patterns of offending looked different in their patterns of psychosocial maturity.

Figure 7.1 shows the pattern of development in the overall psychosocial maturity for each of the identified trajectory groups. Figure 7.2 shows the patterns of overall development of the temperance measure. As hypothesized, individuals in different antisocial trajectory groups differed in their absolute levels of psychosocial maturity as well as the extent to which their psychosocial maturity increased with age. As seen in both figures, offenders who desisted from antisocial activity during adolescence showed significantly greater increases in psychosocial maturity than those who persisted into adulthood.

These analyses regarding patterns of psychosocial development and offending are unique in the field. Despite the centrality of these constructs to how desistance might occur, there has been little work on growth of maturity of judgment and offending. These findings, however, seem to indicate that, just as immaturity is an important contributor to the emergence of much adolescent misbehavior, maturity (especially self-regulation) is an important developmental feature that accompanies the cessation of serious crime. Also, it appears that not all adolescents mature to the same degree; the chronic offenders have markedly blunted development.

The lack of research emphasis on the development of maturity in studies of desistance illustrates a larger set of issues for researchers in this area. First, it highlights the

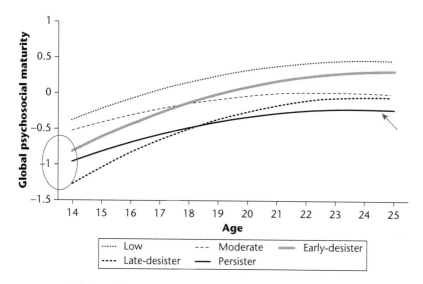

FIGURE 7.1 Global psychosocial change by age for each offending trajectory.

Source: Monahen *et al.* (2014).

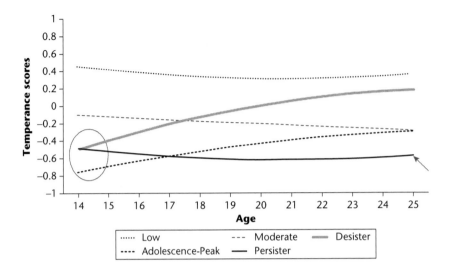

FIGURE 7.2 Temperance scores by age for each offending trajectory.

Source: Monahen *et al.* (2014).

opportunity to enrich our work with trajectory analyses to test connections between patterns of adolescent development and patterns of offending. Trajectory analyses of offending patterns provide ways to group cases that follow the same patterns of offending over time, but this post hoc description is only the first step toward theoretical formulations of how adolescents become or stay involved with offending at different developmental periods. It seems that the field is poised to move beyond description of offending over time toward richer work on explanation of changes in offending. There are approaches in other areas (e.g., developmental psychopathology, Cicchetti and Cohen 2006; substance use careers, Chassin *et al.* 2009) that could provide templates for richer theory about offending based on developmental analyses. While considerable work has been done on what produces variability in the patterns of offending over time, less work has been done on how patterns of change in one area mirror patterns of change in another (e.g., delinquency and substance use; for an illustrative exception, see Sullivan and Hamilton 2007).

Second, the above analyses indicate the potential payoff from integrating developmental science more systematically into work on patterns of desistance. Delinquency theories generally have an implicit "psychology" behind them about why adolescents engage in antisocial behavior or how they change over time (e.g., the idea of age-graded informal social control, Sampson and Laub 1993). Many times, however, these psychological explanations have been largely post hoc, derived from macro-level observations about associations of variables. For example, analyses of the "age–crime" curve are the starting point of Gottfredson and Hirschi's (1990) theoretical formulations about the primacy of self-control as a factor driving involvement in delinquency across different ages. The soundness of fitting psychological theories onto macro-level trends, however, is questionable.

It would seem more useful to look for expected effects on offending related to patterns of psychological development or during certain developmental periods. This would mean *starting* with what is known about adolescent development (about things like the dwindling effects of peer influence or the formulation of "possible selves"; see Oyserman and Markus 1990) and integrating this information into our research design, sampling, measurement, and analyses of delinquent behavior. If information about adolescent development is considered at the beginning rather than the end of inquiries into delinquency, it might point the way toward more focused, less global explanations of how adolescents begin or maintain their involvement in crime. For example, developmental stage (in terms of something like the ability to project into the future) might provide a powerful mediating or moderating variable for inquiries into how perceptions of the costs and benefits of crime affect subsequent offending. It is likely that this type of predictable developmental change could have a powerful effect on how well specific deterrence works with adolescent offenders (a question already explored in the Pathways data, see Anwar and Loughran 2011). More focused inquiries that take developmental features into account could refine the type of information that we generate regarding patterns of adolescent offending and point the way toward theories in line with what is known currently about developmental patterns and progressions.

Issue #3: defining effects and outcomes in terms of the patterns in people's lives and their perceptions of events

Desistance research generally focuses on the processes that promote movement out of an offending or substance-using lifestyle. It is often an attempt to shine a light on a demarcated period of an individual's life to see it more clearly and to identify the major moving parts and their interactions. Our perspective on this process, however, may or may not map onto how the process looks to the individual going through it.

This is not a new insight. As already mentioned, qualitative researchers have enriched the field's views of the process of desistance by recognizing and capitalizing on this reality. They have provided valuable leads about matters such as the importance of personal agency and the need to move in and out of acceptance of new social roles. In addition, Massoglia and Uggen (2007) have stressed the importance of subjective assessments of adulthood status as well as achieved desistance, systematically testing the importance of these factors to behavioral change. Consideration of individuals' perceptions of how a process occurred can identify themes and regularities of experience that guide and enrich quantitatively oriented inquiries. In addition, efforts to measure and test shifts in perceptions open up a rich area of inquiry about the processes of desistance.

Survey-oriented longitudinal researchers have paid less attention to the possible value of taking an individual's perspective into account. Comprehensive longitudinal studies value consistency of definition of constructs both across and within studies. In these types of studies, the researcher is primarily interested in looking for change in a construct over time and relating it to alterations in offending level or pattern over a given time period. For example, one might be concerned with whether increases in parental monitoring reduce subsequent offending. The value of a longitudinal design rests with the ability to place changes in one variable as before, or after changes in another variable. Gathering a sufficient number of observations defined the same way at regular intervals ensures that this can be done.

It is important to note, though, that certain events or periods of behavior may be qualitatively distinct and thus have different effects, depending on when they occur in the stream of experiences constituting an individual's life. We may interpret this variability among the effects of particular experiences as simply "error variance" in our estimation of an effect. Alternatively, it may be a systematic variation related to prior experiences or the situation of the individual at the time of its occurrence. The context of a person's life or their current perspective on an event may go a long way in explaining its impact, and consideration of these types of factors might strengthen analyses of existing longitudinal data sets as well as future data collection efforts.

This point became clear during an interview with a young man in the Pathways study who was confined in the Philadelphia House of Corrections at the time. One section of the interview asked about types of treatment received while in the facility, and this young man said that he had received a certificate for completion of anger management classes while he was there. One of the authors (EM) was interested in whether he could see an impact from this intervention, and inquired if they helped him in some specific ways. His response was telling, "I have six of those damn certificates on my wall and I am sitting here with eight months left on a felony assault charge. How the hell do you think these classes work?" His approach to the classes was obviously filtered by his prior experiences and the thinking about their effect was shortsighted. His first experience with this intervention was in all likelihood very different to his seventh, and the idea that any effect would be uniform across all these experiences, or across all the individuals receiving it, was simplistic.

The general idea here is that experiences, including interventions, occur in the stream of events constituting an individual's life. For instance, it is unlikely that a first institutional placement is experienced in the same way as a second or third institutional placement; the institutional experience itself, coupled with intervening events and the accumulation of new knowledge and skills, provide a new lens through which to view subsequent experiences. This means that analyses may be enriched by taking this possible time varying effect into account. Also, this simple observation implies that some effects may be best considered for their cumulative effects rather than their singular occurrence or disappearance. Having a job for an extended period, for instance, may generate different feelings about and influence from work than having a job for the first time and/or getting a job recently. In desistance research, however, there has been very limited exploration of the effects of extended periods of involvement in a particular behavioral pattern, although the payoffs for these types of analyses could be informative for the design of interventions to promote desistance. Finally, consideration of an individual's impressions about an event can also be integrated into longitudinal research designs to capture perceptions of experiences more directly. It can be argued that the perceptions of an event are as, or more, important than the occurrence of an event "if men define situations as real, they are real in their consequences" (Thomas and Thomas 1928: 572).

A set of analyses done in the Pathways study illustrates the potential value of this last point. In one set of analyses, investigators assessed the impact of placement and longer lengths of institutional stays on subsequent arrests and self-reported offending. These analyses (see Loughran, et al. 2009) used propensity score matching techniques to correct for the selection effect inherent in the placement process, and assessed the impact of an institutional stay on groups with comparable background characteristics. Results indicated that, once 66 background characteristics were controlled, placement in an institution showed no effect on later rates of re-arrest or self-reported antisocial activity. Adolescents on probation in the community had the same rates as adolescents placed in institutions.

Another set of analyses, however, looked at the perceptions of adolescents about aspects of the setting related to a recent institutional stay. Using interviews done close to the time an adolescent exited an institutional placement (on average, 12 days following release), these investigators examined various aspects of the institutional environment from the perspective of the adolescent (e.g., accounts of program operations and services provided, ratings regarding the participant's feelings of their safety in the facility; see Mulvey et al. 2010). The investigators then looked at the relations of these perceptions and adjustment in the community in the year after release from the institution (Schubert et al. 2012), in terms of: (1) system involvement (re-arrest or return to an institutional setting in the year following release); and (2) self-reported antisocial activities over that same time period.

Different perceptions were related to sizeable reductions in each outcome, after antisocial history and background characteristics of the individual adolescent were controlled. For example, system involvement was found to be related to two "structural" aspects of the institutional environment: having a primary caregiver and having someone assigned to help the youth plan for re-entry into the community. Resuming antisocial activity upon release was related to more affectively laden aspects of the institutional environment (e.g., institutional order, harshness) as well as the perception of high levels of antisocial peer influence in the institution. In addition, institutional settings that were rated more favorably across all the dimensions examined produced a much lower likelihood of re-arrest, even after accounting for background characteristics of the adolescent.

In one set of analyses, then, an institutional stay as an event in and of itself appears to have no discernible effect on later offending. This is a finding of great interest to policy makers assessing where to put limited resources. However, when one looks at how an adolescent perceives the environment of the institution during a recent stay, there is a strong relationship with subsequent offending. One could argue that certain individual factors that promote positive reports of an institutional stay also promote less offending in the community, and there is no adequate refutation of this claim. However, it could also be argued that not considering the influence of these perceptions of a setting misses the opportunity to capture an important nuance regarding the impact of an institutional stay on later outcomes, and there is also not currently information to refute this claim. Overall, institutional stays may show no discernible effect on reoffending, but the variability of perceptions of those stays might still be influential in determining their effectiveness.

Nonetheless, this provides an important lesson for researchers. These analyses demonstrate that obtaining data from the primary client within the juvenile justice system is feasible and potentially useful for gauging a setting's "health" as a treatment environment. These perceptions identify variability among institutional settings, and tap into aspects of the institutional environment that affect later outcomes. Current discussions about the use of evidence-based practices in juvenile justice have recognized that significant improvement in service provision will not simply be the result of establishing more "brand name" programs (Lipsey *et al.* 2010). The context within which those programs are delivered appears to be an important consideration as well, and settings can and should be examined with an eye toward improving features that might help innovative programs flourish and youth succeed. Getting perceptions of an individual experiencing an event like an institutional stay may provide an alternative, and programmatically valuable, take on how the impact of that experience unfolds.

Conclusion

Research on desistance is establishing itself as a potentially rich area for inquiry that can shape future theories about involvement in crime and what we can do to improve criminal justice practices and policy. It is a fresh view of what keeps people in or moves people out of lives of crime. It has a commonsense appeal.

At the same time, research on desistance faces formidable challenges. It requires complex field designs as well as sophisticated qualitative and quantitative analyses to tap its potential. Competent desistance research will continue to rest on the ability of researchers to conceptualize the process of interest clearly, measure its dimensions carefully, and analyze its patterns cleanly.

This chapter has called for thinking about how to collect and analyze data in ways that can more closely reflect the complicated processes connected with this phenomenon. Three points are emphasized in this regard. First, we have to recognize the complicated interlocking influences in people's lives. Only by doing this can we construct mediated and moderated models that move us toward accurate portrayals of how people move in and out of criminal involvement. Second, we have to consider developmental science as a starting point for inquiry rather than a post hoc explanation. Analyses can be enriched by thinking about adolescent and young adult development as a powerful backdrop to whatever regularities we might observe in terms of antisocial behavior. Adolescents offenders are, after all, adolescents first and offenders second. Finally, taking an individual's life events and perspective into account can expand our view of how life's regularities and events might influence the desistance process. These steps seem necessary for this line of research to deliver on its enormous potential.

References

Anwar, S. and Loughran, T. (2011), "Testing a Bayesian learning theory of deterrence among serious juveniles offenders," *Criminology* 49(3): 667–698.

Bennett, W., DiIulio, J. and Walters, J. (1996), *Body Count: Moral Poverty and How to Win America's War Against Crime and Drugs*. New York: Simon and Schuster.

Bushway, S. D., Thornberry, T. P. and Krohn, M. D. (2003), "Desistance as a developmental process: A comparison of static and dynamic approaches," *Journal of Quantitative Criminology* 19: 129–153.

Bushway, S. D., Piquero, A. R., Broidy, L. M., Cauffman, E. and Mazerolle, P. (2001), "An empirical framework for studying desistance as a process," *Criminology* 39: 491–515.

Casey, B. J. (2013), "The teenage brain: An overview," *Current Directions in Psychological Science*, pp. 80–81, doi:10.1177/0963721413486971.

Cauffman, E. and Steinberg, L. (2000), "(Im)maturity of judgment in adolescence: Why adolescents may be less culpable than adults," *Behavioral Sciences and the Law* 18: 741–760.

Chassin, L., Hussong, A. and Beltran, I. (2009), "Adolescent substance use," in Lerner, R. M. and Steinberg, L. (eds) *Handbook of Adolescent Psychology, Volume 1, Individual Bases of Adolescent Development*, third edition. Hoboken, NJ: John Wiley & Sons, pp. 723–765.

Cicchetti, D. and Cohen, D. J. (ed.), (2006), *Developmental Psychopathology, Volume 1, Theory and Method*, second edition. Hoboken, NJ: John Wiley & Sons.

Curran, P., Howard, A., Bainter, S., Lane, S. and McGinley, J. (2014), "The separation of between-person and within-person components of individual change over time: A latent curve model with structured residuals," *Journal of Consulting and Clinical Psychology* 82: 879–894.

Edens, J. F., Skeem, J. L., Cruise, K. R. and Cauffman, E. (2001), "Assessment of 'juvenile psychopathy' and its association with violence," *Behavioral Sciences and the Law* 19: 53–80.

Ezell, M. E. and Cohen, L. E. (2005), *Desisting From Crime: Continuity and Change in Long-Term Crime Patterns of Serious Chronic Offenders*. Oxford, UK: Oxford University Press.

Farrall, S. and Maruna, S. (2004), "Desistance-focused criminal justice policy research: Introduction to a special issue on desistance from crime and public policy," *The Howard Journal of Criminal Justice* 43(4): 358–367.

Giordano, P., Cernkovich, S. and Rudolph, J. (2002), "Gender, crime, and desistance: Toward a theory of cognitive transformation," *American Journal of Sociology* 107(4): 990–1064.

Glueck, S. and Glueck, E. (1950), *Unraveling Juvenile Delinquency*. New York: Commonwealth Fund.

Gottfredson, M. R. and Hirschi, T. (1990), *A General Theory of Crime*. Stanford, CA: Stanford University Press.

Hagan, J. and McCarthy, B. (1998), *Mean Streets: Youth Crime and Homelessness*. New York: Cambridge University Press.

Horney, J., Osgood, D. W. and Marshall, I. H. (1995), "Criminal careers in the short-term: Intra-individual variability in crime and its relation to local life circumstances," *American Sociological Review*, 60: 655–673, doi:10.2307/2096316.

Laub, J. H. and Sampson, R. J. (2001), "Understanding desistance from crime," in Tonry, M. (ed.) *Crime and Justice*, volume 28. Chicago, IL: University of Chicago Press, pp. 1–69.

Laub, J. H. and Boonstoppel, S. L. (2011), "Understanding desistance from juvenile offending: Challenges and opportunities," in Feld, B. and Bishop, D. (eds) *The Handbook of Juvenile Crime and Juvenile Justice*. New York: Oxford University Press.

Lipsey, M. W., Howell, J. C., Kelly, M. R., Chapman, G. and Carver, D. (2010), *Improving the Effectiveness of Juvenile Justice Programs: A New Perspective on Evidence-Based Practice*. Washington, DC: Georgetown University, Center for Juvenile Justice.

Loeber, R., Stouthamer-Loeber, M., Van Kammen, W. B. and Farrington, D. P. (1991), "Initiation, escalation, and desistance in juvenile offending and their correlates," *Journal of Criminal Law and Criminology* 82: 36–82.

Loughran, T., Mulvey, E. P., Schubert, C. A., Fagan, J., Losoya, S. H. and Piquero, A. R. (2009), "Estimating a dose–response relationship between length of stay and future recidivism in serious juvenile offenders," *Criminology* 47(3): 699–740.

Maruna, S. (2001), *Making Good: How Ex-Convicts Reform and Rebuild Their Lives.* Washington, DC: American Psychological Association Books.

Massoglia, M. and Uggen, C. (2007), "Subjective desistance and the transition to adulthood," *Journal of Contemporary Criminal Justice* 23(1): 90–103.

Matza, D. (1964). *Delinquency and Drift.* New York: Wiley.

Moffitt, T. E. (1993), "Adolescence-limited and life-course persistent antisocial behavior: A developmental taxonomy," *Psychological Review* 100: 674–701.

Moffitt, T. E. (2003), "Life-course persistent and adolescence-limited antisocial behavior: A 10-year research review and a research agenda," in Lahey, B. B., Moffitt, T. E. and Caspi, A. (eds) *Causes of Conduct Disorder and Juvenile Delinquency.* New York: Guilford Press, pp. 49–75.

Moffitt, T. E. (2006), "Life-course-persistent versus adolescence-limited antisocial behavior," in Cicchetti, D. and Cohen, D. J. (eds) *Handbook of Developmental Psychopathology,* second edition. Hoboken, NJ: Wiley, pp. 570–598.

Moffitt, T. E., Caspi, A., Harrington, H. and Milne, B. J. (2002), "Males on the life-course persistent and adolescence-limited antisocial pathways: Follow-up at age 26 years," *Development and Psychopathology* 14: 179–207.

Monahan, K., Steinberg, L., Cauffman, E. and Mulvey, E. (2014), "Psychosocial (im)maturity from adolescence to early adulthood: Distinguishing between adolescence-limited and persisting antisocial behavior," *Development and Psychopathology* 24(4): 1093–1105.

Mulvey, E. P. (2014), "Using developmental science to reorient our thinking about criminal offending in adolescence," *Journal of Research in Crime and Delinquency* 51(4): 467–479.

Mulvey, E. P., Schubert, C. A. and Odgers, C. A. (2010), "A method of measuring organizational functioning in juvenile justice facilities using resident ratings," *Criminal Justice and Behavior* 37(11): 1255–1277.

Mulvey, E. P., Steinberg, L., Fagan, J., Cauffman, E., Piquero, A. R., Chassin, L., Knight, G., Brame, R., Schubert, C., Hecker, T. and Losoya, S. (2004), "Theory and research on desistance from antisocial activity among serious adolescent offenders," *Youth Violence and Juvenile Justice* 2(3): 213–236.

Nagin, D. S. (2005), *Group-based Modeling of Development.* Cambridge, MA: Harvard University Press.

National Research Council/Institute of Medicine (2001), "Juvenile crime, juvenile justice. panel on juvenile crime: Prevention, treatment, and control," in McCord, J., Widom, C. and Crowell, N. (eds) *Committee on Law and Justice and Board on Children, Youth, and Families.* Washington, DC: The National Academies Press.

National Research Council (2012), "Reforming juvenile justice: A developmental approach. Committee on assessing juvenile justice reform," in Bonnie, R. J., Johnson, R. L., Chemers, B. M. and Schuck, J. A. (eds) *Committee on Law and Justice, Division of Behavioral and Social Sciences and Education.* Washington, DC: The National Academies Press.

Oyserman, D. and Markus, H. R. (1990), "Possible selves and delinquency," *Journal of Personality and Social Psychology* 59(1): 112–125.

Piquero, A. R., Farrington, D. P. and Blumstein, A. (2003), "The criminal career paradigm," in Tonry, M. (ed.) *Crime and Justice: A Review of Research.* Chicago, IL: University of Chicago Press, pp. 359–506.

Sampson, R. and Laub, J. (1993), *Crime in the Making: Pathways and Turning Points through Life*. Cambridge, MA: Harvard University Press.

Schubert, C. A., Mulvey, E. P., Loughran, T. and Losoya, S. (2012), "Perceptions of institutional experience and community outcomes for serious adolescent offenders," *Criminal Justice and Behavior* 39(1): 71–93.

Schubert, C. A., Mulvey, E. P., Steinberg, L., Cauffman, E., Losoya, S., Hecker, T., Chassin, L. and Knight, G. (2004), "Operational lessons from the Pathways to Desistance project," *Youth Violence and Juvenile Justice* 2(3): 237–255.

Scott, E. and Steinberg, L. (2008), *Rethinking Juvenile Justice*. Cambridge, MA: Harvard University Press.

Shaw, C. (1930), *The Jack-Roller: A Delinquent Boy's Own Story*. Chicago, IL: The University of Chicago Press.

Steinberg, L. and Cauffman, E. (1996), "Maturity of judgment in adolescence: Psychosocial factors in adolescent decision making," *Law and Human Behavior* 20: 249–272.

Styve, G. J., MacKenzie, D. L., Gover, A. R. and Mitchell, O. (2000), "Perceived conditions of confinement: A national evaluation of juvenile boot camps and traditional facilities," *Law and Human Behavior* 24(3): 297–308.

Sullivan, C. J. and Hamilton, Z. K. (2007), "Exploring careers in deviance: A joint trajectory analysis of criminal behavior and substance use in an offender population," *Deviant Behavior* 28(6): 497–523.

Sutherland, E. (1937), *The Professional Thief*. Chicago, IL: The University of Chicago Press.

Thomas, W. I. and Thomas, D. (1928), *The Child in America*, second edition. New York: Knopf.

Thornberry, T. P., Giordano, P. C., Uggen, C., Matsuida, M., Masten, A. S., Bulten, E. and Donker, A. G. (2012), "Explanations for offending," in Loeber, R. and Farrington, D. P. (eds) *From Juvenile Delinquency to Adult Crime: Criminal Careers, Justice Policy, and Prevention*. New York: Oxford University Press, pp. 47–85.

Wolfgang, M. E., Figlio, R. M. and Sellin, T. (1972), *Delinquency in a Birth Cohort*. Chicago, IL: University of Chicago Press.

Wright, K. A., Byungbae, K., Chassin, L., Losoya, S. H. and Piquero, A. R. (2014), "Ecological context, concentrated disadvantage, and youth reoffending: Identifying the social mechanisms in a sample of serious adolescent offenders," *Journal of Youth and Adolescence*, DOI: 10.1007/s10964-014-0173-0.

Zimring, F. E. (1998), *American Youth Violence*. New York: Oxford University Press.

Zimring, F. E. and Fagan, J. (eds) (2000), *The Changing Borders of Juvenile Justice: Transfer of Adolescents to the Criminal Court*. Chicago, IL: University of Chicago Press.

8

HOW IMPORTANT ARE LIFE-COURSE TRANSITIONS IN EXPLAINING DESISTANCE?

Examining the extent to which marriage, divorce and parenthood account for the age–crime relationship in former juvenile delinquents

Arjan Blokland and Niek De Schipper

Introduction

Age is one of the strongest predictors of crime (Farrington 1986). After a sudden peak in offending in the late adolescent years, with age follows a more gradual decrease. While some variation exists for different types of crime, this general pattern appears robust across historical time, geographical and cultural location, and across different types of data criminologists have used to study the development of crime over the life-course. The robustness of the age–crime relationship across different contexts has led some researchers to conclude that no contextual factors can explain why crime declines with age, because this would imply that the configuration of these contextual factors needs to be highly similar across time and place as well (Hirschi and Gottfredson 1983). In response, these researchers have turned inward and have explained the winding down of crime with age as a product of the maturation of the individual. Contrarily, the vantage point of life-course criminology is that criminal development cannot be understood in complete isolation from the individual's larger life-course. Instead, life-course criminologists claim that transitions and trajectories in life-course domains other than crime can alter the likelihood of offending (Blokland and Nieuwbeerta 2010). In as far as these transitions bring about a decline in offending and their age trend matches the age trend in crime, these transitions can account for the reduced offending found in adults.

While these different interpretations of the age–crime relationship have given rise to much controversy, surprisingly few studies have directly addressed the issue. This is despite Osgood (2005) offering a clear and readily applied strategy to do so. More specifically, Osgood (2005, 2010) suggests comparing a multilevel model, which includes only the age trend, with a model that besides the age trend also incorporates theoretically relevant time varying covariates. The observed reduction in the coefficients for the age trend between these subsequent models provides a useful basis for judging how much the decline in crime with age is explained by age-related changes in these time varying variables.

Here we use data from the Criminal Career and Life-Course Study (CCLS) to examine desistance from crime during adulthood in a sample of convicted juvenile delinquents. Taking a life-course approach to criminal development, we first assess the impact three major life-course transitions – marriage, divorce and parenthood – have on crime. Next, we examine the extent to which these transitions are able to account for the age trend in offending during the adult years. Finally, we compare our findings across different types of crime.

Defining desistance from crime

Any substantive explanation of a phenomenon requires an adequate definition of the phenomenon to be explained. What do life-course criminologists mean when they talk about desistance? Early criminal career research focused on the termination of offending, defined as the continued absence of criminal behaviour. As the mirror image of the onset of offending, termination marked the end of the individual's criminal career. In addition to the methodological challenges operationalizing termination in empirical research – only the death of the individual would secure no future offending and absolve the researcher from further follow-up – for many offenders, disengaging from crime appeared not to be the overnight event this term suggested. For those embedded in a criminal lifestyle, desisting from crime requires a change in thinking patterns, a change in routine behaviours and a change in the social environment that elicits these thoughts and behaviours – or at least a shift in the perception of that environment – all of which in isolation, but even more so in conjunction, are likely to be gradual rather than sudden events. Referring to these gradual changes, Laub and Sampson (2001) define desistance as the causal process that supports the termination of offending. Defined this way, desistance thus covers some period prior to termination, as well as the period after termination – maintaining the individual's terminated state and preventing future offending. Besides being more grounded in offenders' own experiences, defining desistance as a process has the advantage that it relaxes its operationalization from a complete absence of offending, to that of a marked decrease over time in offending behaviour, regardless of the eventual resulting level of offending (Mulvey et al. 2004). Most commonly, desistance refers to a decline in the frequency of offending, but desistance could in principle also consist of a discernible shift in the other aspects of the criminal career, for example the seriousness, or variety, of offending. Theoretically as well as empirically, desistance under this definition does require some nontrivial level of criminal involvement for offenders to disengage from (Laub and Sampson 2003: 22).

Both aggregate and individual level data suggest that desistance occurs with age. As offenders grow older, they tend to commit fewer crimes. Whether this is true for all offenders, or whether a sub-type of particularly chronic offenders exists that persists rather than desists from crime with age, has been the cause of some debate, but at present the consensus reached seems to be that, while not all at similar rates, all offenders show a decline in offending with age. That is, the same offender at age 48 is generally less active than he or she was at age 18, or even at age 28. While delinquency may be part of growing up, desistance seems to be part of growing old.

Explaining desistance from crime

Three broad theoretical perspectives have been offered to explain why criminal behaviour decreases with age, differing most prominently in the extent to which they allow individual development to divert from the overall downward trend.

First, age theories deny that anything other than age itself can account for desistance. According to these theories, it is the 'inexorable aging of the organism' (Gottfredson and Hirschi 1990: 141) that causes crime to decrease. In fact, desistance is argued as not being explained by anything other than age and to occur regardless of what else happens in the individual's life-course (Wilson and Herrnstein 1985). As the chronological clock ticks at the same speed for everyone, age theory leaves little room for individual variation desistance.

Developmental theories, on the other hand, state that desistance is the product of psychological and biological developments that tend to accompany age (Gove 1985). With age, individuals become better at controlling their impulses, desire less stimulation, grow in their moral reasoning and evaluate their behaviour against a changing self-image. Biological factors that correlate with age, like decreasing testosterone levels, may also contribute to the decreasing trend in offending (Collins 2004). Developmental theories offer more opportunity for individual variation than does age theory. While crime is still seen as something that individuals grow out of, the correlation of psychological and biological factors with age is not perfect: some individuals may be wise for their (chronological) age, whereas others may fail to grow up and act their age. Developmental notions thus allow for individual variation in the processes underlying desistance and therefore in desistance itself. Yet, while the psychological/biological clock may tick at different speeds for different individuals, developmental theories still employ a largely unidirectional conceptualization of development. Like water flowing downstream, falling back to a former state is exceptional – if not impossible – limiting the extent to which individuals can diverge from the normative developmental pattern.

Finally, life-course theory offers the most flexible account of development. Against age theories, life-course theory argues that ascribing development solely to age does not offer any substantive explanation. Age, if not broken down into its developmental components, is nothing but an empty variable (Dannefer 1984). Psychological and biological changes, as recognized by developmental theories, are important components of age, but so are the types and duration of experiences individuals encounter during their life span (Rutter 1989). Life-course research puts emphasis on the plasticity that characterizes human development across the entire life span (Blokland 2015) and also argues against the law-like conception of development present in many developmental accounts of desistance. Instead, regardless of stable or experiential features, human development is thought to remain open to outside influence resulting from random events, introducing a level of unpredictability in the life-course. Thus, unlike age theory, life-course theory interprets change directly by reference to what else happens in the life-course.

According to the life-course perspective, the interwoven nature of the many developmental trajectories that together make up the life-course implies that randomly occurring events and transitions in one trajectory can substantially alter the course of development in another. With regard to desistance from offending, life-course theorists have focused primarily on the effect transitioning to adult social roles has on offending. Transitions to adult social roles, like marriage or parenthood, have the potential to disassociate individuals from their delinquent pasts, provide supervision and social support, change routine activities and offer the opportunity for the personal and social transformation needed to disengage from a criminal lifestyle (Laub and Sampson 2003: 148). Flipside to the susceptibility to outside influence is that events and transitions that decrease supervision and social support, promote criminogenic activities or challenge the conformist self-image can equally affect offending, leading to acceleration rather than deceleration of offending (Blokland 2015). To stay with the clock analogy, over and above chronological and developmental time, life-course theory thus allows life-course transitions to reset the clock – either clockwise or anticlockwise – to an entirely different time zone.

The effects of life-course transitions on offending

Of all life-course transitions theoretically linked to desistance, the good-marriage effect has probably been researched most extensively. Reviews of this research show that marriage generally has a dampening effect on offending, decreasing the likelihood of crime and other types of deviance (Craig *et al.* 2014). Using the full CCLS sample, Blokland and Nieuwbeerta (2005) for example, found that being married reduced convictions by nearly one-third for low-rate offenders, and by over half for moderate rate offenders. This study, however, did not find a marriage effect for the most high-rate offenders. In a follow-up study, the beneficial effect of marriage was found across different marriage cohorts (Bersani *et al.* 2009). Likewise, Sampson and Laub found evidence of marriage promoting desistance in a sample of previously institutionalized boys (Sampson and Laub 1993; Laub and Sampson 2003). Using a counterfactual approach to control for selection effects, Sampson *et al.* (2006) found that married offenders had a 35 per cent lower chance of conviction compared to those remaining single. Furthermore, Laub *et al.* (1998) argued for a snowballing effect of marriage that increased with the growing social bond emerging from continued investment in the union. In support of their argument, their research showed that – over and above the instantaneous effect of being married – the longer offenders were married, the lower their odds of conviction.

While entering a union seems to benefit desistance, experiencing break up may have the opposite effect. Sampson and Laub (1993) found that low marital attachment, as measured by separation and divorce, was associated with higher future crime levels. Using data from the Cambridge Study in Delinquent Development, Farrington and West (1995) found that the men in their sample had a 44 per cent higher crime rate during the times they were divorced than during the times they were married. Blokland and Nieuwbeerta (2005) also found that being separated increased registered offending. Distinguishing between offenders following different offending trajectories, their study showed that even the most frequent and persistent offenders were sensitive to the negative effects of separation. A study by Bersani and Eggleston-Doherty (2013) found that men in their sample were 52 per cent more likely to be arrested in the months after they were divorced. Moreover, this latter study found that the negative effect of divorce was enduring and did not decline – or increase – with additional years of being divorced.

The prior empirical literature on the association between parenthood and desistance is more mixed (Siennick and Osgood 2008). Whereas qualitative studies often pinpoint parenthood as an important transitional event in the lives of former offenders (e.g. McIvor et al. 2004), especially for males, quantitative findings are less conclusive. For instance, while the men studied by Sampson and Laub reported that they experienced becoming a parent as a life-changing event, quantitative analyses showed no effect of parenthood on crime (Laub and Sampson 2003). Likewise, Blokland and Nieuwbeerta (2005) did not find any effect of parenthood. Kerr and colleagues (2011) did find parenthood to have a negative effect on crime, though this effect was limited to self-reported offending and not observed when analysing officially registered offending. These researchers also found that the beneficial effect of parenthood tended to increase over time. Massoglia and Uggen (2007) even found that parenthood increased offending among those with prior arrests.

Finally, some studies suggest that the effects of parenthood may be conditional on the timing of this transition in the life-course. Farrington and West (1995), for example, found that men who had a child within a marital union had lower crime rates compared to men having a child out of wedlock or experiencing a 'shotgun' wedding. Savolainen (2009) also found parenthood to decrease offending, but only for married couples. Finally, in a study of previously institutionalized youths Zoutewelle-Terovan et al. (2012) likewise found the 'full-family-package' of marriage and parenthood to have the largest impact on desistance.

Explaining the age–crime relationship

While a number of previous studies have used a similar approach to explaining the age trend in criminal behaviour as the one we will use here, only two cover the later adult period, and only one of them was based on longitudinal data. In a study of National Youth Survey data on youths born in the 1960s, Warr (1993) found that between ages 11–21, age effects could be eliminated or reversed for underage drinking, smoking marijuana, theft over 50 dollars and burglary, but not for cheating and minor theft, by controlling for time spent with deviant peers. Based on data from the Monitoring the Future study covering the period between ages 18–26 Osgood *et al.* (1996) were able to show that 26.8 per cent of the decline in self-reported criminal behaviour during this time could be attributed to age-related differences in unstructured socializing with peers. Tittle and Grasmick (1997) found that controlling for age trends in self-control, opportunity, community integration, interpersonal integration, religiosity, stress, dissatisfaction and self-esteem each by itself resulted in a maximum drop of 16 per cent (community integration) of the magnitude of the age effect, while the combined effect of these variables together resulted in a 31 per cent decrease in the magnitude of the age effect on major theft. The decrease in the age effect after controlling for these variables was less pronounced for fraud (21 per cent), minor theft (13 per cent), tax cheating (8 per cent) and using or threatening to use force (5 per cent). While the latter study covered much of the adult period, the data used were cross-sectional, preventing the within-individual type of analyses needed to optimally control for selection effects.

In the most comprehensive study to date including many different explanatory variables, Sweeten *et al.* (2013), using data from the Pathways to Desistance study – a US-based longitudinal study of over 1,300 serious juvenile delinquents – found that 69 per cent of the drop in crime from ages 15 to 25 could be explained by co-occurring changes in theoretically relevant concepts like social learning (49 per cent), strain (41 per cent) and social control (26 per cent). Especially relevant for the current study is that of all social control variables, marriage most strongly influenced crime, reducing self-reported crime variety by 28 per cent. While the effect of cohabitation was also negative, being in a dating relationship and becoming a parent tended to have an increasing rather than decreasing effect during the age period under study.

Current study

The current study addresses three related questions. First, we ask to what extent there is desistance from crime in our sample of convicted juvenile delinquents during adulthood, as reflected in a reduced likelihood of conviction with increasing age. Next, we ask to what extent life-course transitions affect the likelihood of conviction. Finally, we assess the extent to which going through these life-course transitions can explain desistance from crime during the adult years. To assess the generalizability of our results, we repeat the above analyses distinguishing between different types of offences.

Data and methods

The CCLS

For our current analysis we use data from the CCLS. The CCLS is based on a 4 per cent sample of all criminal cases either waived by the Dutch public prosecutor or irrevocably disposed of by a Dutch judge in 1977. Due to the large numbers, traffic offences were undersampled at 2 per cent, while less frequent and serious offences, including drug offences, sexual offences and criminal cases pertaining to manslaughter and murder were oversampled. Data from the CCLS have been used in previous work to describe longitudinal patterns of offending far into adult age (Blokland et al. 2005; Blokland and Van Os 2010), to examine the associations between life-course transitions and criminal career development (Blokland and Nieuwbeerta 2005) and to assess intergenerational transmission of crime (Van De Rakt et al. 2008). Previous studies also estimated the (collateral) effects of incarceration (Blokland and Nagin 2012; Nieuwbeerta et al. 2009). Four criminal career trajectories were distinguished in the data, among which was a persistent pathway characterized by an early onset and elevated level of convictions – disproportionately for property crime – far into the adult years (Blokland et al. 2005). Furthermore, evidence of an age–diversity curve emerged, in which diversification between early adolescence and young adulthood was followed by specialization during the later adult years (Nieuwbeerta et al. 2011). The data show evidence of a 'good-marriage effect' on crime for both men and women and across birth cohorts (Bersani and Van Schellen 2014). In turn, crime was found to reduce the likelihood of marriage and increase the likelihood of divorce (Van Schellen et al. 2012). Having an ever-convicted father was shown to increase the likelihood of convictions among the children of the original sample members. Furthermore, in the years directly following a father's conviction, the child's probability of being convicted was temporarily elevated, especially during the child's adolescent years (Van De Rakt et al. 2010). Finally, using matching techniques, a number of studies focused on the detrimental effects incarceration had on subsequent offending and life-course development (Apel et al. 2010; Snodgrass et al. 2011).

Current sample

As we are currently interested in explaining adult desistance – which by definition requires prior criminal involvement – here we select only those individuals within the larger CCLS sample who were aged between 12 – which is the minimum age of criminal responsibility in the Netherlands – and 20 at the time of their 1977 adjudication.

In 2000, and again in 2005, demographical data on the entire sample were gathered from the municipal registry. The Dutch municipal registry has information on all Dutch residents, but not on those not born or officially residing in the Netherlands (e.g. tourists, illegal immigrants). Criminal career data for non-residents are likely to be incomplete, as foreign convictions are not registered. Therefore, offenders not registered in the municipal data were excluded from further analyses. Closer inspection of the municipal data revealed first-degree family relationships among a limited number of original sample members (e.g. father and son, marital partners). To avoid these kinds of dependencies in the data in each case, one individual from these dyads was also excluded.

Based on the above criteria, 1,467 offenders were initially selected who were under age 21 when convicted in 1977 and for whom municipal data were available.

Given that only 75 of these juvenile delinquents were women, here we concentrate on the 1,392 male juvenile delinquents in our sample. Furthermore, as was evident from the municipal data, 118 of these male offenders were already married or had become parents prior to age 21 and thus – by necessity given the above selection criteria – prior to being convicted in 1977. As these offenders had a 100 per cent chance of being convicted at least once while being married or a parent, including them in the analysis would bias the estimated effect these transitions have on crime. Finally, nine of the remaining males did not survive to reach 21 and thus could not contribute to the analysis of desistance past that age. Therefore, we base our analysis on the 1,265 registered male juvenile offenders who lived to become at least 21 years of age and who were not married and did not have any children prior to their 1977 registration.

Criminal career data

The criminal careers for the entire sample were reconstructed based on the General Documentation Files (GDF) from the Criminal Record Office. These GDF include information on all criminal cases the police registered at the Dutch public prosecutor's office, including the date of registration, the nature of the offence, the type of adjudication and – when applicable – the sentence imposed. Only cases that ended in a guilty verdict or a prosecutorial waiver because of policy reasons were counted as convictions, thereby excluding cases ending in an acquittal or those cases waived by the prosecution for technical reasons, such as lack of evidence (see Block *et al.* 2010 for details). The most recent extraction of the GDF was made in 2005, therefore we currently have data available on the conviction history of all juvenile delinquents sampled from age 12 to their age in 2005, or – for those who died prior to 2005 – their age of death. Using these data, a binary variable was created indicating all years in which at least one criminal case was registered. Besides a container measure counting all registrations regardless of the nature of the underlying offence, we also constructed different measures for different subsets of offences, including violent offences (e.g. assault, rape, murder), property offences (e.g. theft, burglary, embezzlement) and traffic offences (e.g. hit-and-run, driving under the influence). Not only are these offences the most prevalent in the adult period in the current sample – making up respectively 10, 43 and 12 per cent of all registered offences during the follow-up – they also intuitively differ in seriousness.

Official data on life-course transitions

Data on life-course transitions were taken from the Dutch municipal registry, a national database containing the dates of marriage and divorce, as well as the birthdates of any children born to the individual under scrutiny. The municipal registry only pertains to officially registered partnerships. In the Netherlands cohabiting partners have been able to register their partnership in the municipal registry since 1998. For the years prior to 1998, the available data thus pertain only to those legally married, excluding all cohabitations; while after 1998 our data also pertain to cohabiting partners who had their union registered in the municipal registry.[1] Similarly, divorce pertains to the ending of any registered relationship, be it marriage or – after 1998 – cohabitation. Also, we do not distinguish voluntary separation from being widowed, both are coded as 'divorce' in our models. Given the age range under study, widowers are unlikely to constitute more than a small proportion of all registered separations. Finally, in the current analysis parenthood refers only to the birth of biological children, excluding stepchildren and foster children. While children born within a marriage are automatically registered to the male partner, children born out of wedlock have to be officially recognized by the supposed father before they are registered as such.[2] We have no information from the municipal register on whether biological children actually lived with and were raised by their biological parents.

Analytic strategy

To address our research questions, the analyses will proceed in three steps. First, to capture desistance from crime in our sample of juvenile delinquents we estimate a multilevel logistic model predicting conviction in each year between ages 21 and 50, allowing for a quadratic age trend. In longitudinal data years are nested within individuals and using a multilevel model allows us to control for the dependence of repeated observations for the same individual. Second, as recommended by Osgood (2010), we estimate the impact of marriage, divorce and parenthood by adding group mean centred exploratory variables to this basic model. To do so, based on the municipal data, we first constructed binary indicators for each state of interest that were coded '1' in each year the person was in the particular state and '0' other-wise. Being single, married or divorced were coded as mutually exclusive categories. Being a parent reflected each year that the person was a parent to at least one biological child under 18. Next, for each person in our sample, we computed the mean for each explanatory variable across the entire follow-up and, for each year, subtracted that mean value from the value of the binary indicator. This way, the explanatory variables have a mean of zero for every respondent and therefore do not refer to between-person differences, but only to within-individual variation in the likelihood of conviction given being in a particular state.

To account for potential gradual effects of these life-course transitions, we also constructed continuous variables that were coded '0' in each year a person entered a particular state, and subsequently increased by one for each year that person remained in that particular state. So, a single person who married in 1980 and got divorced in 1985, would score '1' on the dichotomous marriage variable in 1980, but would score '0' on the marriage duration variable in 1980. While that same person would continue to score '1' on the marriage variables for each year between 1981 and 1984, the marriage duration variable would increase from '1' to '4' within that same period. Both the marriage and marriage duration variable would be reset to '0' in 1985 as a result of the divorce. As such, the dichotomous variables capture the instantaneous effect of transitioning into a particular state, while the continuous variables capture the additional effects of remaining in a particular state for a prolonged period of time. As we are interested in within-individual effects of transitions, the duration variables were also group mean centred.[3] Finally, we assess the extent to which these transitions were able to account for desistance from crime between ages 21 and 50 by comparing the age parameters from the full model to those from the first. To the extent the age coefficients in the latter model are reduced and no longer significant, desistance from crime during the adult years can be said to result from age-graded transitions into adult social roles.

Results

Descriptives

Table 8.1 describes the basic characteristics for our current sample. By definition, age in the sampling year ranges from 12 to 20, with a mean of 17.5 and a median of 18. Given a follow-up of almost three decades, this means our analysis of desistance covers a large part of the adult years. While all individuals in our sample had a criminal case registered before age 21, for a small minority (4.9 per cent) this registration did not pertain to a 'conviction' according to our current definition, but for example to a case that ended in a technical waiver. Well over two-thirds of those registered before age 21, however, had multiple convictions, with an average of 4.77 convictions. The average age of onset – the age of first conviction of any kind – in the current sample was 16.5. Most (70.3 per cent) juvenile delinquents were convicted of property offences, 36.6 per cent were convicted of a violent offence at least once and 25.1 per cent were convicted of a traffic-related offence prior to age 21. In total, the juvenile delinquents in the current sample were registered for 5,739 offences prior to age 21. Of the offence types distinguished in the current study, property offences made up the majority of all juvenile convictions (56.1 per cent), with convictions for violent offences ranking second (13.5 per cent) and traffic offences last (8.8 per cent).[4] As convictions as defined here are the terminus of the criminal justice system, and thus reflect the lower boundary of actual criminal behaviour, these figures aptly illustrate the delinquent character of our current sample.

For many sample members, offending did not stop at age 21, and 78.1 per cent were convicted on at least one additional occasion during their adult years. For those reconvicted as adults, the mean number of reconvictions rose to 14.7, with a median of 6 convictions and a maximum of 314. Of those reconvicted, 36.7 per cent were convicted of at least one violent offence, 45.8 per cent of a property offence and 40.9 per cent of traffic offences.

Desistance during the adult years

Figure 8.1 depicts the percentage decline in the likelihood of conviction with age for the current sample based on the longitudinal data. While far from negligible at the end of the follow-up, between ages 21 and 48 the likelihood of conviction

TABLE 8.1 Descriptives for the current sample of juvenile offenders

	Range	Mean	SD
Demographics			
Male	0–1	1.00	0.00
Age at sample conviction	12–20	17.53	1.82
Convictions prior to age 21			
Any convictions	0–1	0.95	0.22
# of convictions[1]	1–46	4.77	4.95
Age of onset[1]	12–20	16.50	1.97
Violence convictions[2]	0–1	0.37	0.48
# of violence convictions[1]	1–10	1.67	1.16
Age of onset violence[1]	12–20	17.57	1.77
Property convictions	0–1	0.70	0.46
# of property convictions[1]	1–31	3.62	3.75
Age of onset property[1]	12–20	16.33	1.95
Traffic convictions	0–1	0.25	0.43
# of traffic convictions[1]	1–9	1.59	1.15
Age of onset traffic[1]	12–20	18.17	1.67
Convictions from age 21 onwards			
Any convictions	0–1	0.78	0.41
# of convictions[1]	1–314	14.69	23.35
Violence convictions[2]	0–1	0.37	0.48
# of violence convictions[1]	1–32	3.21	3.63
Property convictions	0–1	0.46	0.50
# of property convictions[1]	1–151	10.70	17.28
Traffic convictions	0–1	0.41	0.49
# of traffic convictions[1]	1–46	3.39	4.77
Life-course transitions			
Marriage	0–1	0.65	0.48
# of marriages[3]	1–2	1.12	0.32
# years being married[3]	1–28	15.36	6.91
Divorce	0–1	0.24	0.42
# of divorces[3]	1–2	1.07	0.13
# years being divorced[3]	1–24	10.03	6.27
Parenthood	0–1	0.67	0.47
# years being a parent[3]	1–28	16.73	4.93

Notes

1 For those having at least one conviction of this type during this period.

2 As offenders can engage in multiple types of crime, the percentages for different types of offences do not add up to 100.

3 For those experiencing the transition at least once between ages 21–48.

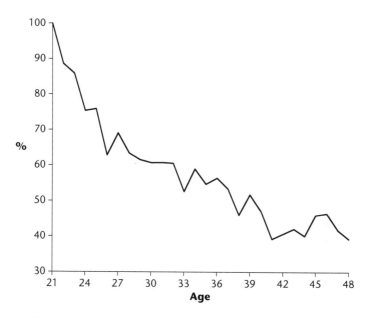

FIGURE 8.1 Percentage decline in the likelihood of conviction by age (any conviction).

TABLE 8.2 Multilevel logistic models explaining the likelihood of conviction from ages 21–48

All

	Model 1				Model 2			
	B		SE	exp (B)	B		SE	exp(B)
Age[1]	−0.055	★★	0.002	0.947	−0.046	★★	0.009	0.955
Age squared	0.002	★★	0.000	1.002	0.001	★★	0.000	1.001
Years single					−0.021	★	0.009	0.979
Married					−0.218	★	0.085	0.804
Years married					−0.005		0.010	0.995
Divorced					0.246	†	0.127	1.279
Years divorced					−0.038	★★	0.012	0.963
Parent					−0.046		0.063	0.955
Years parent					0.027	★★	0.007	1.027
Single★parent					0.086		0.168	1.089
Divorced★parent					0.122		0.227	1.130

Notes
1 Age variables were grand mean centred; all other variables were group mean centred.
N = 1,265 N$_{years}$ = 31,925.
★★ p<0.01, ★ p<0.05, † p<0.10.

(for any conviction) dropped by over 60 per cent, signalling desistance from crime during the adult years. To model the age trend in criminal convictions in our data, we estimate a multilevel logistic model including age and age squared as dependent variables.[5] As expected, and shown in Table 8.2, the linear age effect is negative, reflecting the downward trend in the likelihood of convictions with increasing age.

Effects of life circumstances

Group mean centred indicators of life-course transitions are added in model 2 (Table 8.2). In line with previous studies, we find that being married is associated with a reduced chance of conviction; in this case, the odds of conviction fell by 19.6 per cent. As is reflected by the insignificance of the marriage duration effect, the dampening effect of marriage did not seem to increase as sample members remained married for subsequent years in a row.[6] A divorce seemed to increase the likelihood of conviction – raising the odds of conviction by 27.9 per cent, but this effect seems temporary as is reflected by the negative sign of the divorce duration parameter. After 6 to 7 years of being divorced, the likelihood of conviction was again similar to that of when first being single.

While becoming a parent while being married – as opposed to being a single or divorced parent – may further decrease crime, this effect does not reach significance in the current analysis. As with the effect of divorce, the beneficial effect of parenthood seemed to wane with time and, shortly after becoming a first-time parent, having

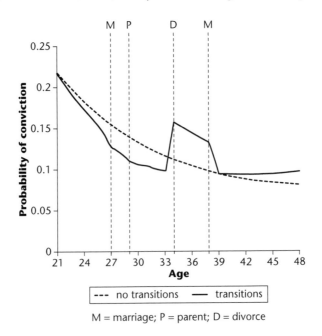

FIGURE 8.2 Effects of life-course transitions on the likelihood of conviction (any conviction).

under-aged children increased rather than decreased the likelihood of conviction. The effects of life-course transitions on the likelihood of conviction are visualized in Figure 8.2. Based on the coefficients of model 2, Figure 8.2 shows the estimated age–crime curve for two archetypical males in our sample; one who stays single and childless during the entire follow-up period, and one who marries, gets divorced and has children, and remarries at the mean ages offenders in our sample make these transitions. The estimates for the latter individual clearly show the effects life-course transitions have on crime. Given the within-individual nature of the current analysis, no stable factor can be responsible for the effects of these life-course transitions.[7]

Distribution of individuals over various life stages by age

For life-course transitions to explain desistance, they must not only have a dampening effect on crime but these beneficial transitions should be prevalent, increase with age and not be offset by transitions that make criminal involvement more likely. Of all juvenile delinquents in the current sample, 64.7 per cent were married at least once during the follow-up. On average, sample members spent 15.4 years of the total follow-up of 28 years in a married state. Nearly one in four (23.6 per cent) of those married experienced at least one divorce during this period, and two-thirds (66.7 per cent) of the sample became a parent.

Figure 8.3 graphically illustrates the (co-)occurrence of the different life-course transitions included in our analyses over the life span. By definition, all sample members were single and childless at the start of the follow-up at age 21. With age, an increasing number of individuals transitioned into marriage and parenthood. By age 30, 42.1 per cent were married and 44.5 per cent had fathered at least one child. With age, however, the proportion of sample members transitioning out of marriage and into the divorced state also increased (to 21.8 per cent by age 48), which for the sample as a whole was likely to offset at least part of the beneficial effects of marriage and parenthood. To the extent that life-course transitions show an age trend similar to that of offending, these transitions have the potential to (partly) explain desistance.

Explaining the age effect

Comparing the age coefficients between models 1 and 2 provides a convenient way to assess the extent to which life-course transitions are able to account for desistance during the adult period. Between models 1 and 2 the linear age coefficient drops by 17.0 per cent (Table 8.3), indicating that life-course transitions account for some, but not a great deal, of the declining likelihood of conviction with age.[8] While decreased in magnitude, the age effect remains significant in the model including life-course transitions, which also indicates that something other than these transitions is driving desistance in the adult years. We can also visualize the extent to which life-course transitions are able to explain desistance by plotting the estimated curve based on the age coefficients for both models, comparing the slopes.

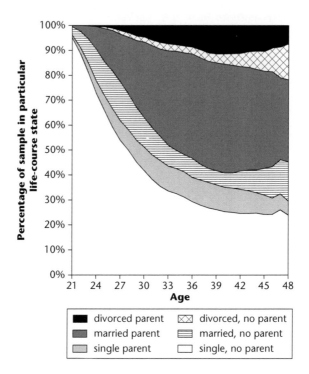

FIGURE 8.3 Life-course transitions by age.

The closer the estimated slope approaches a flat line, the more important are life-course transitions in explaining desistance. Estimated curves for models 1 and 2 are depicted in Figure 8.4. As is evident from Figure 8.4, the estimated curves from models 1 and 2 closely parallel each other, indicating that life-course transitions only capture a limited part of the declining trend. When we directly compare the decline in the estimated likelihood of conviction between models, we find that only 19 per cent of this decline can be attributed to life-course transitions (Table 8.3). Once again, this indicates that something other than the life-course transitions included in our model is driving desistance in the 21–48 age period.

TABLE 8.3 Reduction (in %) in magnitudes of the age coefficients and crime drop between ages 21–48

Conviction type	Age coefficients		
	Linear	Squared	Crime drop
All	0.17	0.24	0.19
Violence	0.20	0.01	0.16
Property	−0.04	−0.11	−0.11
Traffic	0.20	0.33	0.29

Comparisons across different offence types

To test the generalizability of our findings, we repeated the above analysis for convictions for different crime types. Thus within the same sample of juvenile delinquents, we now study separately desistance from violent, property and traffic offences. Relevant coefficients for these models are given in Table 8.4. First, looking at desistance, we find that the decline in the likelihood of conviction is most pronounced in property offending, as is reflected by the magnitude of the linear age coefficient in the unconditional model (model 6). Differences in desistance from these different crime types are also evident when comparing the estimated curves for the unconditional model across the different panes of Figure 8.5.

Being married is associated with a decreased likelihood of property and traffic convictions, but not violence. Prolonged marriages do not have an additional effect. There is not enough evidence for an effect of divorce when offence types are considered separately. Yet, the longer juvenile delinquents spent being divorced, the less likely it seems they would be convicted for a violent or traffic offence. Finally, becoming a parent while married dampens violent and traffic offences, but not property offences. As indicated by the significant interaction effect, having a child out of wedlock increases the likelihood of convictions for property offences. Overall, the models for the different offence types tend to show similar effects of marriage and divorce on crime, while the effects of parenthood may be more different for different types of offending.

Figure 8.5 depicts the age trend in convictions for violent, property and traffic convictions, respectively. As in Figure 8.3, each pane depicts the unconditional curve and that adjusted for the effects of life-course transitions. As for the models

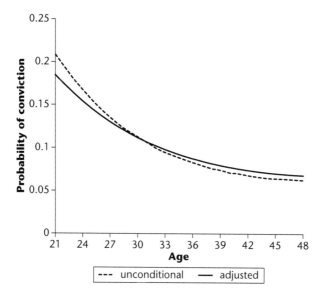

FIGURE 8.4   Unconditional and adjusted desistance curve (any conviction).

TABLE 8.4 Multilevel logistic models explaining the likelihood of conviction from ages 21–48 for violence, property and traffic convictions

| | Violence | | | | | | Property | | | | | | Traffic | | | | | |
| | Model 3 | | | Model 4 | | | Model 5 | | | Model 6 | | | Model 7 | | | Model 8 | | |
	B	SE	exp(B)	B	SE	exp(B)	B	SE	exp(B)	B	SE	exp(B)	B	SE	exp(B)	B	SE	exp(B)
Age[1]	-0.038**	0.004	0.963	-0.030†	0.017	0.970	-0.097**	0.004	0.907	-0.101**	0.016	0.904	-0.055**	0.004	0.947	-0.044**	0.016	0.957
Age squared	0.002**	0.001	1.002	0.002*	0.001	1.002	0.001*	0.000	1.001	0.001*	0.001	1.001	0.003**	0.001	1.003	0.002**	0.001	1.002
Years single				-0.014	0.017	0.986				0.005	0.016	1.005				-0.017	0.016	0.983
Married				-0.192	0.167	0.825				-0.266†	0.138	0.767				-0.435**	0.160	0.647
Years married				-0.006	0.018	0.994				0.010	0.018	1.010				0.003	0.017	1.003
Divorced				0.197	0.232	1.218				0.238	0.195	1.268				0.253	0.226	1.288
Years divorced				-0.038†	0.022	0.963				-0.010	0.019	0.990				-0.043*	0.020	0.958
Parent				-0.219†	0.013	0.803				-0.139	0.100	0.870				-0.239†	0.112	0.787
Years parent				0.0172	0.013	1.017				0.001	0.010	1.001				0.024†	0.013	1.024
Single parent				1.198	0.323	3.314				0.712**	0.269	2.038				0.215	0.288	1.240
Divorced*parent				0.7543	0.411	2.126				0.296	0.348	1.344				0.205	0.373	1.227

Notes

1   Age variables were grand mean centred; all other variables were group mean centred.

N = 1,265. N_{years} = 31,925.

** p<0.01, * p<0.05, † p<0.10.

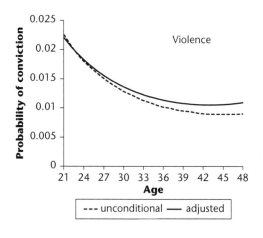

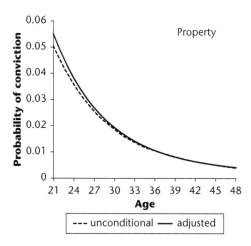

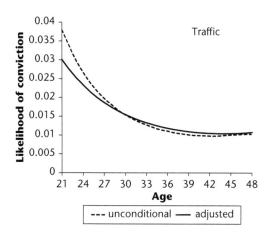

FIGURE 8.5 Unconditional and adjusted desistance curve (violence, property, traffic).

based on convictions for any offence type, Figure 8.5 clearly shows that while marriage, divorce and parenthood are able to explain some of the declining age trend, the estimated trend for the adjusted model is far from a flat line. Between models, the linear age coefficient drops by 20 per cent for violence and traffic convictions, translating into, respectively, 16 per cent and 29 per cent of desistance in these crime types between ages 21–48 being explained by life-course transitions. Surprisingly, the age trend for property convictions increases once controlled for life-course transitions, suggesting that the age effect on property crime becomes even more pronounced when these transitions are taken into account.

Conclusion

The current analyses examined patterns of desistance between ages 21–48 in a sample of registered juvenile offenders. Results show that as these offenders aged, their likelihood of conviction went down by as much as 60 per cent depending on the nature of the offences considered. Next, controlling for stable between-individual differences, we examined the extent to which life-course transitions were associated with changes in the likelihood of conviction. We find that during the years offenders were married, they were less likely to be convicted, while during the years they were divorced, they were more likely to be convicted compared to when they remained single. In the current sample, we find no evidence that staying married for a prolonged period of time additionally decreases the likelihood of conviction. The detrimental effect of divorce, however, seems short lived. The results for parenthood are more equivocal and for some offence types depend on the offender's marital state. Despite the fact that the prevalence of marriage and parenthood increases with age, the extent to which these transitions account for adult desistance in the current sample – while not entirely absent – seems modest.

Effects of life-course transitions on offending were estimated using multilevel models with group mean centred time varying variables. These types of models account for potential selection effects resulting from stable between-individual differences. Therefore, the dampening effect marriage has on offending, or the increase in the likelihood of conviction after experiencing a divorce found in our sample, cannot be explained by between-individual characteristics that make some individuals both more likely to marry and less likely to engage in criminal behaviour, or make some individuals more prone to divorce as well as more liable to conviction. To the extent that these life-course transitions have an independent effect on crime, the results of our analysis support a life-course explanation of adult desistance. Yet, while taking into account stable factors, our models are unable to control for dynamic factors driving both life-course transitions and changes in crime. To the extent that psychological maturation or time varying biological factors influence the occurrence and duration of life-course transitions as well as changes in crime, the current results may overestimate the explanatory power of life-course theories at the expense of developmental theories. In addition, our current models do not account for simultaneity (Osgood 2010: 380). That is, just as marriage influences offending, offending in turn may influence marriage and divorce. Previous analyses using the current dataset have indeed shown that continued offending reduces the likelihood of experiencing the transition to marriage (Van Schellen *et al.* 2012). While reduced in magnitude, Barnes *et al.* (2014) still found a dampening effect of marriage on offending when controlling for the contemporaneous effect of offending on marriage. Again, not controlling for the reciprocity between criminal and marital and parental trajectories may have led the current study to overestimate the effects these life-course transition have on crime.

Despite their marked effect on the likelihood of conviction and their increasing prevalence with age, transitions in and out of marriage and parenthood far from fully account for desistance in our sample of registered juvenile delinquents. While the results for marriage, divorce and parenthood are at odds with age theory, the larger part of the decline in crime with age is left unexplained. This suggests that other factors, be they structural, psychological or biological and which were not included in the current analyses, also contribute to desistance.

The limited explanatory power of life-course transitions with regard to the falling age trend in offending does not readily disqualify life-course explanations of the age–crime relationship. While marriage, divorce and parenthood figure prominently in life-course theories of offending, other important transitions – like obtaining steady employment – have been argued to be pivotal in understanding desistance (Uggen and Wakefield 2008). The current analyses are limited by the availability of official data on different life-course transitions and, because of the lack of computerized data spanning the era under study, do not include employment history. Still, whereas transitioning into the labour market has been shown to have beneficial effects on adult crime, there are good reasons to expect that the extent to which employment explains the age trend in crime is similarly humble. Unlike marriage, which itself could be considered an acme of a growing interpersonal bond, it seems not so much the transition to employment per se, but rather the stability of employment that brings about change in offending (Sampson and Laub 1993). The good fruits of work need time to ripen. However, recent research among previously institutionalized Dutch youths shows that while many do find employment at some point during their adult lives, very few are able to transition into a lasting occupational career (Van Der Geest *et al.* 2011). Instead, the working lives of these youths are spotted – many engaging in short bouts of low quality work – and lack the continuity needed for employment to exert its full influence on crime.

Less prominent in extant life-course criminological theory, but potentially powerful additional factors in explaining desistance, are age-related developments in physical and mental health. Prior research using the CCLS dataset shows that male offenders who spent time incarcerated were more likely to suffer from premature mortality than males in the general population (Dirkzwager *et al.* 2012). More specifically, formerly imprisoned offenders were two times more likely to die of natural causes and almost eight times more likely to die of unnatural causes. While the main causes of death were cancer and cardiovascular diseases in both populations, the premature manifestation of these ailments in the imprisoned population may be linked to deleterious conditions – e.g. stress, substance abuse – that characterize a criminal lifestyle. Furthermore, ex-prisoners also experienced an increased risk of suicide, which may signal accumulating mental health problems in the lives of these offenders. Within the offender population, mortality risk is linked to the frequency and duration of offending careers, corroborating the idea that those most embedded in a criminal lifestyle run the highest risk of experiencing health problems (Nieuwbeerta and Piquero 2008). Qualitative accounts of desistance also refer to health issues as a reason to disengage from offending. Premature aging as a result of deteriorating physical and mental health may therefore account for a substantial part of the age trend in criminal offending that is as yet unexplained.

A final limitation to the current analyses is that they are based on official records regarding the conviction histories of the members of our sample. As is widely recognized, official records reflect only the proverbial tip of the iceberg when it comes to actual offending behaviour. Many offences go unnoticed and many that are noticed remain unsolved. Whether or not a particular offence results in a conviction depends on many factors, including the type and circumstances of the offence, offender characteristics and police priority and capacity. To the extent that older offenders tend to engage in offences that have a low probability of being caught, or engage in crimes in the private realm, they are better able to mask their involvement in the offence, or force their victims to refrain from pressing charges, or they tend to receive less police attention than do their juvenile counterparts. Therefore, adult desistance as found in official data may be false.

To extend the number of life-course trajectories that can be linked to desistance, and to remedy the possibility of forced and false desistance explaining the declining age trend in adult crime, additional data will be needed to cover a broader spectrum of life-course domains and encompass self-reported criminal behaviour in old age. In response to these needs and to be better able to account for the way offending develops during the adult years, we are currently in the process of augmenting the existing CCLS data with retrospective self-report information gathered by means of life event calendars. The life event calendar method is especially suited to gathering this type of information, limiting retrospective bias due to memory issues.

Finally, prior qualitative studies on desistance have highlighted the importance of the scripts and narratives offenders use to ascribe meaning to their lived experiences, the ways these narratives are tied to class and gender, and how these ascribed meanings guide individual decisions shaping the life-course (e.g. Maruna 2001; Carlsson 2013). By making the realities of the lives of offenders tangible, these studies help to identify the specific mechanisms by which crime interacts with the individuals' larger life-course. Therefore, to better capture the conscious and unconscious choices that led juvenile offenders in the CCLS sample to desist from crime and deviance, in-depth interviews will be conducted with a subsample of those who participated in the life event calendar part of the study. Separately, but especially in combination, these data will allow us to dig deeper into the lives of the offenders in the CCLS sample and help us to unearth the causal processes driving development and the way these processes link development across different life-course domains.

Beyond the CCLS study, future research on desistance would benefit from broadening its scope to include cohorts from different historical periods, respondents of different social and cultural backgrounds, and other than 'run-of-the-mill' crimes, to assess the generalizability of the current findings and the theories that have been offered in explanation. Life-course development is governed by age-graded expectations of both the timing and sequence of important events. These norms may differ between societies and within societies between social and cultural groups, which in turn may lead to different patterns of desistance. Over the past decades for example, many Western countries have witnessed an increase in the average age of marriage and parenthood. These demographic shifts have given rise to what Arnett (2015) has labelled the period of emerging adulthood; a period during which the individual enjoys more freedom than during adolescence, yet still lacks many of the responsibilities that characterize the adult years. To the extent that desistance from crime is linked to adult roles and responsibilities, the 'emergence' of the emerging adult period may have altered patterns of desistance in more recent cohorts. Likewise, desistance may differ across social or cultural groups. For women, the age–crime curve appears less skewed than for men, and many women are convicted only when they are adults (Block et al. 2010). Recent research also suggests that the age–crime curve may be different for minority groups. The age–crime curve for Dutch citizens with Caribbean roots, for example, drops less steeply during the period between ages 20–40 than it does for native-Dutch, which to a large extent seems attributable to Caribbean-Dutch males cohabiting less often with a female partner (Jennissen 2014). Finally, studies on desistance have usually dealt with common crimes like theft, burglary and assault. Research on desistance from specific crime types, like sexual offending (Blokland and Van Der Geest 2015) or organized crime (Van Koppen et al. 2010) is still scant.

While not without limitations, the results of the current effort speak to theory as well as practice. To the extent that life-course transitions can discernibly alter the course of criminal development and promote desistance in adult offenders, a life-course approach to desistance trumps a more deterministic maturational account of desistance. Future research efforts – both quantitative and qualitative – directed to establishing the precise nature of the causal mechanisms that underlie the influence life-course transitions have on offending, will allow researchers to establish better the relative weight of these transitions compared to other developmental changes taking place with age in explaining the decline of criminal behaviour during the adult years. Likewise, this research will be able to ascertain which life-course transitions hamper rather than promote desistance from crime, and why. The finding that life-course transitions affect criminal offending and account for at least some part of the downwards trend in offending during the adult period, supports current efforts aimed at actively promoting desistance in active offenders. The more is learned about the causal mechanisms that bring about change in offending, the better these efforts can be tailored to achieve this ultimate goal. Current findings on the detrimental effects divorce has on offending may also serve to remind us of the potentially deleterious effects interventions may have. Prudence is ever needed when dealing with a complex phenomenon such as desistance from offending.

Notes

1 Data from Statistics Netherlands show that between 1998 and 2005, the percentage of all newly registered unions pertaining to non-marital partnerships rose from around 5 per cent in 1998 to over 13 per cent in 2005.
2 Data from Statistics Netherlands indicate that for approximately 5 per cent of all children born in the Netherlands in 2005, the father was registered as being 'unknown'.
3 To control for differences in exposure time, we also included two variables reflecting imprisonment in our models. Years in which the person was imprisoned for the entire duration of the year were coded as '1' whereas all other years were coded as '0'. In a similar way to the other transitions, prison duration was a continuous variable reflecting the number of subsequent years the person spent imprisoned.
4 The low prevalence of traffic offences during the juvenile period – but not in the adult period – likely results from age 18 being the minimum driving age in the Netherlands during the 1970s.
5 The quadratic form of the age trend is appropriate in our analysis as reflected by the close match between the shape of the predicted curve and observed data.
6 Remaining single for a prolonged period does seem to decrease the likelihood of conviction somewhat.
7 Two important sources of bias, however, remain: within-individual models as used here are not able to control for possible time-varying confounders, and remain subject to simultaneity bias – when convictions affect life-course transitions and not the other way around (Osgood 2010).
8 As we estimated a logistic model, the percentage decrease in the age coefficient does not represent an equal decrease in the probability of conviction.

References

Apel, R., Blokland, A., Nieuwbeerta, P. and Van Schellen, M. (2010), 'The impact of imprisonment on marriage and divorce: A risk set matching approach', *Journal of Quantitative Criminology* 26: 269–300.

Arnett, J. J. (2015), *Emerging Adulthood: The Winding Road from Late Teens through the Twenties*, second edition. New York: Oxford University Press.

Barnes, J. C., Golden, K., Mancini, C., Boutwell, B. B., Beaver, K. M. and Diamond, B. (2014), 'Marriage and involvement in crime: A consideration of reciprocal effects in a nationally representative sample', *Justice Quarterly* 31(2): 229–256.

Bersani, B. E. and Eggleston-Doherty, E. (2013), 'When the ties that bind unwind: Examining the enduring and situational processes of change behind the marriage effect', *Criminology* 51(2): 399–433.

Bersani, B. E. and Van Schellen, M. (2014), 'The Effectiveness of marriage as an intervention in the Netherlands', in Humphrey, J. A. and Cordella, P. (eds) *Effective Interventions in the Lives of Criminal Offenders*. New York: Springer, pp. 101–120.

Bersani, B. E., Laub, J. H. and Nieuwbeerta, P. (2009), 'Marriage and desistance from crime in the Netherlands: Do gender and socio-historical context matter?', *Journal of Quantitative Criminology* 25(1): 3–24.

Block, R., Blokland, A. A. J., Van Der Werff, N., Van Os, R. and Nieuwbeerta, P. (2010), 'Long-term patterns of offending in women', *Feminist Criminology* 5(1): 73–107.

Blokland, A. A. J. (2015), 'Theoretical perspectives on delinquent development: Propensity, plasticity and range', in Krohn, M. D. and Lane, J. (eds) *Juvenile Delinquency and Juvenile Justice Handbook*. Chichester, UK: Wiley-Blackwell.

Blokland, A. A. J. and Nieuwbeerta, P. (2005), 'The effects of life circumstances on longitudinal trajectories of offending', *Criminology* 43(4): 1203–1240.

Blokland, A. A. J. and Nieuwbeerta, P. (2010), 'Life course criminology', in Shoham, S. G and Knepper, P. (eds) *International Handbook of Criminology*. Boca Raton, FL: CRC Press/ Taylor and Francis, pp. 51–94.

Blokland, A. A. J. and Van Os, R. (2010), 'Life span offending trajectories of convicted Dutch women', *International Criminal Justice Review* 20(2): 169–187.

Blokland, A. A. J. and Nagin, D. S. (2012), 'Estimating the effects of imprisonment: Intended and unintended consequences of incarceration', in Malsch, M. and Duker, M. (eds) *Incapacitation: Trends and New Perspectives*. Surrey, UK: Ashgate: pp. 221–236.

Blokland, A. A. J. and Van Der Geest, V. (2015), 'Life course transitions and desistance in sex offenders: An event history analysis', in Blokland, A. and Lussier, P. (eds) *Sex Offenders: A Criminal Career Approach*. Chichester, UK: Wiley, pp. 219–242.

Blokland, A. A. J., Nagin, D. and Nieuwbeerta, P. (2005), 'Life span offending trajectories of a Dutch conviction cohort', *Criminology* 43(4): 919–954.

Carlsson, C. (2013), 'Masculinities, persistence, and desistance', *Criminology*, 51: 661–694.

Collins, R. E. (2004), 'Onset and desistance in criminal careers: Neurobiology and the age–crime relationship', *Journal of Offender Rehabilitation* 39(3): 1–19.

Craig, J. M., Diamond, B. and Piquero, A. R. (2014), 'Marriage as an intervention in the lives of criminal offenders', in Humphrey, J. A. and Cordella, P. (eds) *Effective Interventions in the Lives of Criminal Offenders*. New York: Springer, pp. 19–37.

Dannefer, D. (1984), 'Adult development and social theory: A paradigmatic reappraisal', *American Sociological Review* 49: 100–116.

Dirkzwager, A., Nieuwbeerta, P. and Blokland, A. A. J. (2012), 'Effects of first-time imprisonment on post-prison mortality: A 25-year follow-up study with a matched control group', *Journal of Research in Crime and Delinquency* 49(3): 383–419.

Farrington, D. P. (1986), 'Age and crime', in Tonry, M. and Morris, N. (eds), *Crime and Justice: An Annual Review of Research*, Volume 7. Chicago, IL: University of Chicago Press, pp. 189–250.

Farrington, D. P. and West, D. (1995), 'Effects of marriage, separation and children on offending by adult males', in Hagan, J. (ed.) *Current Perspectives on Aging and the Life Cycle. Vol. 4: Delinquency and Disrepute in the Life Course*. Greenwich, CT: JAI Press, pp. 249–281.

Gottfredson, M. and Hirschi, T. (1990), *A General Theory of Crime*. Palo Alto, CA: Stanford University Press.

Gove, W. R. (1985), 'The effect of age and gender on deviant behavior: A biosocial perspective', in Rossi, A. S. (ed.) *Gender and the Life Course*. New York: Aldine, pp. 115–144.

Hirschi, T. and Gottfredson. M. (1983), 'Age and the explanation of crime', *American Journal of Sociology* 89(3): 552–584.

Jennissen, R. (2014), 'On the deviant age–crime curve of Afro-Caribbean populations: The case of Antilleans living in the Netherlands', *American Journal of Criminal Justice*, 39: 571–594.

Kerr, D. C. R., Capaldi, D. M., Owen, L. D., Wiesner, M. and Pears, K. C. (2011), 'Changes in at-risk American men's crime and substance use trajectories following fatherhood', *Journal of Marriage and the Family*, 73(5): 1101–1116.

Laub, J. H. and Sampson, R. J. (2001), 'Understanding desistance from crime', in Tonry, M. (ed.) *Crime and Justice: An Annual Review of Research*, Volume 28. Chicago, IL: University of Chicago Press, pp. 1–69.

Laub, J. H. and Sampson, R. J. (2003), *Shared Beginnings, Divergent Lives. Delinquent Boys to Age 70*. Cambridge, MA: Harvard University Press.

Laub, J. H., Nagin, D. S. and Sampson, R. J. (1998), 'Good marriages and trajectories of change in criminal offending', *American Sociological Review* 63: 225–238.

Maruna, S. (2001), *Making Good. How Ex-Convicts Reform and Rebuild Their Lives*. Washington, DC: American Psychological Association.

Massoglia, M. and Uggen, C. (2007), 'Subjective desistance and the transition to adulthood', *Journal of Contemporary Criminal Justice* 23: 90–103.

McIvor, G., Murray, C. and Jamieson, J. (2004), 'Desistance from crime: Is it different for women and girls?', in Maruna, S. and Immarigeon, R. (eds) *After Crime and Punishment: Pathways to Offender Reintegration*. Portland, OR: Willan Publishing, pp. 181–197.

Mulvey, E. P., Steinberg, L., Fagan, J., Cauffman, E., Piquero, A. R., Chassin, L., Knight, G. P., Brame, R., Schubert, C. A., Hecker, T. and Losoya, S. H. (2004), 'Theory and research on desistance from antisocial activity among serious juvenile offenders', *Youth Violence and Juvenile Justice* 2: 213–236.

Nieuwbeerta, P. and Piquero, A. R. (2008), 'Mortality rates and causes of death of convicted Dutch criminals 25 years later', *Journal of Research in Crime and Delinquency* 45: 256–286.

Nieuwbeerta, P., Nagin, D. and Blokland, A. A. J. (2009), 'Assessing the impact of first-time imprisonment on offenders' subsequent criminal career development: A matched samples comparison', *Journal of Quantitative Criminology* 25(3): 227–257.

Nieuwbeerta, P., Blokland, A. A. J., Piquero, A. and Sweeten, G. (2011), 'A life-course analysis of offence specialization: Introducing a new method for studying individual specialization over the life course', *Crime and Delinquency* 57(1): 3–28.

Osgood, D. W. (2005), 'Making sense of crime and the life course', *Annals of the American Academy of Political and Social Science* 602: 196–211.

Osgood, D. W. (2010), 'Statistical models of life events and criminal behavior', in Piquero, A. R. and Weisburd, D. (eds) *Handbook of Quantitative Criminology*. New York: Springer, pp. 375–396.

Osgood, D. W., Wilson, J. K., Bachman, J. G., O'Malley, P. M. and Johnston, L. D. (1996), 'Routine activities and individual deviant behavior', *American Sociological Review* 61: 635–655.

Rutter, M. (1989), 'Age as an ambiguous variable in developmental research: Some epidemiological considerations from developmental psychopathology', *International Journal of Behavioral Development* 12(1): 1–34.

Sampson, R. J. and Laub, J. H. (1993), *Crime in the Making. Pathways and Turning Points through Life*. Cambridge, MA: Harvard University Press.

Sampson, R. J., Laub, J. H. and Wimer, C. (2006), 'Does marriage reduce crime? A counterfactual approach to within-individual causal effects', *Criminology* 44(3): 465–508.

Savolainen, J. (2009), 'Work, family and criminal desistance', *British Journal of Criminology* 49: 285–304.

Siennick, S. E. and Osgood, D. W. (2008), 'A review of the research on the impact on crime of transitions to adult roles', in Liberman, A. M. (ed.) *The Long View of Crime: A Synthesis of Longitudinal Research*. New York: Springer, pp. 161–187.

Snodgrass, G. M., Blokland, A. A. J., Haviland, A., Nieuwbeerta, P. and Nagin, D. (2011), 'Does the time cause the crime? An examination of the relationship between time served and reoffending', *Criminology* 49(4): 1149–1194.

Sweeten, G., Piquero, A. R. and Steinberg, L. (2013), 'Age and the explanation of crime, revisited', *Journal of Youth and Adolescence*, 42: 921–938.

Tittle, C. R. and Grasmick, H. G. (1997), 'Criminal behavior and age: A test of three provocative hypotheses', *Journal of Criminal Law and Criminology* 81: 309–342.

Uggen, C. and Wakefield, S. (2008), 'What have we learned from longitudinal studies of work and crime?', in Liberman, A. M. (ed.) *The Long View of Crime: A Synthesis of Longitudinal Research*. New York: Springer, pp. 191–219.

Van De Rakt, M., Nieuwbeerta, P. and De Graaf, N. D. (2008), 'Like father, like son? The relationship between conviction trajectories of fathers and their sons and daughters', *British Journal of Criminology* 48(2): 538–556.

Van De Rakt, M., Ruiter, S., De Graaf, N. D. and Nieuwbeerta, P. (2010), 'When does the apple fall from the tree? Static versus dynamic theories predicting intergenerational transmission of convictions', *Journal of Quantitative Criminology* 26: 371–389.

Van Der Geest, V., Bijleveld, C. and Blokland, A. A. J. (2011), 'The effects of employment on longitudinal trajectories of offending: A follow up in high risk youth from ages 18 to 32', *Criminology* 49(4): 1195–1234.

Van Koppen, V., De Poot, C. J., Kleemans, E. and Nieuwbeerta, P. (2010), 'Criminal trajectories in organized crime', *British Journal of Criminology* 50: 102–123.

Van Schellen, M., Poortman, A. R. and Nieuwbeerta, P. (2012), 'Partners in crime? Criminal offending, marriage formation, and partner selection', *Journal of Research in Crime and Delinquency* 49(4): 545–571.

Warr, M. (1993), 'Age, peers, and delinquency', *Criminology* 31: 17–40.

Wilson, J. Q. and Herrnstein, R. J. (1985), *Crime and Human Nature*. New York: Simon and Schuster.

Zoutewelle-Terovan, M., Van Der Geest, V., Liefbroer, A. and Bijleveld, C. (2012), 'Criminality and family formation: Effects of marriage and parenthood on criminal behavior for men and women', *Crime and Delinquency* 60(8): 1209–1234.

9

TIMING OF CHANGE

Are life course transitions causes or consequences of desistance?

Torbjørn Skardhamar and Jukka Savolainen

Theoretical background

The capacity of life course transitions, such as employment and marriage, to modify offending trajectories is a central concern of life course criminology (Fagan and Freeman 1999; Uggen and Wakefield 2008; Bushway 2011). Echoing the socio-logical distinction between structure and agency (Bottoms *et al.* 2004), the desistance literature offers two basic accounts of how life course transitions may exert causal influence on criminal behaviour: the *turning point* and the *hook-for-change* hypotheses (Sampson and Laub 1993; Giordano *et al.* 2002). In addition, challenging the causal interpretation, the *maturation perspective* expects transitions to adult social roles to follow rather than precede desistance from crime (Hirschi and Gottfredson 1983; Morizot and Le Blanc 2007).

As articulated in the age-graded theory of informal social control, the turn-ing point hypothesis treats life course transitions as exogenous events with the potential to set in motion the process of desistance (Sampson and Laub 1993; Laub and Sampson 2003). Although Laub and Sampson recognize the role of indi-vidual agency, they maintain that '*most offenders* desist in response to *structurally induced* turning points that serve as the catalyst for sustaining long term behavioural change' (Laub and Sampson 2003: 147; emphasis added). According to this per-spective, desistance happens as an inadvertent response to changes in objective life circumstances. Laub and Sampson (2003: 278–279) use the term *desistance by default* to describe this process, 'Many men made a commitment to go straight without even realizing it. Before they knew it, they had invested so much time in a marriage or a job that they did not want to risk losing their investment'.

The strong causality suggested by the turning point hypothesis has been quali-fied by scholars who view subjective change as a precondition for successful exits from a criminal lifestyle (Maruna 2001; Giordano *et al.* 2002; LeBel *et al.* 2008).

For example, Bushway and Reuter (1997) have argued that employment is unlikely to facilitate desistance in the absence of true commitment to reform. Giordano and colleagues have advanced a theory of cognitive transformation, which argues that actors themselves must recognize the need to change and make a commitment to realistic plans to that effect (Giordano *et al.* 2002). According to this perspective, life course transitions are unlikely to result in lasting changes in behaviour without a strong personal desire to undertake a conversion effort. However, in order for these intentions to materialize, it may be important to find tangible 'hooks for change' in the everyday environment. Thus, under this theory, marriage and employment have the potential to sustain and reinforce the emerging process of desistance.

Additional strands of criminological theory are skeptical of causal interpretations of either variety (Glueck and Glueck 1940; Hirschi and Gottfredson 1983; Morizot and Le Blanc 2007). These perspectives explain the longitudinal association between life course transitions and declining criminal activity as a spurious function of *maturational reform*, i.e. the age-varying process of 'settling down' (Massoglia and Uggen 2010). Under this model, it would be unrealistic to expect successful adult transitions to occur during an active phase of the criminal trajectory. Individuals who persist in criminal offending often face serious obstacles in the labour market as a direct result of their criminal lifestyle (Pager 2003) and may not be perceived of as attractive spousal candidates in the marriage market (Van Schellen *et al.* 2012). Moreover, as observed by Massoglia and Uggen (2010), active offenders are unlikely to regard themselves as capable of taking on social roles associated with mature adulthood. The maturation perspective goes one step further than the hook-for-change hypothesis in that it assumes sustained behavioural transformation, not mere psychological readiness, as a precondition for successful labour market transitions.

Regardless of their positions on causality, each of these three perspectives predicts a negative longitudinal association between life course transitions and crime: the average rate of offending is expected to be higher during the pre-transition period under each perspective. As described in Figure 9.1, the main point of contention has to do with the *timing* of change in this process. The turning point hypothesis predicts gradual reductions in offending after the transition. The hook-for-change hypothesis expects transitions to follow the *onset* of desistance, but suggests that a strong marriage or a positive job experience may help reinforce the process. Finally, the maturation perspective expects marriage and employment transitions to *follow* a period of sustained desistance with no appreciable consequences for the offending rate thereafter. This is illustrated in Figure 9.1, which depicts *ideal–typical* renditions of these processes.

Although there is ample (albeit inconsistent) evidence regarding the 'effect' of both employment and marriage on desistance, the evidence on *timing* is largely lacking and limited mostly to conflicting accounts from qualitative studies of retrospective narratives (Maruna 2001; Giordano *et al.* 2002; Laub and Sampson 2003). The typical approach in quantitative studies of desistance is to use only one dummy variable to capture the average crime rates in states of (non)marriage and (un)employment. This approach is problematic, because it ignores any dynamics

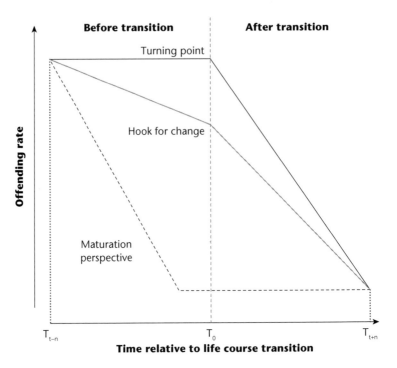

FIGURE 9.1 Three ideal–typical trajectories derived from theory.

Source: Adapted from Skardhamar and Savolainen (2014).

within the period in each state.[1] As one can see from Figure 9.1, each of the hypothesized trajectories implies lower average levels of offending under each state of institutional 'bonding', although the underlying processes are assumed to be very different.

Probably the most unique contribution of our research using Norwegian registry data is that we have examined the timing of change quantitatively. Specifically, we have focused on two issues that have received limited attention in prior (non-experimental) studies of desistance from crime: (1) the timing of life course transitions in the criminal trajectory, specifically the offending behaviour in the period leading up to the transitions; and (2) the pattern of the criminal trajectory following the point of transition. It is important to understand that the purpose of our agenda is not to estimate the *causal effect* of life course transitions on crime. We want to be absolutely clear that our research designs are not suitable for removing selection bias (regardless of available potential controls). In this sense, our results are merely 'descriptive'. The purpose is to examine which theoretical model (see Figure 9.1) is most consistent with the data and which one(s) are not, in terms of the timing of change. Of course, the question of time order is a critical component of causal inference. In this sense, our results are directly relevant for causal theory.

A note on registry data

Contrary to most studies of desistance, our research is not based on one discrete longitudinal sample. Rather, for each research study, we have created a specific sample drawn from the total population data available through Statistics Norway. In each situation, the sample was selected with the research questions in mind. In what follows, we will not discuss the details of the specific samples used in our research. Instead, we describe the Norwegian system of individual-level registry data more generally. Readers interested in the samples used in any given study are encouraged to read the relevant sections of the cited articles.

The administrative records available in Denmark, Finland, Norway and Sweden provide rich opportunities for quantitative longitudinal research using large samples. In these Nordic countries, all residents are assigned a personal identification number (PIN), which is routinely used for identification in administrative records, such as the population register, education registers and tax registers, as well as records from the police, courts and the prison administration. These administrative systems are not linked together at the administrative offices, so that each agency usually only has access to their own data. However, as these data are routinely sent to Statistics Norway for the production of official statistics, they can be linked there using the PIN. In Norway, the production and use of individual-level data sets using this approach are regulated in the Norwegian Statistical Act and controlled by the Data Inspectorate. Importantly for our purposes, any given individual with a PIN can be assessed across multiple domains of life and over time (Lyngstad and Skardhamar 2011).

The data on recorded crime used in the Norwegian studies discussed in this chapter are based on police records. This has been the preferred choice, because this source includes the most detailed information on the offence. The records include information about all solved cases where the perpetrator has been identified and a judicial decision has been rendered, resulting in an official criminal record. The judicial decision is typically a conviction, but could also be a waiver of prosecution. The main advantage is that police records provide information on each offence, when it was committed and the judicial decision reached by the authorities. By contrast, the sentencing records tend to pool information about multiple offences, some of which are not necessarily committed on the same day. Due to this limitation, sentencing data are less well suited to analyse the timing of criminal offending in a precise way.

Although there is a strong tradition of registry-based research in Norwegian social sciences, criminological studies of this kind are relatively recent and are mainly focused on life course studies of desistance (Lyngstad and Skardhamar 2011). Adhering to the research programme associated with Sampson and Laub's age-graded theory of informal social control (Sampson and Laub 1993; Laub and Sampson 2003), a number of these studies have examined the effects of such life course transitions as marriage, parenthood and employment. Sampson and Laub (1993) have famously argued that bonds to *good marriages* and *stable employment* have the capacity to set in motion the process of desistance from crime. Both marriage and work have received considerable attention in subsequent research (Siennick and Osgood 2008; Uggen and Wakefield 2008; Craig *et al.* 2014; Skardhamar *et al.* 2015).

The theoretical argument is causal, but because these life course events are not randomly assigned, but rather exhibit a great deal of self- and social selection, establishing causality becomes challenging with observational data. Although it is difficult to estimate truly causal effects with non-experimental data, it is possible to evaluate which causal claims are consistent with observational data and which ones are not. As noted above, most perspectives expect that the average offending rates are lower during states of marriage and (stable) employment. The critical difference has to do with the timing of change. The Norwegian register data are particularly well suited to address this issue, because they allow us to observe short-term changes in offending and various life course circumstances over long periods of time.

Main findings on desistance from Norwegian registry data

Our main contribution to this literature has been to evaluate which of the three theoretically proposed trajectories described in Figure 9.1 offers the best approximation of the empirical reality. The methodological approach is to compare offending patterns before and after the life course transition (e.g. marriage or employment) in a way that captures the dynamics *within* each state.

Marriage and other family-related transitions

When we first started to examine the association between marriage and crime (Skardhamar and Lyngstad 2009; Lyngstad and Skardhamar 2013), two issues stood out as critically important. First, although the interpretation of the evidence was heavy on causal language, there were no studies that came close to demonstrating a causal effect. Second, hardly any studies paid proper attention to well-documented changes in family formation patterns over the past decades. We thought it was important (even if obvious) to keep in mind that, in contemporary societies, most couples tend to cohabit before they get married. This is especially commonplace in the Nordic countries, but is also quite typical elsewhere. In most advanced Western societies, cohabitation is considered as not only 'normal' but perhaps even a normative part of the family formation process. Cohabitation is seen as a stepping stone towards marriage. Thus, any restraining effects flowing from the spouse (social control, attachment, routine activities, etc.) are likely to emerge prior to the point of marriage.

Focusing on males, Lyngstad and Skardhamar (2013) examined annual changes in offending, as recorded by the police, before and after transition to marriage. Because cohabitation is not a formal event recorded in the official statistics, the study did not have information about the timing of union formation. However, the logic of the analysis is based on the realistic assumption that a period of cohabitation typically precedes the date of marriage. The study consisted of the total population of men who got married for the first time in Norway between 1997 and 2001 (N=90,019). For these men, crime rates were calculated for each of the years in the five-year periods before and after the year of marriage. The results showed that, although these men had lower levels of crime during the time they were married, the decline in offending took place in the period leading up to marriage (see Figure 9.2). As this change occurred gradually, a comparison of average levels between the two periods would have masked the dynamics in the pre-marriage period. Note that no additional decline in offending was observed in the period following the transition to marriage, suggesting no marriage effect. If the declines were associated with union formation, they imply a cohabitation or 'courtship' effect. However, because the data could not address the timing of these demographic events, it would be premature to assign any causal meaning to these patterns. While our findings do not contradict the hypothesis that a romantic relationship restrains male offending, the study suggests that the date of marriage is probably not a good measure of capturing *when* this potential effect occurs.

In a subsequent study, we found these patterns to vary depending on the spouse's criminal record. The data were similar to those used by Lyngstad and Skardhamar (2013), but also included information about the criminal records of the spouses. Unexpectedly, the pre-marriage decline in offending was more substantial among those with a criminal spouse (Skardhamar *et al.* 2014). These results contradict

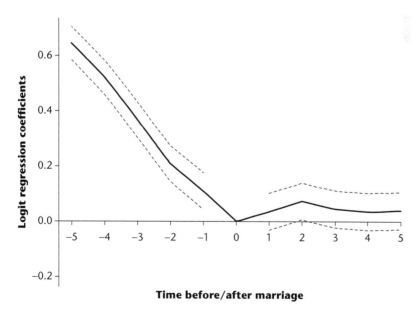

FIGURE 9.2 Logistic regression parameters for the probability of offending each year before and after the year of marriage.

Source: Lyngstad and Skardhamar (2013).

the assumption that desistance is conditional upon marrying a law-abiding wife. Note that those who married a criminal wife were also more criminal themselves and thus had a higher baseline of offending from which to decline. This could be the most parsimonious explanation of the unexpected finding.

Parenthood is another family transition that has received attention in the desistance literature (Laub and Sampson 2003; Savolainen 2009; Kreager *et al.* 2010). In Norway the majority of first-births occur outside marital unions, which makes this a transition that typically occurs before marriage and during cohabitation. Monsbakken *et al.* (2013) used data on all first-time parents (males and females) between 1997 and 2001 (N=208,296). The study found that becoming a parent is strongly correlated with desistance from crime, but, as with marriage, most of the decline had taken place in the five years before the first child was born. The pattern was found to vary by union status at the time of childbirth. For married parents and cohabiting fathers, the change was gradual over the five preceding years, but for cohabiting mothers and mothers not residing with the child's father, the decline was more abrupt, starting around one year prior to childbirth. Among men who did not reside with the child's mother, there was no decline in the probability of offending in the years before the birth, but a gradual decline thereafter. The decrease in offending for women was more abrupt and occurred closer to the timing of pregnancy and birth, followed by an *increase* thereafter. This increase was clear, but did not reach the levels of offending observed prior to becoming a mother. For mothers, the magnitude of the increase varied by union status. It was smallest for mothers who were not residing with the father of the child.

Transition to employment

Although the evidence from longitudinal studies of employment and crime is somewhat inconsistent, most studies find a negative association between states of employment and rates of offending (Sampson and Laub 1993; Uggen and Wakefield 2008; Savolainen 2009; Van Der Geest *et al.* 2011; Skardhamar and Telle 2012). At least one study has found crime to increase during periods of employment (Horney *et al.* 1995). The evidence from labour market experiments offers the most persuasive evidence of causal influence. In general, experimental evidence has failed to demonstrate that providing jobs to offenders makes them reduce their criminal activities. On the other hand, most theories of desistance do not expect temporary low-paying 'dead-end' jobs to serve as turning points, especially among clients who are not psychologically ready to go straight. Labour market experiments may suffer from low external validity, because they typically offer unattractive jobs to an offender population of varying levels of motivation. Observational data may be the only option to study transitions to attractive jobs among offenders who are motivated to change.

In a recent article, we investigated the timing of change in criminal offending relative to the point of job entry (Skardhamar and Savolainen 2014). Our methodological approach was more sophisticated than before. The sample was focused on males (born in 1960–1974) with a serious history of criminal offending, who made transitions to stable employment between 2001–2006 (n=783). The purpose was to identify a group with the potential to desist in response to a positive change in the employment situation. To address the quality of the employment experience, we limited the analysis to employment entries lasting six months or more.[2] Using monthly measures of employment and crime, we described changes in offending 36 months before and after the point of job entry. Similar to the studies of family transitions, the main finding was that crime rates declined before job entries, with no additional declines after the point of transition (Figure 9.3a). Moreover, most of those who became employed lost their jobs within a relatively short period of time after the initial six-month period built in to the research design. In addition, we investigated whether these patterns varied by age; they did not. Finally, we used group-based modelling techniques (Nagin 2005) to see if we could identify subgroups with offending trajectories more consistent with causal influence. We found that, at best, only 2 per cent of the sample conformed to a pattern consistent with the turning point hypothesis, by which we mean a trajectory where the employment transition occurred during a period of criminal activity with notable reductions in offending following the transition (Figure 9.3b).

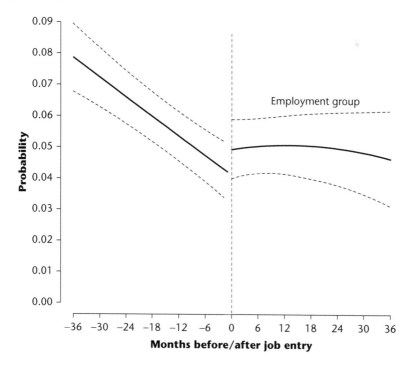

FIGURE 9.3a   Predicted probabilities of offending in each month in the 36 months leading up to and following job entry: average results.

Source: Skardhamar and Savolainen (2014).

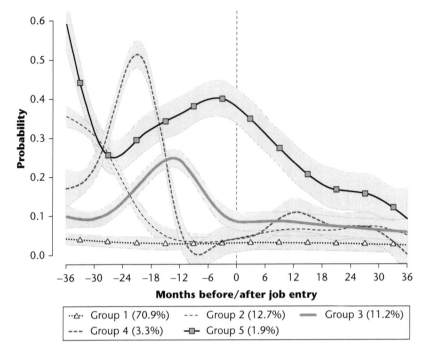

FIGURE 9.3b Predicted probabilities of offending in each month in the 36 months leading up to and following job entry: results by latent trajectory groups.

Source: Skardhamar and Savolainen (2014).

Implications

Across each study from this research agenda, we found consistently that crime rates had already declined before the transitions. This pattern contradicts the hypothesis that marriage or employment *leads to* desistance. Rather, it appears that marriage and employment should be viewed as consequences of desistance. It appears that most individuals are resistant or unable to make these transitions unless they are already far along in the desistance process.

Although the *conclusions* from our research have challenged those reported in a number of widely cited studies, it is critically important to recognize that our *empirical findings* are entirely consistent with those same studies. The main difference, we contend, has to do with standards of causality applied in the interpretation of the results. It seems that other studies are more comfortable assigning causal meaning to 'effects' estimated with methods – such as propensity score matching or fixed effects models of intra-individual change – that undoubtedly reduce selection bias, but can never eliminate it. The main difference between our studies and previous studies is that we describe the timing of change rather than compare average rates before and after the life course transition of interest. We wish to reiterate here that each of the hypothetical trajectories presented in Figure 9.1 implies reductions in the *average* crime rates. It is conceivable that patterns observed in our research would also appear in other data sets if they were examined from the same timing of change perspective.

There are some prior studies that have focused on timing of change in relation to marriage, although perhaps not as systematically as we have. Contrary to our results, Laub *et al.* (1998) did not find any decline before marriage, but reported a gradual decline in the post-marriage period.[3] Duncan *et al.* (2006) found evidence of initial declines in marijuana use in the period leading up to marriage, followed by a more substantial decline during the state of marriage. On the other hand, Beijers *et al.* (2012) and McGloin *et al.* (2011) reported evidence of declines in offending in the period preceding marriage. In sum, the results from prior research are not consistent, and it remains uncertain if the discrepancies are related to methodology or differences in the social context, for example. Our main concern, however, is that timing of change has been given far too little attention in the literature, and it is likely that the average differences around the point of transition reflect processes that have taken place *before* the transition. Our results underscore the importance of the timing issue and suggest that future research should move away from reporting changes in the average rates of offending.

Our findings must be interpreted against the fact that Norway represents a very specific type of macro-social context. The Norwegian welfare state provides a strong and comprehensive socio-economic safety net by comparative standards. Due to its strong economy, labour market conditions have been exceptionally advantageous and stable over a long period of time. The patterns and norms of family formation in Norway are similar to other Nordic countries, which can be described as more liberal or 'progressive' than in most other countries. The same goes for the criminal justice system: Norway is among the least punitive and most supportive in social context when it comes to law enforcement and sentencing (Pratt 2008; Savolainen 2009). It is quite possible that our findings are specific to this particular social context.

While our research does not rule out that marriage, parenthood or employment exert some influence on crime, we find these transitions to be unlikely to occur without behaviourally demonstrated ability to curb criminal offending. Importantly, all of these transitions require the willingness of *another* person, other than the offender, to support the transition. For example, an employer must be willing to hire a person with a criminal background. We contend this is more likely if the employer has reason to believe the applicant has turned over a new leaf. In a similar vein, romantic others are more likely to proceed to marriage and parenthood with a crime-prone person only with some evidence suggesting the criminal behaviour belongs in the past and not in the future. To be sure, these arguments apply only under the assumption that the employer or the romantic partner is a conventional other with the capacity to act as an effective source of prosocial bonding. Clearly, not all romantic partners or employers have these characteristics; some may not care if the boyfriend or employee persists in criminal behaviour.

Our agenda might be viewed as rejecting the idea that transitions to conventional adult social roles influence crime. This would be a misleading takeaway. It is true that we are skeptical of the idea that these events have the potential to set desistance in motion. We believe that if there are 'turning points', such events have to be quite rare. Contrary to Laub and Sampson (2003), we do not think most offenders desist as an inadvertent response to exogenous changes in their objective life circumstances. It seems obvious to us that individuals may drop out of crime without strong bonds to family or work. Our results suggest that if these life course transitions have a causal effect on crime, the effect is one of sustaining the process. In other words, marriage and employment might be important for maintenance of the desistance process. In this causal model, *relapse* to crime constitutes the counterfactual outcome.

Our findings do not support the assumptions of the turning point hypothesis; we do not find any evidence of desistance triggered by transitions to marriage, parenthood or employment. The gradual decline in offending prior to each transition is more consistent with the hooks-for-change and maturation hypotheses. The fact that we tend to observe little change following these transitions is more in line with the maturation hypothesis, but some of our findings do show additional declines in offending as predicted by the hooks-for-change hypothesis. It should be acknowledged that the turning point hypothesis could be salvaged if one is willing to argue that the actual turning point occurred *before* the formal point of transition. For example, one of the Glueck men is quoted as saying his turning point occurred when he *met* his wife (Laub and Sampson 2003: 134), which in all likelihood took place before the date of marriage. Perhaps there are equivalent pre-employment turning points, such as vocational training or social service intervention (Cook *et al.* 2015). In order for such claims to amount to more than ad hoc hypotheses, the theory needs to be specified and tested accordingly.

Our general concern with this literature (including our contributions) is its dominant focus on transitions occurring in a single domain, such as employment or marriage. This approach seems misplaced given that most theoretical perspectives view desistance as a complex process of incremental change. In addition, quantitative studies of desistance seem to aim at estimating causal effects without exogenous variation in the treatment variable of interest. This approach is not well suited to establishing effects that are likely to be related to other treatments or conditions. For example, we find it realistic to assume that employment may help with desistance depending on the state of mind of the offender, the characteristics of the job and other environmental factors that support the employment transition (peers, housing, family, etc.). If all of these auxiliary factors are important for the employment effect to occur, failure to attend to them introduces selection bias in the estimate. On the other hand, the goal of creating quantitative research designs that adequately address these complex and interdependent factors is daunting.

Directions for future research

Our agenda presents a number of challenges for future research, the most obvious of which has to do with our argument about timing. We think studies should pay more attention to the timing of change in criminal offending with respect to life course transitions. The approach we suggest is to describe the shape of offending trajectories before and after the transition. This can be accomplished in a number of ways from simple descriptions of trends to more advanced regression modelling. At the very least, we hope scholars will become more aware of the limitations associated with the approach that compares average offending rates around the point of transition. Future research should be sensitive to the timing issue and avoid making conclusions that are not warranted by the empirical results. Scholars should understand that results that are consistent with, say, the turning point hypothesis might also be consistent with competing models of desistance. Tests of any given theory should derive hypotheses that are unique to that theory.

We would like to see more detailed discussions of types of causal effects. For example, one should distinguish between whether life course transitions are expected to *initiate* or to *sustain* desistance. Studies should be more sensitive to the possibility that the effect of a given life course transition might vary across subgroups. The idea that the effect of employment may depend on age is well recognized in the literature (Uggen 2000). In addition, there are theories suggesting that psychological states (maturity, cognitive transformation, etc.) may moderate the effect of objective life course transitions. There has been very little quantitative research pursuing this hypothesis.

Future research should avoid making strong causal claims unless the evidence warrants it. If there is no exogenous variation in the data, no amount of methodological sophistication will be sufficient to justify a leap from associational to causal conclusions. We think there are too many loose claims about the effect of marriage and, to a lesser extent, employment on crime. With the exception of evidence from randomized job experiments, none of those studies serve counterfactual causal estimates. As such, they do not meet current methodological standards of causality (Morgan and Winship 2007).

One productive goal for observational research is to establish whether the *conditions* for a causal effect assumed by theory are actually present. This would not provide direct evidence of the hypothesized effect, but it would assess the plausibility of the theoretical claim. For example, acts of social control by the spouse are assumed to be an important mechanism for producing the marriage effect on crime. To our knowledge, there are no longitudinal studies documenting such behaviours and whether they are related to reduced levels of offending. Neither is there any empirical evidence evaluating the assumption that marriage generates prosocial capital through informal ties to the extended family of the spouse (Laub and Sampson 2003). The widely cited article by Warr (1998), which documents a shift in peer associations following marriage, is a paradigmatic example of this line of research. Wadsworth's (2006) study of job characteristics and desistance is less well known, but an equally compelling example of an effort to investigate the mechanisms expected to produce the employment effect.

As discussed above, we think quantitative studies of desistance tend to be too narrowly focused on discrete life course transitions. This approach ignores the possibility of multiple 'hooks for change' operating simultaneously in a mutually reinforcing process. If we take seriously the idea of desistance as a process, it might be better to focus on sequences of events rather than a single transition. Under this approach, factors that are typically treated as selection effects become an integral part of the explanatory model. In conclusion, findings from our research challenge popular beliefs about the impact of life course transitions on desistance from crime. We are particularly doubtful as to the validity of the turning point hypothesis; we do not think this perspective is the future of desistance research. Criminologists should continue to pay attention to these kinds of life course events, but in a far more nuanced fashion.

Notes

1 This criticism does not apply to studies based on randomized experiments. Under experimental conditions, timing of the treatment is an explicit part of the research design. There are no experimental studies of marital transitions, but there is an extensive literature on labour market experiments. These studies tend to find that providing jobs for crime-prone individuals does not reduce their rates of criminal offending (Wilson *et al.* 2000; Visher *et al.* 2005).
2 This definition of the analytic sample is somewhat arbitrary, but we repeated the analysis several times using alternative sample specifications. The findings were virtually identical across the different sampling criteria, including the definition of 'stable' employment. Thus, we concluded that the results are robust. The details are provided in the original article.
3 Although the study by Laub *et al.* (1998) has been highly influential, it has a major methodological limitation. By using latent trajectory classes estimated for the entire observational period, they are in effect making their findings conditional on future outcomes, which may have biased the results.

References

Beijers, J., Bijleveld, C. and Van Poppel, F. (2012), '"Man's best possession": Period effects in the association between marriage and offending', *European Journal of Criminology* 9(4): 425–441.
Bottoms, A., Shapland, J., Costello, A., Holmes, D. and Muir, G. (2004), 'Towards desistance: Theoretical underpinnings for an empirical study', *The Howard Journal of Criminal Justice* 43(4): 368–389.
Bushway, S. (2011), 'Labour markets and crime', in Wilson, J. Q. and Petersilia, J. (eds) *Crime and Public Policy*. New York: Oxford University Press.
Bushway, S. and Reuter, P. (1997), 'Labour markets and crime risk factors', in Sherman, L., Gottfredson, D., MacKenzie, D., Eck, J., Reuter, P. and Bushway, S. (eds) *Preventing Crime: What Works, What Doesn't, What's Promising. A Report to the United States Congress*. College Park, MD: University of Maryland, Department of Criminology and Criminal Justice.

Cook, P. J., Kang, S., Braga, A. A., Ludwig, J. and O'Brien, M. E. (2015), 'An experimental evaluation of a comprehensive employment-oriented prisoner re-entry program', *Journal of Quantitative Criminology* 31(3): 351–382.

Craig, J. M., Diamond, B. and Piquero, A. R. (2014), 'Marriage as an intervention in the lives of criminal offenders', in Humphrey, J. A. and Cordella, P. (eds) *Effective Interventions in the Lives of Criminal Offenders*. New York: Springer.

Duncan, G. J., Wilkerson, B. and England, P. (2006), 'Cleaning up their act: The effect of marriage and cohabitation on licit and illicit drug use', *Demography* 43(4): 691–710.

Fagan, J. and Freeman, R. B. (1999), 'Crime and work', *Crime and Justice* 25: 225–290.

Giordano, P. C., Cernkovich, S. A. and Rudolph, J. L. (2002), 'Gender, crime, and desistance: Towards a theory of cognitive transformation', *American Journal of Sociology* 107(4): 990–1064.

Glueck, S. and Glueck, E. (1940), *Juvenile Delinquents Grown Up*. New York: Commonwealth Fund.

Hirschi, T. and Gottfredson, M. (1983), 'Age and the explanation of crime', *The American Journal of Sociology* 89(3): 552–584.

Horney, J., Wayne Osgood, D. and Haen Marshall, I. (1995), 'Criminal careers in the short-term: Intra-individual variability in crime and its relation to local life circumstances', *American Sociological Review* 60(5): 655–673.

Kreager, D. A., Matsueda, R. L. and Erosheva, E. A. (2010), 'Motherhood and criminal desistance in disadvantaged neighborhoods', *Criminology* 48(1): 221–258.

Laub, J. H. and Sampson, R. J. (2003), *Shared Beginnings, Divergent Lives: Delinquent Boys to Age 70*. Cambridge, MA: Harvard University Press.

Laub, J. H., Nagin, D. S. and Sampson, R. J. (1998), 'Trajectories of change in criminal offending: Good marriages and the desistance process', *American Sociological Review* 63(2): 225–239.

LeBel, T. P., Burnett, R., Maruna, S. and Bushway, S. (2008), 'The "chicken and egg" of subjective and social factors in desistance from crime', *European Journal of Criminology* 5(2): 131–159.

Lyngstad, T. H. and Skardhamar, T. (2011), 'Nordic register data and their untapped potential for criminological knowledge', in Tonry, M. and Lappi-Seppälä, T. (eds) *Crime & Justice: A Review of Research*. Chicago, IL: Chicago University Press.

Lyngstad, T. H. and Skardhamar, T. (2013), 'Changes in criminal offending around the time of marriage', *Journal of Research in Crime and Delinquency* 50(4): 608–615.

Maruna, S. (2001), *Making Good: How Ex-Convicts Reform and Rebuild Their Lives*. Washington, DC: American Psychological Association.

Massoglia, M. and Uggen, C. (2010), 'Settling down and aging out: Toward an interactionist theory of desistance and the transition to adulthood', *American Journal of Sociology* 116(2): 543–582.

McGloin, J. M., Sullivan, C. J., Piquero, A. R., Blokland, A. and Nieuwbeerta, P. (2011), 'Marriage and offending specialization: Expanding the impact of turning points and the process of desistance', *European Journal of Criminology* 8(5): 361–376.

Monsbakken, C. W., Lyngstad, T. H. and Skardhamar, T. (2013), 'Crime and the transition to parenthood: The role of sex and relationship context', *British Journal of Criminology* 54(4): 129–148.

Morgan, S. L. and Winship, C. (2007), *Counterfactuals and Causal Inference: Methods and Principles for Social Research Analytical Methods for Social Research*. New York: Cambridge University Press.

Morizot, J. and Le Blanc, M. (2007), 'Behavioural, self, and social control predictors of desistance from crime: A test of launch and contemporaneous effect models', *Journal of Contemporary Criminal Justice* 23: 50–71.

Nagin, D. S. (2005), *Group-Based Modeling of Development*. Cambridge, MA: Harvard University Press.

Pager, D. (2003), 'The mark of a criminal record', *American Journal of Sociology* 108(5): 937–975.

Pratt, J. (2008), 'Scandinavian exceptionalism in an era of excess. Part I: The nature and roots of Scandinavian exceptionalism', *British Journal of Criminology* 48(2): 119–137.

Sampson, R. J. and Laub, J. H. (1993), *Crime in the Making: Pathways and Turning Points through Life*. London: Harvard University Press.

Savolainen, J. (2009), 'Work, family, and criminal desistance: Adult social bonds in a Nordic welfare state', *British Journal of Criminology* 49(3): 285–304.

Siennick, S. E. and Wayne Osgood, D. (2008), 'A review of research on the impact on crime of transitions into adult roles', in Liberman, A. M. (ed.) *The Long View of Crime: A Synthesis of Longitudinal Research*. New York: Springer.

Skardhamar, T. and Lyngstad, T. H. (2009), 'Family formation, fatherhood and crime', in *Discussion Papers*. Oslo, Norway: Statistics Norway.

Skardhamar, T. and Telle, K. (2012), 'Post-release employment and recidivism in Norway', *Journal of Quantitative Criminology* 28(4): 629–649.

Skardhamar, T. and Savolainen, J. (2014), 'Changes in criminal offending around the time of job entry', *Criminology* 52(2): 263–291.

Skardhamar, T., Monsbakken, C. W. and Lyngstad, T. H. (2014), 'Crime and the transition to marriage. The role of the spouse's criminal involvement', *British Journal of Criminology* 54(3): 411–427.

Skardhamar, T., Savolainen, J., Aase, K. N. and Lyngstad, T. H. (2015), 'Does marriage reduce crime? A review of research', in Tonry, M. (ed.) *Crime and Justice*, Volume 44. Chicago, IL: University of Chicago Press.

Uggen, C. (2000), 'Work as a turning point in the life course of criminals: A duration model of age, employment, and recidivism', *American Sociological Review* 67: 529–546.

Uggen, C. and Wakefield, S. (2008), 'What have we learned from longitudinal studies of work and crime?', in Liberman, A. M. (ed.) *The Long View of Crime*. New York: Springer.

Van Der Geest, V. R., Bijleveld, C. and Blokland, A. A. J. (2011), 'The effects of employment on longitudinal trajectories of offending: A follow-up of high-risk youth from 18 to 32 years of age', *Criminology* 49(4): 1195–1234.

Van Schellen, M., Poortman, A.-R. and Nieuwbeerta, P. (2012), 'Partners in crime? Criminal offending, marriage formation, and partner selection', *Journal of Research in Crime and Delinquency* 49(4): 545–571.

Visher, C. A., Winterfield, L. and Coggeshapp, M. B. (2005), 'Ex-offender employment programs and recidivism: A meta-analysis', *Journal of Experimental Criminology* 1(3): 295–316.

Wadsworth, T. (2006), 'The meaning of work: Conceptualizing the deterrent effect of employment on crime among young adults', *Sociological Perspectives* 49(3): 343–368.

Warr, M. (1998), 'Life-course transitions and desistance from crime', *Criminology* 36(2): 183–216.

Wilson, D. B., Gallagher, C. A. and MacKenzie, D. L. (2000), 'A meta-analysis of corrections-based education, vocation, and work programs for adult offenders', *Journal of Research in Crime and Delinquency* 37(4): 347–368.

SECTION III

Criminal justice and state interventions

Policy makers in some jurisdictions have shown considerable interest in some of the ideas developed by those studying desistance. In short, their interest stems from the possibilities for the criminal justice system of 'piggy-backing' on desistance processes so as to speed its progress, or at least maintain its momentum. If some processes of change occur outwith the ambit of the criminal justice system, what can the criminal justice system do to allow and encourage such changes, and also what ought it to refrain from doing which might endanger or impede desistance? This section of the book looks at the relation between desistance and criminal justice systems and processes. Does supervision by the probation service have any effect on desistance, from the desister's own perspective, or is desistance 'all their own work'? How can aftercare from prison and conditions on licence potentially set back intentions to desist, or cement them? Distinguishing offences from legitimate conduct is an important purpose of the criminal law. But do the labels that the criminal justice system applies to those who offend then themselves become obstacles to desistance? Depending upon how those processes associated with desistance occur, will different proposed policy mechanisms be likely to have any effect, negative or positive, on desistance? In sum, the chapters in this section all consider the degree to which we can reconceive penal policy to support desistance and build on offenders' strengths without damaging what is, for some, a very fragile and contingent process.

10

UNDERSTANDING DESISTANCE IN AN ASSISTED CONTEXT

Key findings from tracking progress on probation[1]

Stephen Farrall

Introduction

My aim in this brief chapter is to outline some of the main findings from a longitudinal project, which started in the very late 1990s and which sought to explore the impact (in terms of assisting people towards desistance) of probation supervision. The project has outlived its original brief (it was designed as a project which would last no more than three to four years) and is now one of two longitudinal projects into desistance currently being run by staff in the Centre for Criminological Research at the University of Sheffield (the other is that run by Tony Bottoms and Joanna Shapland, see Chapter 6 in this volume). As well as outlining this project, its methodology and some of the key findings, I will devote some time to sketching an agenda for future research in this field.

Study outline

Tracking Progress on Probation (and later Tracking Progress after Probation) is a longitudinal study of almost 200 men and women who started probation supervision in 1997. When they commenced supervision, probation orders in England and Wales typically lasted between 6 and 24 months. As well as getting what was known as 'straight' probation (i.e. supervision with a named probation officer, with or without the requirement to repay damages to the victim, undertake particular programmes and so on) some people were given what were known as combination orders, which included the above and a set number of hours of community service. It was these sorts of community disposals, which the sample members were given.

All members of the sample were aged 17 to 35 years old at the start of their sentences, and none of the orders were to be for longer than 24 months. The number of previous convictions, their gender and the nature of their charging offences were not factors for inclusion. Sample members and their supervising officers were interviewed for the first time shortly after their probation orders had started. Officers and those being supervised were not interviewed together, but rather in parallel. Two more sweeps of interviews were completed whilst the sample was being supervised. The second sweep took place about 6–7 months after the first (which meant that some had formally completed their supervision), and the third sweep interview was timed to coincide with the end of their orders. Again, during the second and third sweeps, probation officers were interviewed. This phase of the project lasted from 1997 to 1999 and was reported in Farrall (2002a). A fourth sweep of interviews took place in late 2003 to mid-2004. This sweep was a smaller undertaking, with just a quarter of the sample targeted for interview. Although some of the sample were back on probation, there were no interviews with supervising officers. This phase of the fieldwork was reported in Farrall and Calverley (2006). Finally, in 2010 to 2013 we conducted interviews with as many of the sample as we could find (in all 105 interviews were completed, with some information about offending career and/or lifestyle gleaned from conversations, official records or online searches for a further 39).

Some of the main lessons learnt

The project made a contribution to knowledge in a number of ways. In some ways, one of the main lessons was that research projects like this could be conducted successfully with those on probation. Prior to this project, many studies of the effectiveness of probation supervision were large-scale quantitative undertakings, which placed an emphasis on those processes and interventions about which the criminal justice system retained data. As such, these sorts of projects focused on the types of interventions completed, the 'dosage' of these, any notes which the probation staff had recorded in their records of supervision, etc. Data collected from the perspective of the recipients of such interviews or about other factors (such as motivation to change, changes in social circumstances and so on) were not a key part of this tradition. An example of this tradition of research might be Lloyd *et al.*'s (1994) Home Office study. Alternatively, those studies that had interviewed probationers (or former probationers) tended to be rather small scale (e.g. Brown 1998) or selected cases on the dependent variable (e.g. Leibrich 1993). Such studies sought to collect data on the experiences of those men and women who had served a probation order and had made (or were making) some form of progress towards desistance. In this respect the Tracking project represented evidence that novel forms of research could be undertaken with quite large numbers of respondents (sufficient with which to conduct some quantitative analyses). In this respect, the project demonstrated that *technically* this could be completed and that *conceptually* exploring desistance (rather than reconviction) made sense, even with a group of adjudicated offenders. The project also made some contributions to the *operationalisation* and *measurement* of desistance (a slippery phenomenon to deal with). Since the completion of further rounds of interviews, the project has been able to make contributions to the methodological discussions around maintaining contact with members in a cohort sample and on how to maintain good levels of sample retention (Farrall *et al.* 2015). We also contributed to the small literature on why people fail to maintain contact with their probation officers (Farrall 2002b), the victim–offender overlap (Farrall and Maltby 2003) and the relationship between self-reported and officially recorded offending (Farrall 2005). In this respect, some of what is summarised below relates directly to interventions aimed at encouraging desistance, whilst some of it relates to the non-interventional drivers of desistance.

The role of probation in desistance

Turning to the substantive findings, rather than the contribution to methodological matters, the project has explored a number of issues. Whilst the main explanations of reasons for desisting, such as employment, family formation, motivation and overcoming drug and alcohol problems were confirmed, the project also contributed to our knowledge about how probation supervision contributed to 'assisted desistance'. Initially, the findings suggested that many members of the sample had not taken a lot from probation supervision (Farrall 2002a). This impression was gained via data from both the probationers themselves and the probation officers, and was formed on the basis of the first three sweeps of interviews (1997–1999). The drivers of desistance were a combination of motivation on the part of the probationer and changes in their personal and social circumstances. The fourth sweep of interviews reiterated this message (albeit just from the former probationers, some of whom had avoided further trouble, others of whom had not – see Farrall and Calverley 2006). Yet this sweep of interviews also showed something new, namely that some former probationers who had previously dismissed the idea that probation supervision had helped them, were now less damning in their assessments of what they had taken from probation. In this respect, we had the first signs that the impact of probation supervision was a slow-moving one.

When we returned to as many of the sample as we could find and interview for a fifth sweep, a subtly new story emerged. There were still some who reported that probation had been of little or no use to them in terms of encouraging or facilitating desistance (some had stopped offending relatively quickly without, they felt, much assistance from probation, whilst others were still offending at quite a high rate of frequency and/or were in prison at the time of interview). However, there were far more who now reported that probation supervision *had* indeed helped them. The main explanation for this appeared to be that the advice, which they had been given by probation staff, had lain 'dormant' for many years. Our sample members had required changes in objective social and personal circumstances to emerge (i.e. for relationships with girlfriends or boyfriends to develop into marriages and/or to result in children, or for entry-level jobs to develop into possible careers) before they could start to use some of this advice. As these changes took hold, the former probationers concerned started to cast about for advice which would enable them to move away from engagement in crime. Some of the advice they recalled came from family members, friends, drug and social workers, and some of it from their probation officers. Figure 10.1 is an attempt to chart these processes diagrammatically (see also Farrall *et al.* 2014, chapter 5). Figure 10.1 describes the processes (social, interpersonal and in terms of their outlook), which someone with a high degree of embeddedness in offending and (initially) minimal desire to change may, over time, undergo and which shift them towards desistance. So, for example, Jasper recounted to us how advice from his girlfriend's father (who had said to him, 'you live by the sword you'll die by the sword'), the birth of his second child (his third child in all) with his girlfriend ('was the day I said, I'm getting a job tomorrow' he reported), and being threatened with a gun in a pub (he had recently beaten someone up very badly) had encouraged him to stop offending. Even when interviewed several years later, Jasper could recall the earlier advice of his probation officer:

> She just said to me 'listen, where do you want to be in five years' time?'. She said 'I'll speak to you in five minutes and see what you think'. Went away, left me to it, and she came back and she asked me the same question again. And I'd thought about it and I thought 'Well, I don't want to be in the same position I'm in now, I want to be respected but I don't want to be feared. I mean there's a difference'.

As such, as Jasper's life unfolded, so he reflected on the advice given to him by his probation officer and started to use some of the insights he had gained from probation and the practical assistance they had offered him in terms of employment skills in order to ensure that his imagined future life some five years off in the future was different to his (then) current life. In this respect, 'trigger points' (perhaps a better term than 'turning points', Carlsson 2012) in his social and personal life encouraged Jasper to try to refashion his future, and in so doing necessitated adopting the advice he had been given by proximal others, including (but not limited to) his probation officer. Of course, such influences need not be limited to either probation or desistance. Prison, arrest, appearance in court may also encourage processes of change, which unfold slowly (i.e. have what may be termed lagged effects). Similarly, numerous other interventions in the criminal justice system (such as victim counselling, compensation or both social and situational crime prevention) may also have lagged effects.

The spatial dynamics of desistance

Our studies, and the length of time over which we have been able to study the lives of the men and women we have interviewed, have, as well as affording us insights such as the above, also allowed us to draft interviews, which have taken account of findings that have emerged unexpectedly in earlier sweeps. One such topic has been the spatial dynamics of desistance from crime. Whilst interviewing one cohort member (Anthony) who lived within the same town, but moved home within it as his offending appeared to lessen (see Farrall *et al.* 2014: 177–179), I started to wonder about the degree to which desistance from crime also went

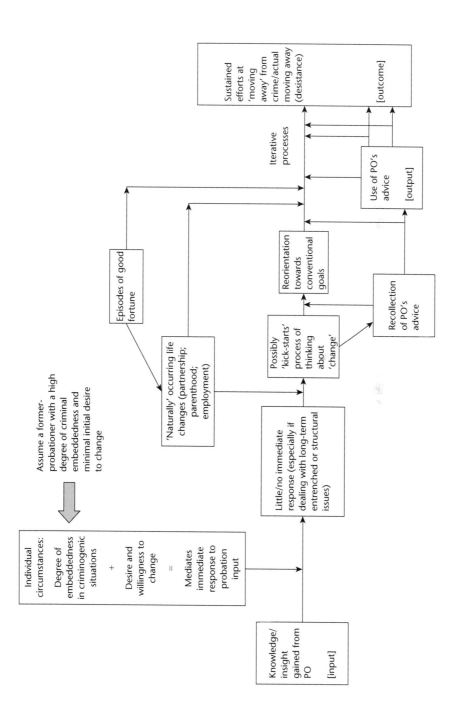

FIGURE 10.1 Model of impact of probation supervision.

hand-in-hand with a change in daily routines and the spatial emplacements these require. Anthony, it struck me, changed his use of his local town centre. Where once it had been a place in which to reside, go drinking, take recreational drugs, go to nightclubs, 'pick-up girls', get into fights and enjoy watching others embroiled in the carnival of the night-time economy, after Anthony had moved to the suburbs, was living with a new partner and was much more thoroughly engaged in the labour market, the town centre became a place he visited infrequently and only during the day time and then only to visit his bank or go shopping. In short, his relationship with that physical location changed as his lifestyle became more conventional.

This started me wondering about the extent to which this was also the case for others and so, in the fifth sweep, we asked a series of questions, in part inspired by the work, which Wikström and his colleagues had undertaken (see Wikström *et al.* 2010), but also drawing on the work of 1960s existential geographers like Anne Buttimer and David Seamon (see Buttimer 1976; Seamon 1980) about sample members' time-space budgets. When we came to analyse these data, they suggested not only that there were indeed different spatial dynamics for desisters and persisters (in itself hardly a surprise since family and employment routines are spatially as well as temporally restricting) but that these spatial dynamics operated at different levels for those with different offending careers. Anthony, for example, whose offending had all been related to street-crimes (fighting, minor chequebook and card frauds, conveying drugs for friends, taking recreational drugs and so on) had never lived away from the town I referred to above. Markey, on the other hand, had had a very long injecting drug career. His moves of home had been across whole regions of the UK as he undertook (unsuccessfully) residential drug treatment programmes. Eventually, one of these resulted in him getting off drugs and he settled in that city, some hours away from his home city. Now free of drugs, Markey returned to his home city when his own son started to become involved in minor episodes of anti-social behaviour and came to the attention of the police. At this point, Markey got a job as a drugs counsellor in his home city and settled there.

We found many similar spatially as well as temporally configured offending and desistance trajectories amongst others like Anthony and Markey. As such, the scale of the moves they had made was, in part but not totally defined by, the nature of their offending careers (see Farrall *et al.* 2014, chapter 6). We also found that desisters and persisters inferred something about 'who' they were from the physical places in which they found themselves. Nick, a former injecting drug user, reflected on his experiences of finding himself in 'normal' places, as opposed to those sorts of places he used to hang around in:

> Like last year, we went swimming every other Saturday, I went swimming and so did the kids, it was the first time the kids had been swimming. So we go swimming, McDonalds, just normal family stuff but sometimes when I am out and stuff and I am there with my kids and stuff I think back, you know, years, 'I am in a McDonalds and I used to be a smackhead', fucking all sorts. And now I am with normal people doing normal stuff what normal people do, but it freaks me out a little bit, you know, because of what I have been like in the past.

As such, there was much for us to learn about how places came to symbolise to individuals the degrees to which they had changed (or were still changing in some cases). As I mentioned above and we outline in more depth elsewhere (Farrall *et al.* 2014, chapter 6), we were greatly aided by insights from existential geography in this respect and found evidence of the ways in which the daily operating procedures of probation offices, medical practices, drug drop-in centres, social welfare offices, dealer networks and such like create time-space rhythms for drug users. In this respect, where one is, the time one is in that particular place, where one has travelled to that place from and where one will go to next are functions of all sorts of processes, which operate above and beyond the control of many of those who are supervised in one way or another in the community – and these 'place-ballets' have consequences for self-identity.

Citizenship, voting and inclusion

Another issue we explored in sweeps four and five has been the degree to which desisters and persisters are engaged in activities, which one might consider reflective of the degree to which they are citizens. We asked our cohort members the degree to which they agreed with the following seven statements:

1. *People should not rely on the government, they should take responsibility for themselves.*
2. *It does not really matter if you lie when dealing with state officials.*
3. *Being a citizen is about becoming involved in your community.*
4. *The government does not listen to people like me.*
5. *People should obey the law.*
6. *People should accept that others have a right to be different.*
7. *Local government officials don't really care about what happens to people like me* (not asked during sweep four).

TABLE 10.1 t-Tests of citizenship statements

Statement number and description	Mean scores	N	Sig.
1 Responsibility	D 2.43	78	0.002
	P 3.41	31	
2 Honesty	D 5.08	78	0.001
	P 3.84	32	
3 Involved in community	D 2.57	78	0.049
	P 3.37	32	
4 Not listened to	D 3.53	78	0.000
	P 2.28	32	
5 Obey law	D 1.88	78	0.000
	P 3.22	31	
6 Tolerate differences	D 1.75	78	0.011
	P 2.22	31	
7 Local government doesn't care	D 4.02	70	0.030
	P 3.14	28	

Note: D = desisters; P = persisters.

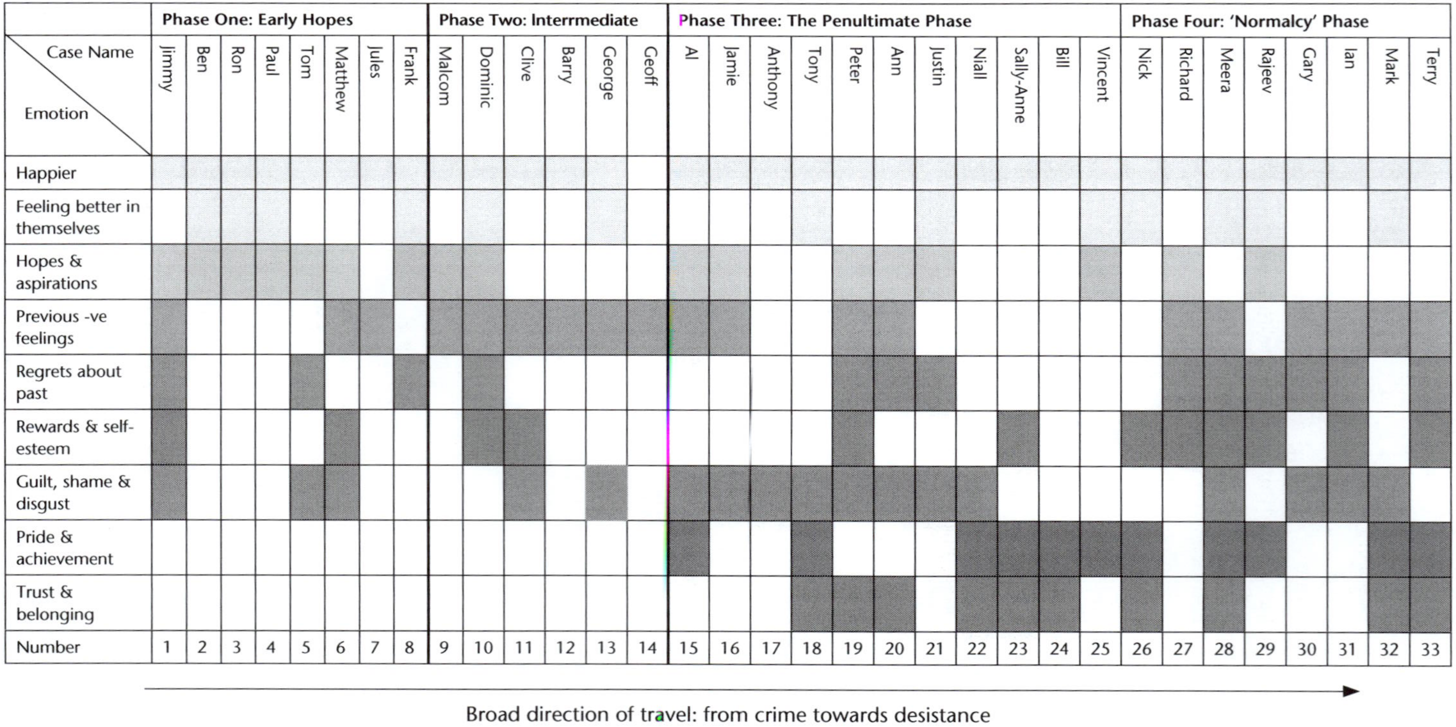

Phase One: Early Hopes — Jimmy (1), Ben (2), Ron (3), Paul (4), Tom (5), Matthew (6), Jules (7), Frank (8)

Phase Two: Intermediate — Malcom (9), Dominic (10), Clive (11), Barry (12), George (13), Geoff (14)

Phase Three: The Penultimate Phase — Al (15), Jamie (16), Anthony (17), Tony (18), Peter (19), Ann (20), Justin (21), Niall (22), Sally-Anne (23), Bill (24), Vincent (25)

Phase Four: 'Normalcy' Phase — Nick (26), Richard (27), Meera (28), Rajeev (29), Gary (30), Ian (31), Mark (32), Terry (33)

Emotion (rows):
- Happier
- Feeling better in themselves
- Hopes & aspirations
- Previous -ve feelings
- Regrets about past
- Rewards & self-esteem
- Guilt, shame & disgust
- Pride & achievement
- Trust & belonging

Broad direction of travel: from crime towards desistance

FIGURE 10.2 Emotional trajectory of desistance (sweep 4).

Respondents were encouraged to discuss their answers, which were subsequently coded on a seven-point scale (strongly agree to strongly disagree). We found, following the appropriate coding (some items needed to be reverse scaled, for example), that desisters were more likely than persisters to agree with statements 1, 3, 5 and 6, and more likely to disagree with statements 2, 4 and 7 (see Table 10.1 above).

Additionally, desisters were more likely than persisters to be registered to vote (70 per cent vs 39 per cent, p = 0.009) and were also more likely to have voted in the past two years (42 per cent vs 14 per cent, p = 0.006). We think, therefore, that there is considerable evidence to suggest that desisters' citizenship values are more 'liberal' than those of persisters, and that desisters are more likely to be engaged in the kinds of activities we would associate with liberal citizenship. What our data suggested to us was that the desisters in our cohort sought out ways of expressing their citizenship, which transcended simple mechanisms such as voting, and in so doing did some considerable social good. In this respect, formal agencies need, we feel, to recognise that part of the process of rehabilitation is about both helping others and playing a part in decision-making processes. Attempts to curtail the civic engagement of current or formerly incarcerated men and women strike a chord which is at odds with our data: 'citizenship' is about, amongst other things, inclusion. As such, attempts to deny former offenders the right to vote strike us as curtailing one avenue of the expression of this form of reintegration (see Farrall et al. 2014, chapter 9).

The emotional trajectory of desistance

By rank ordering our cohort members in terms of the degree to which they had desisted (or were on the route to desistance), we were able to explore two further issues. The first, which I shall touch on only briefly, concerns the emotional trajectory of desistance (see Figure 10.2), and the second concerns the relationship between victimisation and desistance. Using the data collected during sweep four, Adam Calverley and I (see Farrall and Calverley 2006) were able to identify an emotional trajectory of desistance. (We revisited this during sweep five, but the data, being based on a large number of cases do not lend themselves to a cursory summary such as this one.) Figure 10.2 shows the feelings reported during interviews (the rows) with those who we had interviewed (the columns). Shading indicates the presence of a report of that emotion during the interview. What one sees (again I shall skip over some of the details), is a shift over time from reports of hopes and aspirations (common in the early phase), to feelings of pride and achievement and feelings of being trusted and belonging (common in the final phase). Similarly, previous negative feelings and regrets about the past fade away as people become more established desisters. We found similar, albeit more nuanced, trends when we repeated this exercise using the data we collected during sweep five.

Victimisation, offending and desistance

We have asked cohort members about their experiences of victimisation three times: during sweeps two, four and five. At sweep four (when we first explored the relationship between desistance and victimisation), we found that desisters had the same probability of victimisation as persisters. This suggested that desistance did not 'protect' individuals from victimisation. Initially, this appeared to be the case with the sweep five data. However, this ignores a key point, namely that desisters are *not* best thought of as a homogenous group. When we analysed the data and separated those who were just *starting* the process of desistance from those who had progressed to the point where their desistance was largely beyond doubt, we found differences in their rates of victimisation. We divided desisters into 'recent' and 'established' desisters (i.e. those who had desisted for less than three years and those who had desisted for longer than three years). This division left us with three groups: 30 'recent desisters', 38 'established desisters' and 28 persisters. For our analyses we combined the recent desisters and persisters. This produced dramatically different findings: established desisters were much *less* likely than the rest of the sample to have been the victims of either damage (11 per cent vs 30 per cent, $p = 0.025$) or theft (22 per cent vs 47 per cent, $p = 0.012$). (The differences for threats and assault were not statistically significant, but did suggest substantive differences: 16 per cent of established desisters vs 26 per cent of recent desisters/persisters had been assaulted, $p = 0.198$, whilst the same figures for threats were 22 per cent vs 28 per cent, $p = 0.344$.) When we compared the *number of times* established desisters had been victimised compared with recent desisters/persisters, the results were just as stark: established desisters were victimised on average 0.86 times in the past year, compared to 5.2 times for recent desisters/persisters (t-test, $p = 0.009$). What is striking, when the data are represented visually, is that recent desisters appear to have been victimised *more frequently*, even when compared to persistent offenders for three out of the four offence types we asked about (Figure 10.3).

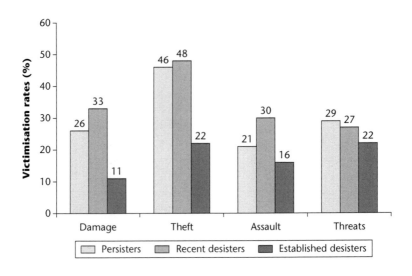

FIGURE 10.3 Victimisation rates (percentages) by desistance status.

Perhaps this apparent increase in their victimisation was part of their desistance story.[2] Had the victimisation that they suffered recently pushed them towards wanting to change their lifestyle? To throw further light on this matter, we explored a number of related themes, including how the neighbourhoods in which our sample lived, the people with whom they spent their time, and their efforts to desist, impacted upon their victimisation experiences via case studies. This suggested that recent desisters had indeed experienced quite dramatic victimisation (both episodic and serial), which appeared to have propelled them towards initiating efforts to desist (see Farrall *et al.* 2014, chapter 8).

Failing to maintain contact with probation

Probation supervision will only assist people to stop offending if they engage in the work being undertaken and remain in contact with their officer. Of the 199 probationers in the project, 40 (20 per cent) did not maintain contact with their supervising probation officers for extended periods of time. In several cases, these absences lasted for many months, and in some instances, over a year. A minority of probationers re-established contact, whilst others remained unsupervised until the (planned) end of their orders. A range of factors and their relationship to losing contact were explored via bivariate cross-tabulations. These included the probationer's social and personal circumstances; their offending since the start of the order (self- and officer-reported); their motivation to stop offending; obstacles to stopping offending; and previous criminal history. The results of these are shown in Table 10.2. Disappointingly (from the perspective of being able to identify potential absentees at the outset of their orders), few of the variables, which probation services routinely collected at that point in time, were found to be related to absence

TABLE 10.2 Variables associated with absence

Variable	Reported by . . . (Chi. Sq. Sig.)
Finances: a cause of the offence	Probationer (★★) and officer (★)
Finances: a problem at the offence	Probationer (★★) and officer (★★)
Finances: a problem at the first interview	Probationer (★)
Drugs: a cause of the offence	Officer (★)
Drugs: a problem at the offence	Probationer (★)
Drugs and/or alcohol: obstacles	Probationer (★)
Depressed/anxious: a cause of the offence	Officer (★★)
Depressed/anxious: a problem at the offence	Probationer (★)
Employment: a problem at the offence	Probationer (★)
Previous custodial experience	– (★)
Property offender	– (★)
OGRS >50%	– (★)

Notes

N = 199.

★ = sig. at 0.05 level, ★★ = sig. at 0.01 level.

df = 1 for cross-tabulation cells upon which table is based.

TABLE 10.3 Modelling absence

	Beta	Df	Sig.
Previous custody	1.0087	1	0.0498
Finances: cause	1.4401	1	0.0057
Finances: problem at 1st interview	1.1866	1	0.0293
Depression: cause	1.7574	1	0.0066
Constant	−5.9584	1	0.0000
Cases correctly predicted	76%		

(the grey cells at the bottom of Table 10.2). The length of the order, starting probation for a violent offence, a drug offence or another indictable offence, and previous
number of convictions were all found to be unrelated to absence, as were gender
and age. Having had a previous custodial sentence and being on probation for a
property offence were both weakly associated with later absence, however.

However, as can also be seen from Table 10.2, financial problems, problematic
drug usage and depression were commonly associated with absences. Attempts
were made to produce a model of absence (using the variables listed in Table 10.2).
Some variables were unsuitable for inclusion in regression modelling (as they were
too highly correlated with other variables) and so only four variables were used in
attempts to model absence. These were: previous custodial experience; financial
problems as a cause of offending; financial problems at the time of first interview
(both probationer-reported); and depression as a cause of offending (officer-
reported). All of these variables entered the model, described in Table 10.3.

The model suggests that those probationers who said that their finances had
been a cause of their offending and whose officers had said that the probationer
feeling 'down, depression and anxious' had been a cause of their offending were
particularly likely to absent themselves. Additionally, those who had previous
prison experiences and who said that their finances were a problem (at the first
interview) were likely to disappear, although these were less strongly associated.
Such findings could be used to identify those 'at risk' of losing contact with probation staff and offering them extra support.

Theoretical implications

This project has also attempted to make a contribution to the theoretical understanding of desistance from crime (and persistence in offending). We have tried to
develop a theoretical model which:

- has retained a focus on structural processes (including the criminal career itself
  as a form of structuring);
- can explore what it feels like to stop offending (or to continue) and to have
  once been an offender;
- can retain an acceptance of agency, but which takes seriously the idea that
  there are various social, legal, cultural and economic processes which influence crime, offending desistance and circulating ideas and images about these;

- can incorporate changing beliefs about some inputs (such as probation), which may develop over time as those subject to these reflect on their lives;
- incorporates a spatial element when examining desistance from crime;
- is capable of exploring other (in some case, consequential) dimensions of desistance (such as feelings of citizenship);
- allows us to move away from 'one size fits all' theoretical models of desistance, but instead recognises that there are differing trajectories of criminal careers and hence variations in routes 'out'.

Space constraints preclude a full outlining of our approach, which can instead be found in Farrall *et al.* (2010, 2011, 2014). Our model is summarised as a diagram in Figure 10.4. Let us start with the three bands of general influence, which run across the top of the diagram and represent different macro-level influences. The influences in the top band are those which are broadly unchanging, or very slowly changing (for example, social institutions such as 'the family', even if the definition of what constitutes a family may alter over time, and the idea that there are acts, which are labelled as 'crimes'). Below this are macro-level influences which change less slowly (such as social values) and finally, amongst the macro-level influences, are the shocks to the system, which emerge with little warning (such as sudden economic downturns). On the left-most side of Figure 10.4 are individual-level influences, such as gender and ethnic identity, which can shape the opportunities that are presented to them throughout their life.

Another factor that influences the character of pathways out of crime is the nature and length of the previous criminal career. For individuals with intensive criminal careers, desistance from crime may well require a greater degree of 'rebuilding' of their core selves (and hence many turn to religion or to quasi-religious forms of belief in order to make such changes possible, intelligible and sustainable). At the bottom of Figure 10.4 is an oval, which represents routine social interactions and relationships between individuals over time. It is an oval as not all relationships extend far backwards in time (some people we have only known briefly) and neither will all last for the rest of one's lifetime. Cutting into this is a column ('Situational Contexts') representing specific circumstances, chapters, events or processes in individuals' lives. These may be short-lived episodes, or they might represent extended periods, such as time spent in prison or living in a particular city.

Running from left to right are four further rows. The bottom two rows relate closely to ongoing social relationships and deal with subjective views of structures, of relationships and of one's own abilities, and changes in personal values and cognitive orientations to the world and the way it works, the 'habitus' (Bourdieu 1977). Relationships, of course, are dynamic and can change and develop over time and extend into the future, influencing hopes and desires. The top two rows across the centre of Figure 10.4 relate to experiences of the criminal justice system. Few ex-offenders, in our experience, go on to become 'professional exes' or develop a new pro-social identity based on their previous criminal identities (although see Maruna 2001). Of course, in some cases, repeated and prolonged exposure to the criminal justice system may become *so* dramatically cumulative to

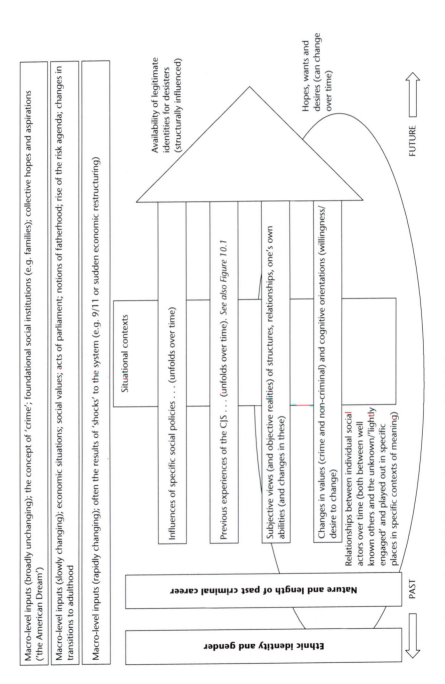

Macro-level inputs (broadly unchanging); the concept of 'crime'; foundational social institutions (e.g. families); collective hopes and aspirations ('the American Dream')

Macro-level inputs (slowly changing); economic situations; social values; acts of parliament; notions of fatherhood; rise of the risk agenda; changes in transitions to adulthood

Macro-level inputs (rapidly changing); often the results of 'shocks' to the system (e.g. 9/11 or sudden economic restructuring)

Availability of legitimate identities for desisters (structurally influenced)

Hopes, wants and desires (can change over time)

Situational contexts

Influences of specific social policies . . . (unfolds over time)

Previous experiences of the CJS . . . (unfolds over time). *See also Figure 10.1*

Subjective views (and objective realities) of structures, relationships, one's own abilities (and changes in these)

Changes in values (crime and non-criminal) and cognitive orientations (willingness/desire to change)

Relationships between individual social actors over time (both between well known others and the unknown/'lightly engaged' and played out in specific places in specific contexts of meaning)

Nature and length of past criminal career

Ethnic identity and gender

PAST

FUTURE

FIGURE 10.4 Structural and individual level processes and criminal careers.

the point that even if an individual does cease to offend, they carry with them a legacy of their earlier sentences. Similarly, we have uncovered evidence that some criminal justice workers leave *imprints* on offenders (see above) and this is located within this row of our model.

Finally, on the right-hand side of Figure 10.4 is a triangle, which represents the idea that lives are lived *into* the future and that humans are often involved in ongoing projects of the self, which they project forward into the unlived future as part of their immediate day-to-day lives and as part of their concern for their own future over longer time periods. Of course, the extent to which ex-offenders can achieve their desires and goals is partly dependent on the availability of legitimate identities. In societies that prevent ex-offenders from full engagement in social and economic life, we imagine that more would-be desisters will return to their old (criminal) behaviours.

Future directions

In closing, I would like to propose that the future of research into desistance from crime move in two directions (which can each be done separately from one another, or simultaneously). The first is that more studies of this nature are needed, by which I mean that we need more studies of how particular interventions, which seek to aid and support desistance from crime, actually operate. Such studies are going to need to be designed as longitudinal from the outset (the Tracking project evolved into a longitudinal study fairly painlessly). Such projects I see differently from evaluations, since the latter are more tightly focused on the degree to which an intervention was delivered, operated and 'measured-up' against certain performance indicators, largely in absentia of any consideration of wider contexts (Pawson and Tilley 1997). The sorts of research projects I have in mind are far more open-ended in that they would explore not just the intervention but the degree and manner to which social and personal circumstances aided or thwarted the formal work undertaken. The nature of probation supervision has changed enormously since the fieldwork for the Tracking project was planned (at least in England and Wales), and future projects in this field will need to recognise those changes. Along with colleagues, I have elsewhere described the sorts of attributes which such projects ought to aim for (see Farrall *et al.* 2014, chapter 1).

However, in addition to this, and not necessarily needing to include formal attempts at aiding desistance, there ought to be more comparative studies of desistance from crime. We have seen how comparing different ethnic groups within the same country can yield additional insights into how local social, cultural and economic structures influence desistance (Finestone 1967; Calverley 2013), so we need to extend these sorts of comparisons to incorporate both different sorts of criminal justice systems and different sorts of belief, economic, social and cultural systems. For example, the following projects would, I think, contribute greatly to our understanding of desistance. The first would be a comparison of the supervision of offenders in the community in Scotland, and England and Wales. In terms of social values, I am not sure that there is much to distinguish between north and south of the border, although there will be some differences, no doubt. However, in terms of the organisation of the criminal justice system, things are very different. Scotland did not lose the social work basis of offender supervision and did not embrace probation services (and hence did not have these in effect privatised, as has happened south of the border). This, then, would be a comparison of the ways in which criminal justice organisations and the institutions, which they reproduce and are shaped by themselves, shape desistance from crime. A second example might be a study of community sentences in two or more countries. Whilst one would need to think carefully about which countries one was studying and why one had chosen that country and not another, this would allow one to explore how cultural practices and belief systems affected desistance from crime. The key – whichever of these two possible ways forward one is considering – is to have a theory about why one might expect to see variations, rather than just to take countries on an opportunity sampling basis. In this regard, one might want to select two countries, which share similar criminal justice or legal frameworks (for example, as a result of colonialisation), but which have very different religious, cultural and social practices and beliefs. A comparison of Britain and India might be one example of this sort of model. Alternatively, one might select countries, because they had different criminal justice and legal systems, but had reasonably similar social, cultural and religious norms (a comparison of, say, France and Ireland might be an example of this approach). Alternatively, still, one might compare countries which had very different welfare states or modes of delivery of community supervision (privatised or state-led). The opportunities are seemingly endless, but each speaks to Figure 10.4 above, in that each study would be an attempt to understand how the three bars running along the top of that figure and some of the other factors referred to in it can shape and mould the experiences of and opportunities for desistance. For my money, cross-cultural studies of desistance are the 'next move' which this field needs to take, for in so doing we learn more about how to structure our criminal justice systems in such a way that they might better facilitate desistance from crime.

Such future directions ought to seek to embrace both quantitative and qualitative research methodologies and to be prospective and longitudinal in design. Studies which can include the insights of informants, collect data from respondents with a range of socio-demographic characteristics in sufficient quantities to enable meaningful analyses to be conducted, follow people well beyond the peak age of offending in their jurisdictions, and incorporate officially recorded data, will be all the more likely to make lasting contributions to knowledge in this area. Farrall *et al.* (2014, chapter 1) outlines these issues in far greater detail.

Notes

1 I would like to extend my thanks to Tony Bottoms, Adam Calverley, David Gadd, Ben Hunter, Shadd Maruna, Fergus McNeill, Gwen Robinson, Joanna Shapland and Gilly Sharpe, with whom I have been working during the lifespan of the project detailed herein, and whose ideas have shaped my own thinking in ways too numerous to mention. Numerous probation staff during the course of the fieldwork, or during presentations of the findings from the project, have been kind enough to assist with both practical and

analytical matters and I would like to thank these individuals for taking the time to engage with the project and its findings. I would also like to thank the anonymous reviewer of this chapter who helped me clarify some of the points I make.

2 It is impossible to know for sure that they had actually experienced an increase in their *rates* of victimisation, as we would need to have data for each case for at least another year or two before the most recent year in order to assess if there had been an increase on previous years. Hence, our findings remain suggestive, but not conclusive.

References

Bourdieu, P. (1977), *Outline of a Theory of Practice*. Cambridge, UK: Cambridge University Press.

Brown, I. (1998), 'Successful probation practice', in Faulkner, D. and Gibbs, A. (eds) *New Politics, New Probation?*, Probation Studies Unit Report No. 6. Oxford, UK: University of Oxford, pp. 57–76.

Buttimer, A. (1976), 'Grasping the dynamism of the life world', *Annals of the Association of American Geographers* 66(2): 277–292.

Calverley, A. (2013), *The Cultures of Desistance*. London: Routledge.

Carlsson, C. (2012), 'Using "turning points" to understand processes of change in offending', *British Journal of Criminology* 52(1): 1–16.

Farrall, S. (2002a), *Rethinking What Works With Offenders*. Cullompton, UK: Willan Publishing.

Farrall, S. (2002b), 'Long-term absences from probation: Officers' and probationers' accounts', *The Howard Journal of Criminal Justice* 41(3): 263–278.

Farrall, S. (2005), 'Officially recorded convictions for probationers: The relationship with self-report and supervisory observations', *Legal & Criminological Psychology* 10(1): 121–131.

Farrall, S. and Maltby, S. (2003), 'The victimisation of probationers', *The Howard Journal of Criminal Justice*, 42(1): 32–54.

Farrall, S. and Calverley, A. (2006), *Understanding Desistance from Crime*. Buckingham, UK: Open University Press, Crime and Justice Series.

Farrall, S., Bottoms, A. and Shapland, J. (2010), 'Social structures and desistance from crime', *European Journal of Criminology* 7(6): 546–570.

Farrall, S., Sharpe, G., Hunter, B. and Calverley, C. (2011), 'Theorising structural and individual-level processes in desistance and persistence: Outlining an integrated perspective', *Australian and New Zealand Journal of Criminology* 44(2): 218–234.

Farrall, S., Hunter, B., Sharpe, G. and Calverley, A. (2014), *Criminal Careers in Transition: The Social Context of Desistance from Crime*. Oxford, UK: Oxford University Press, Clarendon Studies in Criminology.

Farrall, S., Hunter, B., Sharpe, G. and Calverley, A. (2015), 'What "works" when retracing sample members in a QLR study? Some thoughts on how to minimize attrition', *International Journal of Social Research Methodology* (only available as advanced access).

Finestone, H. (1967), 'Reform and recidivism amongst Italian and Polish criminal offenders', *American Journal of Sociology* 72(6): 575–588.

Leibrich, J. (1993), *Straight to the Point*. Dunedin, New Zealand: Otago University Press.

Lloyd, C., Mair, G. and Hough, M. (1994), *Explaining Reconviction Rates: A Critical Analysis*. Home Office Research and Planning Unit Report No. 136, London: HMSO.

Maruna, S. (2001), *Making Good: How Ex-Convicts Reform and Rebuild Their Lives*. Washington, DC: American Psychological Association Books.

Pawson, R. and Tilley, N. (1997), *Realistic Evaluation*. London: Sage.

Seamon, D. (1980), 'Body-subject, time-space routines and place-ballets', in Buttimer, A. and Seamon, D. (eds) *The Human Experience of Space and Place*. London, UK: Croom Helm, pp. 148–165.

Wikström, P. O. H., Ceccato, V., Hardie, B. and Treiber, K. (2010), 'Activity fields and the dynamics of crime', *Journal of Quantitative Criminology* 26(1): 55–87.

11

IN SEARCH OF DESISTANCE

Notes from an Australian study[1]

Mark Halsey

The aim of this chapter is to explicate one of the key themes emerging from a decade-long study of repeat offending and desistance from crime among young male offenders in South Australia. That theme centres on the disparity between personal need and systemic offerings – what young men repeatedly narrate as key to getting desistance going (let alone sustaining it) as against the resources and approaches used by authorities to manage the 'risk' of reoffending. Here, the privileging of expert knowledge (psychological, managerial, actuarial) over personal need (the hopes and fears of young men in custody and beyond) meant that desistance was rare in the study cohort (n=14) and emerged in spite of, not because of, correctional practices and wider cultural conditions.

Context and design

In late 2013, I completed a 10-year study of the link between desistance from (serious) crime and generative commitment and action among 14 young men.[2] At July 2009 (the mid-point of interviews for the majority of participants), half of the cohort evinced good degrees of generative commitment (wanting to be a good parent, a good partner, a good provider and the like) (Halsey and Harris 2011). Ten were in prison, three were under community supervision (including a four-year parole period, a home detention bail and a community service order with matters pending), and one was 'free' from any order. Of those in prison, four were due for release within several months and a further three within a year. The mix of earliest release dates permitted the opportunity to continue closely mapping the process of 'starting again' – for documenting the personal and social factors hindering or supporting moves towards desistance. The average age of each participant on first being admitted to custody was 13 years, and all, by age 18, had experienced at least 10 prior release episodes (some over 30) from a custodial facility. Collectively, they had committed a wide range of offences including, but not limited to, motor vehicle theft, home invasion (burglary break and enter), armed robbery, serious assault, drug possession and supply and more. At the end of 2013, they had served in excess of 33,000 custodial days. Their familial backgrounds, circumstances of offending and life histories are described in detail elsewhere (Halsey and Deegan 2015).[3]

Each young man nominated up to three significant others capable of narrating the challenges of incarceration and release from an 'external' viewpoint (Halsey and Deegan 2012, 2014). Here, 15 males and 26 females were nominated, resulting in 95 interviews. One-off interviews were also completed with the managers (wardens/governors) (n=7) and intervention (rehabilitation) managers (n=6) of each adult male custodial facility in South Australia. Interviews with 40 prison officers (10 female, 30 male), with varying levels of service, also formed part of the project data. In total, 284 interviews were completed with and in relation to the 14 young men.[4] Two key questions framed the research: (1) Who or what is it possible for young offenders to care about within and beyond custody?; and (2) What are the events and processes which nurture and/or interrupt generativity and desistance from crime in the lives of these young men?

Of the 14 young men, only 3 (Billy, Charlie and David) are 'on track' in terms of desistance. In these cases, minor breaches have occasionally occurred, but generally, they self-report as committing few if any offences for the last 3 to 5 years. Official data confirm as much as well. Eleven are caught in various degrees of persistence and desistance. Of these, four are in what I term a state of 'recurring breakdown' (Joel, Paul, Reggie and Ben), two have suffered 'major derailments' (Matt and Lee) and three have taken a 'catastrophic turn' (Sam, James and Chris).[5]

Study location

South Australia has a population of around 1.6 million, with the majority (80 per cent) residing in the capital city, Adelaide. Less than 2 per cent of the South Australian population are indigenous (i.e. identify as Aboriginal or Torres Strait Islander) but as a group, make up 50 per cent and 25 per cent, respectively, of juvenile and adult custodial numbers. The overall incarceration rate in South Australia is roughly 170 per 100,000 relevant population. This puts it more or less on par with states such as Maine and Minnesota in the US and with the incarceration rate of the UK generally. Like most cities, Adelaide evinces some stark disparities between its wealthier and economically marginalised communities. By the most conservative estimate, about 12 per cent of Adelaide's population live below the poverty line (Australian Council of Social Service 2012) rising to 20 per cent when a slightly different threshold of disposable income is invoked. All the young men in the research grew up in suburbs or towns with high rates of youth unemployment, high rates of public housing of varying but typically dilapidated condition, high rates of crime and low accessibility to good schools, adequate public transport, good leisure activities, cultural pursuits and the like. Large-scale blue-collar industries – revolving particularly around automobile manufacture – have come and gone or are soon to go. A recent national report rated Adelaide's northern suburbs as the third worst area nationally in terms of youth unemployment (Brotherhood of St Laurence 2014). The majority of research participants lived in such suburbs and returned to them time and again following release from custody. These locations seem also to be disproportionately home to families experiencing significant levels of intergenerational incarceration. Halsey and Groves (unpublished) found almost half of 240 prisoners reporting two or more generations of incarceration grew up in just three marginalised areas (Port Adelaide, Elizabeth and Noarlunga). Research participants describe certain streets in these places as akin to 'the Bronx'.

Personal need versus systemic offerings

In terms of impediments to, and facilitators of, desistance, at least four major themes emerge from longitudinal interview data: (1) *parentification* or the damage done to children who bring themselves and/or their siblings up from a very young age; (2) *steadfast belief in the unified self* or young men's reluctance to reach out to a trusted other (or service) before or when things turn bad; (3) *managing the scorned self* or humiliation as both a catalyst for offending and as reproduced by prison and post-prison environments; and (4) *personal need versus systemic offerings* or the disconnect between what is required to desist from crime compared with what is available to support this process. It is the last of these that is the focus in this chapter.

Without exception, all the young men spoke consistently of needing some*one* (such as a mentor) instead of some*thing* (such as a program addressing criminogenic needs) to help steer their way through the myriad of challenges posed by incarceration and release. In fact, their 'needs' were typically very humble and entirely reasonable, encompassing such matters as assistance to get to appointments on time, or obtaining a driver's licence, or getting shared custody over children, or help in finding (and keeping) accommodation. One young man observed, 'The criminal needs a [different] footstep to follow instead of . . . the footstep of [the] criminal life or gangster life . . . He needs someone to show him a straight path, not the crooked path' (Lee). Despite the quite modest nature of their needs, the young men persistently told of the lack of systemic support for the 'individual' and highlighted, in particular, the pressure for staff within and beyond prison to treat people as if they were components on an assembly line.

> There's not much support . . . You've probably got . . . two social workers that are running around the whole gaol trying to see . . . so many prisoners a day that they're not actually getting the time to sit down [properly] with [each] prisoner. They've just got to rush through everything . . . Even while they're out . . . like [when they're on] parole . . . I can probably vouch for every prisoner [that they'd] be sick of signing in to parole – just how strict parole is . . . It's just the way they do it, it's just all crap . . . Most criminals [are] not making [enough] money . . . to get through day-to-day . . . Some

can't even afford a bus ticket to get to parole half the time [and] if they don't have that money for a bus ticket they . . . can't sign that piece of paper . . . for their freedom. (Paul)

So often the views of (ex)prisoners are interpreted with suspicion (Maruna and Mann 2006) and/or recast as attempts to neutralise individual responsibility for crime. But Paul has some very powerful allies – namely, senior correctional personnel. As one prison manager remarked:

We've actually released prisoners here with a tent and a sleeping bag . . . And that's been the best we can do to address the accommodation needs for them . . . We had a chap who . . . we did that to and he had mental health issues . . . The best we could get for him to move forward . . . as a valued member of the community was that he had a tent. He was going to try and find somewhere along the river where he could pitch his tent . . . and . . . to try and find work picking grapes or picking oranges . . . And [all the while] we're saying . . .,'In no time he'll be back in' . . . Before long we had him back again and [we asked him] what happened? 'Oh, well, you know, this happened and that, someone stole my sleeping bag and tent, so I had nowhere to go, so I caught up with some friends and ended up staying at their house. They went out to do a [house] break [i.e. burglary break and enter]. They told me to come along with them, so I went along with them and I was the one the police found outside the house' . . . And, you know, that happens so often.

Numerous studies have noted the way people emerging from prison are set up to fail (Petersilia 2003; Travis 2005; Wacquant 2009). This continues, in my view, to be one of the enduring issues surrounding prisoner reentry and reintegration (see Thompkins 2010). If things get off to a bad start for those already at the limits of economic stress and social marginalisation, then the chance of these same people getting on track (i.e. not having to resort to crime) is poor at best. As James commented during one of his many attempts to hold things together:

At the moment [I'm] living [way up north of the city but] everything I feel comfortable with – the only Centrelink [i.e. social security office] I feel comfortable with – is [way down south of the city] . . . So here I am [risking my curfew by] going all the way out of my way from [the north] to [the south] just to feel comfortable . . . because I feel like I'm just going to get up and walk out [of any other social service agency].

Across all interviews, I found time and again that the correctional system provokes risky behaviour in those under its remit. And it does this not out of any ill-will or malice towards young offenders – or offenders generally – but because it is in fact *a system within a system*. Correction is beholden to all manner of political forces and is always just one step away from being judged in the court of public opinion about how it manages the 'dangerous' among us (Pratt 2007). The corrections industry itself is under strain and this strain is passed on in all kinds of ways to prisoners and their families (where such exist) (Comfort 2003, 2007; Halsey and Deegan 2014). More critically, the system is a highly irrational one. It does things that could only be described as senseless – high risk. James, again, gives the following example.

P: They released me [at] 2.30 in the afternoon with no paperwork . . . [Instead], they've given me a cab fare to go to the local Centrelink and I've rocked up . . . and I said that I've just been released from prison and they said, 'Prove it'. . . [So] I said, 'Ring the prison'. And they said, 'Oh, we could be ringing anyone and anyone could answer the phone and tell us you've just got released'. So I had to go from [mentions location] Centrelink back to [the] prison . . . to the . . . admin guy and say, 'You didn't give me no papers saying that I was released'. [The papers would have helped me get my Emergency Bank Transaction] . . . I [then had] to go from Centrelink, back to [the prison and from the prison] back to Centrelink.

I: What if it was closed?

P: Exactly. That's the thing . . . If I had walked to [the prison] and then walked back again, Centrelink would have been closed by the time I got back . . . It's only luck that I ran into people that I've known for a long time . . . and they understood my situation and said, 'Yeah, no worries', and took me back to [the prison] and brought me back down [to Centrelink] . . . If it wasn't for that . . . there was a good chance that I would have stolen a car or . . . did a runner or something.

Lee also tells of a major mistake in terms of his progression through custody into the community following a five-year stint behind bars.

> I didn't get any resocialisation. I didn't get [to go to the pre-release centre]. I didn't get a job. I didn't save up no money. I was back and forth from medium to high security because someone that had the same name as me . . . had 14 house break charges . . . and that stuffed up my chance [to go to the low security prison] . . . They had the wrong person. I [had to go] down to the . . . magistrates court just for them to have both of us there and say, 'Yeah, we have the wrong person'. [But] by then . . . I'd already thrown . . . my hopes and dreams out the [window]. Like, 'Stuff it. I've been doing the right thing . . . [but] I'm not going anywhere. I'm not progressing [towards a lower security rating and my release]'.

In a system (at the state level) that manages around 2,500 prisoners (and roughly 3,000 probationers/parolees) on any day, mistakes are bound to happen. But in the end we are talking of people and their futures, however precarious those futures might appear. Prisons undeniably impact the attitudes of prisoners post-release

(Contreras 2012: 85–86). Ben, in his late twenties, describes a recent 'short stay' in Yatala Labour Prison's notorious 'G Division' – the most secure and sparsest place for prisoners in South Australia.

P: I forgot to sign in on my bail . . . [so] I handed myself into the police station. They gave me bail again through the courts . . . At first it was with a guarantor and I had to get that sorted because my phone was flat and I didn't have any of my numbers . . . They put me in Yatala [Labor Prison] for six days even though I had bail. It was just because I couldn't get hold of a guarantor and then I went back to court. While I was in Yatala I tried to kill myself . . . With everything going on, getting screwed over by [my ex-girlfriend], my bail [problems], and my mate dying [from a criminal gunshot wound to the head] . . . I [was] burning inside, and, yeah, [I] slashed up. [So they put me in] G Division [because I] was going a bit loopy.

I: Right . . . Did that make things worse?

P: It did . . . I told them before they put me in there too, they've gone, 'You're going to G Division'. I was like, 'That's a punishment place. Like, I need help. I don't need to be punished'. No one was listening to me when I was asking for help. No one was listening to me about the way I felt inside . . . I just lost it. They just stripped me down and put me in a canvas skirt and put me in a room with the light on 24 hours a day, a prison officer sitting at the full glass door . . . So you've got a prison guard watching you all day plus a camera, the light's on 24 hours a day, and you're in a skirt. It was pretty [terrible].

I: What's in that G Division cell?

P: Nothing. You don't even have a mattress or a pillow or anything. Just a wooden board to lay on and then there's a hole in the floor and when you go to the toilet you've got to squat over the hole . . . It's disgusting.

I: And the bed scenario?

P: Wood slats, yeah.

I: No pillow?

P: No . . . I was that cold and uncomfortable. I had a sore back for weeks after that. They treated me like I was the worst person in the world when all I really needed was some help . . . Out of all the . . . years I've done, that six days was probably the lowest point . . . Very inhumane in there. Yatala's the worst prison out of them all.

For someone who, as it turns out, was in the midst of a psychotic breakdown, this was the best 'care' the prison could show Ben. The day after he was released he called me in a highly distressed state saying he felt himself slipping into mental disarray – he said, specifically, that he felt like his mind was 'caving in on itself'. I asked if there was any mental health plan in place for him. There wasn't. Had the prison put him in touch with a service, with anyone who could help? They hadn't. I made some calls and did what I could. But it shouldn't have to work like that. There are thousands of people who don't have a university researcher's personal mobile number at their disposal and the potential connection to networks of expertise and support that stem from such. Ben had tried to call me from prison, but he was reputedly denied the right to phone calls. Again, we needn't take Ben's word regarding his situation. As one intervention manager commented, 'the provision of psych[ological and psychiatric] services . . . is a huge issue for us. We have many people incarcerated . . . that need access to psychs. We only get a psych two and a half days a month'. It is a strange irony that psychological and psychiatric expertise so thoroughly informs the risk inventories used to assess and manage prisoners, but that actual psychiatric and psychological services are next to non-existent in custodial facilities. Another intervention manager remarked that 'bed space takes all priority over rehabilitation and rehabilitation programs'.

The problem of systemic offerings versus personal need doesn't end with the young men. As with many (ex)prisoners, their network often extends to those struggling with their own battles to keep abreast of correctional rules and court-related matters. By way of example, one of Reggie's nominated significant others (Jane) suffered a major and unnecessary hardship due to the overzealous 'risk crazed' (Carlen 2008) approach to managing parolees – even those who, in this case, had not put a foot wrong for many years.

P: [I was on parole and] I had a breakdown . . . I was nervous about flying on big planes . . . to Sydney . . . I was just so nervous . . . and I wanted to see my granddaughter [and] be there for her first birthday . . . And I just had a bit of a breakdown and [was] accused [by my parole officer] of not taking my medication . . . And apparently the Parole Board approved my two weeks in Sydney . . . [but] I wasn't told until the last minute . . . And when I did find out, I booked all my plane fares and I was getting phone calls [from corrections] to say, 'Well, you'd better not get connecting flights so you're not hanging around in Melbourne cos we don't know who you're associating with' . . . And it was just stress, stress, stress, stress . . . The warrant was out for two days before I was picked up at my house [and] transferred to . . . prison.

I: How long were you in . . . prison before you [were permitted] to appear before the Parole Board?

P: Three and half months . . . [And] the breach was never proven . . . It was just, 'You are now free to go' . . . [Not even] a simple, 'Sorry . . . We fucked up your life'. [But] it's not [just] my life. It's my granddaughter's, it's my parent's, it's my daughter's [life as well], you know?

Jane called me just prior to being taken away by the police. I had some idea of what was at stake: her house, her mental health, her relationship with her daughter and granddaughter, her hitherto impeccable contribution to building 'community' – in short, her continued desistance. With Jane's full knowledge and permission, I contacted the Executive Director of Community Corrections suggesting to him that Jane's current parole officer was causing more problems than it was worth (the

inexperienced officer had recently arrived in Australia from the UK probation service, whereas Jane was a lifer released to ten years on parole). A more experienced
officer was assigned. The relief in Jane's voice and the change in her demeanour
upon seeing her some months later were palpable. Her family was so incredibly
thankful – they knew they could have struggled for years, literally, to get the same
result. Again, getting good support shouldn't have to be this hard. It shouldn't
depend on some kind of social lottery – whether you happen to be involved in a
research project or not.

It would be a mistake to lay the blame for these kinds of problems solely at
the feet of the Parole Board. Instead, it's the whole conception of what parole is
or should be about that's the central issue. Just as there are problematic parolees
who snub their nose at the various chances given them, there are also problematic parole and probation officers. These officers are driven by checklists and
seem rarely to spend time getting to know 'clients' (people). And yet there is evidence suggesting that parole officers *can* make meaningful differences in people's
capacity and motivation to desist. This might not be explicitly acknowledged
by parolees at the time of their supervision, but in time there is a tendency to
look back and view the community corrections officer as at least *partly* important to reducing or stopping offending (Farrall and Calverley 2006). Still, in my
South Australian cohort, even 'success stories' like David, Billy and Charlie had
to engage in a difficult if not risky dance with the parole system. It was a system,
which, in their eyes, generally failed to understand that *compliance is not the same
thing as reintegration*.

> They expect you to report [to corrections every week] . . . It was impos-
> sible . . . I was working five days a week or more, six [days], sometimes
> seven . . . Please, I can't [report] there every week. [But] [i]f they were open
> until six [pm], I would be there every week. (David)

Like many ex-prisoners, David felt he had little option but to persist at a particular
type of offending (driving while disqualified) in order to desist from other more
serious types of offending (motor vehicle theft, high speed pursuits, burglary, illicit
drug use). Ben had a similar experience of being prohibited from doing things he
knew would strengthen his involvement in positive networks.

> I got in contact with my DJ again and there's some gigs coming up that I can't
> do because of the parole. There was a couple [of gigs] in Sydney . . . which
> would be good . . . Everyone's been waiting for me to get out and continue
> on again . . . But I'm not allowed in licensed premises.

At the other end of the spectrum, some young men surrendered the possibility of
early release in favour of getting out 'end of order'. There were, apparently, too
many rules to follow and so it was better to stay in prison than to be brought back
for a minor breach.

I: So did you have to go before the Parole Board?

P: No, I just wrote them a letter saying, 'Look, I don't want my parole back, fucking don't let me get out early' . . . I put in there, like, 'Parole's just a pathetic excuse for fucking following me around and telling me how to do my business and run my life and . . . tell[ing] me I have to be at this course and do that course and then pick up rubbish on this main road'. Nah.

Lee, admittedly a more serious offender, also found parole to be a strange and unhelpful experience:

> You see, I'm not even meant to be here . . . [in a café] . . . [Corrections say] to us, 'Tell us two to [or] three days ahead if we [want to] go to a licensed premises'. [But] everywhere's a licensed premises. I haven't even gone clubbing since I got out. I haven't even gone partying since I've been out. I haven't gone anywhere . . . I've been eating at home . . . the majority of the time . . . And they say, 'If you feel like going somewhere, just ring us two days before'. [But] when you go out [and] you want to eat something, you don't [think] two days [in] advance, 'I want to eat that' . . . It's weird.

What these excerpts show is that the subject of parole is not the kind of person that inhabits society writ large. Parole – especially for those deemed 'high risk' requires a heavily managed subject – someone who is consistently reminded of their 'offenderhood' through surveillance of their whereabouts (place), the things they consume (drugs, alcohol) and the people they converse with or meet (co-offenders and other parolees are deemed particularly problematic). Across all interviews (including those conducted with my earlier and larger sample of 54 young men), it is hard to find a parolee who tells of the *right* kind of support – someone who has found a point where the system appropriately balances personal need and systemic offerings. There is either over-supervision or under-supervision. Interviews with intervention managers bear this out.

> We kick them out the front door and say, 'See you later'. And there's absolutely very minimal follow-up . . . If a prisoner is on parole, community corrections, in my opinion, are just overwhelmed. There are an unrealistic number of supervisions . . . per case officer . . . And so they quickly move them from a high-intensity level of reporting and monitoring to a much lower level. They do that as quickly as possible, with just the sheer numbers that they have, and so you get people falling through the cracks at that point.

Here, the pressure involved in managing large caseloads exacerbates the very problem one is trying solve – people repeatedly coming back to prison. This is the *derailment of desistance by design* (see Barry 2013). There are few better illustrations of this than putting people back into known criminogenic circumstances – the precise contexts that all the prison-based and community programs tell offenders to avoid at all costs. James and Paul capture, respectively, this circumstance.

When I was at [the] Drug Court house at [mentions suburb], I really did feel that it was no better than gaol. I was surrounded by people – next door, in my house, [the] other side of me – that were in and out of prison, that had drugs around [them], that were using . . . [There was] no difference between that Drug Court house and the gaol cell that I'm in now.

[The suburb I was in was] not a bad area. [But] the block of units [I was living in] was bought by [Offender Aid and Rehabilitation Services to house people] released . . . from gaol . . . [So] you're usually surrounded by dickheads . . . [engaging in] drunk and disorderly behavior . . . I was . . . bringing . . . my kids . . . there [and] just wanted to do my family thing. But it's hard being surrounded by that. And across the road from th[e] units was another set of townhouse units and they're all for mental patients . . . So I was surrounded by a lot of criminals and dickheads. And I was surrounded by loopy criminal dickheads.

These situations would be laughable were the stakes not so high. Housing – stable living arrangements in good streets and suburbs – ranks as probably the most important material thing a prisoner needs post-release (see Baldry *et al.* 2006; Halsey 2007b). Through a decade of interviewing, accommodation came up time and again as central to getting desistance going. Employment, education, getting off drugs and learning to adjust to life in the 'free world', also featured prominently. But having a place of one's own was central to sustaining these other events. It is no coincidence that the only young men who could rightly be said to be progressing along a desistance path all found somewhere stable and safe to reside following years of being in and out of custody.

There are also real questions to be asked surrounding the purpose of imprisonment. South Australia, for example, has the highest remand rate of any state or territory in Australia (around 35 per cent of the daily prison population fall into that category). Some remandees are refused bail not because they are a flight risk (as was the historical intent of bail) but because they cannot give an appropriate (bona fide) residential address (recall Ben's predicament above). And many are coming back to prison for breaches as opposed to new offences (roughly 15 per cent of the daily prison population in South Australia fall under this category) (Australian Bureau of Statistics 2013). The real story here is the economic and social costs attached to reincarcerating people for non-violent matters. As Reggie (formerly one of the state's most notorious car thieves) comments:

P: I went in to get a pack of cigarettes from the shop in the car . . . And got caught driving disqualified.
I: And how far . . . would you have driven from the house to get the cigarettes?
P: It would have been quicker to walk there . . . than take the car . . . It wasn't as if the cigarettes were even for me. I had cigarettes. I was getting them for my brother's girlfriend because she's got no ID.

Given that bed space is known to get in the way of doing rehabilitation, the use of prison in such circumstances has to be seriously queried. One intervention manager concurred, saying 'finding people being remanded in custody for minor offences – you've just got to question, "Is that what a place like this should be for?"' Many of the stories relayed by the young men tell of the damage done when people are brought back to prison for minor infractions. Relationships, accommodation, jobs – the motivation to stay out – are all adversely impacted. Again, prison managers – not just prisoners – can see the game for what it is.

> We had . . . [a] fellow that came . . . into prison for something relatively minor. [Well], his wife [subsequently] left him because she was sick of him always being arrested. [She] took his kids away [and] didn't tell him where they'd gone to. [Before being locked up], he was in a Housing Trust house [which was then taken] . . . away from him. His employer said, 'Look, I can't hold your job for you', so he lost his job. Eight weeks he was [in prison for] . . . So this guy, he went out and he [had] nowhere to live. Nothing. [His] family has fallen apart. [He] got into the drugs again, [and] finished up doing . . . a massive amount of break and enters [i.e. burglaries] and [has] just come back to us for three years. Now, this was a mature . . . 30 [year] old chap who basically [had] just got his head together, but because we brought him back in for eight weeks, we cost him everything.

This harks back to the irrationality of the correctional enterprise. In truth, it doesn't correct so much as induce new problems and aggravate old ones. Those on parole get caught up in a bizarre world of checks and balances such that the main goal of (re)integration recedes from view. Lee told of this Kafkaesque scenario.

> [One time] I had a urine [test] at DASSA [Drug and Alcohol Services South Australia] and [while I was there my parole officer] rang [me] up [and] . . . I said [to him], 'Yeah, I'm at DASSA giving a urine'. And then the [parole officer told the DASSA worker that I needed to give another urine in an hour's time to the Parole Board at 9.30am] . . . [I was worried] because [I thought I] might not be able to [urinate] because [I've] just [urinated at DASSA] . . . Then I go [to the Parole Board] and . . . they make me sit there for an hour . . . [And then when I gave them the urine], they said to me, 'This is a bit clear'. I said, 'What do you mean? I drank a lot of water. I knew I was going to get urined . . . and I've just done a urine, right?' I said, 'How else was I going to [urinate]?' And [the Parole Board] goes, 'If [your urine] keeps coming [back] like this we can [write up] your dilute[d] [urine] as a dirty [urine]'. I said, 'What? If I can't give it, it's a breach. [But] if I give [it] too clean, it's a breach. Come on, make up your mind'.

Trying to read 'progress' from a urine sample is like trying to assess artistic greatness from a child's drawing. It's possible, but mostly fraught with inaccuracy and conceit. Technology – whether electronic bracelets, urine analysis, mouth swabs, random phone calls – does not really substitute for consistent, respectful and individualised support (McNeill and Maruna 2008). As James put it, 'You've got to treat each kid differently'. Wacquant (2010) writes:

> If the authorities were serious about 'reentry', they would . . . start by reestablishing the previously existing web of programs that *build a bridge back to civilian life* – furloughs, educational release, work release, and half-way houses – which has atrophied over the past two decades and avoid locating 'reentry services' in decrepit facilities located in dangerous and dilapidated inner-city districts rife with crime and vice.
>
> *(Wacquant 2010: 614; emphasis added)*

Beyond the US, this remedy has direct relevance in Australia and other locales. Without such efforts, many (ex)prisoners – young men like those in my research – will continue to be stuck in what Rose (2000: 324) calls the 'circuits of exclusion' where 'exclusion itself is effectively criminalized . . . [such that] . . . individuals [cycle] from probation to prison because of probation violations, from prison to parole, and back to prison because of parole violations' (Rose 2000: 336).

Concluding remarks and future directions

Life, as Deleuze (1994) says, is characterised by *alterity* – a kind of radical difference that refuses attempts to serialise the diversity of personal biography. Past, present and future concerns cannot be usefully captured in Likert scales or inventories of criminogenic need. The most important bits, as illustrated above, tend always to fall outside the parameters of standardised 'intervention' and 'service delivery'. The purpose of longitudinal qualitative research, I believe, is to show something of the complexity and 'underlying' troubles investing real people's lives and to demonstrate that one life is *never* reducible to another. Yes, the 14 young men 'graduated' from juvenile to adult custodial facilities, and yes, most lacked a stable parental figure, were kicked out of school for bad behaviour, lived in the most economically depressed suburbs, had slept rough on occasion, had been wards of the state, battled their own and others' problems with drugs and alcohol, and commenced offending to 'escape' the turmoil of their lives. To an extent, they *are* cut from the same cloth. But in so many ways their circumstances are different and this difference requires carefully calibrated responses that no sentence or program seems capable of delivering. Again, as Deleuze (2007: 216) writes, 'There is no beginning, there is no end. We always begin in the middle of something'. Wherever agencies intervened in the lives of the 14 young men, they singularly failed to grasp the nature of the 'middle' – the nature of the personal and social milieux in which each resided and would most likely return subsequent to arrest or release from custody. As one prison manager remarked, '[W]e send them out quite often in the early stages [of their offending career] without getting intervention.

We send them back to the same environment that we took them out of, usually into the same house with the same peers'.

Perhaps most tellingly, so much of what happened to the 14 young men within and beyond custody only heightened their sense of disempowerment and personal humiliation. When incarcerated as juveniles they swung between the poles of *infantalisation* ('You cannot know what is best since you are still a child') and *responsibilisation* ('As a young man, you need to take control over your life'). How could a capable well-adjusted young person ever emerge from this 'Alice in Wonderland' scenario (Maruna *et al.* 2004)? When incarcerated as adults, things got worse with the tag 'career criminal' entrapping the majority more deeply in what Reich (2010) terms the 'Game of Outlaw'. By their mid-twenties, half of the young men's identities had been 'nailed down as one' by authorities (Deleuze and Guattari 1996: 159).

Putting young men in prison is sometimes necessary. But it's typically not going to put them on the path to primary, less, secondary desistance. Most leave such environments not knowing how to cope in legitimate ways beyond the perimeter of the facility. The archetypal example of personal need being consistently forsaken by systemic offerings, occurred in relation to Chris (now in his mid-twenties and serving a minimum of ten years). As part of some serialised production line attempt at rehabilitation he was made to do all manner of programs, 'Anger Management'; 'Challenging Offending'; 'Victim Awareness'; 'Drugs and Alcohol'. The list went on and on. He did them all many times over – most often as a hurdle requirement for (early) release rather than out of genuine commitment to any of them. In fact, at interview, Chris's needs, as 'complex' as they were at one level, proved quite straight-forward. He needed basic life skills – a means for learning, internalising and practising the basic building blocks for managing in the community. He didn't need more cognitive behavioural therapy or 'Thinking Straight' programs. The following extended excerpt explains the incredible social deficits in Chris's life, which, in retrospect, contributed to his extreme sense of feeling like an 'outsider' when he so very much wanted to be 'normal':

P: What I need is a job. [But] I won't get that [situation in here of] having a job where I work six, seven hours a day, go home, [and] you're that stuffed you don't feel like doing any [crime] cos you got to go to work again.

I: Let me drill down on that [in terms of life beyond prison]. Do you know how to cook yourself a meal? . . . Like a healthy, good meal?

P: No.

I: There's no shame in that. I'm not judging you . . . Do you know how to shop, for instance?

P: No.

I: Do you know how to get the phone connected, or pay a phone bill, or do you know how to get the gas connected?

P: No.

I: Do you know how to buy a bus ticket?

P: Yeah.

I: You can do that, OK. Do you know how to go about organising housing . . . getting somewhere to stay?

P: No . . . I never learnt how to do Centrelink [i.e. how to claim housing assistance or social security payments while unemployed, etc.] . . . I don't even know the way to talk to them.

I: Have you ever had, or would you like it, for instance, if someone [like your parole officer or a mentor] said, 'Chris, the first day you're out . . . we're going to drive to Centrelink and I will stand with you in line. I will do a lot of the talking. I will help you fill out the form?'

P: Yeah. If someone was there with me, talking for me, [it would help], because I get frustrated when I feel that that person [behind the counter] might not understand what I'm saying . . . But [with] someone standing there with me in line . . . then I'd be able to do it.

I: Do you know how to use a washing machine?

P: No . . . I don't know how – and I'm going to be honest with you – how to pay for petrol . . . I don't even know how to use a mobile phone.

I: You see, that's the reason I started this conversation . . . It's important, really important, that you said what you said. Yeah, doing a lot of gaol and then coming out and trying to somehow live normally is almost impossible [for you].

P: It's impossible.

There is so much to take from this excerpt. But the main point is that Chris – like so many young men struggling to desist from crime – never got schooled in how to be a citizen. He missed that train in its entirety. He couldn't cook, pay a bill (he never even received a bill to pay), connect the phone, buy clothes or a host of other essential things for surviving in modern day life. But he could get a sawn off shotgun at a moment's notice, he could outwit police at high speed while driving the most ramshackle vehicle, he could get whatever quantum of illicit drugs he needed, he could play the prison system to ensure he was housed away from the madding crowd and he could intimidate enemies in the community from behind prison walls. Chris, in short, had many 'skills'. It's just that they were overwhelmingly centred on criminal and anti-social endeavours. How desistance could ever find a footing in such circumstances is an incredibly difficult question. But the answer lies in strategies that don't reduce solely to the epistemologies and logics of the psy-complex (Foucault 1977; Rose 1989). *Desistance requires that social and political risks be more readily taken to counteract the stigmatizing focus on offender risk* (see Uggen and Blahnik, Chapter 12, this volume). This is one of the only ways to give people who've done significant custodial time meaningful opportunities to transform from 'prisoners back into citizens' (Maruna 2011: 4).

Incarceration and release are too often humiliating and disenabling processes – the excerpts throughout this chapter overwhelmingly testify to this (but see Soyer 2014). Katz (1988: 30) writes:

> Humiliation is a painful awareness of the mundane future, a vivid appreciation that once I get out of the current situation I still will not be able to get away from its degradation. I become humiliated just as I discover that despite my struggles to do so, I cannot really believe that the meaning of the moment is temporary.

To extend the analogy, 'I know that the lull in my offending is a by-product of my incarceration and that my release will only offer further proof of such'. Desistance is and always will be about hope and the will to fashion a future that is distinct but linked to the past. But it also requires the loosening of systemic and cultural factors that continually threaten even the strongest desire to make good.

It is impossible, finally, to delve sufficiently here into the full range of future directions for desistance-oriented research. The very fact that most if not all of desistance scholarship to date has focused on 'street'/violent crime as opposed to white-collar/corporate offenders, suggests that desistance has in a sense been 'captured' by a particular imagining of whose behaviour it is most important to study. There is surely an argument to say that in terms of the quantum of harm caused, the offending and desistance trajectories of major corporate companies (and individuals in such companies) should form a more meaningful part of the desistance oeuvre. But more specifically, and on the basis of the ten-year study cited throughout, at least three ideas spring to mind. First, better understanding of the psycho-social factors, which combine to derail seemingly steady progress towards desistance, is needed (see Weaver 2015). In short, why do people who appear to have so much to gain (and so much to build on) fall back into crime in more and less serious fashion? Do they, for example, 'self-sabotage' in the face of their own 'success'? Does a kind of fatalism creep into their lives? If so, why and under what circumstances? More importantly, what do those who *severely* relapse say about what might have prevented them from going seriously awry? Second, a far more detailed understanding is needed of how the psy-complex (psychologists, psychiatrists and social workers) fits into desistance pathways. It is too often taken as given that any and all involvement of such professionals in the lives of would-be desisters is a good and useful thing. In fact, very little research has been published on precisely how such professionals engage, operationalise or disregard insights generated by the desistance literature. The same could be said of police, lawyers and the judiciary and, to a lesser extent, of probation and parole officers (Farrall 2002). In short, what kinds of 'truth games' (about the causes of crime and ways of (re)habilitating/(re)integrating offenders) are being played by various stakeholders within and around the criminal justice system? How and to what degree do these games produce unintended consequences for those who are asked to do the heavy lifting when it comes to *doing* (living) desistance? Is it not possible that many 'clients' feel themselves pulled this way and that such that the path(s) to desistance start(s) to resemble a puzzle devoid of a clear and workable solution? Third, the ten-year longitudinal study, as well as my current research on intergenerational incarceration, suggests it is critically important to ask questions about how processes of desistance might differ in essential ways for indigenous offenders (see Sullivan 2012). With the rate of Aboriginal incarceration doubling since the mid-2000s, coupled with the continued diminution (through early/unforeseen death, alcoholism, chronic unemployment, homelessness and the like) of family members in the community capable of supporting loved ones released from custody, there is an urgent need to understand the struggle to desist among such people. Indeed, it is probably necessary to ask whether desistance even resonates as a concept in particular quarters. After all, like the practice of imprisonment, the concept of desistance is a recent invention and therefore needs explication in a culturally nuanced and appropriate fashion. There is much to do on that count alone.

Notes

1 This chapter is drawn and adapted, with permission, from the book *Young Offenders: Crime, Prison and Struggles for Desistance* (Halsey and Deegan 2015).
2 The relevant projects are: *Negotiating Conditional Release: A Pilot Study of the Factors Affecting Recidivism Rates of Young Men in Secure Care* (funded by Flinders University); *Understanding Recidivism and Repeat Incarceration among Young Male Offenders: A Biographical and Longitudinal Approach* (funded by the Australian Research Council DP0556471); and *Generativity in Young Male (Ex)Prisoners: Caring for Self, Other, and Future within Prison and Beyond* (funded by the Australian Research Council DP094562). Results have been widely published (Halsey 2006, 2007a, 2007b, 2008a, 2008b, 2008c; Halsey and Armitage 2009; Goldsmith and Halsey 2013). Nine of the 14 were first interviewed in 2003/04, 4 in 2005, and 1 in 2008. At the end of 2013, they were aged 22 to 29 years (1=22; 1=24; 1=25; 4=26; 2=27; 1=28; 4=29). Twelve identified as Caucasian, one as Aboriginal and one as Asian.
3 Across all projects, the distribution of interviews ended up as follows: 1 young man was interviewed on 5 occasions; 3 on 7 occasions; 2 on 9 occasions; 2 on 10 occasions; 3 on 11 occasions; 2 on 12 occasions; and 1 on 14 occasions (n=135 interviews with the 14 young males). Of these, 31 took place in non-secure settings (houses, public parks, university premises). The remainder were conducted in various custodial facilities.
4 This includes 234 interviews for the *Generativity in Young Male (Ex)Prisoners* project and 50 interviews with the 14 young men from 2003 to 2008 on previous projects (see Note 1).
5 Two of the 14 have not been contactable for over a year and therefore have not been categorised for the purposes of this chapter.

References

Australian Bureau of Statistics (2013), *4517.0 Prisoners in Australia, 2013*, available at http://www.abs.gov.au/AUSSTATS/abs@.nsf/Lookup/4517.0Main+Features100022013? OpenDocument (accessed 27 May 2014).
Australian Council of Social Service (2012), *Poverty in Australia*, available at http://www.acoss.org.au/uploads/html/ACOSS_PovertyReport2012.html (accessed 10 May 2014).
Baldry, E., McDonnell, D., Maplestone, P. and Peeters, M. (2006), 'Ex-prisoners, homelessness and the state in Australia', *Australian and New Zealand Journal of Criminology* 39(1): 20–33.
Barry, M. (2013), 'Desistance by design: Offenders' reflections on criminal justice theory, policy and practice', *European Journal of Probation* 5(2): 47–65.
Brotherhood of St Laurence (2014), *Youth Unemployment Jumps 67 per cent in South Australian Areas*. Media release, available at http://www.bsl.org.au/Media-centre/Media-Releases?id=1032 (accessed 10 May 2014).

Carlen, P. (2008), 'Imaginary penalties and risk crazed governance', in Carlen, P. (ed.) *Imaginary Penalties*. Cullompton, UK: Willan, pp. 1–25.

Comfort, M. (2003), 'In the tube at San Quentin: The "secondary prisonization" of women visiting inmates', *Journal of Contemporary Ethnography* 32(1): 77–107.

Comfort, M. (2007), 'Punishment beyond the legal offender', *Annual Review of Law and Social Science* 3: 271–296.

Contreras, R. (2012), *The Stickup Kids: Race, Drugs, Violence and the American Dream.* Oakland, CA: University of California Press.

Deleuze, G (2007), *Two Regimes of Madness – Texts and Interviews 1975–1995*, edited by Lapoujade, D. (trans. M. Taormina and A. Hodges). New York: Semiotext(e).

Deleuze, G. (1994), *Difference and Repetition* (trans. P. Patton), New York: Columbia University Press.

Deleuze, G. and Guattari, F. (1996), *A Thousand Plateaus*, Minneapolis, MN: University of Minnesota Press.

Farrall, S. (2002), *Rethinking What Works with Offenders: Probation, Social Context and Desistance from Crime.* Cullompton, UK: Willan.

Farrall, S. and Calverley, A. (2006), *Understanding Desistance from Crime.* London: Open University Press.

Foucault, M. (1977), *Discipline and Punish.* London: Penguin.

Goldsmith, A. and Halsey, M. (2013), 'Cousins in crime: Mobility, place and belonging in indigenous youth co-offending', *British Journal of Criminology* 53(6): 1157–1177.

Halsey, M. (2008a), 'Pathways into prison: Biographies, crimes, punishment', *Current Issues in Criminal Justice* 20(1): 95–110.

Halsey, M. (2008b), 'Narrating the chase: Edgework and young people's experience of crime', in Anthony, T. and Cunneen, C. (eds) *The Critical Criminology Companion.* Sydney, Australia: Federation Press, pp. 105–117.

Halsey, M. (2008c), 'Risking desistance: Respect and responsibility in custodial and post-release contexts', in Carlen, P. (ed.) *Imaginary Penalties*. Cullompton, UK: Willan, pp. 218–251.

Halsey, M. (2007a), 'On confinement: Client perspectives of secure care and imprisonment', *Probation Journal* 54(4): 339–368.

Halsey, M. (2007b), 'Assembling recidivism: The promise and contingencies of post-release life', *Journal of Criminal Law and Criminology* 97(4): 1209–1260.

Halsey, M. (2006), 'Negotiating conditional release: Juvenile narratives of repeat incarceration', *Punishment and Society* 8(2): 147–181.

Halsey, M. and Armitage, J. (2009), 'Incarcerating young people: The impact of custodial care', in McNeill, F. and Barry, M. (eds) *Young People, Crime and Justice.* London: Jessica Kingsley, pp. 154–175.

Halsey, M. and Deegan, S. (2015), *Young Offenders: Crime, Prison and Struggles for Desistance.* London: Palgrave.

Halsey, M. and Deegan, S. (2014), '"Picking up the pieces": Female significant others in the lives of young (ex)incarcerated males', *Criminology & Criminal Justice*, available at http://crj.sagepub.com/content/early/2014/03/12/1748895814526725.ref.html (accessed 13 March 2014).

Halsey, M. and Deegan, S. (2012), 'Father and son: Two generations through prison', *Punishment & Society* 14(3): 338–367.

Halsey, M. and Groves, A. (unpublished), 'Intergenerational incarceration: Emerging issues from a mid-range Australian State', Flinders University, Australia: Law School.

Halsey, M. and Harris, V. (2011), 'Prisoner futures: Sensing the signs of generativity', *Australian and New Zealand Journal of Criminology* 44(1): 74–93.

Katz, J. (1988), *Seductions of Crime: Moral and Sensual Attractions In Doing Evil*. New York: Basic Books.

Maruna, S. (2011), 'Reentry as a rite of passage', *Punishment and Society* 13(1): 3–28.

Maruna, S. and Mann, R. (2006), 'A fundamental attribution error?: Rethinking cognitive distortions', *Legal and Criminological Psychology* 11(2): 155–177.

Maruna, S., LeBel, T. P., Mitchell, N. and Naples, M. (2004), 'Pygmalion in the reintegration process: Desistance from crime through the looking glass', *Psychology, Crime & the Law* 10(3): 271–281.

McNeill, F. and Maruna, S. (2008), 'Giving up and giving back: Desistance, generativity and social work with offenders', in McIvor, G. and Raynor, P. (eds) *Developments in Social Work with Offenders*. Series: Research Highlights in Social Work (48), London: Jessica Kingsley, pp. 224–339.

Petersilia, J. (2003), *When Prisoners Come Home: Parole and Prisoner Reentry*. Oxford, UK: Oxford University Press.

Pratt, J. (2007), *Penal Populism*. London: Routledge.

Reich, A. D. (2010), *Hidden Truths: Young Men Navigating Lives in and out of Juvenile Prison*. Berkeley and Los Angeles, CA: University of California Press.

Rose, N. (2000), 'Government and control', *British Journal of Criminology* 40(2): 321–339.

Rose, N. (1989), *Governing the Soul: The Shaping of the Private Self*. London: Routledge.

Soyer, M. (2014), 'The imagination of desistance: A juxtaposition of the construction of incarceration as a turning point and the reality of recidivism', *British Journal of Criminology* 54(1): 91–108.

Sullivan, K. (2012), 'Motivating and maintaining desistance from crime: Male Aboriginal serial offenders' experience of "going good"', a thesis submitted for the degree of Doctor of Philosophy, Australian National University, available at http://www.healthinfonet.ecu.edu.au/key-resources/bibliography/?lid=25058 (accessed 12 March 2015).

Thompkins, D. (guest editor) (2010), 'Special issue: The prison reentry industry', *Dialectical Anthropology* 34(4): 427–620.

Travis, J. (2005), *But They All Come Back: Facing the Problem of Prisoner Reentry*. Washington, DC: The Urban Institute Press.

Uggen, C. and Blahnik, L. (forthcoming), 'The increasing stickiness of public labels', in *Global Perspectives on Desistance: Reviewing What We Know and Looking to the Future*. London: Routledge (Chapter 12 of this book).

Wacquant, L. (2010), 'Prisoner reentry as myth and ceremony', *Dialectical Anthropology* 34(4): 605–620.

Wacquant, L. (2009), *Punishing the Poor*. Durham, NC: Duke University Press.

Weaver, E. (2015), *Offending and Desistance: The Importance of Social Relations*. London: Routledge.

12

THE INCREASING STICKINESS OF PUBLIC LABELS

Christopher Uggen and Lindsay Blahnik

Contemporary criminology offers compelling evidence that the distinction between "criminal" and "non-criminal" is largely a matter of time. Yet crime discourse and policy remain rooted in the notion of criminality as an immutable individual characteristic. This chapter contrasts the fluidity in criminal behavior with the growing stickiness of public labels, drawing from an experimental study of low-level criminal records, a demographic analysis of the population bearing such records, and their spillover effects on health care and other institutions. After summarizing key U.S. policy interventions on stigmatization and crime, we conclude by introducing a new study of restorative alternatives in a radically different legal and social context.

There has been a tremendous revolution in life course criminology, as careful longitudinal research has shown us how criminal behavior changes from month to month and year to year. We now have clear evidence that pretty much "all offenders eventually desist" (Laub and Sampson 2003: 582), yet our laws, policy, and public discourse have all lagged behind this revolution in scientific knowledge. Public discourse continues to proceed as though there are two kinds of people in the world—the good and the bad—and if we would simply lock up the bad guys forever, the rest of us will be safe. We thus continue to affix a more or less permanent label on people who engage in crime.

But a *second* revolution has transformed the stickiness of these labels. We will argue here that new and disruptive information technologies now make these labels more accessible and consequential, blurring the boundaries between public and private information. People now know more about their fellow citizens than ever before, such that labels are increasingly difficult to "peel off," dissolve, and remove. This juxtaposition is causing all sorts of difficulties, particularly in regard to the dual imperatives of public criminology. How do we enhance the quality of justice while also improving and protecting public safety? And how does the increasing stickiness of public labels affect the prospects for truly reintegrative approaches to public safety (Braithwaite 1989)?

Below we will present some examples of fluidity from our own research and then discuss how labels retain their stickiness. Making extensive use of graphics and figures, we will show the demographic growth of felon and ex-felon populations in the United States and discuss how these populations spillover to affect other social institutions. Next, we identify some reintegrative interventions that may facilitate desistance from crime, versus stigmatizing collateral sanctions that likely constitute "piling on" (Uggen and Stewart 2014). Finally, we will move beyond the U.S. context and raise more dramatic alternatives, as well as more modest or incremental reforms.

Age, crime, and fluidity

There is a pronounced empirical relationship between age and crime for a great range of criminal activities. The age–crime curves in Figure 12.1, prepared from U.S. Uniform Crime Reports data, show a somewhat flatter age profile for rape arrests than for burglary arrests (Nyseth Brehm et al. 2012).[1] Nevertheless, arrest certainly remains much more likely in the teens and twenties than in the thirties and forties. These smooth curves, of course, mask great intra-individual movement.

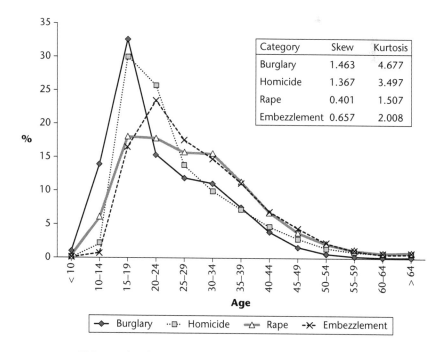

Category	Skew	Kurtosis
Burglary	1.463	4.677
Homicide	1.367	3.497
Rape	0.401	1.507
Embezzlement	0.657	2.008

FIGURE 12.1 U.S. age distribution of arrest.

Source: Adapted from Nyseth Brehm *et al.* (2012).

When we look more closely at individual offending patterns, we observe that desistance unfolds in fits and starts. With Melissa Thompson (2003, 2013), Uggen has been investigating what is happening in people's lives when they are in higher and lower periods of illegal earning activity. One study considered monthly patterns for the 4,927 participants in the National Supported Work Demonstration Project, an experiment that provided jobs to both people leaving prison and other people with barriers to employment. Figure 12.2 below charts the pattern for Paul, a participant from Oakland, California. Paul had been using cocaine and was incarcerated for at least a portion of the first month of the program. He also perceived frequent illegal earning opportunities, and he self-reported making about $867 illegally that month (or $200 per week). He was living with his spouse or partner, but was not employed. He began working in a Supported Work job in the sixth month. Nevertheless, he was rearrested in the eighth month, his substance use escalated to include heroin in month ten, his illegal earnings escalated to over $3,000 per month, and he was no longer partnered or working in either a program job or a regular job.

Although Paul's level of illegal earnings is relatively high, this was not an unusual pattern among participants in the first year of the program. There is more of the same at the start of Paul's second year, as shown in Figure 12.3, and one would have to be fairly pessimistic about his prospects. He was earning about $2,500 per month illegally, and he was still using cocaine and heroin. His reported substance use, however, stopped abruptly after 18 months. At that point he was either reunited with his spouse or he was with another spouse or partner. Still, he reported no work and only a tiny amount of unearned legal income (likely to be General Assistance support).

Finally, after two full years, he picked up some regular (unsubsidized) work, and he began reporting steady legal earnings of about $1,000 a month. As shown in Figure 12.4, he was no longer being arrested, he was steadily employed, and he was in a stable relationship. In short, he is the very picture of the change that most reintegration programs are trying to induce.

Of course, whether we consider Paul a recidivism success or failure depends on *when* we look at him. This sort of fluidity in offending is well understood by every desistance researcher, yet it remains poorly understood by the public and in policy circles. In the first year, Paul was involved in a great deal of criminal activity, which might merit arrest and incarceration. By the third year, however, he appeared to be living a completely different life—it would have been a colossal waste to incarcerate him at this point, as society would be forgoing all his productive economic activity and bearing the costs of his incarceration. But what about that second year? Would re-incarceration have slowed or undone the reintegrative progress that Paul had been making, prolonging the cycle of recidivism and incarceration? Such questions are difficult to answer in desistance research, but timing clearly matters.

While the distinction between criminal and non-criminal is largely a matter of time, desistance research also shows us how other life course markers map onto this process. In "Settling Down and Aging Out" (2010), Mike Massoglia and Uggen considered how crime and punishment affect our subjective sense of ourselves as

	1	2	3	4	5	6	7	8	9	10	11	12
Drugs and money												
Drug use	coke	coke	coke	coke	coke	coke	coke	coke	coke	coke heroin	coke heroin	coke heroin
Earned legal $	867					433	433	433	433			
Eamed illegal $		867					867	867	867	867	3342	3342
Uneamed legal $									84	146	146	146
Opportunity structure												
Incarceration	yes	yes										
Unemp. rate	11.6	11.6	11.6	11.2	11.2	11.2	11.0	11.0	11.0	10.6	10.6	10.6
Illegal opportunities	high	high	high	high	high	high	high	high	high	high	high	high
Crim. embeddedness												
Unemp/deviant friend									yes	yes	yes	yes
Arrest experience	8			8	8	8	8	10	10	10	10	10
Age	33.0	33.1	33.2	33.3	33.3	33.4	33.5	33.6	33.7	33.8	33.8	33.9
Conv. embeddedness												
Spouse/partner	yes		yes	yes	yes	yes	yes	yes				
Regular employment												
Program employment					yes	yes	yes	yes	yes			
School attendance												
Subj. risks & rewards												
Perceived risk of prison	low	low	low	low	low	low	low	low	low	low	low	low
Earnings expectations	350	350	350	350	350	350	350	350	300	300	300	300

Key: Absence of characteristic: [ ]   Lower levels: [ ]   Higher levels: [ ]

FIGURE 12.2   Year 1 array of legal and illegal activities.

Source: Adapted from Uggen and Thompson (2003).

	13	14	15	16	17	18	19	20	21	22	23	24
Drugs and money												
Drug use	Coke heroin	Coke heroin	Coke heroin	Coke heroin	Coke heroin							
Earned legal $												
Earned illegal $	2475	2475	2475	2475	2475	2475	2475	2475				
Unearned legal	146	146	146	146	146	146						
Opportunity structure												
Incarceration												
Unemp. rate	9.3	9.3	93	1.6	8.6	8.6	8.3	83	83	7.6	7.6	7.6
Illegal opportunities	high	high	high	high	high	med.	med.	med.	med.	med.	med.	med.
Crim. embeddedness												
Unemp/deviant friend	yes	yes	yes	yes	yes							
Arrest experience	10	10	10	10	10	10	10	10	10	10	10	10
Age	34	34.1	34.2	34.3	34.3	34.4	34.5	34.6	34.7	34.8	34.8	34.9
Conv. embeddedness												
Spouse/partner						yes	yes	yes	yes	yes	yes	yes
Regular employment												
Program employment												
School attendance												
Subj. risks & rewards												
Perceived risk of prison	low	low	low	low	low	high	high	high	high	high	low	low
Earnings expectations	300	300	300	300	300	300	300	300	300	300	300	300

Key: Absence of characteristic: Lower levels: Higher levels:

FIGURE 12.3   Year 2 array of legal and illegal activities.

Source: Adapted from Uggen and Thompson (2003).

	25	26	37	28	29	30	31	32	33	34	35	36
Drugs and money												
Drug use												
Earned legal $	1066	1066	1066	840	840	840	840	840	840	840	840	840
Earned illegal $												
Unearned legal $												
Opportunity structure												
Incarceration												
Unemp. rate	6.2	6.2	6.2	5.6	5.6	5.6	6.9	6.9	6.9	5.1	5.1	5.1
Illegal opportunities	med.	med.	high	high	high	high	high	high	high	high	high	high
Crim. embeddedness												
Unemp/deviant friend		yes	yes	yes	yes	yes	yes	yes	yes	yes	yes	yes
Arrest experience		10	10	10	10	10	10	10	10	10	10	10
Age	35.1	35.1	35.2	35.3	35.3	35.4	35.5	35.6	35.7	35.8	35.8	35.9
Conv. embeddedness												
Spouse/partner	yes	yes	yes	yes	yes	yes	yes	yes	yes	yes	yes	
Regular employment	yes	yes	yes	yes	yes	yes	yes	yes	yes	yes	yes	
Program employment												
School attendance												
Subj. risks & rewards												
Perceived risk of prison	high	high	med.	med.	med.	med.	med.	med.	med.	med.	med.	low
Earnings expectations	300	300	800	800	800	800	800	800	800	800	800	260

Key: Absence of characteristic: [ ]   Lower levels: [ ]   Higher levels: [ ]

FIGURE 12.4 Year 3 array of legal and illegal activities.

Source: Adapted from Uggen and Thompson (2003).

TABLE 12.1 Predictors of subjective desistance

REFERENCE GROUP DESISTANCE, SUBJECTIVE DESISTANCE, AND SUBJECTIVE ADULT STATUS: LOGISTIC REGRESSION ESTIMATES

Variable	Model 1	Model 2	Model 3	Model 4	Model 5
Reference group desistance	.472** (.168)	.245 (.200)			.096 (.215)
Subjective desistance			.626*** (.183)	.557** (.221)	.518** (.235)
Arrest (1 = arrest in 2000–2002)		−1.491*** (.406)		−1.552*** (.406)	−1.537*** (.408)
Male		−.304 (.199)		−.236 (.202)	−.238 (.202)
White		.035 (.237)		.015 (.238)	.023 (.239)
Marriage		−.013 (.219)		−.040 (.218)	.049 (.220)
Educational attainment		−.187 (.215)		−.207 (.216)	−.201 (.216)
Self-sufficiency		.407* (.218)		.402* (.219)	.405* (.219)
Children		.860*** (.225)		.823*** (.225)	.817*** (.226)
Voting		.521** (.221)		.451* (.222)	.452* (.223)
Prior adult status (1999)		2.171*** (.220)		2.223*** (.224)	2.226*** (.224)
Missing dummy for prior adult status		.157 (.278)		.091 (.281)	.084 (.280)
Intercept	.630*** (.125)	−1.082** (.415)	.457*** (.154)	−1.247*** (.426)	−1.268*** (.426)
−2 log likelihood	841.72	663.78	837.04	656.12	655.47

Source: Massoglia and Uggen (2010).

adults. In this study we fielded some questions on a longitudinal survey,[2] asking people in their early thirties questions such as, "Do you feel like an adult most of the time?" (Table 12.1). Standard life course markers, including having children, completing school, and getting married were quite predictive. What was interesting, however, was that the effect of being arrested was at least as strong as any of these life course markers in terms of *not* feeling like an adult. Both "subjective desistance" (slowing down relative to yourself five years ago) and, to a lesser extent, reference group desistance (slowing down relative to others your age) had similar effects. By any measure, then, continued criminality appears to have a juvenilizing effect that delays the assumption of adult status.

This line of research led to an ongoing project investigating how institutions affect the transition to adulthood: the Minnesota Exits and Entries Project. Like many desistance projects, this study targets people leaving prison between the ages of 18 and 25. To provide a more comparative perspective on reentry, however, we are comparing the experiences of the ex-prisoners with individuals leaving jail,[3] juvenile corrections,[4] mental health treatment, drug treatment, foster care, and the armed forces. Pre-release interviews were conducted with participants at their respective institutions, and post-release interviews were conducted 90 days after they reentered the general population. In total, more than 250 individuals were interviewed for this project. We have thus far seen more commonality between these groups than one might anticipate, although the correctional groups (those leaving prison, jail, and juvenile corrections) have been more likely to be re-incarcerated. Nevertheless, we have also observed great fluidity *across* these groups—a participant might begin in foster care, then do time in a juvenile correctional facility or a drug treatment center, before eventually winding up in the county jail or state prison. It thus became very difficult to isolate these treatment settings from corrections, especially when so many clients enter treatment institutions through the criminal courts. The "sticky" criminal label has thus been affixed to a broader set of institutions and their clients.

Stickiness and marginality

In contrast to the relative fluidity of criminal offending, criminal records are notoriously "sticky." We will argue, however, that these criminal records are growing increasingly stickier with each passing year. In Erving Goffman's (1963) terms, those who cannot hide a stigmatizing characteristic are considered "discredited," in contrast to "discreditable" individuals whose stigmatizing information can be concealed in interaction. As criminal records have become cheaper to access *and* more widely accessible in recent years, millions have moved from the category of "potentially discreditable" to the category of "formally discredited." It has now become normative for U.S. firms to conduct background checks, with over 60 percent of employers indicating that they always check the criminal backgrounds of applicants (Raphael 2010; Society for Human Resource Management 2010). These checks often yield information on arrests as well as convictions, such that applicants for housing and employment must now routinely account for misdemeanor arrests that were never prosecuted. At the same time, we have witnessed a corresponding explosion in the creation of such records. Robert Brame and colleagues (2014) now estimate that 30 percent of Americans are arrested by the age of 23, a number that increases to 49 percent for African American males.

While felony-level criminal records are quite consequential in hiring and other areas (see, e.g., Devah Pager's experimental audit studies (2007)), there has been far less research on more common or prosaic misdemeanor arrests. Figure 12.5 below shows a breakdown of the 14 million U.S. arrests in 2007. Only about 16 percent involved the Uniform Crime Reports Part I "index" offenses. As can be seen in the breakout section of the pie chart below, Part I offenses are the category of crimes considered the most serious, such as homicide, robbery, and rape. The upper left section of the pie chart represents the much larger proportion of substance use and drug law violations, while the hatched region represents a mix of minor and miscellaneous offenses such as trespassing. About 5 percent of the total arrests involved disorderly conduct, the low-level offense we chose to examine in our audit study that is documented below.

As with incarceration, arrest is quite unevenly distributed by race. Figure 12.6 below compares arrest and imprisonment rates in the state of Minnesota, where we conducted our audit study. The annual American Indian and Alaskan Native arrest rate was an astounding 158 per thousand in 2007, and the African American arrest rate was even higher, at 227 per thousand that year. The latter figure is over

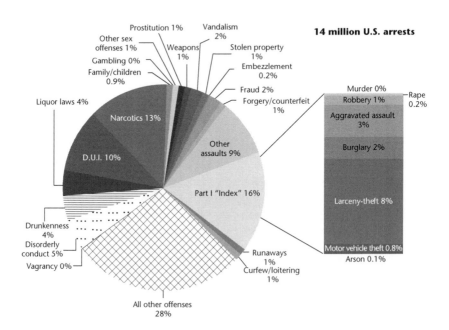

FIGURE 12.5 The offense distribution of U.S. arrests, 2007.

Source: Adapted from Uggen *et al.* (2014).

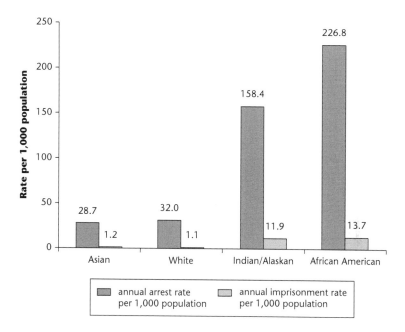

FIGURE 12.6   Minnesota arrest and imprisonment rates, 2007.

Source: Adapted from Uggen *et al.* (2014).

16 times the corresponding African American imprisonment rate and about 7 times the rate of arrest for Whites and Asian Americans. Because some individuals are arrested multiple times per year, this does not correspond to 22.7 percent of all African Americans being arrested. Nevertheless, arrest records affect a very large share of the total African American and American Indian populations.

To explore what effects these arrest records may have on hiring decisions, we conducted an audit study testing the "Edge of Stigma." We sent matched pairs of young men to apply for 300 entry-level jobs in Minnesota, assigning one member of the pair a three-year-old disorderly conduct arrest (Uggen *et al.* 2014). Figure 12.7 below shows the no-record (control) and arrest record (treatment) for our White and African American pairs. There was about a four percentage point difference between the control and treatment groups in the rate of positive "callbacks" by employers—a much more modest effect than Pager (2007) observed for felony prison records. Nevertheless, the minor arrest record caused a 15 percent drop in the likelihood of callback for African Americans and an 11 percent drop for Whites.

Younger cohorts must now navigate a world in which stigmatizing information about themselves is increasingly accessible to potential employers. In contrast, the first author's own arrest records were largely invisible to the University of Wisconsin when he applied as a student in the 1980s—and they were largely invisible

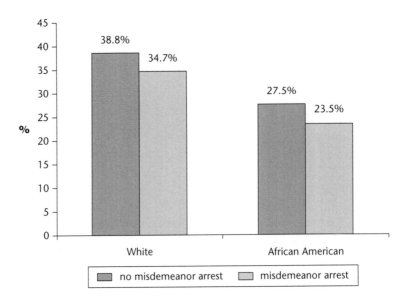

FIGURE 12.7   Employer "callbacks" by race and arrest record.

Source: Adapted from Uggen *et al.* (2014).

to the University of Minnesota when he applied for a faculty position in the 1990s. Today, this situation has changed dramatically and has made the mark of a criminal record—or even an arrest record—all the more "sticky."

More people with more records

The story of the American punishment boom has been well-documented by many sources. As Figure 12.8 shows, the number of people under correctional supervision (prison, jail, probation, or parole) grew from under 2 million in 1980 to over 7 million in 2011.

With Sarah Shannon *et al.* (2014), we have been developing estimates of the corresponding growth in the number of former felons. Our demographic life table estimates (Figure 12.9) suggest that there are approximately 20 million people in the United States who have been convicted of felonies—about 5 million are currently under correctional supervision and about 15 million have a felony-level conviction history but have completed their sentences.

The story of these sticky records is both racial and spatial. We estimate that in 2010 about 6.4 percent of the U.S. adult population shared a felony conviction history. As seen in Figure 12.10, this rate was far higher in states such as Georgia and Florida, relative to Northeastern states such as Maine, New Hampshire, and New York. In Florida (12.6 percent) and Georgia (11.4 percent), more than 10 percent of the total adult population had spent time incarcerated and/or under correctional supervision for felonies in 2010.

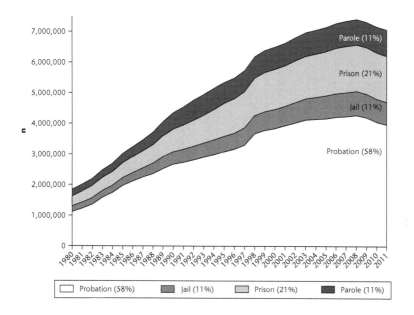

FIGURE 12.8 U.S. correctional populations, 1980–2011.

Source: Adapted from U.S. Department of Justice data.

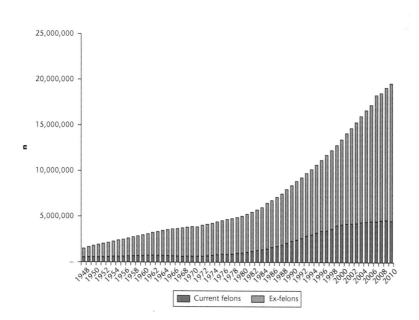

FIGURE 12.9 Number of U.S. citizens with a current or past felony conviction, 1980–2010.

Source: Shannon *et al.* (2014).

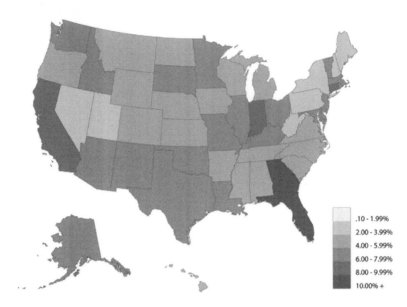

Legend:
.10 - 1.99%
2.00 - 3.99%
4.00 - 5.99%
6.00 - 7.99%
8.00 - 9.99%
10.00% +

FIGURE 12.10   Spatial distribution of U.S. felon population as percentage of voting age population.

Source: Shannon *et al.* (2014).

For at least the past 160 years, African Americans have been incarcerated at disproportionately high rates in America. Figure 12.11 presents the rate of African American ex-felons in the US, showing that every state had at least 4 percent of the adult African American population under felony supervision in 2010. Moreover 12 states had African American ex-felon rates in excess of 20 percent, meaning that one in five African American adults in these states had at some point been under felony supervision (California, Connecticut, Florida, Indiana, Kansas, Massachusetts, New Jersey, New Mexico, Ohio, Oklahoma, Rhode Island, and Washington).

The combination of more people with records and greater public visibility of these records exerts "spillover effects" on a great range of social institutions— including labor markets, political institutions, health care, education, and housing markets. For example, Jeff Manza and Chris Uggen have shown how felon disenfranchisement affects election outcomes (2002, 2006). Using data from legal sources, election studies, and inmate surveys, their counter-factual analysis found that felon disenfranchisement led to Republican victories in numerous U.S. Senate elections and even the 2000 presidential election. Because felons are often drawn from disadvantaged communities and communities of color, their disenfranchisement has led to lost votes for Democratic candidates.

To explore other "spillover effects," an ongoing project with Jason Schnittker examines how the density of former prisoners in an area affects the health choices

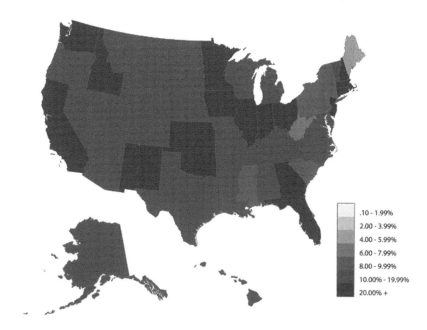

FIGURE 12.11 Spatial distribution of African American felons as percentage of voting age population.

Source: Shannon *et al.* (2014).

of all citizens—everything from annual testing to the availability of mammograms (Schnittker *et al.* 2015). This study uses data from the Community Tracking Study to show how a large number of ex-prisoners in the population increases the percentage of uninsured individuals, which, in turn, increases the number of emergency room visits and reduces the number of available hospital beds. These secondary or tertiary spillovers are illustrated in Figure 12.12. Criminal labels thus affix themselves to broader communities and constituencies, not just the individuals convicted of crime.

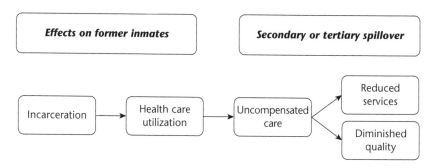

FIGURE 12.12 Secondary or tertiary spillovers on health care.

Reintegrative strategies versus "piling on"

So how might we better intervene to capitalize on the fluidity in criminal offending? During the recession of the 1970s, the National Supported Work experiment provided jobs to those leaving prison and drug treatment. Sarah Shannon and Chris Uggen reanalyzed the data (2014) and found that those given jobs had a significantly lower rate of arrest than the randomly assigned control group. After 18 months in the program, about 74 percent of the treatment group had yet to be arrested, relative to about 68 percent of the controls (Figure 12.13).

Of course, people can be arrested for many offenses. We were especially interested in whether the jobs reduced more predatory crimes, such as robbery and burglary. Indeed, providing a basic entry-level job almost cut the rate of robbery and burglary arrests in half among these former drug users—a 46 percent reduction (Figure 12.14).

As criminologists, we do not often find randomized experiments that yield a 46 percent reduction in offending. Why has the program's success not been more widely reported and emulated? The answer lies in the next chart (Figure 12.15), which shows the time until cocaine and heroin were used among these same participants. As this chart demonstrates, the program had no effect on drug relapse. If anything, those who were working in the program jobs relapsed at somewhat quicker rates than the control group.

This pattern of results raises an absolutely critical policy question: Is it wise to invest in employment programs that reduce crime, even if participants may spend some of their earnings on drugs? This is the fulcrum of debates over "harm reduction"

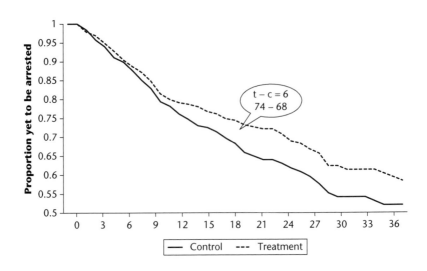

FIGURE 12.13 Time to arrest among drug treatment group.

Source: Adapted from Uggen and Shannon (2014).

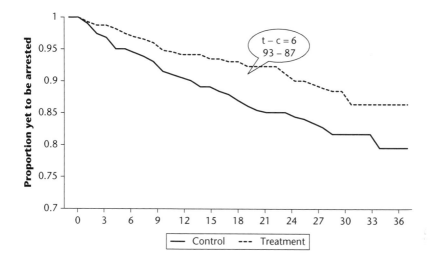

FIGURE 12.14 Time to robbery/burglary arrest.

Source: Adapted from Uggen and Shannon (2014).

programs more generally, such as the controversial choice between "wet" programs and more traditional "dry" approaches that enforce abstinence-only policies. By opening work and housing opportunities to a broader set of clients, perhaps such harm reduction efforts can facilitate a transition from a sticky and totalizing criminal label to one that more accurately reflects the complex and transitional nature of the desistance process.

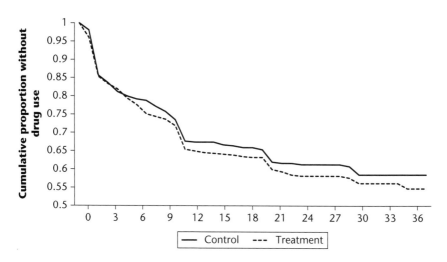

FIGURE 12.15 Time to cocaine or heroin use.

Source: Uggen and Shannon (2014).

While supported employment might serve as an example of reintegrative interventions, other policy interventions have been far more stigmatizing. In a separate study with Melissa Thompson (Thompson and Uggen 2013), we have been examining the effects of a federal policy that places restrictions on public assistance for those individuals convicted of drug felonies. Since 1996, U.S. states could opt out of this federal ban on public assistance for drug felons or choose to implement partial bans (e.g., on food assistance and/or cash transfers) that allowed individuals to continue receiving assistance if they met certain conditions. We are now examining how these interventions affected female arrest rates. We use pooled time-series models with fixed state and year effects from 1990 to 2010, testing whether state-specific welfare bans affected the female arrest rates reported in the Uniform Crime Reports the following year. Figure 12.16 shows the total female arrest rate before and after states imposed the ban. We observed a sharper increase in female arrests among states that imposed the full ban relative to those that opted out or imposed a partial ban.

We saw this pattern for property arrests and, particularly, for violent arrests, as shown in the chart below (Figure 12.17). The female violent arrest rate rose at a much steeper rate immediately after the 1996 changes took effect.

This pattern of results implies that the change was consequential. The only type of crime that was clearly *unaffected* by the felony drug ban was the drug arrest rate. For all other categories, we saw an increase in female arrests among states that cut the benefits of people who had been convicted of drug crimes. When we first presented this information to a group of economists, they were initially quite skeptical of the story that a welfare ban could increase arrests. Some found it easier to understand when we asked which group of recipients we would cut off if we had intended to *increase* crime. Wouldn't we target those with the greatest "criminal capital" and networks for illegal activity? If our goal is instead to hasten desistance, we would really want to reduce these unnecessary collateral sanctions.

We refer to policies such as the welfare ban as "piling on," because they lack a meaningful crime control function or motivation (see Uggen and Stewart 2014). In American football, "piling on" occurs when one or more players jumps atop a downed player after a tackle has been made. It is illegal because it is unnecessary, slows the progress of the game, and often results in serious injury. We might also think of "piling on" in terms of the thick stack of criminal labels stubbornly affixed to so many domains of social life—from employment, to education, to public assistance, to online dating, to family relationships, to housing, to restrictions on physical movement, to voting, to volunteering, and to other public service (Uggen and Stewart 2014). The effects of these criminal labels extend far beyond the individuals who bear them, however. A denial of benefits will also affect their families (Uggen and McElrath 2014), denying these individuals and their communities the assistance that they may require. As discussed previously, families and communities are also affected by this "piling on" when spillover effects venture beyond individual offenders to affect political elections and the health outcomes of individuals *without* criminal labels (Uggen and Stewart 2014).

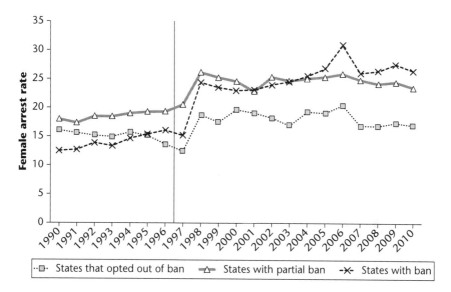

FIGURE 12.16 Female arrest rates by welfare ban implementation.

Source: Thompson and Uggen (2013).

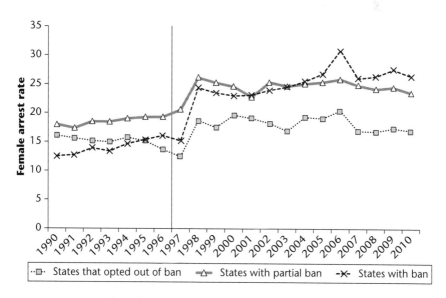

FIGURE 12.17 Female violent arrest rates by welfare ban status.

Source: Thompson and Uggen (2013).

New models

After two decades of studying crime and desistance in the United States, we have become increasingly convinced of the need for more radical ideas and approaches. With Hollie Nyseth Brehm and Damas Gasanabo (2014), we have begun a project in Rwanda, a nation that experienced a devastating 1994 genocide that left 1 million of its 7 million citizens dead. We analyzed the 1.96 million cases in the hybrid *gacaca* court system devised by the nation to try over 60,000 organizers, 577,000 killers, and 1.3 million other individuals who were accused of property offenses during the genocide. Rwanda's devastated legal infrastructure could never process so many cases, so the *gacaca* courts used an adapted version of a traditional restorative justice practice based on elected lay judges and a mixture of restorative and punitive sanctions.

For property offenses, we found that about 87 percent of those found guilty were fined (Nyseth Brehm *et al.* 2014). The *gacaca* courts also used apologies, negotiated settlements, agreements, and restitution as sentences for these crimes. For those who planned the genocide, the modal sentence length was 25 to 30 years in prison. For killing, the modal sentence length ranged from 10 to 15 years in prison. Furthermore, 29 percent of these convicted individuals were eligible

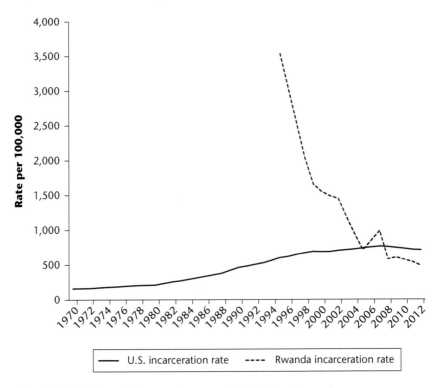

FIGURE 12.18 Estimated incarceration rates in the US and Rwanda.

Source: Brehm and Uggen (2014).

for early release (up to a 50 percent reduction of their sentence). Although the *gacaca* process has been criticized for not meeting the due process standards of the liberal legal model (Apuuli 2009; Ingelaere 2009), it is likely to have been under-appreciated for its ability to do justice with relatively few resources. It is clearly a promising model for other cases of mass atrocity, but elements of the *gacaca* system may also be a useful model for community courts or other restorative justice settings. Importantly, Rwanda has experienced an astounding *decarceration* since the genocide, which has been accompanied by relatively little social disruption. Figure 12.18 above shows the estimated peak rate of incarceration at 3,500 per 100,000 people in the wake of the genocide—a figure that overwhelms even the outsized U.S. prison incarceration rate by a factor of 7. Only 20 years past the genocide, is it possible that the label of "genocide perpetrator" is less sticky in Rwanda than the label of "criminal" in twenty-first-century America?

Conclusion

As we learn more about desistance patterns, the old "two kinds of people" argument has become increasingly untenable. We criminologists now spend our time thinking about how to effect or smooth transitions, rather than how to identify individual offenders and quarantine them from non-offenders. Age–crime curves show that the likelihood of desistance increases with age for all crimes, while individual life course trajectories reveal that offending is quite fluid, with recidivism dependent on when in the life course an individual is viewed. This holds particular significance, as criminal labels have become "stickier," with criminal history information more readily available to everyone from employers, to landlords, to potential romantic partners. These labels have myriad consequences for individuals, including a decreased likelihood of gaining employment, numerous health effects, and restrictions on accessing public assistance. More so, many of these sanctions have spillover effects on families and communities, affecting an even larger population's health and access to needed assistance. As the number of individuals under correctional supervision increases, especially for communities of color, a greater percentage of Americans are affected by the long-lasting consequences of a criminal record. Criminal labels have indeed become increasingly "sticky."

The time has thus come for a reasoned critique of excess punishment. As research has shown, providing jobs to individuals leaving prison and drug treatment can yield a marked decrease in predatory crimes, even if such programs have no effect on drug relapse. Thus, policy makers must weigh which outcomes they consider most important when evaluating such programs. Harm reduction and "wet" programs may not be "cure all" solutions, but if they are successful at achieving desired results, then they should at least receive consideration. The case of Rwanda also provides at least one example showing how "mass decarceration" of an enormous number of former prisoners will not necessarily bring about rampant crime and social disorder. Thus, even though the United States contains a large number of people who bear the mark of a criminal record, large-scale and successful reintegration is a realistic and achievable goal. To achieve this, however, requires greater scientific and policy acknowledgement that criminal labels need not be so sticky.

Notes

1 This manuscript tests a life-course model of genocide participation for the 1994 Rwandan genocide, comparing the crimes committed during the genocide to analogous criminal offenses in the United States. The United States data come from the FBI's Uniform Crime Reporting Program, which collects nationwide arrest data.
2 This paper uses data from the Youth Development Study, a longitudinal survey of 1,000 students who attended public schools in St. Paul, Minnesota in the 1980s. Respondents were asked about subjective adulthood when they were 26 to 27 years old and again when they were ages 29 to 30.
3 In the United States, jails differ from prisons in jurisdiction and sentence length. Prisons are under the jurisdiction of the federal or state government, while jails are run by county sheriff's departments. Also, prisons hold individuals convicted of crimes who are serving longer sentences, while individuals awaiting trial or serving shorter sentences, usually of less than a year, are held in jails.
4 In most U.S. states, the age of juvenile court jurisdiction extends to 18 years old, such that juvenile correction facilities typically house youth who were adjudicated as adolescents.

References

Apuuli, K. P. (2009), "Procedural due process and the prosecution of genocide suspects in Rwanda," *Journal of Genocide Research* 11: 11–30.

Braithwaite, J. (1989), *Crime, Shame, and Reintegration*. Cambridge, MA: Cambridge University Press.

Brame, R., Bushway, S. D., Paternoster, R. and Turner, M. G. (2014), "Demographic patterns of cumulative arrest prevalence by ages 18 and 23," *Crime & Delinquency* 60: 471–486.

Goffman, E. (1963), *Stigma: Notes on the Management of Spoiled Identity*. Englewood Cliffs, NJ: Prentice-Hall, p. 41.

Ingelaere, B. (2009), "Does the truth pass across the fire without burning? Locating the short circuit in Rwanda's gacaca courts," *The Journal of Modern African Studies* 47: 507–528.

Laub, J. H. and Sampson, R. J. (2003), *Shared Beginnings, Divergent Lives: Delinquent Boys to Age 70*. Cambridge, MA: Harvard University Press.

Manza, J. and Uggen, C. (2006), *Locked Out: Felon Disenfranchisement and American Democracy*. New York: Oxford University Press.

Massoglia, M. and Uggen, C. (2010), "Settling down and aging out: Toward an interactionist theory of desistance and the transition to adulthood," *American Journal of Sociology* 116: 543–582.

Nyseth Brehm, H., Uggen, C. and Gasanabo, J.-D. (2012), *Genocide and the Age Distribution of Crime*. Paper presented at the Annual Meetings of the American Society of Criminology, Chicago, IL.

Nyseth Brehm, H., Uggen, C. and Gasanabo, J.-D. (2014), "Genocide, justice, and Rwanda's gacaca courts," *Journal of Contemporary Criminal Justice* 30: 333–352.

Pager, D. (2007), *Marked: Race, Crime, and Finding Work in an Era of Mass Incarceration*. Chicago, IL: University of Chicago Press.

Raphael, S. (2010), "Improving employment prospects for former prison inmates: Challenges and policy," National Bureau of Economic Research: Working Paper w1(5874). Available at URL: http://www.nber.org/papers/w15874 (accessed 7 January 2016).

Schnittker, J., Uggen, C., Shannon, S. and McElrath, S. (2015), "The institutional effects of incarceration: Spillovers from criminal justice to health care," *Milbank Quarterly* 95(3): 516–560.

Shannon, S. and Uggen, C. (2014), "Visualizing punishment," in Hartmann, D. and Uggen, C. (eds) *Crime and the Punished*. New York: W. W. Norton, pp. 42–62.

Shannon, S., Uggen, C., Schnittker, J., Thompson, M., Wakefield, S. and Masoglia, M. (2014), "Growth in the U.S. ex-felon and ex-prisoner population 1948–(2010)," Unpublished manuscript.

Society for Human Resource Management (2010), *Background Checking: Conducting Criminal Background Checks*. Alexandria, VA: SHRM.

Thompson, M. and Uggen, C. (2013), *How Welfare Reform Drove Up Female Arrest Rates*. Paper presented at Institute for Research on Poverty Summer Workshop, in Madison, WI, 26 June. Available at http://www.soc.umn.edu/~uggen/Thompson_Uggen_WelfareReform_WP.pdf (accessed 7 January 2016).

Uggen, C. and Manza, J. (2002), "Democratic contraction? The political consequences of felon disenfranchisement in the United States," *American Sociological Review* 67: 777–803.

Uggen, C. and Thompson, M. (2003), "The socioeconomic determinants of ill-gotten gains: Within-person changes in drug use and illegal earnings," *American Journal of Sociology* 109: 146–185.

Uggen, C. and McElrath, S. (2014), "Parental incarceration: What we know and where we need to go," *Journal of Criminal Law and Criminology* 104: 597–604.

Uggen, C. and Shannon, S. (2014), "Productive addicts and harm reduction: How work reduces crime—but not drug use," *Social Problems* 61: 105–130.

Uggen, C. and Stewart, R. (2014), "Piling on: Collateral consequences and community supervision," *Minnesota Law Review* 99(5): 1871–1912.

Uggen, C., Vuolo, M., Lageson, S., Ruhland, E. and Whitham, H. (2014), "The edge of stigma: An experimental audit of the effects of low-level criminal records on employment," *Criminology* 52: 627–654.

13

UNDERSTANDING AND IDENTIFYING DESISTANCE

An example exploring the utility of sealing criminal records

Megan C. Kurlychek, Shawn D. Bushway and Megan Denver

Introduction

The development of a criminal lifestyle has long captured the imagination and scientific attention of criminology. Indeed, when we talk about criminological theory, we are almost exclusively referring to a body of literature developed studying the behavior of adolescent males and their onset into delinquency (Shaw and McKay 1942; Cohen 1955; Hirschi 1969; Sutherland and Cressey 1984). It was not until the 1980s that more careful attention was provided to another phenomenon—persistence in crime. The now classic criminal career approach (Blumstein *et al.* 1986) was the first to examine patterns of continuation of crime over the lifespan and to draw attention to the fact that most offenders do not persist in crime, but at some point exit, or desist, from this lifestyle. The notion of desistance as an independent topic of study, however, did not gain the attention of scholars until the late 1980s and 1990s and even then often branched off of studies initially designed to examine "recidivism"—or recorded criminal events after release from prison or treatment programs.

Since this time, the examination of desistance as an event (Blumstein *et al.* 1986) or process (Fagan 1989; Laub *et al.* 1998; Maruna 2001, 2007; Kurlychek *et al.* 2012) has become more viable with access to longitudinal data. Researchers are now able to view offending behavior beyond the adolescent years and into middle, and even late, adulthood (Wolfgang *et al.* 1987; Sampson and Laub 1993). However, as this line of inquiry is still in its infancy, there is abundant room for growth. In particular, we propose that researchers need to develop more thorough theoretical explanations for the desistance process, including explanations of how and why desistance starts, and why desistance persists for some individuals while others may suddenly return to crime.

One group of theorists suggests that desistance can be studied and understood using existing theories of crime—that is, those risks and needs that brought someone into crime in the first place (Andrews *et al.* 1990; Uggen and Piliavin 1998). Indeed, Laub and Sampson (2001) go as far as to suggest that "desistance cannot be understood apart from the onset of criminal activity and possible continuation in offending over time" (Laub and Sampson 2001: 3).

Other theorists argue, however, that what brought someone into crime may have little to do with what brings one out of crime. For example, desistance may simply be linked with a maturation or aging process (Matza 1964; Hirschi and Gottfredson 1983). In this model, individuals begin offending in early adolescence. Their offending behavior peaks in late adolescence, and declines thereafter until they reach the point of zero offending. While the magnitude of individual offending will differ across people based on propensity for crime, this overall pattern will exist for all individuals. Other theories suggest a different explanation for this age–crime curve. For example, Lemert (1951) argues that almost all individuals temporarily experiment with primary deviance as teenagers and would exit voluntarily had they not been forced into a life of crime by society's labels. Thus, while most will commit acts of primary deviance as teenagers, desistance is the natural or expected state if one is not labeled a criminal. Those labeled would then remain in a life of crime unless some event allowed this label/stigma to be removed before they accepted their identity as a criminal.

Still other theorists argue for a much more complicated and individualistic path toward desistance. For example, Sampson and Laub (1993) focus on specific, influential, positive life events that lead to a gradual accumulation of positive social bonds, which eventually lead to desistance. Still other theoretical perspectives stress the importance of dissatisfaction with one's current identity (Paternoster and Bushway 2009), or emotive and cognitive changes (Maruna 1997, 2001; Giordano *et al.* 2007) that lead one to redefine one's self and make a purposeful exit from crime. These latter two explanations emphasize the role of human agency.

Whether desistance is conceptualized as an event or a process, each of these theoretical perspectives has been derived from the observation or tracking of a sample of subjects over time. That is, researchers have developed primarily inductive theoretical knowledge drawn from direct observation. Each theory can then in turn be used to help us deduce ideas about how desistance should look if this theory is, in general, a true picture of the desistance process. We therefore believe that the logical next step of inquiry for desistance researchers is to find ways to differentiate between these theoretical predictions. By doing so, we can design true empirical tests of each theory. Current policies implemented to encourage desistance and ease the reentry process provide unique opportunities to conduct such tests. Put simply, different theories make very different predictions about how these policies will affect behavior. Subsequent empirical work, therefore, can not only evaluate the impact of various policies but also shed direct light onto the validity of the various theoretical models of desistance. In this chapter, we provide specific ideas and examples of how evaluation of existing policies intended to impact the employment of individuals with criminal histories provides a unique opportunity to make progress in this direction. We start with a focused examination of exactly what each of these theories suggests about the individual desisting from crime and the link between this event/process and the opening up of employment opportunities. Then, we describe how each theory predicts how individuals will be affected by three different policies that regulate the use of criminal background screenings for employment determinations. For practical purposes, we situate our discussion to policies existing in one state, New York, USA; however, it should be readily evident that the implications of each policy and its evaluation have extensions far beyond this jurisdictional boundary.

Theories of crime and images of the desister

We agree with the premise that policies designed to promote desistance must begin with a theoretical basis for how and why desistance happens. Only upon this base of knowledge can effective interventions and strategies be formed. Otherwise, as suggested by Hoffman and Beck (1984), "we are really only identifying events of recidivism rather than understanding and identifying true desistance from crime." However, the difficulty in designing and testing policy is that different theories offer very different and even contradictory explanations of desistance. In the following section, we refer to these as "images" of the desister.

Maturational desistance

Perhaps the most straightforward explanation of desistance was provided by David Matza (1964), who suggested that most youth simply undergo a process of "maturational reform," or put more simply, they outgrow crime. Supported by the invariability of the age–crime curve (Hirschi and Gottfredson 1983), this image of the desister is one who undergoes a natural process of maturation in which risk-taking and criminal involvement both decline with age. Policy aimed at promoting desistance would then be futile, as it will occur only when the individual has reached a given state of maturity (arguably mid-twenties for males and early twenties for females). While this is encouraging in that we need to do little as a field to promote desistance, as it will occur as one matures and decision-making capabilities and risk/benefit calculations change as part of the maturational process, this idea is inherently pessimistic—we cannot promote desistance, but must helplessly sit and wait for people to "age out."

Natural desistance

Labeling theory provides a different image of the desister, but perhaps similar policy recommendations. Here again desistance is a natural occurrence as it happens for most after experimenting with a few acts of primary deviance as adolescents. So, instead of placing focus on what *causes* desistance, this theory instead provides an explanation of what *prevents* it. In this perspective, formal labels from social agents in the criminal justice system can cause additional criminal activity (Lemert 1951;

Garfinkel 1956; Matza 1964; Paternoster and Iovanni 1989). Employers and other social agents who use and respond to the label provided by the criminal justice system as if it is an accurate reflection of the individual's character send a continued message to the individual that he/she is indeed a criminal. Eventually, the label becomes part of the person's identity, and deviance a part of the individual's response to the label so-called secondary deviance (Lemert 1951).

Applying this theory to desistance would then suggest that policies that avoid the initial label of delinquent or criminal would have a positive impact on desistance. That is, if two people had equal propensity to initially commit a crime, but one received a formal label upon committing the crime and one did not, this theory would predict that the second individual would be more likely to desist from crime. This notion has been tested recently by Chiricos *et al.* (2007) in a study that takes advantage of a Florida law that allows judges essentially to seal felony convictions for offenders who are found guilty, but sentenced to probation. They found judges applied this option to about 40 percent of the felony convictions sentenced to probation in their sample. This creates a situation in which one can identify two people convicted of the same crime where one is burdened with the stigma of a criminal record and the other is not. This research supports the premise of labeling theory, finding a strong correlation between having a formal criminal record and later likelihood of recidivism (measured as a new felony conviction during a two-year follow-up period). This second image of the desister is then one for whom policy need not promote or cause desistance, but merely provide the opportunity by removing stigmatizing labels before they have the chance to create secondary deviance and "trap" an individual in a persistent life of crime.

Social bonds and desistance

More recent theory situates desistance in the transition from adolescence to adulthood. Here the process is dependent upon acquiring adult social bonds such as stable relationships and employment. Rooted in social control theory (Hirschi 1969), the underlying assumptions are based in a Hobbesian view of humanity in which individuals are essentially out for themselves and will do whatever it takes to get what they want. Thus, criminality itself is a natural state of an individual unless he/she is controlled by formal and informal mechanisms. Hirschi emphasized the importance of attachment, commitment, involvement, and beliefs as they relate to the formation of bonds to one's family of origin, school, and peers during adolescence in providing such controls. In adulthood, Sampson and Laub (Sampson and Laub 1993, 2003; Laub *et al.* 1998) extend these controls to the formation of a new family unit through marriage, and the importance of school is replaced by employment. Here the image of the desister develops out of the image of the delinquent. The youth who enters into delinquency in adolescence is one without strong social bonds to family, school, and peers. He/she has little to lose because he/she does not have conventional "stakes in conformity" (Toby 1957). Desistance from crime can only happen then through the formation of new social bonds that create ties to conventional society.

Laub and Sampson (1993) test this notion using the Glueck and Glueck (1950) data to explore the role of marriage in desistance from crime. They find that the formation of a stable marital bond in adulthood inhibits criminal activity over time (Laub *et al.* 1998). Horney *et al.* (1995) also provide empirical support for the relationship between adult social bonds such as employment and marriage, and reductions in offending. In this examination of patterns of offending among a sample of convicted felons, they constructed life-history calendars through retrospective interviews with offenders and demonstrated that periods of reduced self-reported offending or no offending were connected with spells of employment and time in meaningful relationships and that the loss of such bonds was related to increases in offending behavior.

This image of the desister is one who is in need of something in order to desist—in need of a turning point that will change the life trajectory away from a continued life of crime. Effective policy for this desister would then not only be to avoid a label, which might stigmatize the youth in a way that would prevent such bonds (employment), but would include efforts to increase positive social bonds such as stable relationships and employment. Here too, we note that the image of desistance is one of a process: as one's ties to society increase, criminal activity will decrease, until ultimately reaching a point of non-offending. *This is a critical point for empirical research designed to examine desistance and desisters.* As previously noted, much of the research on desistance has grown from studies aimed at assessing the effectiveness of treatment programs in reducing recidivism. As such, most research looks at only the first recidivism event rather than examining prior and post rates and patterns of offending that would better capture desistance as a "process."

Motivated desistance: going straight, emotive/cognitive change, and identity theories

In addition, there is a remaining debate over "the chicken or the egg." That is, which comes first? Does an individual desist from crime because of a stable marriage and employment? Or must he or she first make a decision to change and then, as a consequence of this change, stop offending and thus become a better potential employee and marital partner? While life-course theory implies that employment and stable adult social bonds "cause" desistance, other theories suggest an individual change or decision to desist must occur first. These theories place more emphasis on human agency and the actor rather than on an external act.

Perhaps the best-known work on the role of human agency in the desistance process is that of Maruna (2001) in which he describes the process of going straight from qualitative interviews with 55 male and 10 female offenders. In this research, Maruna highlights themes that emerge indicating that those successful in desisting from crime see themselves as a truly new or different person. This process often involves separating from past peers or even moving to new environments. Moreover, this research suggests that, contrary to the age-graded life-course theory of crime, obtaining a job or getting married would have little effect on criminality void of a redefinition of the self. That is, there is nothing inherent in the event that makes it a "turning point," but rather it is the reaction of the individual to the event.

Giordano *et al.* (2007) also suggest that a change must occur within the individual before desistance begins, here focusing on emotive rather than cognitive changes. Proposing a "neo-Meadian perspective" on continuity and change in offending, this research criticizes traditional social control models for focusing too heavily on an act (or turning point) rather on changes in the actor. Indeed, the authors go as far as to suggest that this process of emotive change happens "independent of the major role transitions typically emphasized in sociological studies of the life course" (Giordano *et al.* 2007: 1603). According to this symbolic interactionist perspective on the emotive self, traditional pro-social bonds such as marriage and employment are rather catalysts (or "hooks," Giordano *et al.* 2007: 1607) for potential change in one's perspective of the self and the situation. For example, positive appraisals of the self by a pro-social spouse can lead to a change in one's self perspective as well as definitions of desirable social roles. However, contrary to Maruna's notion of a "new self," desistance may not always be a straightforward process. In their examination of emotive states such as depression and anger, this research also suggests that the desistance path may be fraught with potential "derailments" (Giordano *et al.* 2007: 1608), as the current self always incorporates versions of the past self. In this way, this theory proposes to explain how someone with a history of violent behavior who has controlled or tempered his or her anger for years can have a violent encounter upon a substantial negative emotional event (Giordano *et al.* 2007).

This approach to desistance takes emphasis off of social policy and places it back on the individual actor. While not discrediting the importance of *opportunities* for change as chances to redefine the self and try new roles, these perspectives do suggest that the timing of such policies is crucial to their success. Moreover, this timing cannot be clearly defined by age or time since last crime, but rather must be defined by the individual when he/she is ready for a change.

Bushway and Apel (2012) provide an interesting new take on how one might define such a time using "signaling theory" from economics. In this piece, the researchers suggest that those who participate in, and fully complete, employment programs may be signaling to potential employers that they are good employees. In a response paper, Maruna (2012) joins this notion of signaling with aspects of symbolic interactionist theory. He points to the differences between a reform "or" sign, which is applied to an individual from outside, and rehabilitation and "signals," which require action on the part of the individual. While it is impossible for outsiders to know what is in one's emotive or cognitive self, the logical extension of the signaling approach is that those individuals who actively seek out and complete various treatment programs are signaling they are "going straight" and are therefore good candidates for renewed opportunities. By combining notions of emotive/cognitive change with signaling, we develop a fourth image of the desister, one who is motivated and actively ready to make a change in him/herself.

Rock bottom and the feared self

Building on this agentic model of desistance, Paternoster and Bushway (2009) propose that as an individual accumulates negative consequences from involvement
in crime, he/she eventually reaches a decision point that crime is not worth it and
makes a conscious choice to adopt a new identity and desist. This idea is similar to
the Giordano *et al.* (2007) model, but puts less emphasis on the emotional component and instead stresses the agentic selection of a new identity.

One unique aspect of the Paternoster and Bushway (2009) model is the emphasis on the accumulation of negative experiences that lead to a decision to move
away from the "feared self" that the person sees they are becoming. This harkens
back to one of the first descriptions of a desistance process in the literature by
Fagan (1989), who suggested that desistance is a three-stage process. The first stage
involves the accumulation of both formal and informal negative consequences
that lead to the motivation to quit the behavior. This is followed by the formal
decision and/or statement to "quit." Finally, the third stage is maintenance of
this new behavior. It is at this last stage that Fagan suggests the formation of new
positive social networks is crucial for the individual actually to maintain a state of
desistance.

This image of the desister is in direct opposition to that provided by labeling
theory and strict maturational theory, which both suggest there is little to nothing
policy makers can do to encourage desistance. This theory suggests that negative consequences, and perhaps even stigma, are important in the individual reaching "rock
bottom," or that point at which he or she is ready to change. Until this point,
relationships will not be stable and employment may do little except create opportunities to offend. Similar to the motivated desister described above, Paternoster and
Bushway's (2009) theory suggests individual change must occur first, but it places the
roots of this change in the accumulation of negative consequences.

However, Paternoster and Bushway (2009) also point out the relative unpredictability of these "rock bottom" moments, which suggests that policies specifically
designed to create rock bottom moments may be misplaced, and may even be
harmful if they instead create more intransigence or further disadvantage. The
problem, from a policy perspective, is not how to instigate hitting rock bottom, but how to be responsive to the decision to change if, and when, it comes.
Responding before it comes might actually delay desistance by delaying the realization of the "feared self."

Employment and the desistance process

Although there are many theories to suggest a positive link between employment
and desistance from crime, empirical studies of this effect have been far less convincing. Research has consistently found a significant but weak causal relationship
between individual employment and crime (Thornberry and Christenson 1984;
Farrington *et al.* 1986; Sampson and Laub 1993; Needels 1996). Piquero (2012)

characterizes employment as merely a "presumed correlate" of desistance that is "not routinely and convincingly demonstrated" (Piquero 2012: 51).

We suspect this mixed literature regarding the value of employment and employment programs may be linked back to the various notions of desistance itself. Therefore, instead of providing an exhaustive discussion of the literature on employment and crime, in the following sections we demonstrate how the images of the desister presented above lead to vastly different recommendations for employment policy as well as the timing and measuring of desistance.

To recap, the images of the desister provided above can be summarized as:

a. the **maturational desister** who will simply age out of crime;
b. the **natural desister** who will desist from crime *unless* stigmatized and led further into a life of crime, i.e., secondary deviance;
c. the **controlled desister** who initially engaged in crime due to a lack of social controls and who will only desist from crime upon the formation of positive social bonds/controls;
d. the **motivated desister** who must reach a point at which he or she is motivated to change;
e. the **"rock bottom" desister** who must experience enough negative consequences from crime that he/she decides to adopt a new identity, and then benefits from assistance to maintain this state.

The policies we discuss take different approaches to removing the stigma of a criminal record at the time of employment decisions. In general, such policies can be situated at the beginning of one's delinquent activities, at any time during one's interactions with the criminal justice system, or later in life once a person has been free of contact with the criminal justice system for some time. In addition, policies can be automatic, or require little effort or substantial effort on the part of the individual.

The following section describes three specific renditions of restrictions on the use of criminal records in employment decisions in New York State, USA, and their projected impact on each of the above "desisters." For clarity and practical reasons, we focus our discussion on one type of policy and one jurisdiction—restrictions on the use of criminal records in employment background screening in New York State. However, we believe our points are generalizable across jurisdictions and policy initiatives.

Pathways to opening up employment opportunities for offenders

Path 1: proactive policies

According to several of the theories above, and most notably labeling theory, it would be best for a young individual to avoid the stigmatization of a criminal record from the start. That is, desistance will occur naturally for most people if we simply keep the system from interfering with their life and identity. In fact, involvement with the system would prevent desistance and further lead one into a life of crime. In line with this perspective, most states maintain procedures that keep the records of juvenile offenders private and allow for them to be sealed or expunged after a period of time. Most states also offer some type of sealing or expungement opportunities for adult offenders as well, although these policies vary drastically by jurisdiction. New York has been identified as having one of the most liberal sealing policies in the USA, most likely because New York is one of only a handful of states that processes all 16- and/or 17-year-olds automatically as adults. This policy, originating in the state's Youthful Offender Law, is designed to offer a true second chance to young offenders, as described in more detail below. While the following section provides detail on the specific New York policy, this is just one example of a class of policies that we would define as proactive policies. By proactive we mean those policies that *avoid* the initial stigmatization of a criminal record and thus any negative impact of such a record on employment opportunities.

The youthful offender seal

The New York Youthful Offender Act (NY CPL. Law § 720.10) provides the opportunity for youthful offender (YO) status to any defendant between the ages of 14 and 18 (as determined by age at the time of offense) who has no prior felony convictions, no prior felony YO adjudications, and no prior juvenile delinquent adjudications for certain designated felonies. The youth is not automatically eligible if the current offense of indictment is an A-I or A-II felony (murder), an armed violent felony, rape in the first degree, a criminal sexual act in the first degree or aggravated sexual abuse. As with any law, however, there are exceptions to these rules. A judge can still grant a defendant YO status if he/she is charged with an armed violent felony or any of the sex crimes listed above, or even if he/she has a prior record if the judge finds reasons for mitigation. In these cases, YO status can be extended to the youth if the court determines that "the interest of justice would be served by relieving the eligible youth from the onus of a criminal record" (CPL. § 720.20(1)(a)).

There are many benefits for a youth who is eligible for and receives such status. First, the hearings are sealed, which means that they are held in private and upon YO adjudication, the official records are also sealed. Because the offender is determined a YO instead of a "criminal," the individual retains his/her qualification for possible public employment, service in public office, and continued eligibility to seek and receive licenses granted by public authorities that may impact future employment opportunities. The absence of an adult conviction record also means the individual can continue to report no convictions on job applications, college applications, and student loan applications.

In addition to avoiding burdensome collateral consequences of an adult conviction, YO status also extends the benefits of mitigation at sentencing by restricting the maximum sentence that can be handed down by the judge from a maximum of 4 years for a felony offense (rather than up to 25 years for an adult convicted of a class B felony), and a maximum of 6 months (rather than 2 years for an adult conviction) for a misdemeanor YO adjudication. This policy therefore eliminates the stigma of an adult criminal record, keeps open all job/educational possibilities for the offender, and mitigates the punishment associated with the act. Table 13.1 depicts our projected impact of this policy on each "desister." Its impact is assessed against simply "doing nothing," which would allow an employer to see and use all criminal history information in making an employment determination. We therefore assume that the "doing nothing" approach would restrict employment opportunities and that this policy, and the other policies discussed, help the individual gain employment.

The maturational desister, who simply matures out of crime, would not be impacted by this policy. Instead, he or she would simply continue along the traditional age–crime curve, engaging in delinquency and crime in the mid-teens, peaking by the late teens, and then gradually declining in criminal activity. The greatest impact of this policy would be for the natural desister, who without this policy would be led further into crime via a stigmatization process. However, if the record is sealed, this individual is able to look like a non-offender to others; they would not adopt a criminal identity; and thus naturally desist from crime. We also project a positive impact for the controlled desister who needs to form pro-social bonds in order to leave a life of crime. Not having to report a criminal record on job applications or having a criminal record appear during a background check should open up more job opportunities for this individual, serving as a turning point that changes the person's criminal trajectory. Our fourth desister type, the motivated desister, would only be impacted by this policy if it happened at a point when he or she was intrinsically motivated to change. Since this policy occurs early on in an offending career (age 16–18), we would predict this policy would probably be applied before such motivation may occur, and as it takes no effort or action on the part of the individual, there is not a chance for the desister to signal such motivation. However, in Table 13.1 we allow for the possibility that this policy would have a positive impact *if* such motivation were present.

This policy would have the worst impact for our last desister type, the rock bottom desister, for whom this criminal event has not instigated rock bottom. This person may feel they have gotten away with something, and therefore continue on a negative path. For this individual, this policy would at best delay desistance

TABLE 13.1 The proposed impact of the youthful offender seal on desistance

	Positive impact	Negative impact	No impact
Maturational			✓
Natural	✓		
Controlled	✓		
Motivated	✓		✓
Rock bottom		✓	

and at worst increase criminality, as the offender believes his/her criminal actions are without real consequence. On the other hand, if the involvement with the criminal justice system instigates a realization of the "feared self," the sealing could be perfectly timed to correspond with the change in identity. The problem, from a policy perspective, is that it is not possible in real time to know whether the person is in the process of adopting a new identity.

Path 2: reactive policies

A second set of popular policies does not avoid the original stigmatization or other consequences of a criminal record, but rather relies on the fact that experiencing such consequences of crime will eventually deter someone from committing offenses. In this case, the original punishment and stigmatization were perhaps necessary to deter the individual from continuing in a life of crime. The individual has reached a point at which he or she is tired of the consequences of crime and a criminal record, and has made the choice to desist from crime. Then, after a period of time refraining from crime, the individual is offered a second chance.

This type of policy is probably the most popular in Europe and is often referred to as "legal rehabilitation." According to Boone (2011), "these policies assume that the passage of time itself demarks rehabilitation." How much time must pass? Reviews of the laws of several European countries highlighted in a special issue of the *European Journal of Probation* reveal the time frame can be as little as 6 months after conviction in Spain (Larrauri 2011) or, in extreme circumstances, to a maximum of the individual's 80th (Netherlands) or 100th (France) birthday for the most serious offenses (Boone 2011; Herzog-Evans 2011).

In the United States the policies are even more diverse across states, offering what has been referred to as a "hodge-podge of inaccessible and over-lapping provisions" for expungement (Love 2003: 113). In the broadest summary, almost all states allow for criminal records to be sealed after certain time periods and under certain circumstances, but the vast array of time periods and circumstances are too broad for summary herein. As it relates directly to the use of criminal records in employment determinations, several states have begun to address this issue through legislation as well.

Again, it is evident that these policies differ across jurisdictions both in regard to the time that must pass and the extent of the sealing. Therefore, we again select a single "reactive" policy to use as an example for our predictions below.

The time mandated "seal"

Article 23-A of the New York State Correction Law (§§ 750–755), which is designed to guide employer criminal background screening and prohibit employer discrimination, requires employers and licensing agencies in the state to consider criminal convictions (including all felonies and misdemeanors) for applicants on a case-by-case basis. The law requires employers to consider eight factors.

Two of these factors are broad in scope, and indicate a state interest in increasing employment opportunities for individuals with criminal history records, while also acknowledging employers' interests in protecting both property and people. The other six factors are more specific and include job duties/responsibilities, the bearing of the criminal convictions on the individual's suitability to perform the duties of the job, the age of the individual at the time of the offense, the time since the last offense, the seriousness of the offense, and any information provided by the individual regarding his or her rehabilitation.

While Article 23-A does not specify the exact time frame for consideration, it suggests that some period of time must have passed since the last offense. As one example, here we turn to the New York State Department of Health (DOH), which conducts one of the largest and most comprehensive mandatory background screenings in the state. In 2005, based on federal statute, the DOH started conducting criminal history background checks for certain direct access care positions in certified or licensed home health/home care agencies and long-term home health care programs through a new Criminal History Record Check Legal Unit (CHRCLU). In 2006, New York amended their state statutes to provide legal guidance for the CHRCLU program. Section 402 of the New York Codes, Rules and Regulations (NYCRR), Title 10 (Health), was revised to accommodate the legal mandates under Public Health Law Article 28-E and amendments to the state executive law, and these changes took effect in September (2006).

Section 402.7 of NYCRR specifies the crime types and timeframe that should automatically exclude[1] a provisionally hired employee from working in one of these healthcare agencies. For example, certain crime types—a felony conviction for a sex offense, any class A felony, endangering the welfare of an incompetent or physically disabled person in the first degree (section 260.25 of NYS penal law), or certain class D or E felonies, including, but not limited to, assault, larceny, or robbery—are considered too severe regardless of the amount of time that has passed. However, for a large group of crime types, such as a violent felony or any class B or C felony conviction, the law specifies that DOH should disapprove the person for employment when the conviction occurred "within the past 10 years." This means in real terms that essentially the criminal record is "sealed" after 10 years.

In Table 13.2, we review how the policy might impact most pathways to desistance. The basic conclusion is that this policy will have little to no direct impact on the observed behavior of offenders under most theories of desistance.

TABLE 13.2 The proposed impact of the time mandated seal on desistance

	Positive impact	Negative impact	No impact
Maturational			✓
Natural			✓
Controlled	✓		✓
Motivated			✓
Rock bottom			✓

The maturational desister moves along on his/her own trajectory regardless of the policy. The second desister type, the natural desister who was positively impacted by the previous policy, would also not be impacted by this policy as the ten-year policy requires one to desist for a considerable period of time before removing stigma. Thus, the primary deviant is saddled with the formal criminal record on all job applications early in life, in a similar way as if no sealing policy existed at all. Therefore, this person is unlikely to ever experience ten years of non-offending, almost by definition. The impact of the policy on the controlled, motivated, and rock bottom offender is also most likely negligible, but for the opposite reason. After a ten-year period without another contact with the criminal justice system has passed, their identity as desisters is already fairly cemented. As a result, it would be surprising if their offending behavior were to change after the seal. However, they may well benefit from the additional opportunities provided by the removal of the employment ban, given that they are now in the position to take advantage of these additional employment opportunities. The problem from a policy perspective is that these seals come too late in the process to support or encourage the new identities of these individuals, identities that, in all likelihood, are well developed after ten years without an additional contact with the criminal justice system. In this context, what is needed is a positive response from the system earlier in the process, when the identity may not be well established.

Path 3: individual initiated policies

Several of the theories noted above place the action inside the individual as an active change that involves the adoption of a new identity. A seal that happens after ten years without another criminal event in all likelihood will only occur after that identify has solidified. There is room for policies that encourage and support the desistance behavior, but only if these policies are directed at individuals who have reached the point of change. As noted above, positive steps to aid desistance will largely be lost on motivated or rock bottom desisters who have not yet reached the point where they are willing to adopt a new identity. In fact, these attempts may even be harmful if they delay the process by which the person reaches rock bottom. Accordingly, for these desister types, a reactive policy that encourages or rewards desistance early in what Fagan (1989) described as stage 3 could be helpful.

The concept of signaling might be particularly useful here. Motivated or rock bottom desisters form a relatively small segment of the population with recent criminal histories. They will be eventually revealed as desisters by the length of their periods of non-involvement with the criminal justice system. After ten years of no involvement with the criminal justice system, the information problem facing policy makers and employers is much simpler—most of the people who have made it that long without another mark on their record are desisters. In the short run, the problem for policy makers is how to target resources only to the minority of individuals with records who have made the individual decision to change and would therefore benefit from opportunities to maintain desistance.

Signals are actions taken by the individual that can identify them as someone who has hit stage 2 and is on the path of desistance (i.e., is motivated and eager to shed their "feared self"). Valid signals should be more costly to provide by people who have yet to hit this stage, but might otherwise want to receive the benefits offered under this policy. To be a valid signal, only individuals who have made the decision to change should make the choice to provide the signal. After receiving the signal, the policy makers can be more confident that the benefits or services that correspond to the signal will benefit the individual. Valid signals could include attending rehabilitative programming, making the effort to obtain letters of recommendation from others, maintaining stable employment, and/or going through sometimes complex legal processes to obtain legal documents of reform or rehabilitation. Unlike the Youthful Offender Seal or Time Mandated Seal noted above, all of these policies require distinct effort on the part of the individual and would fall into a category that Maruna (2011) refers to as "active" rehabilitation policies. To give an example of one such policy and expectations for its impact, we turn again to New York State Correction Law, Article 23.[2]

Contesting the decision

For those offenders who do not have a sealed criminal record and who are denied employment based upon their record, Article 23-A requires the employer to consider evidence of rehabilitation and to provide reasons for a denial in writing to the individual. Thus, upon receipt of a negative finding, the individual may then submit evidence of rehabilitation if this was not included in the original application. The formality of this review process varies greatly even within New York State agencies, so again here we focus in on the specific process of the New York DOH in conducting state-mandated background checks. The policy utilized by this agency officially declares to the denied candidate that he/she has 30 days in which to submit proof of rehabilitation. Proof may include, but is not limited to, certificates of program completion for programs such as anger management counseling, drug and alcohol rehabilitation, job training programs, and letters of reference from past employers.

New York State also offers two official documents of rehabilitation that are specifically referenced in Article 23-A: a Certificate of Relief from Disabilities and a Certificate of Good Conduct. A Certificate of Relief from Disabilities is specific to a conviction. Therefore an individual must apply for a Certificate of Relief for a specific conviction (often the most recent or the most serious), or they may undergo the process of applying for separate Certificates of Relief for each conviction. However, Certificates of Relief do not restore one's ability to hold public office or a gun license. Also, Certificates of Relief are not offered to anyone with more than one felony conviction. If an individual wants to restore public office or gun rights, or has been convicted of more than one felony, he/she may apply for a Certificate of Good Conduct. This certificate requires a five-year waiting period for a class A/B felony and a three-year waiting period for a class C-E felony, with the waiting period calculated from either date of conviction for the most serious felony if no confinement time was served, or date of release from jail/prison if confinement time was served. The applications for both ask for evidence of rehabilitation including recent employment, education, etc. In addition, the Certificate of Good Conduct requires an in-home interview by a parole officer who will then make the final recommendation to a judge.

This process may be particularly meaningful in a redefinition of the self as it is a judge who first assigns the original formal label of convicted criminal and decides the associated punishment, and it is a judge who officially awards the symbol of rehabilitation in the Certificate of Good Conduct. Thus, the message from a judge that one is rehabilitated may not only send a signal for a potential employer that this individual is a good candidate for employment but it provides a positive appraisal of the self as non-criminal to the individual as well. If the contest process is successful and employment thus gained, the individual also now has the opportunity to try on this new social role (i.e., Giordano *et al.* 2007) and gain a positive and conventional adult social bond (i.e., Sampson and Laub 2003). This process itself is also interesting as it requires action/effort on the part of the individual to obtain some form of proof to submit.

Unlike the Youthful Offender Seal, however, which occurs immediately and thus could be indicated at an approximate point in the life span, this process and/ or the granting of a Certificate of Relief or Good Conduct occurs at different times for different individuals. Table 13.3 depicts our projected impact of a *successful* contest on each type of desister, as compared to not having contested the decisions or having an unsuccessful outcome.

For the maturational desister, maturation occurs as a process as does the reduction in offending, and at some point along this process the individual reaches the point of zero offending, or total desistance. We might assume that as one matures (somewhere in one's mid- to late twenties) an individual realizes that having a criminal record is negatively impacting his/her search for employment, housing, etc. At some point, this person would then probably begin to contest negative employment decisions, and if unsuccessful, after years of desistance, apply for a Certificate of Good Conduct. Thus, the contest might help to open up employment opportunities for this individual, but would have no impact on the actual desistance process itself.

TABLE 13.3 The proposed impact of successfully contesting the decision on desistance

	Positive impact	Negative impact	No impact
Maturational			✓
Natural	✓		✓
Controlled	✓		✓
Motivated	✓		
Rock bottom	✓		

There are two possible paths for the natural desister. In one rendition, the youth experimenting with crime and deviance would realize the folly of his/her ways and immediately take steps to remedy this by attending treatment programs, counseling, and/or applying for a Certificate of Relief from these minor transgressions. That is, the individual did not accept the label of criminal. Thus, desistance would occur abruptly and early in the life span. On the other hand, if the person were already stigmatized by their interaction with the system to the point he/she has accepted the identity of "criminal," then he or she would not take steps to remedy or change that identity. Thus, the youth who was just experimenting with primary deviance and who would have naturally desisted if not impacted by the system, would persist in a life of crime due to the stigmatization of label and negative employment determination.

Our predictions of the effect of this policy on the controlled desister are also tricky, as this approach to desistance does not focus on human agency such as the actions needed to contest a negative employment decision. Thus, for the controlled desister, our policy predictions again have two possible impacts: a positive impact or no impact. Most simply, assuming this individual contested the decision successfully, this would support the growing stake in conformity that would help the individual along the desistance process. However, it is a bit tricky to predict if this particular type of desister would or would not invoke efforts to rehabilitate him/herself and to contest negative employment decisions. Perhaps the decision to apply for employment in the first place indicates that this individual would take the next steps needed to obtain such an adult social bond. Perhaps another positive social bond such as marriage or parenthood has encouraged one to seek employment and stable income; thus, this process becomes part of an already started desistance process. Or, perhaps the individual would just accept the rejection of employment and continue on his/her previous trajectory, indicating that this policy could have no impact for this desister.

It is hard to imagine this policy having anything but a positive impact for the motivated desister. Once motivated to change, it can be assumed the individual would take steps toward such change including participating in rehabilitative programming and seeking relief from one's past self (e.g., Certificate of Relief or Good Conduct). Allowing the individual to use such evidence as a signal of change, thus opening up more employment opportunities, allows the individual the opportunity to succeed in this process and avoid "derailment" (Giordano et al. 2007).

Our final desister, the rock bottom desister, has continued along in crime until enough negative consequences are obtained to make him/her declare the decision to change. This person is responding to their negative perception of the "feared self" that they have become, and makes a conscious choice to make the necessary changes to adopt a different identity. Desistance happens as a rather abrupt event for this type of desister, and after some time, he or she would be able to contest negative decisions and apply for Certificates of Relief or Good Conduct to help maintain the state of desistance. Thus, this policy would have a positive impact on helping this individual maintain the final and ultimate state of desistance, although it would not impact the accumulation of negative events that ultimately led the person to their own personal "rock bottom."

However, what about unsuccessful contests? As noted, the New York policy only requires the employer to consider evidence of rehabilitation, but gives no guidance as to what items should carry weight and to which individuals employment should be granted. Thus, we would be amiss if we did not at least anticipate that some intrinsically motivated individuals might have their hopes dashed by an unsuccessful process. Such a negative event could have significantly detrimental effects for the natural desister who has just had the label of criminal reconfirmed, and for the motivated desister who could be led into a negative emotional state and potential derailment from the desistance process. On the other hand, if decision makers were able to accurately identify the criminal risk/employment opportunity trade-off for each individual, negative decisions could actually *benefit* those not yet ready to desist by removing potential opportunities to commit crime. Ideally, the process would be created such that only motivated individuals on the path to desistance would find it worthwhile to make the application in the first place, allowing high success rates and eliminating the potential harm from rejected contests.

Informing policy: designing studies that inform theories of desistance

It was our intention in the above discussion to draw attention first to how different theories of desistance lead to very different assumptions of what ultimately causes an offender to exit from crime. We then used these various assumptions to create images of different types of desisters to indicate how a policy could have diverse effects dependent upon which image of the desister we believe to be true. In this discussion, however, we are not assuming that there is only one pathway to desistance, but rather we are trying more formally to state the assumptions about desistance inherent in each theory or approach to desistance. This then sets the stage for research to better connect tests of policy to the theory or theories upon which it draws.

We provide a fair amount of detail on these different desistance perspectives and connect them to specific, tangible policies for several reasons. First, our discussion should draw attention to the importance of considering the scope and timing of a policy. Should policies be created to open up opportunities to all? Or should they be reserved for those showing clear signs of desistance? Should they be automatic, or should the individual have to apply a significant amount of effort to achieve redemption to signal that he or she is ready for employment? The process that we discussed above involved using the Certificate of Relief process in New York State as evidence of rehabilitation. While it is our understanding that this process used to be quite demanding, recent interviews with officials at the Department of Corrections and Community Supervision have revealed that these certificates are becoming more automatic, with individuals receiving certificates as they leave prison or parole supervision. This change in procedure could have a positive impact if many simply did not know about the availability of the certificates or did not have the means to navigate the complicated process. On the other hand, if exerting the effort to gain such a certificate was itself part of the rehabilitation/ signaling process, then this policy change would be inherently negative. As with much policy in this area, however, its implementation moves forward void of empirical evidence of its utility.

Second, it should be noted that many of the theories discussed herein view desistance as a process. This process might be a gradual decline in offending behavior until it eventually reaches "zero" (Bushway *et al.* 2001), or, as depicted by the neo-Meadian perspective (Giordano *et al.* 2007), it might be a more harried path marbled with successes and failure. Yet most desistance research still follows the traditional model of looking to the first new arrest or conviction event. If desistance is a more complex process, *all* of this research misses the concept of desistance and instead identifies only the first failure, or the final and last "sign" of total desistance. As the one policy example above that relies on such a sign has the least potential to positively impact desistance, this is of serious concern. If research continues blindly to apply survival models looking only to the first event as the primary method of identifying desistance, most policies will appear ineffective and could potentially be abandoned.

Similarly, policy research must give more thought to the timing of when to look for desistance regardless of whether it is believed to be a process or an event. The research by Sampson and Laub (2003) suggests that desistance does not necessarily occur the day someone gets married, or even as a more gradual process that begins the day one gets married, rather it is a gradual process that happens as one becomes more committed to the other individual and has, in a traditional social control language, more to lose. As more and more couples live together for significant periods of time before getting married, the timing of the start of such a process may actually occur well before marriage. Waiting to examine the impact of relationships until an official marriage occurs may indeed miss much of the action. On the other hand, looking for too sudden or dramatic an impact, as we suggested above with survival models, could also miss the mark in the opposite direction.

This brings us to our last, and perhaps, most important point. As the field works to develop models that better identify and describe the true nature of desistance, we should be working hand in hand with practitioners and policy makers rather than waiting for a post hoc call to evaluate a policy already pushed into place. In our own research, we have worked diligently since the mid-2010s to develop such "forward" collaborations with officials at New York's Division of Criminal Justice Services (DCJS), Department of Labor, Department of Corrections and Community Supervision, and DOH. Through this effort, we have created a truly unique research opportunity utilizing a database of provisionally hired employees subject to the state-mandated background check by the DOH as noted above. Through connections with DCJS, the data have been augmented to include complete criminal history records including sealed records (primarily Youthful

Offender Seals) and three years of complete recidivism data. The Department of Labor, working with these agencies, has for the first time in its history provided researchers with access to employment and earnings data, allowing us to assess the impact of employment on not only crime but also individual earnings and employment stability. This analysis will be able effectively to study the role of all three policies discussed in this chapter as they relate both to opening up employment opportunities and later offending behavior. Interestingly, we have found that these collaborations have not only benefited us through access to unique data but have our collaborators excited as well as they approach us with new questions and insight that continue to shape our research agenda and potential future desistance policy.

In conclusion, we hope to have highlighted the importance of connecting desistance research, particularly policy evaluation, to underlying theories of desistance. We encourage the use of new statistical approaches that assess spells of desistance and declines in offending rates, rather than mere failure events, and stress the importance of timing the projected policy impact. Finally, we propose the proactive development of collaborations between academia, practitioners, and policy makers that leads to an open communication network to encourage continued research and to provide formal feedback loops to ensure empirical findings are translated into effective practice.

Notes

1 The law has an important caveat, "unless the Department determines, in its discretion, that the prospective employee's employment will not in any way jeopardize the health, safety or welfare of patients, residents or clients of the provider." This is where other pieces of Article 23-A may become relevant in the background check decision, such as rehabilitative information.
2 It should be noted that policy types can become intertwined here, as some legal documents require waiting periods and thus may resemble the back-end sealing process.

References

Andrews, D. A., Bonta, J. and Hoge, R. D. (1990), "Classification for effective rehabilitation: Rediscovering psychology," *Criminal Justice and Behavior* 17: 19–52.
Blumstein, A., Cohen, J., Roth, J. and Visher, C. (eds) (1986), *Criminal Careers and "Career Criminals"*. Washington, DC: National Academy Press.
Boone, M. (2011), "Judicial rehabilitation in the Netherlands: Balancing between safety and privacy," *The European Journal of Probation* 3(1): 63–78.
Bushway, S. and Apel, R. (2012), "A signaling perspective on employment-based reentry programming: Training completion as a desistance signal," *Criminology and Public Policy* 11(1): 21–50.
Bushway, S., Piquero, A., Broidy, L., Cauffman, E. and Mazerolle, P. (2001), "An empirical framework for studying desistance as a process," *Criminology* 39: 491–516.
Chiricos, T., Barrick, K., Bales, W. and Bontrager, S. (2007), "The labeling of convicted felons and its consequences for recidivism," *Criminology* 45(3): 547–581.
Cohen, A. K. (1955), *Delinquent Boys: The Culture of the Gang*. Free Press.

Fagan, J. (1989), "Cessation of family violence: Deterrence and dissuasion," in Ohlin, L. and Tonry, M. (eds) *Family Violence, Volume 11 of Crime and Justice: A Review of Research*. Chicago, IL: University of Chicago Press.

Farrington, D. P., Gallagher, B., Morley, L., St. Ledger, R. J. and West, D. J. (1986), "Unemployment, school leaving, and crime," *British Journal of Criminology* 26: 335–356.

Garfinkel, H. (1956), "Conditions of successful degradation ceremonies," *American Journal of Sociology* 6: 420–424.

Giordano, P. C., Schroeder, R. D. and Cernkovich, S. A. (2007), "Emotions and crime over the life course: A neo-Meadian perspective on criminal continuity and change," *American Journal of Sociology* 112(6): 1603–1661.

Glueck, S. and Glueck, E. (1950), *Unraveling Juvenile Delinquency*. New York: Commonwealth.

Herzog-Evans, M. (2011), "Judicial rehabilitation in France: Helping with the desisting process and acknowledging achieved desistance," *European Journal of Probation* 3(1): 4– 19.

Hirschi, T. (1969), *Causes of Delinquency*. Berkeley, CA: University of California Press.

Hirschi, T. and Gottfredson, M. R. (1983), "Age and the explanation of crime," *American Journal of Sociology* 89: 552–584.

Hoffman, P. B. and Beck, J. L. (1984), "Burnout-age at release from prison and recidivism," *Journal of Criminal Justice* 2: 617–623.

Horney, J., Osgood, D. W. and Marshall, I. H. (1995), "Criminal careers in the short-term: Intra-individual variability in crime and its relation to local life circumstances," *American Sociological Review* 60: 655–673.

Kurlychek, M. C., Bushway, S. D. and Brame, R. (2012), "Long-term crime desistance and recidivism patterns-evidence from the Essex County convicted felon study," *Criminology* 50(1): 71–103.

Larrauri, E. (2011), "Conviction records in Spain: Obstacles to reintegration of offenders," *The European Journal of Probation* 3(1): 50–62.

Laub, J. H. and Sampson, R. J. (2001), "Understanding desistance from crime," *Crime and Justice*: 1–69.

Laub, J. H., Nagin, D. S. and Sampson, R. J. (1998), "Trajectories of change in criminal offending: Good marriages and the desistance process," *American Sociological Review* 63: 225–238.

Lemert, E. (1951), *Social Pathology*. New York: McGraw-Hill.

Love, M. C. (2003), "Starting over with a clean slate: In praise of a forgotten section of the model penal code," *Fordham Urban Law Journal* 30(1): 101–136.

Maruna, S. (1997), "Going straight: Desistance from crime and life narratives of reform," in Lieblich, A. and Josselson, R. (eds) *The Narrative Study of Lives*, volume 5. Thousand Oaks, CA: Sage.

Maruna, S. (2001), *Making Good: How Ex-Convicts Reform and Rebuild Their Lives*. Washington, DC: American Psychological Association.

Maruna, S. (2007), "Amputation or reconstruction? Notes on the concept of 'knifing off' and desistance from crime," *Journal of Contemporary Criminal Justice* 23(1): 104–124.

Maruna, S. (2011), "Judicial rehabilitation and the 'clean bill of health' in criminal justice," *The European Journal of Probation* 3(1): 97–117.

Maruna, S. (2012), "Elements of successful desistance signaling," *Criminology & Public Policy* 11(1): 73–86.

Matza, D. (1964), *Delinquency and Drift*. New York: Wiley.

Needels, K. (1996), "Go directly to jail and do not collect? A long-term study of recidivism," *Journal of Crime and Delinquency* 33: 471–496.

Paternoster, R. and Iovanni, L. (1989), "The labeling perspective and delinquency: An elaboration of the theory and an assessment of the evidence," *Justice Quarterly* 6: 359–394.

Paternoster, R. and Bushway, S. (2009), "Desistance and the 'feared self': Toward an identity theory of criminal desistance," *The Journal of Criminal Law and Criminology* 99(4): 1103–(1156).

Piquero, A. R. (2012), "Obeying signals and predicting future offending," *Criminology and Public Policy* 11(1): 51–59.

Sampson, R. J. and Laub, J. H. (1993), *Crime in the Making: Pathways and Turning Points through Life.* Cambridge, MA: Harvard University Press.

Sampson, R. J. and Laub, J. H. (2003), "Life-course desisters? Trajectories of crime among delinquent boys followed to age 70," *Criminology* 41(3): 555–592.

Shaw, C. R. and McKay, H. D. (1942), *Juvenile Delinquency and Urban Areas.* Chicago, IL: University of Chicago Press.

Sutherland, E. H., Cressey, D. R. and Luckenbill, D. (1995), "The theory of differential association," in Herman, N. J. (ed) *Deviance: A Symbolic Interactionist Approach.* Lanham, MD: AltaMira Press, pp. 64–68.

Thornberry, T. P. and Christenson, R. L. (1984), "Unemployment and criminal involvement: An investigation of reciprocal causal structures," *American Sociological Review* 49(3): 398–411.

Toby, J. (1957), "Social disorganization and stake in conformity: Complementary factors in the predatory behavior of hoodlums," *Journal of Criminal Law and Criminology* 48(1): 12.

Uggen, C. and Piliavin, I. (1998), "Asymmetrical causation and criminal desistance," *Journal of Criminal Law and Criminology* 88: 1399–1422.

Wolfgang, M. E., Thornberry, T. P. and Figlio, R. M. (1987), *From Boy to Man, from Delinquency to Crime.* Chicago, IL: University of Chicago Press.

14

THE FUEL IN THE TANK OR THE HOLE IN THE BOAT?

Can sanctions support desistance?

Fergus McNeill

Introduction

To a certain extent, desistance research has – since the start of the twenty-first century – helped to change some of the questions that we ask about criminal sanctions. Desistance scholars have tended to encourage us to ask first, how and why people change with respect to their involvement in offending, and (only) second, what sorts of criminal sanctions help them and hinder them in these processes? As the Gluecks asked many decades ago (Glueck and Glueck 1966 [1937]), the issue isn't just whether or not people 'grow out of crime'; it is whether we can do anything to accelerate rather than impede these processes of maturation and human development.

The nautical metaphors in the title of this chapter illustrate these concerns in several helpful respects. First, they remind us that desistance from crime is usually a journey or a process, rather than an event. Second, they suggest, albeit implicitly, that people on that journey can make active (and agentic) choices about how they navigate from here to there; they can be captains of their own lives as it were, rather than being tossed hither and thither by the waves. Conversely, they also remind us of the power of the environment and the weather in influencing our journeys; at best, they can speed us on our way; at worst, they can conspire to sink our ship. Extending the metaphor, we might conceive of criminal sanctions and 'correctional' interventions as contributing fuel and other resources for the journey, or conversely as actively (even if unintentionally) depleting and damaging people's resources.

For example, scholars have suggested that imprisonment can both prompt and sabotage desistance. Many ex-offenders' accounts point to imprisonment as a 'turning point', although for most this is typically in spite of, rather than because of, its reformative intentions and efforts (see, e.g. Schinkel 2015). In spite of these accounts, researchers more typically highlight the potentially criminogenic (and hence desistance-frustrating) effects of imprisonment, whether pointing to delays in maturation, to damaged social ties or to the confirmation of negative identities (see, e.g. McNeill and Weaver 2007).

Initially, at least, research exploring the relationships between desistance and probation was no more encouraging (Leibrich 1994; Farrall 2002). However, since the early 2000s, a number of scholars have made a concerted attempt to explore what *forms* of community supervision might play a more positive role in prompting and sustaining desistance. In this chapter I aim to review and advance these debates about and prescriptions for 'desistance-focused' practice. As well as reviewing arguments about a 'desistance paradigm', I examine the relationships between that paradigm and other conceptions of evidence-based practice or 'What works?'. In conclusion, however, I argue that more attention needs to be paid to the institutional and cultural contexts of 'correctional' practices, especially if we are to avoid adverse and unintended consequences of the popularization of desistance research.[1]

Sailing away: what works and what helps

Helping people get from A (offending) to B (desistance) is a central aim of correctional practice in most jurisdictions and working out the best ways of doing so has long been a preoccupation of correctional research within and beyond criminology. The question that has usually been asked is 'What works?' (to reduce reoffending). Although that is a good and important question, it also has some limitations.

'What works?' is inescapably a question concerned first and foremost with interventions, systems and practices – the mechanisms which we expect (somehow) to produce the outcomes that we are after; or in our nautical metaphor, the boat that we must take to get from A to B. The intervention is what *causes* us to get from A to B. Some boats are slow and some are fast; some are just not seaworthy and should not be embarked upon.

Since the 1980s, a great deal has been learned about what sorts of boats to trust if we want to arrive at a place of reduced offending, and there is little doubt that those designed in line with the familiar principles of risk, need and responsivity (RNR) (Bonta and Andrews 2010) have come to be seen by many as state of the art vessels (see Polaschek 2012; McNeill 2012a). Briefly, those principles imply that the level of correctional service provided should be commensurate with the level of risk of reoffending; that the focus of interventions should be those needs associated with offending; and that the manner of intervention should be consistent with the learning style of the 'offender'. However, the implementation of these principles tends to require correctional services to weigh the costs and benefits of running a few large ships that are a reasonable fit for a large number of travellers, as opposed to a large fleet of bespoke craft carefully adapted for each individual.

Some desistance researchers (whose work I will discuss in more detail below) and a number of criminologists have been somewhat critical of RNR-based approaches to rehabilitation and of 'What works' research in general. Whereas some critics have focused less on the model and more on its somewhat ham-fisted implementation in the UK (within the context of broader public sector reform – McNeill 2001), others argued from a principally sociological perspective that the RNR model of offending (and implicitly of desistance) neglected social causes and contexts, colluding with the reductive 'responsibilization' of 'offenders' and ignoring diversity issues in the process (Kendall 2004; Hannah-Moffat 2005). Returning to our metaphor, these critics draw attention to broader questions about where the desistance journey begins (typically in a place of adversity, which is at least partly a product of *social* inequality and injustice); they compel us to question why some people are not fit for the journey; and they question the appropriateness of compelling people to travel in vessels that are insensitive and ill-adapted to their differences (for example, of gender or ethnicity). In these circumstances, they might say, it is unsurprising that people jump overboard and swim back to point A, or suffer even worse fates.

Some desistance researchers have raised similar concerns. First of all, they have argued that more attention needs to be paid to the person's motivation and to the impact of their social context on the outcomes of the intervention (Farrall 2002) – in other words on what the individual brings to the journey and what is the effect of the wider context or climate in which they experience it. Second, it is now well understood that there is more to effective programmes or vessels than designing them well; they also need to be run well and that requires the right organizational arrangements, the right staff skills and the right sort of qualities in the relationships between travellers and crew – not just while on board, but also before and after travelling (Raynor 2004a, 2004b, 2008).

Arguably, the delay in recognizing the significance of these sorts of additional ingredients in the recipe for effective correctional practice (or sailing in our metaphor) is a result of thinking too narrowly about interventions or programmes (or ships) and not broadly enough about the change processes (or journeys) that they exist to support. Of course, this is precisely the focus of desistance research: it seeks to understand and explain these change processes. Note the change in the verbs used in the last sentence; this body of evidence is not about *evaluating* practices, systems or techniques – it is about *understanding* and *explaining* the processes that practices, systems and techniques exist to support.

This different framing of interests can be illustrated again with reference to the nautical metaphor. From the perspective of desistance research, it's not so clear that the correctional intervention is properly seen as the main vehicle for the desistance journey or the main mechanism for 'producing' change. As other chapters in this volume will illustrate, other vehicles might include, for example, maturational processes, the development or re-development of social bonds (like work or intimate relationships or parenting) or broader changes in self-identity. Perhaps more likely, all of these factors, (and many others) such as correctional interventions, might provide certain resources for the journey, but none is *the* vehicle or vessel. Indeed, perhaps it makes best sense to think of the traveller as mattering more than the vessel.

In the last few years, and after a period of polarization between 'What works?' and 'desistance-based' perspectives, there has been some evidence of a rapprochement between the two (e.g. McNeill 2012a). In part, this arises from becoming clearer about the proper claims that each form of research (evaluative and explanatory) can make and about how these claims relate to one another. Indeed, as long ago as 2000, Shadd Maruna proposed a marriage between the two perspectives, in which 'What works?' might provide general principles for interventions, while desistance research enabled a richer understanding of the micro-mechanisms of change; of *how and why* change happens.

More recently, for example, Friedrich Lösel (2012) has argued that there is no inherent conflict between the two perspectives. More specifically, he suggests that deficit-oriented and strength-oriented perspectives (respectively associated with 'What works?' and desistance) should not be juxtaposed so carelessly since it is evident that 'both are needed for an adequate explanation of behavioural outcomes' (Lösel 2012: 1005). Again, returning to our metaphor, Lösel is surely correct that any traveller facing an arduous journey will have both assets and liabilities, although I might add that it is not just personal assets and liabilities, deficits and strengths that matter for desistance. Lösel is also right that some of the well-documented obstacles faced by would-be desisters 'are targeted by motivational modules, cognitive interviewing or applications of the cycle of change in correctional programmes' (Lösel 2012: 1006). This is to say, in our metaphor, that such interventions can and do develop skills or assets that are necessary for the journey. However, from a desistance perspective, it is important to add that social resources (or the lack of them) are at least as important as personal resources. Training a person to sail is extremely important, but it doesn't make up for the lack of any wind in the sails. Similarly, an unfit person may be able to face a long journey with a supportive companion, but not alone. Also, journeys are easier if someone goes ahead and removes unnecessary obstacles.

To sum up, the central difference between the two perspectives is that a desistance perspective requires us to reframe the effects of interventions as accelerating or impeding positive changes in offending behaviour, rather than causing them. It is not just and perhaps not mainly the intervention that gets the traveller from A to B; the journey is much more complex than that. The question is not so much 'What works?' as 'What helps?'.

Supervision and sabotage[2]

Before going on to examine the question of 'What helps?' (or more modestly 'What might help?') in more detail, it is worth pausing to ask 'What hinders?'. There are perhaps three forms of sabotage that might sink the desistance ship, as it were, although only two of them relate directly to supervision.

First, the state might sabotage desistance through its approach to economic and social policy. Though the development of this sort of argument is beyond the scope of this chapter, it is worth noting that the life trajectories of 'offenders' (like those of all citizens) are likely to be more affected by approaches to market de/regulation or to social welfare retrenchment than they are by penal policy. These sorts of policy choices will have profound effects on the social contexts in and through which offending emerges and in which desistance is attempted. As both Wacquant (2010) and De Giorgi (2014) suggest, in these social contexts, many ex-prisoners face 'the myth of reentry' or 'reentry to nothing'. I return to this issue below, since it begs an important question about how we might best imagine the destination of the distance journey.

Focusing more directly on penal policy, the second form of sabotage relates to how systems of supervision are ordered and to what effect. I began the last section by arguing that supporting desistance is a common aim of correctional supervision, but even if it is, that aim might be pursued in a number of quite different ways. For example, correctional systems might seek to promote desistance through deterrence or even incapacitation. It is at least arguable that this approach is common in the USA (see Taxman *et al.* 2010) and that the effect of 'tail them, nail them and fail them' approaches has contributed to mass incarceration. Cecilia Klingele (2014) has recently argued this case forcefully, not least by noting that half of all admission to jails and more than a third of all admissions to federal prisons in the USA are for probation or parole revocations. If we accept that imprisonment is, at best, a problematic context for supporting desistance and, at worst, criminogenic, then these alarming rates of supervision revocation raise important issues about the proper targeting of supervision (in ways which contribute to decarceration rather than net-widening) and about the effective management of compliance issues (see Robinson and McNeill 2008; McNeill and Robinson 2012; Phelps 2013). Wider aspects of penal policy – like the way in which disclosure of criminal convictions is managed – are also likely to have significant effects on labour market participation and thus on desistance (see, for example, McGuinness *et al.* 2013).

A third form of sabotage might be found in the practice and the experience of supervision itself. If, for example, the practice of supervision is mediated through the sometimes pathologising language of risks and needs, then this epistemic framing may serve to undermine people's resources for desistance and to construct or cement their identities as 'hopeless offenders'. As labelling theory suggests, discourses that reflect and predict failure may well provoke it (Maruna and LeBel 2003, 2010).

Summing up again in metaphorical terms, the state can make social policy choices that whip up a storm for our weary travellers, or it can calm the waves. Those that run the correctional support vessels can carry supplies and help with navigation, or they can torpedo any desistance vessel that looks a little wayward. And the crews of these supportive vessels can encourage travellers or they can tell them (directly or indirectly) that their journeys are doomed.

Fuelling the tank? Supervision and desistance[3]

Stephen Farrall and Shadd Maruna, and in particular their books *Rethinking What Works with Offenders: Probation, Social Context and Desistance from Crime* (Farrall 2002) and *Making Good: How Ex-Convicts Reform and Rebuild their Lives* (Maruna 2001), have made key contributions to debates about desistance and how best to support it. Both drew on and developed earlier work by Ros Burnett in her *Dynamics of Recidivism* study (Burnett 1992). Another important study of 'assisted desistance' (as opposed to spontaneous or unaided desistance) was undertaken by Sue Rex (1999), who argued that '[t]he knowledge we are beginning to acquire about the type of probation services which are more likely to succeed could surely be enhanced by an understanding of the personal and social changes and developments associated with desistance from crime' (Rex 1999: 366).

Thus even during Farrall and Maruna's research projects, publications (like Rex's) had begun to engage directly with the question of how desistance theory and research might inform supervision. An early example of the genre was an edition of *Offender Programs Report* (volume 4, issue 1) which, amongst several interesting short articles, included a paper from Maruna (2000) in which he argued for a marrying of the desistance and 'What works?' literatures (as noted above).

The romance proved short-lived when Farrall's (2002) book was published. Farrall challenged both the implementation of 'What works?' research and aspects of its methodological underpinnings. Farrall's study (based on a qualitative longitudinal study of 199 probationers and their supervising officers) suggested that motivation and social context were more clearly associated with desistance than supervision, and that the focus of supervision (on risk factors and 'criminogenic needs') neglected the crucial roles of relationships and social capital in the desistance process. Farrall's (2002) prescription was that supervision should focus less on 'offence-related factors' (or 'criminogenic needs') and more on 'desistance-related needs'. The nature of the difference between the two approaches is well captured by one of the probationers in his study, in response to a question about what would prevent him from reoffending:

> Something to do with self progression. Something to show people what they are capable of doing. I thought that was what [my officer] should be about. It's finding people's abilities and nourishing and making them work for those things. Not very consistent with going back on what they have done wrong and trying to work out why – 'cause it's all going around on what's *happened* – what you've already been punished for – why not go forward into something . . . For instance, you might be good at writing – push that forward, progress that, rather than saying 'well look, why did you kick that bloke's head in? Do you think we should go back into anger management courses?' when all you want to do is be a writer. Does that make any sense to you at all? *Yeah, yeah. To sum it up, you're saying you should look forwards not back.* Yeah. I know that you have to look back to a certain extent to make sure that you don't end up like that [again]. The whole order seems to be about going back and back and back. There doesn't seem to be much 'forward'.

(Farrall 2002: 225)

In my own subsequent work (McNeill 2003; McNeill and Batchelor 2004), drawing on a range of desistance studies (*as well as* on 'What works?' research), I sought to further elaborate what 'desistance-focused probation practice' might look like. I suggested that such practice would require careful individualized assessment, focused on the inter-relationships between desistance factors (linked to age and maturation, to social bonds and to shifts in narrative identity), which built towards clear plans to support change. It would entail engaging, active and participative supervisory relationships characterized by optimism, trust and loyalty, as well as interventions targeted at those aspects of each individual's motivation, attitudes, thinking and values, which might help or hinder progress towards desistance. Crucially, in my assessment – and drawing on Laub and Sampson's (2003) seminal work, it would require work not just to develop personal capabilities but also advocacy to support access to opportunities for change, for example, around labour market participation.

Beyond these prescriptions, and inspired by Farrall (2002), McNeill and Batchelor (2004: 66) went on to further elaborate the shift in practice dispositions or perspectives that desistance research seemed to us to suggest (see Table 14.1).

Table 14.1 below contrasts two notional 'ideal types' of practice. We were clear that this was intended only as a heuristic device; arguably, neither of these approaches could or should exist in practice in a 'pure' form. Necessarily, an offence focus must be appropriate, of course, given that it is offending that occasions and justifies penal intervention. However, as I have already noted above, being overly offence-focused might in some senses tend to amplify precisely those

TABLE 14.1 Ideal-type contrasts – offence-focused and desistance-focused practice

	Offence-focused practice	*Desistance-focused practice*
Orientation	Retrospective	Prospective
Problem locus	Individual attitudes and behaviours	Individual problems and behaviours in social context
Practice focus	Individual attitudes and behaviours	Personal strengths and social resources for overcoming obstacles to change
Medium for effective practice	Rehabilitative programmes (to which offenders are assigned on the basis of risk/needs assessment instruments)	Individual processes and relationships
Worker's roles	Risk/needs assessor, programme provider, case manager	Risk/needs/strengths assessor, advocate, facilitator, case manager
Intended outputs	Enhanced motivation, pro-social attitudinal change, capacity/skills development	Enhanced motivation, changes in narrative/self-concept, development of inclusion opportunities
Intended outcomes	Reduced reoffending	Reduced reoffending, enhanced social inclusion

aspects of a person's history, behaviour and attitudes, which intervention aims to diminish. It may also tend towards misidentifying the central problems of desistance as problems of individual or personal 'malfunctioning':

> By contrast, being 'desistance-focused' implies an orientation towards the purpose and aspiration of the intervention rather than the 'problem' that precipitates it. It also requires recognising the broader social contexts and conditions required to support change. Thus, where 'being offence-focused' encourages practice to be retrospective and individualised, being desistance-focused allows practice to become prospective and contextualised.
>
> *(McNeill and Batchelor 2004: 67)*

Maruna's (2001) book was less directly focused on the implications of his Liverpool Desistance Study for supervision, but his ideas (developed along with Tom LeBel) about 'strengths-based' approaches to reentry and corrections were already developing in similar directions, informed both by desistance research and by a wider range of influences (Maruna and LeBel 2003, 2009, 2010). In essence, Maruna and LeBel (2003) exposed the limitations and problems associated with both risk-based and support- (or needs-) based narratives for reentry. The former, they argued, casts the offender ultimately as a threat to be managed; the latter as a deficient to be remedied by the application of professional expertise. By contrast, 'strengths-based or restorative approaches ask not what a person's deficits are, but rather what positive contribution the person can make' (Maruna and LeBel 2003: 97). I have already noted Lösel's (2012) argument that these contrasts may be somewhat overblown, but they perhaps represented a necessary corrective to then prevailing practice models.

In a slightly later paper, Maruna *et al.* (2004) did engage more directly with the implications of his study for supervision, but reached similar conclusions. They suggested that supervision should move away from risks and needs and towards strengths, seeking to support and encourage redemptive and generative processes, such as those involved in community service at its best. They averred that such a discursive shift could signal the true potential of probationers not just to themselves but equally importantly to their communities. Although Maruna *et al.* (2004) supported Farrall's call for a more explicitly prospective or future-oriented form of practice, they also stressed the need for people to make sense of their pasts. They therefore suggested the need for rehabilitative processes that could support a reconstruction of personal narratives, one which recognized and repaired wrongdoing, but which refused to define or delimit the person by their previous conduct.

By 2006, there seemed enough emerging evidence to propose 'A desistance paradigm for offender management' (McNeill 2006). This reflected a peculiarly British debate about how probation practice should be redesigned in the light of both changing evidence and normative arguments. I therefore used both empirical (desistance) research and normative arguments to critique what I perceived as the misappropriation and misinterpretation of evidence in a managerialized and reductionist 'What works' paradigm that dominated probation policy and practice in England and Wales at that time. I summed up these paradigms in Table 14.2.

Presaging the arguments developed in the preceding sections of this chapter, my central argument ran as follows:

> Unlike the earlier paradigms, the desistance paradigm forefronts processes of change rather than modes of intervention. Practice under the desistance paradigm would certainly accommodate intervention to meet needs, reduce risks and (especially) to develop and exploit strengths, but . . . subordinated to a more broadly conceived role in working out, on an individual basis, how the desistance process might best be prompted and supported. This would require the worker to act as an advocate providing a conduit to social capital as well as a 'treatment' provider building human capital . . . Critically, such interventions would not be concerned solely with the prevention of further offending; they would be equally concerned with constructively addressing the harms caused by crime by encouraging offenders to make good through restorative processes and community service (in the broadest sense). But, as a morally and practically necessary corollary, they would be no less preoc-cupied with making good to offenders by enabling them to achieve inclusion and participation in society (and with it the progressive and positive refram-ing of their identities required to sustain desistance).
>
> *(McNeill 2006: 56–57)*

More recently, Maruna and LeBel (2010) have again engaged directly with the promise of developing and employing a desistance paradigm for correctional prac-tice. They begin with the recognition that evaluation evidence is not the only

TABLE 14.2 Probation practice paradigms

	A what works paradigm	*A desistance paradigm*
Purpose of the intervention	Intervention required to reduce reoffending and protect the public	Help in navigating towards desistance to reduce harm and make good to offenders and victims
Approach to assessment	'Professional' assessment of risk and need governed by structured assessment instruments	Explicit dialogue and negotiation assessing risks, needs, strengths and resources and offering opportunities to make good
Focus of supervisory relationship	Compulsory engagement in structured programmes and case management processes as required elements of legal orders imposed irrespective of consent	Collaboratively defined tasks, which tackle risks, needs and obstacles to desistance by using and developing the offender's human and social capital

Source: Adapted from McNeill (2006).

form of evidence that matters in developing evidence-based practice. Following Lewis (1990), they argue for a shift in focus 'from programmes to lives', rejecting a medical model of change.

By better understanding the change process, Maruna and LeBel (2010) argue, we may be able to better adapt supervision to contribute to (but not to 'produce') the process. It follows that a desistance paradigm must place the person changing and *their* change process (in our metaphor, the traveller and the journey) centre-stage. Notably, this is a message that finds support amongst prisoners and probationers themselves, who are often resistant to being 'treated' through programmatic interventions (Harris 2005). Although the views and voices of 'offenders' are often much too marginalized in correctional work and research, the problems of supervision violation referred to above (and of programme 'dropout'), suggest that correctional practitioners and researchers would do well to hear and attend carefully to the views of those they are seeking to influence. One of the central contributions of desistance research is that it provides one way (and only one way) in which these voices can be heard. Maruna and LeBel sum up their argument for a desistance paradigm as follows:

> [t]he desistance paradigm argues that the search for 'what works' should not begin with existing expert models of crime reduction, but rather should begin with an understanding of the organic or normative processes that seem to impact offending patterns over the life course. That is, if turning 30 is the 'most effective crime-fighting tool' (Von Drehle 2010), then we should seek to learn as much as we can about that process and see if we can model these dynamics in our own interventions.
>
> *(Maruna and LeBel 2010: 72)*

Recognizing that the practical implications of such a perspective remain seriously under-developed (see also Porporino 2010), Maruna and LeBel (2010) go on to suggest one form of desistance-based intervention. Drawing on labelling theory, and on their earlier work (Maruna and LeBel 2003), they make the case for an approach to supervision, which employs pro-social labelling. As well as avoiding negative labelling, this requires practices and systems that expect, invite and facilitate positive contributions and activities from people subject to supervision, and which then certify and celebrate redemption or rehabilitation – de-labelling and de-stigmatising the reformed offender.

I have similarly argued (McNeill 2012b), further to my proposals for a desistance paradigm, that the field of corrections needs its own 'Copernican correction' – one in which supervision and support services revolve around the individual change process, rather than requiring offenders' lives to revolve around programmes and interventions. Moreover, I suggest a shift away from seeing the 'offender' as the target of the intervention (the 'thing' to be fixed) to seeing the broken relationships between individuals, communities and the state as the breach in the social fabric (or breach of the social contract) that requires repair. Importantly, this casts correctional agencies less as agents of 'coercive correction' and more as mediators of social conflicts. The objective becomes not the correction of the deviant so much as the restoration of the citizen to a position where they can both honour the obligations and enjoy the rights of citizenship. I return to these issues in closing below.

Captains and navigators

Recalling the two ways in which supervision might sabotage desistance (via systems and via practices), the arguments reviewed in the previous section are perhaps more concerned with *reframing* systems of supervision than with *redesigning* supervisory practices. The clearest attempts at tackling the latter challenge are perhaps to be found in reports I prepared for the Scottish Government and the National Offender Management Service of England and Wales respectively (McNeill 2009; McNeill and Weaver 2010). Both reports responded to policymaker and practitioner requests for more explicit articulation of the practical implications of desistance research for supervision practice; both share a similar reticence in responding to these requests.

Towards Effective Practice in Offender Supervision (McNeill 2009), was an attempt to summarize evidence about both desistance and 'What works?' in order to inform practice development. Instead of proposing a predesigned and therefore homogenized intervention, I tried to articulate the range of issues and questions with which a reflective practitioner would have to engage in seeking to support desistance in individual cases. The resultant 'offender supervision spine' explains in broad terms how to approach the preparatory, relationship-building stage of supervision, as well as assessment, planning, intervention and evaluation. My suggestion was that a supervisor, working their way along this spine in partnership with the supervisee, should continually develop and test 'theories of change', seeking to work out together, 'why and how we think that doing what we propose to do will bring about the results we seek', and then to implement that plan and evaluate its progress.

Beyond such emergent models of the supervision process, a number of broader practical implications of desistance research have been identified in the literature. In a recent overview, for example, McNeill *et al.* (2012b) identify eight broad principles, the genesis of which is perhaps already apparent in the discussion above.

First, it is clear that desistance, for people who have been involved in persistent offending, is a complex process. Criminal justice supervision must be realistic about these difficulties and find ways to manage setbacks and difficulties constructively. It needs to be recognized that it may take considerable time for supervision and support to exercise a positive effect. Second, and relatedly, since desistance is an inherently individualized and subjective process, approaches to supervision should accommodate and address issues of identity and diversity.

Third, desistance research also suggests that the development and maintenance of hope may be key tasks for supervisors (see Farrall *et al.* 2014). Fourth, hope may feed the discovery of self-efficacy or agency, which may also be important in desistance processes. Interventions are most likely to be effective where they encourage and respect self-determination; this means working *with* would-be desisters, not *on* them.

Fifth, desistance can only be properly understood within the context of human and social relationships; not just relationships between supervisors and offenders (though these matter a great deal) but also between offenders and those who matter to them (Weaver 2015). Interventions based only on developing the capacities and skills of people who have offended (human capital) will not be enough. Sixth, it follows that supervision must address developing social capital and with it the opportunities to apply these skills, or to practice newly forming identities (such as 'worker' or 'father').

Seventh, although a focus on risks and needs is necessary, desisters also have strengths and resources that they can use to overcome obstacles to desistance – both personal strengths and resources, and strengths and resources in their social networks. Supporting and developing these capacities can be a useful dimension of supervision. Finally, the language of practice should reflect this recognition of potential, striving to more clearly recognize positive potential and development, and should seek to avoid identifying people with the behaviours we want them to leave behind.

This eight-principle summary was produced as part of a recent UK Economic and Social Research Council-funded project, which aimed to develop a much more comprehensive and innovative response to the challenge to 'operationalize' desistance (explained more fully in McNeill *et al.* 2012a). The partners in this project sought to foster a dialogue about supporting desistance involving academics, policymakers, managers, practitioners, ex/offenders and their families and supporters. The project was entitled 'Discovering Desistance',[4] and was partnered in the USA by Professor Faye Taxman's Center for Advancing Correctional Excellence (http://www.gmuace.org/). It aimed to explore the experience and knowledge of these different stakeholders in relation to desistance from crime and how correctional supervision in the community can best support it.

Though intended to be focused on redesigning supervision, the ideas and proposals generated in and through this dialogue extended far beyond supervision practice and into much broader aspects of reintegration. For example, the participants called for the criminal justice system to make greater use of reformed offenders, not least through service user (i.e. supervisee) involvement in the design, delivery and improvement of policies and provision across the criminal justice system. Participants argued that greater involvement of ex/offenders in mentoring schemes should be a key part of this involvement.

More generally, they argued both for a reorientation towards a more holistic and humanistic form of supervision and for correctional services to become better connected with the local communities, playing a greater role in mobilizing wider community support networks to support desistance and reintegration. They called for services to work to challenge inequality and promote equality; equalizing life chances and contributing to social justice (pursuing both substantive equality and equality in the criminal justice process), suggesting that this required a new approach to public and community education about the process of leaving crime behind and the lives of current and former service users in order to break down the 'them' and 'us' mentality. This, the participants suggested, would ensure better public understanding that people are capable of change and that we all have a part to play in supporting change. Criminal justice agencies ought to model and promote the belief that positive change is possible and show that it is common, focusing on this rather than 'risks'.

Two more structural changes were routinely proposed in the workshops, both of which echo the arguments above. First, the participants called for a reduction in the reliance on imprisonment as a sanction (especially for women, black men, those with mental health issues and those on short sentences), calling for the money saved to be reinvested in community justice. Second, they argued the need to redraft the [UK] Rehabilitation of Offenders Act 1974 (which governs disclosure of criminal convictions) so as to both encourage and recognize rehabilitation, rather than standing in the way of it.

Perhaps most fundamentally, they called for a criminal justice system that gives people hope and shows them they have a future. Given that this last prescription seems so at odds with some of the broader economic and social barriers to desistance discussed above, it is to these barriers that I return in conclusion.

Conclusions

Even if desistance scholars remain divided on the relative priority of individual and structural aspects of the process, there is little disagreement over the significance of social bonds, social capital and social relations in the process. Although these social factors must be apprehended individually and thus subjectively in order to motivate and stimulate change, and even if some elements of cognitive restructuring might precede that apprehension, the fact remainh have been a mistake at the outset to define desistance as the destination. It is better to conceive of desistance as the process of moving from offending to successful social integration (and with it compliance with the law and social norms) (Kirkwood and McNeill 2015).

The Sheffield Desistance Study suggests the importance of this more careful consideration of the destination of desistance journeys in a particularly bleak and powerful way. If, as Tony Bottoms (2013) has argued, some people desist through a form of extreme 'situational self-binding', which amounts effectively to self-incarceration and social isolation – then it seems obvious to me that even if desistance can be approached and achieved as an individual project of cognitive transformation and behavioural change, integration requires something more. Although Bottoms (2013) notes that self-imposed social isolation was rare in the Sheffield study, evidence from other studies might suggest that it is not so unusual for those whose desistance journeys are undertaken ill-equipped and undersupported. Adam Calverley's (2009) exploration of ethnicity and desistance, for example, suggests that black and dual heritage respondents in this study faced the greatest structural and cultural obstacles to desistance – and that they tended to desist through isolation. Two recent Scottish studies of very different populations (released long-term prisoners and young people exiting an intensive support service) also found common pains of desistance linked to isolation and goal failure (see Schinkel and Nugent, forthcoming).

Integration (or reintegration or reentry) is inescapably a relational and social process. It follows that however effectively and diligently correctional practitioners work with individuals to support their change processes, these efforts may be hamstrung by failure to attend to these social dynamics. I have argued elsewhere (McNeill 2012a, 2014; Kirkwood and McNeill 2015) that a serious engagement with the meanings of rehabilitation and reintegration compels us to develop models, policies and practices that attend not just to correctional processes aimed at individual transformation but to moral reparation (or restoration), judicial rehabilitation and social reintegration too. In most cases – and particularly for people with serious and/or long offending histories, I suspect that these four processes are almost always intertwined. It follows that if we want to support desistance, we have as much work to do with communities, judges and politicians (to name but a few), as we have to do with (other) 'offenders'.

Notes

1 With respect to these 'adverse and unintended consequences', readers might wish to examine a recent publication commissioned by the Criminal Justice Alliance (CJA) in England and Wales (*Prospects for a Desistance Agenda*. Available at http://criminaljusticealliance. org/wp-content/uploads/2015/02/ProspectsforDesistanceAgendaExecSummary.pdf (accessed 23 April 2015)). This paper reports a piece of research in which 20+ 'in-depth interviews' were carried out with policymakers and other stakeholders, asking them what they thought were the prospects of promoting a desistance agenda in criminal justice. The paper identifies and reveals a number of problems with the understanding of research and responding to the research in policy and practice.
2 This section and the subsequent section of this chapter draw somewhat on McNeill *et al.* (2014).
3 This section draws upon an earlier co-authored paper (McNeill *et al.* 2014). I am grateful to my co-authors and editors for permission to further develop the material here.
4 The project was funded by the UK Economic and Social Research Council, award no. RES-189-25-0258.

References

Bonta, J. and Andrews, D. (2010), *The Psychology of Criminal Conduct*, fifth edition. London and New York: Routledge.
Bottoms, A. (2013), 'Learning from Odysseus: Self applied situational crime prevention as an aid to compliance', in Ugwudike, P. and Raynor, P. (eds) *What Works in Offender Compliance: International Perspectives and Evidence-Based Practice*. Basingstoke, UK: Palgrave.
Burnett, R. (1992), *The Dynamics of Recidivism*. Oxford, UK: University of Oxford Centre for Criminological Research.
Calverley, A. (2009), *Cultures of Desistance: Rehabilitation, Reintegration and Ethnic Minorities*. London: Routledge.

De Giorgi, A. (2014), 'Returning to nothing. Urban survival after mass incarceration', *Social Justice blog* 28 May 2014, available at http://www.socialjusticejournal.org/?p=2273 (accessed 23 April 2015).

Farrall, S. (2002), *Rethinking What Works with Offenders: Probation, Social Context and Desistance from Crime*. Cullompton, UK: Willan Publishing.

Farrall, S., Hunter, B., Sharpe, G. and Calverley, A. (2014), *Criminal Careers in Transition: The Social Context of Desistance from Crime*. Oxford, UK: Oxford University Press.

Glueck, S. and Glueck, E. (1966 [1937]), *Later Criminal Careers*. New York: Kraus.

Hannah-Moffat, K. (2005), 'Criminogenic needs and the transformative risk subject: Hybridizations of risk/need in penality', *Punishment and Society* 7(1): 29–51.

Harris, M. K. (2005), 'In search of common ground: The importance of theoretical orientations in criminology and criminal justice', *Criminology & Public Policy* 4(2): 311–328.

Kendall, K. (2004), 'Dangerous thinking: A critical history of correctional cognitive behaviouralism', in Mair, G. (ed.) *What Matters in Probation*. Cullompton, UK: Willan Publishing.

Kirkwood, S. and McNeill, F. (2015), 'Integration and reintegration: Comparing pathways to citizenship through asylum and criminal justice', *Criminology & Criminal Justice* 15(5): 511–552.

Klingele, C. (2014), 'Rethinking the use of community supervision', *The Journal of Criminal Law and Criminology* 103(4): 1016–1070.

Laub, J. and Sampson, R. (2003), *Shared Beginnings, Divergent Lives*. Boston, MA: Harvard University Press.

Leibrich, J. (1994), 'What do offenders say about supervision and going straight?', *Federal Probation* 58(2): 41–46.

Lewis, D. A. (1990), 'From programs to lives: A comment', *American Journal of Community Psychology* 18: 923–926.

Lösel, F. (2012), 'Offender treatment and rehabilitation: What works?', in Maguire, M., Morgan, R. and Reiner, R. (eds) *The Oxford Handbook of Criminology*, fifth edition. Oxford, UK: Oxford University Press.

Maruna, S. (2000), 'Desistance from crime and offender rehabilitation: A tale of two research literatures', *Offender Programs Report* 4(1): 1–13.

Maruna, S. (2001), *Making Good*. Washington, DC: American Psychological Association.

Maruna, S. and LeBel, T. (2003), 'Welcome home? Examining the "re-entry court" concept from a strengths-based perspective', *Western Criminology Review* 4(2): 91–107.

Maruna, S. and LeBel, T. (2009), 'Strengths-based approaches to reentry: Extra mileage toward reintegration and destigmatization', *Japanese Journal of Sociological Criminology* 34: 58–80.

Maruna, S. and LeBel, T. (2010), 'The desistance paradigm in correctional practice: From programmes to lives', in McNeill, F., Raynor, P. and Trotter C. (eds) *Offender Supervision: New Directions in Theory, Research and Practice*. Cullompton, UK: Willan Publishing.

Maruna, S., Porter, L. and Carvalho. I. (2004), 'The *Liverpool Desistance Study* and probation practice: Opening the dialogue', *Probation Journal* 51(3): 221–232.

McGuinness, P., McNeill, F. and Armstrong, S. (2013), *The Use and Impact of the Rehabilitation of Offenders Act (1974): Final Report*, Scottish Centre for Crime and Justice Report 02/2013, University of Glasgow, available at http://www.sccjr.ac.uk/publications/the-use-and-impact-of-the-rehabilitation-of-offenders-act-1974final-report/ (accessed 23 April 2015).

McNeill, F. (2001), 'Developing effectiveness: Frontline perspectives', *Social Work Education* 20(6): 671–687.

McNeill, F. (2003), 'Desistance-focused probation practice', in Chui, W.-H. and Nellis, M. (eds) *Moving Probation Forward: Evidence, Arguments and Practice*. Harlow, UK: Pearson Education.

McNeill, F. (2006), 'A desistance paradigm for offender management', *Criminology and Criminal Justice* 6(1): 39–62.

McNeill, F. (2009), *Towards Effective Practice in Offender Supervision.* Glasgow, UK: Scottish Centre for Crime and Justice Research, available at http://www.sccjr.ac.uk/documents/McNeil_Towards.pdf (accessed 23 April 2015).

McNeill, F. (2012a), 'Four forms of "offender" rehabilitation: Towards an interdisciplinary perspective', *Legal and Criminological Psychology* 17(1): 18–36.

McNeill F. (2012b), 'Counterblast: A Copernican correction for community sentences', *The Howard Journal of Criminal Justice* 51(1): 94–99.

McNeill, F. (2014), 'Punishment as rehabilitation', in Bruinsma, G. and Weisburd, D. (eds) *Encyclopedia of Criminology and Criminal Justice*, pp. 4195–4206, DOI 10.1007/978-1-4614-5690-2, Springer Science and Business Media: New York. (A final draft version of this paper is available open access online at http://blogs.iriss.org.uk/discoveringdesistance/files/2012/06/McNeill-When-PisR.pdf.)

McNeill, F. and Batchelor, S. (2004), 'Persistent offending by young people: Developing practice', *Issues in Community and Criminal Justice*, Monograph No. 3, London: National Association of Probation Officers.

McNeill, F. and Weaver (2007), *Giving Up Crime: Directions for Policy.* Edinburgh, UK: Scottish Consortium on Crime and Criminal Justice, available at http://www.sccjr.ac.uk/publications/giving-up-crime-directions-for-policy/ (accessed 6 January 2016).

McNeill, F. and Weaver, B. (2010), *Changing Lives? Desistance Research and Offender Management.* Glasgow, UK: Scottish Centre for Crime and Justice Research, available at http://www.sccjr.ac.uk/publications/changing-lives-desistance-research-and-offender-management/ (accessed 6 January 2016).

McNeill, F. and Robinson, G. (2012), 'Liquid legitimacy and community sanctions', in Crawford, A. and Hucklesby, A. (eds) *Legitimacy and Compliance in Criminal Justice.* Abingdon, UK: Routledge.

McNeill, F., Farrall, S., Lightowler, C. and Maruna, S. (2012a), 'Reexamining "evidence-based practice" in community corrections: Beyond "a confined view" of what works', *Justice Research and Policy* 14(1): 35–60.

McNeill, F., Farrall, S., Lightowler, C. and Maruna, S. (2012b), *How and Why People Stop Offending: Discovering Desistance.* Insights: Evidence summaries to support social services in Scotland, no. 15, April 2012, Institute for Research and Innovation in Social Services, available at http://www.iriss.org.uk/sites/default/files/iriss-insight-15.pdf (accessed 6 January 2016).

McNeill, F., Farrall, S., Lightowler, C. and Maruna, S. (2014), 'Desistance and supervision', in Bruinsma, G. and Weisburd, D. (eds) *Encyclopedia of Criminology and Criminal Justice.* New York: Springer Science and Business Media, pp. 958–967.

Phelps, M. (2013), 'The paradox of probation: Community supervision in the age of mass incarceration', *Law & Policy* 35(1/2): 51–80.

Polaschek, D. (2012), 'An appraisal of the risk-need-responsivity (RNR) model of offender rehabilitation and its application in correctional treatment', *Legal and Criminological Psychology* 17(1): 1–17.

Porporino F. (2010), 'Bringing sense and sensitivity to corrections: From programmes to "fix" offenders to services to support desistance', in Brayford, J., Cowe, F. and Deering, J. (eds) *What Else Works? Creative Work with Offenders.* Cullompton, UK: Willan Publishing.

Raynor, P. (2004a), 'Rehabilitative and reintegrative approaches', in Bottoms, A., Rex, S. and Robinson, G. (eds) *Alternatives to Prison: Options for an Insecure Society.* Cullompton, UK: Willan Publishing.

Raynor, P. (2004b), 'Opportunity, motivation and change: Some findings from research on resettlement', in Burnett, R. and Roberts, C. (eds) *What Works in Probation and Youth Justice.* Cullompton, UK: Willan Publishing.

Raynor, P. (2008), 'Community penalties and Home Office research: On the way back to "nothing works"?', *Criminology & Criminal Justice* 8(1): 73–87.

Rex, S. (1999), 'Desistance from offending: Experiences of probation', *The Howard Journal of Criminal Justice* 36(4): 366–383.

Robinson, G. and McNeill, F. (2008), 'Exploring the dynamics of compliance with community penalties', *Theoretical Criminology* 12(4): 431–449.

Schinkel, M. (2015), *Being Imprisoned. Punishment, Adaptation and Desistance*. Basingstoke, UK: Palgrave.

Schinkel, M. and Nugent, B. (forthcoming), 'The pains of desistance', *Criminology & Criminal Justice*.

Taxman, F., Henderson, C. and Lerch, J. (2010), 'The sociopolitical context of reforms in probation agencies: Impact on adoption of evidence-based practices', in McNeill, F., Raynor, P. and Trotter, C. (eds) *Offender Supervision: New Directions in Theory, Research and Practice*. Cullompton, UK: Willan Publishing.

Von Drehle, D. (2010), 'Why crime went away: The murder rate in America is at an all-time low. Will the recession reverse that?', *Time Magazine*, 22 February: 22–25.

Wacquant (2010), 'Prisoner re-entry as myth and ceremony', *Dialectical Anthropology* 34: 605–620.

Weaver, B. (2015), *Offending and Desistance. The Importance of Social Relations*. London: Routledge.

DIVERSITY OR CONGRUENCE?

Sketching the future: an afterword

Joanna Shapland, Stephen Farrall and Anthony Bottoms[1]

The aim of this book was to bring together the leading researchers from key studies of desistance from around the world. In particular, we believed that several of the major longitudinal studies of criminality over the life course had now reached the point where their subjects were in their twenties, thirties and older, so that many were reducing their commission of crime, rather than increasing it. It means that we have reached a time at which it is possible to compare and contrast studies and findings from different countries, different populations and different cultural and economic contexts. Are findings similar? Is there one process of desistance? How is desistance mediated or affected by life events such as acquiring a stable life partner, or changes in employment? How do societal changes impinge? What influence do the person's own decisions and agency bring to bear?

We asked each of the contributors to this volume to summarise their own research findings and those of their colleagues over the course of their studies. For some of them, this was a major endeavour, given the very considerable number of publications on that study – and we are very grateful for the succinct, theoretically informed work that has resulted. We also asked them to indicate what they felt to be the key next questions for desistance research – what we don't know, where there are gaps, where theories need to be tested further.

In this afterword, we cannot attempt to summarise all the insights that have resulted. That would be an impossible task. We believe, though, that we can point out some of the insights that have resulted from the discussions between the attendees at the conference of the papers that have given rise to the chapters in this volume, and also reflect on some of the distinctions between desisters' experiences in different countries and from different perspectives. In doing so, although there are three authors named at the head of this afterword, there are in fact some 50 contributors, because this stems from all the discussions between presenters and those commenting, brought together in a number of 'ideas' sessions during the conference.

In attempting these tasks, we are very aware that we are writing at one point in history and so our conceptions of societal influences are culturally and politically biased to this point in time. Studies of desistance are largely based on Western countries, in particular on Europe, North America and Australia – there is at present very little known about processes of desistance in other parts of the world, so there is no possibility of any universal theory or set of explanations. Second, this is a time immediately after the world's financial systems have gone through a series of shocks and in which there is real austerity in a number of countries. That austerity has increased unemployment and is often increasing economic inequality, in terms of the gap between more and less economically successful members of society. Desisting offenders tend to be towards the bottom of the economic pile – and as people desist, necessarily the amount by which their household budget is constituted by criminally acquired income decreases. Desistance may often go hand in hand with decreased income. In periods of austerity, any job is hard to come by for any young (or older) person. For those marked by criminal records and often without the skills or paper qualifications others will have, it is even harder.

As structural inequality increases, prospects for desisters will tend to decrease. What we do not know is the extent to which the advantages of desistance (particularly less attention from criminal justice) still outweigh its disadvantages (particularly its economic difficulties during times of precarious employment). Desistance studies unfortunately have not covered previous periods of austerity (as in the last century, for example). Hence, we do not know exactly how this may be affecting desisters' choices and opportunities. Both the contributions to this volume and this afterword have to be seen as products of their place and time. Neither can we predict the future. We know there is a relationship between structural conditions and the opportunities for desistance (Farrall *et al.* 2010), but we do not know whether current increasing uncertainties through financial shocks, migration and disorder will continue to lead to growing inequality (a band of the wealthy and the comfortable sitting on top of a large underclass), or whether we will, for example, see a growth in alternative modes of living or gaining income (through barter systems, or the informal economy).

In comparing and contrasting between the results of different studies and their theoretical underpinnings at this moment in time, we need to set out both what forms a shared understanding between desistance researchers – congruence – and where there is disagreement or difference between the experiences of those in different places or at different ages – diversity. We shall start by trying to set out the congruent elements.

Moving forward in understanding desistance

Perhaps the most far-reaching realisation, which has affected criminological thinking in the last decade or two, is that desistance occurs. Put another way, it is now clear that most people desist from the commission of crime, however minor or persistent their offending may be. Criminology has been marked by the amount of attention paid in the twentieth century to people's progress *into* crime – particularly in adolescence (Rutter *et al.* 1998). It is now a truism to say that many different elements to do with genetics, individual attitudes and morals, families, schools, societal structures and peer groups contribute to the path into crime and the rise in the likelihood that young people will commit crime in adolescence. It is also clear that individual and areal factors interact in that progression into crime (Wikström *et al.* 2012). Much less attention has been paid to those in their twenties, thirties, forties and above. It has sometimes been assumed, particularly in the popular media, that once a criminal, always a criminal. Until recently, we have had very little idea of what influences offending or non-offending in adulthood – and as a result, it was not known who was desisting from crime and with what this was associated.

Empirically, the age–crime curve shows that participation in crime after late adolescence or the early twenties starts to decline – and this is true in many countries. Given the very small proportion of persistent offenders in the general population, however, there still remained the question as to whether persistent offenders – those who have offended several times and often come to the attention of criminal justice – also are likely to desist, or whether it is only those who dip their toes into offending who then give up, leaving it to the persistent. The longitudinal studies reported in this volume indicate clearly that the persistent can and usually do desist – however deeply someone is into crime at one point in their life, they can extract themselves later on. This makes the study of those who do desist, and how and why, far more important.

It is, though, much more difficult for those who have been more persistent in offending to desist than those who have fewer convictions or offences. This is clear from trajectory life-course studies and also from more qualitative work. The reasons for the greater difficulty for the persistent are clearly multiple. It may be because of the problem of breaking out of habitual behaviour, or being stuck in geographical neighbourhoods where criminal opportunities and challenges abound (Bottoms and Shapland, Chapter 6, this volume). Or it may be because of the smaller number of opportunities to gain legitimate work, or the reduced opportunities for those who have started their work career in prison, or the continued attention of criminal justice authorities (Halsey, Chapter 11, this volume), or the lower social capital of those whose friends can provide criminal opportunities but not other opportunities (Healy, Chapter 3, this volume).

The challenge then for desistance research is to chart these paths to desistance and to see whether it is likely that societal interventions, particularly those by criminal justice personnel, will accelerate or slow up progress towards desistance. If, for example, desistance is governed largely by agency, by the individual's decisions, then however helpful a societal intervention is, it will only be likely to have an effect if it comes at the point at which that individual has decided to at least try desistance. It is clear that agency does play a considerable part in desistance (see, for example, Carlsson, Chapter 2, this volume). What then affects individuals' decision making? Past research has majored on the influences of partners, employment and societal events such as war, which may act as 'turning points', affecting individuals' decisions (for example, Laub and Sampson 2003). However, more recent research has raised queries about the timing of such events and their causal pathways (Skardhamer and Savolainen, Chapter 9, this volume). Does marriage constitute a turning point? Or does the individual need to move towards desistance to become a marriage-eligible prospect? Some researchers have seen such causal turning points occur for some desisters, but their work and that of others suggests that a causal turning point seems relatively rare, with individual agency and environmental elements interacting, such that the environmental elements (partner, family, employment) may act to support desistance rather than occasion it (Cid and Marti, Chapter 4, this volume; Skardhamer and Savolainen, Chapter 9, this volume; Farrall, Chapter 10, this volume; Bottoms and Shapland, Chapter 6, this volume). There seems as yet little evidence that criminal justice interventions have major effects on agency and decisions, though prison clearly can provide a spur to thought about one's future life, and probation supervision, when desisters look back, may be having an influence (Farrall, Chapter 10, this volume).

Are we beginning to understand what kinds of environmental and structural elements or factors may be important in the road to desistance? It is becoming clearer that there are elements which support desistance, amongst which, prominently, are those that address the economic difficulties of desistance (i.e. filling the hole in the household's finances, which previously was filled by criminal activity). So offers of employment; social capital, which provides initial offers of employment or work experience (e.g. Calverley 2013); training, which leads to employment; and social capital, which helps in matching up employer and desister (e.g. probation officers, see Healy, Chapter 3, this volume) can all help fill that gap. Criminal justice interventions, which 'seal' criminal records to mitigate their negative effects on acquiring legitimate income similarly will help (see Uggen and Blahnik, Chapter 12, this volume; Kurlychek et al., Chapter 13, this volume), whilst policies which tighten the effect of past criminal records (such as making employers undertake criminal records checks) will be unhelpful (Farrall et al. 2010).

Social influences are also obviously key. Having offending peers, even if one has made a firm decision to desist, provides temptation, which may prove too much. Having pro-social influences around, if those influences are important to the individual, particularly at times of stress, is also key. So, having a partner and the transitions to roles such as being married (or divorced) or being a parent are important, though they do not form the whole explanation (Blokland and De Schipper, Chapter 8, this volume). Equally, the support of families for those in prison was significant in Cid and Marti's study (Chapter 4, this volume). Whatever the final view on the timing problem, having pro-social partners around maintains the impetus to desist, whether or not it directly causes desistance.

We know less, though, about areal influences, except in as far as they are synonymous with the presence or absence of important others. The important strand of work on the path into crime, which shows interactions between individual and neighbourhood (e.g. Wikström et al. 2012), is as yet absent from desistance research. There may be several reasons for this. One is that the relatively regimented regime to which Western children are subject (with its separations in place and time of home, school and leisure pursuits) becomes much more fluid after school age, if the person is not attending further education. Offenders, and so desisters, typically have poor educational records and few qualifications and, at least at the start of desistance, are unlikely to be in educational establishments, training or employment and so have sharply place-defined lives.

In the Sheffield Desistance Study (Bottoms and Shapland, Chapter 6, this volume), we found that it was very difficult to replicate the space–time diaries that have been so fruitful in adolescence studies – because our persistent offenders' lives were often full of day-to-day problems, so in retrospect they could not remember exactly what they were doing on a given day (see also Mulvey and Schubert, Chapter 7, this volume). Yet environmental criminology shows us that place is key to criminal opportunities and, we would venture to suggest, possibly legitimate opportunities as well.

If desistance is learning to live a non-criminal (or at least much less criminal) life outside carceral institutions, then desistance must also be about forging new spatial pathways in one's environment. To our knowledge, there has been little research which tracks persisters and desisters across space. Is it the case that desisters tend to go through a process of diachronic self-control (deliberately not going to offending-related places so that one is not subsequently subjected to temptation – Bottoms and Shapland, Chapter 6, this volume)? Or do desisters limit their lives to 'safe' places like their home? Do those who continue to offend travel more or less widely than those who are desisting? What are the spatial proportions of any distance involved? Do variations in the spatial dynamics of desistance play out at neighbourhood level, the level of the city or at regional levels?

One study which has attempted to throw further light on these matters is that by Farrall et al. (2014), who found that desisters (when compared to persisters) spent more time at work, more time engaged in family routines and/or undertaking voluntary activities, whilst persisters tended to spend more time relaxing at home, out socialising and/or doing 'not much'. Similarly, former injecting drug users made quite large 'leaps' between cities and regions (in their efforts to 'get clean'), whilst those who continued to use street drugs reported feeling 'entrapped' by social and criminal justice workers in neighbourhoods blighted by crime (Hunter and Farrall 2015).

A further factor may be that desisters may be less likely to travel, for purely economic reasons (lack of funds). Is this another obstacle to desistance, in that it may be particularly difficult for desisters, without the support of others, to move into new environments and learn less-offending pathways?

Differences in paths to desistance

Some congruent elements to desistance can, therefore, be seen from the progress of research into desistance. Yet there is clearly fluidity in paths to desistance. There seems to be no one identical track followed by every person who desists. Some may be majorly influenced by external events; others primarily take their own agentic path. Some may 'knife off' (Maruna 2001) their former selves as almost another person – 'what I did when I was younger'. Others may have a smoother transition in self-identity – or even never have seen themselves as an offender at all – 'offender' was a label applied by others (Shapland and Bottoms 2011).

It is also important to be open to the possibility that, as well as individual differing paths, different demographic or cultural groups may follow different paths to desistance (or the same path at a different pace, or for different reasons). The quest for *one* theory of desistance may be a chimera, because, for example, women's paths may be fundamentally different to those of men, or those of the young to those adopted by the older. Equally, they may vary by cultural beliefs and practices (that is to say, the presence or absence of a religious belief, the 'rehabilitative tone' of that belief, or differing levels of penetration in the labour market, or ways of organising families). For example, Adam Calverley's (2013) work suggests that religious belief was absent in the narratives of Black-British men as they desisted, whilst for British-Indian men religious events (such as weddings) offered chances for networking and securing employment, whilst for British-Bangladeshi men Islam provided a 'script' and set of personal goals (being a good Muslim, getting married, having a family), which fostered reform. Perhaps what is needed is a theory, which is sufficiently flexible to remain universal whilst retaining the ability to deal with diversity.

Research on the path *into* crime has tended to suggest that this is mostly similar for different adolescents, at least in the West (though there is still much debate about the major differences in criminality between young men and young women). However, this may be an effect of societal similarity in the lives of adolescents (driven by mandatory school attendance ages, school curricula and the media). There may be greater differences in adulthood and so, as well as multiple influences on desistance there may be multiple paths *out of* crime. But these differences may be subtle: for example, whilst much research suggests that men find employment schemes useful in finding work and hence desistance, other studies suggest that women find similar schemes important – but largely for the social networks they build rather than for the jobs they may lead to. Similarly for women, what may be key may be leaving intimate relationships, which have led to offending in the past, rather than building new relationships, with the latter appearing to be important for many men. In 'ideas sessions' at the conference, which spawned this volume, we encouraged delegates to debate the extent to which their studies showed there was one path, or several, depending on the demographics of age, gender, social capital and country.

Age and maturation

The chapter by Loeber *et al.* (Chapter 5, this volume) reminds us that desistance does not merely occur in the twenties or thereafter (on the downslope of the age–crime curve), but starts early in life. There is desistance for some in childhood and in adolescence, at a time when others may be increasing their criminality. Desistance is hence a concept, which is applicable from relatively early childhood (in terms of, for example, aggressive behaviour) to the end of life. Does it, though, have the same meanings and influences at different times of life? Is someone in late adolescence scared away from further criminality by the same portrayal of their 'feared self' (Paternoster and Bushway 2009) as someone in their fifties? If sent to prison for the first time at age 18, does this provoke the same reflection as at age 30?

We suspect that influences on agentic decisions and the environmental obstacles to desistance do vary with age, simply because both societally valued activities and social positions vary with age. Influences such as partners and being a father or mother become more relevant into one's twenties. Providing economically for dependants also tends to become more of a pressing need in the mid- or late twenties and thirties. Yet, all these elements can actually be concentrated in a very few years of young adulthood. Does their meaning then change as they become more familiar pressures, or everyone around also feels them later on in life? In other words, does it matter when the agentic decisions are made – can they be approached at any age, or is there a peak time period, after which one's life course is more set? Considering whether paths to desistance or persistence are the same at different ages in adulthood is an area where there is need for more research. Only very few studies have considered the path to desistance up to the seventies.

It is also important to bear in mind that chronological age is not the same as developmental age. As Mulvey and Schubert (Chapter 7, this volume) remind us, there is continuing psychosocial development throughout adolescence and onwards, so that the potential for desistance for individuals, biologically and psychologically, changes. Maturation, or active maturation (to encompass the agentic element) is therefore potentially an important part of explanations of desistance. Accordingly, a strong case can be made that desistance researchers, in the future, should not only take account of chronological age (and the question whether paths to desistance vary with age) but also should pay greater attention to data about both physiological and psychological maturity.

Gender: is men's desistance different from that of women?

The social and structural position of women in society is clearly different to that of men. Women's offending rates are also much lower, proportionately, to those of men, and their offending profile is different. Loeber *et al.* (Chapter 5, this volume) also point out that girls' developmental curves peak earlier than those of boys. Do these differences play through, though, into desistance? There is relatively little research into women's desistance, but from what there is, we can see that it may be helpful to distinguish between paths to desistance and the obstacles men and women may face in achieving desistance.

Giordano (Chapter 1, this volume) has argued that there may be few differences between men and women in terms of the cognitive and emotional processes of desistance themselves, though these will clearly be individual to that person and represent a constant dynamic between agency, the perceived world and identity. Similarly, the route out of addiction for those who are addicted to illegal drugs may also be similar to those of men. So, as well as thinking about gender, ethnicity, age, cultural values and so on, we need to explore the extent to which past offending careers (their nature, length and 'depth') act as structuring forces in desistance (Farrall *et al.* 2014).

However, the obstacles facing women who have offended and now wish to desist may be very different. Women with a criminal record may find it harder to find a pro-social partner – and their partner, if also offending or taking drugs, may be able to control the woman's life and behaviour. The effects of stigma on women may also be different in terms of types of employment being sought (white collar job employers may be less prone to give a chance to someone with a criminal record). Moreover, as has been pointed out, in terms of the path into offending, women who offend are often doubly stigmatised, as law-breaker and as violating social norms about the correct female role. When released from prison, they will perhaps be expected to provide care and support for others (such as children), rather than receiving care and support themselves.

We do not currently know whether desistance processes are the same for men and women, though we have no conclusive evidence to suggest the opposite. However, it is clear that it is societal pressures, structures and assumptions which play a large role in shaping the course of desistance. In as far as these are different for women than men, the obstacles and opportunities for women desisters – and the support they will need – are also likely to be different.

Social capital and country differences and similarities

Those who persistently offend are often those who have little conventional human or social capital. They have few qualifications and a poor employment record. They are not tuned into networks of contacts who will provide them with opportunities for employment or where to live. It follows that those who are desisting also start from the same point. However, it is possible to acquire social capital – contacts, support and signposting – from others close to them, or even from criminal justice and social agencies.

One of the key advantages to bringing together the scholars whose work is included in this volume is that it has rendered feasible talking comparatively – comparing the results of different longitudinal studies conducted in different countries, which thereby have been situated in different social structures and indeed philosophies about encouraging desistance. We are very aware that we come from England and Wales, which has, since the 1980s, stressed individual responsibility for offending and the task of the individual to desist (Farrall and Calverley 2006; Farrall *et al.* 2014). The effects of this in terms of social structures is that obstacles to desistance have tended to increase, with the increased stress on employers and landlords checking criminal records, dearth of employment for the low-skilled and so on. Supervision practices by the probation service have also become very much more attuned to desistance as an 'individualised project',[2] with home visits being rare and probation staff focusing on individual cognitive deficits and lifestyles, rather than including families, partners, peer groups or local organisations such as employers or faith groups (Shapland *et al.* 2012).

Engaging in comparative research is of course a hard task, with the dangers that one may misunderstand other cultures or social structures (Nelken 2002). However, bringing together researchers who themselves have been studying desistance in different societies brought into sharp focus the different societal and penal philosophies even between Western countries.

Cid and Marti's work (Chapter 4, this volume) indicates, for example, the importance of families in assisting rehabilitation and desistance for those in prison and released from prison. Prisoners who had active family ties and whose family took on board this duty were far more likely to desist. This was despite the very precarious economic situation in Spain and high rates of unemployment. Healy (2010 and Chapter 3, this volume) interviewed prisoners in the Republic of Ireland during the 'Celtic Tiger' economic growth phase and during the subsequent deep recession. She looked at whether prosperity promoted desistance and found that when the recession hit Ireland this had a real impact on prisoners' job prospects – but that here too family could, through the opportunities it could create and the social capital and support it provided, have an important protective effect.

Different perceptions of the state's role in promoting welfare, rehabilitation and building on the strengths that offenders have can also serve to reduce obstacles to desistance. McNeill (Chapter 14, this volume) indicated that he has noticed political discourse in Scotland shifting as a result of the discussion around possible independence, from more punitive criminal justice policies to more welfarist policies, which take a more strengths-based approach to prisoners and supervision (i.e. to build on prisoners' strengths to achieve desistance, rather than concentrating upon the original offence and prisoners' deficits). Skardhamar and Savolainen (Chapter 9, this volume) report that in Norway the government guarantees that it will support people into work, so that the Ministry of Justice is focused on getting people into employment, rather than on reconviction.

In practice, some of these differences may be more about words than deeds, but in the field of desistance words themselves can be important in providing encouragement and maintenance of agentic desistance. As Bottoms commented in the conference discussion, language can indicate the place of the offender in criminal policy – whether those words be about individualisation, responsibilisation and risk, or about support, opportunities and potential. Uggen also commented that the words can show the degree of 'othering' that the state (and society) wish to ascribe to offenders – and so the potential, or lack of potential, for reintegration. Moreover, those words can turn into expectations – that offenders will reoffend, but citizens will not, or that welfare claimants will scrounge, whereas those looking for work will strive.

In some countries, words have turned into programmes to try to support re-entry into mainstream society. This is the case in the USA, where there has been considerable investment in re-entry programmes (supporting employment, for example), but unfortunately little evaluation and some lack of implementation. However, the recent turn against continuing mass incarceration, although driven by cost factors, has allowed far greater discussion now of new ways to support prisoners upon re-entry and to encourage continued desistance. The moves to 'seal' criminal records (Kurlychek *et al.*, Chapter 13, this volume) and to consider the effects of records upon employment (Uggen and Blahnik, Chapter 12, this volume) are part of this.

Given that the ethos of criminal justice is that it is about offending, or preventing and discouraging re-offending, it may seem strange that we have only rarely mentioned the influence of criminal justice measures and policies on desistance. One reason may be that criminal justice policies are still largely national policies (or sub-national policies, as in the USA or Germany). Hence, research and evaluations, which take a national remit, cannot investigate variation in those deep-seated cultural assumptions and policies that form the essence of criminal justice in that place. There may be specific initiatives promoted by criminal justice or state welfare institutions, which may have some effect on the offenders who participate in them (such as employment programmes or substance abuse programmes). But promoting desistance may be about viewing offenders differently per se – not as continuing outcasts from that society, but to be brought back in and reintegrated. That may require almost a revolution in justice policy making and very different ways of thinking from practitioners in criminal justice. Currently, it is likely that practitioners and policy makers may not be very familiar with either desistance theories, or the practical implications of taking a more desistance-oriented approach (e.g. working with offenders to plan individual rehabilitation, emphasising strengths, working with the social context of offenders and those supporting them – Moffatt 2015). Working out the direction that revolution might take will require cross-national study, in which it is possible to consider different criminal justice policies and practices.

Let us take one or two examples. Farrall and colleagues (2014 and Farrall, Chapter 10, this volume) have shown that probationers, looking far back to the time they were supervised by probation staff, could recall what those staff were doing, and that they were continuously encouraging the probationers to move towards the pro-social, or desist, whilst discouraging the antisocial. Importantly, they reported that this work had 'sown the seeds' of their later desistance. In general, it would appear that probationers generally value an encouraging, but firm, approach by probation staff, which also seeks to help them overcome the practical obstacles they face in desisting (a place to stay, family problems, debt, employment) (Shapland *et al.* 2012). Probation staff value much the same things, but in England in the late 2000s they were not emphasising the need to help with practical obstacles (Robinson *et al.* 2013). Is that because probation staff were having to focus more on risk than on change? Similarly, moving towards supporting the family links that Spain and Ireland have found beneficial would mean a mind-change regarding the focus of supervision – that it should be the whole family, not the individual offender. In Ireland, Healy (Chapter 3, this volume) indicates that the probation service sees itself as having a role in enhancing desisters' use of agency. Is that compatible with the more controlling, limiting and electronically monitored tasks of probation and parole staff in much of the USA? In order for people to desist, they need (to some degree) to 'own' their desistance and that requires trusting them (and showing that one trusts them), and allowing them to learn, sometimes via trial and error, their own ways and techniques of staying out of trouble. Holding that observation at the front of one's mind when thinking about criminal justice policies, procedures and interventions, radically changes that nature of those activities.

These questions, in short, ask 'how can criminal justice (and associated state welfare agencies) impede or support desistance?'. Fundamentally, that question boils down to how criminal justice regards and is oriented towards offenders, whether as those who are likely to desist (but may not, and may periodically offend in any event), or as those who are 'dangerous', 'risky' or 'troublesome'. From the answers to that question stems a further question about whether the state wishes to put 'sticky labels' onto offenders or take them off and find ways of making them 'constructive labels'. The answers to these questions embody how the state and criminal justice systems (and other social systems) will see offenders, and so, to some extent, how they will see themselves and their role in what might be termed the 'co-production of desistance'. Perhaps also this is a question for criminology. If we are criminologists, then are we expecting crime? If, however, we are desistance scholars, then our focus may shift towards charting and explaining how desistance occurs and the interactions between agency and societal processes in shaping that journey. As well as changing what we may come to expect from the criminal justice system, the study of desistance may therefore change what we come to expect from the craft of criminology.

Notes

1 We would like to thank Keir Irwin Rogers, who diligently took notes of the discussions throughout the conference and so has enabled us to have a record from which to bring together this afterword.
2 Of course, desistance in many ways will always be an individualised project – no one can desist for you. The point we wish to stress, though, is that whilst this is true, and whilst we believe that those working with potential desisters need to attune their actions to the individual concerned, this ought not to lead to the neglect of wider organisations and institutions. Individualised provisions and responses are quite acceptable, but individuals live, work, rest and play in wider social, economic and cultural contexts, which need to be recognised and mobilised.

References

Calverley, A. (2013), *Cultures of Desistance*. Routledge: London.
Farrall, S. and Calverley, A. (2006), *Understanding Desistance from Crime*. Basingstoke, UK: Open University Press.
Farrall, S., Bottoms, A. and Shapland, J. (2010), 'Social structures and desistance from crime', *European Journal of Criminology* 7(6): 546–70.
Farrall, S., Hunter, B., Sharpe, G. and Calverley, A. (2014), *Criminal Careers in Transition: The Social Context of Desistance from Crime*. Oxford, UK: Oxford University Press.
Healy, D. (2010), *The Dynamics of Desistance: Charting Pathways through Change*. Cullompton, UK: Willan Publishing.
Hunter, B. and Farrall, S. (2015), 'Space, place and desistance from drug use', *Sortuz: Oñati Journal of Emergent Socio-legal Studies* 5(3): 945–968.

Laub, J. H. and Sampson, R. J. (2003), *Shared Beginnings, Divergent Lives*, Cambridge, MA: Harvard University Press.

Maruna, S. (2001), *Making Good: How Ex-Convicts Reform and Rebuild Their Lives*. Washington DC: American Psychological Association.

Moffatt, S. (2015), *Prospects for a Desistance Agenda*. London: Criminal Justice Alliance, available at http://criminaljusticealliance.org/wp-content/uploads/2015/03/Prospects-for-a-Desistance-Agenda-Full-report.pdf (accessed 15 October 2015).

Nelken, D. (2002), 'Comparing criminal justice', in Maguire, M., Morgan, R. and Reiner, R. (eds) *The Oxford Handbook of Criminology*, third edition. Oxford, UK: Oxford University Press.

Paternoster, R. and Bushway, S. (2009), 'Desistance and the "feared self": Toward an identity theory of criminal desistance', *Journal of Criminal Law and Criminology* 99: 1103–1156.

Robinson, G., Priede, C., Farrall, S., Shapland, J. and McNeill, F. (2013), 'Understanding "quality" in probation practice: Frontline perspectives in England & Wales', *Criminology and Criminal Justice* 14(2): 123–142.

Rutter, M., Giller, H. and Hagell, A. (1998), *Antisocial Behaviour by Young People*. Cambridge, UK: Cambridge University Press.

Shapland, J. M. and Bottoms, A. E. (2011), 'Reflections on social values, offending and desistance among young adult recidivists', *Punishment and Society* 13: 256–282.

Shapland, J. M., Bottoms, A. E., Farrall, S., McNeill, F., Priede, C. and Robinson, G. (2012), *The Quality of Probation Supervision: A Literature Review*. Sheffield, UK: University of Sheffield, Centre for Criminological Research Occasional Paper no. 3, available at http://www.shef.ac.uk/polopoly_fs/1.159010!/file/QualityofProbationSupervision.pdf (accessed 15 October 2015).

Wikström, P-O., Oberwittler, D., Treiber, K. and Hardie, B. (2012), *Breaking Rules: The Social and Situational Dynamics of Young People's Urban Crime*. Oxford, UK: Oxford University Press.

INDEX

Aboriginal Australians 219
active maturation 101, 108, 288; *see also* maturation
adolescents 5, 126, 245, 284, 287; developmental processes 133–137, 140; masculinity 73–74; maturation 288; Pathways to Desistance study 127–131, 134–135, 138, 139–140, 149; peak periods of desistance 88; Peterborough Adolescent Development Study 121n25; Stockholm Life-Course Project 32; transition to adulthood 105–108, 247; typologies of desisters 89; *see also* delinquency; young people
adult status 224–229
advice 189–190, 191
African Americans 230–231, 234, 235
age 145–146, 148–149, 163, 245, 287–288; age–crime curves 91, 95–96, 136, 155–162, 165, 223, 241, 246, 253, 284; diversification with 150; life-course transitions 152–162; as predictor of crime 144–145; Sheffield Desistance Study 105; transition to adulthood 105–108, 119, 147; *see also* maturation
agency 5, 28–49, 63, 127, 245, 248–249; concept of 43, 50; coping behaviour 56; definitions of 28, 35; gender differences 288; hope 275–276; Ireland 54–55; life history interviews 37–41, 45;

probation supervision 198, 291; Sheffield Desistance Study 109, 119; social and political context 41–42; Stockholm Life-Course Project 29–35; turning points 284–285; understanding 35–37
aggression: children 86, 88–89, 95; desistance rates 92; gender differences 95; psychosocial maturity 134
Ahonen, Lia 85–98
alcohol 189, 215, 219
Alexander, J. C. 36
alterity 215
American Indians 230–231
anger management 138, 270
Annison, H. 3, 6n1, 6n2
anxiety 197
Apel, R. 249
appeals process 257–260
Arnett, Jeffrey 107, 121n17, 122n27, 165
arrests 223, 230–231, 236, 238–239
aspirations 106, 194, 200
assault 151, 165, 205, 255; *see also* violence
'assisted desistance' 4, 189, 270
asymmetric causation 104–105
attachment 21, 79n17, 247
austerity 52, 53, 283
Australia 204–221

Baicker-McKee, C. 90
Bandura, A. 106

Banner, Michael 117, 118
Barnes, J. C. 163
Barnett, A. 93
Batchelor, S. 271–272
Baumeister, R. 17
Beck, J. L. 246
Becker, H. S. 38, 43
Beijers, J. 179
Bersani, B. E. 148
biological factors 146
Blahnik, Lindsay 222–243
Blokland, Arjan 105, 144–169
Blumstein, A. 76
Boone, M. 254
boredom 56–57, 115–116
Bottoms, Anthony 1–7, 43, 99–125, 187, 277, 282–293
Brame, Robert 230
Brassard, R. 119n3
Brehm, Hollie Nyseth 240
broken windows theory 86
burglary 22–23, 165; age–crime relationship 148, 223; Australia 205, 214; Criminal Career and Life-Course Study 151; impact of employment on 236–237; *see also* property crime
Burnett, Ros 115, 270
Bushway, Shawn D. 171, 244–264; 'desired self' 106, 109; 'feared self' 33, 75, 109, 250; identity change 14, 15, 17, 36; negatives 17, 23
Buttimer, Anne 192

Calverley, Adam 78n8, 188, 195, 278, 287
Cambridge Study on Delinquent Development (CSDD) 86, 90, 94, 102, 120n10, 120n11, 148
capacity to offend 95
Carlsson, Christoffer 20, 28–49, 73, 74
causality 248, 285; asymmetric causation 104–105; life-course transitions 170–171, 172, 174, 178, 180, 181
CCLS *see* Criminal Career and Life-Course Study
ceiling effects 87–88
Center for Advancing Correctional Excellence 276
Certificates of Relief 257–261

change: agency 31, 43, 127; correctional intervention 267; criminal justice agencies 277; desistance-focused practice 271, 272; desistance paradigm 273; early stages of 60; emotive 249; 'hooks' for 14–22, 34, 69, 170, 171–172, 180, 182, 249; identity 14–15, 17; longitudinal design 137–138; micro-mechanisms of 268; narratives of 71, 73; Pathways to Desistance study 129; probation supervision 190, 191; readiness to 250; Sheffield Desistance Study 105; signaling theory 256–257; theories of 275; timing of 171–172, 174, 176–179, 181; turning points 83, 170; *see also* cognitive transformation
children 86, 88–89, 95; *see also* adolescents; young people
Chiricos, T. 247
Cid, José 66–82, 290
citizenship 193–195, 275
CJA *see* Criminal Justice Alliance
Clausen, J. S. 36
cognitive coping strategies 56–57
cognitive distortions 25, 59
cognitive transformation 13–25, 56, 69, 71, 77, 109–110, 171, 277
cohabitation 66, 149, 151–152, 166n1, 174–175, 176
commitment 204, 247
communication 25
community context 130
community sentences 202, 204, 277
comparative research 289, 290
compensation 190
'complete respectability package' 12
complexity of people's lives 131–133
compliance 99, 100, 113, 211
conduct problems 85–86, 88–89, 90
conformity 76, 115
coping 54, 55, 56–60
counselling 57, 61
CRIME PICS II 51
crime prevention 1, 190
Criminal Career and Life-Course Study (CCLS) 145, 147, 149–162, 163, 164
criminal career approach 244
Criminal Justice Alliance (CJA) 3–4, 6n1, 278n1

criminal justice system 3–4, 5–6, 185, 291, 292; cross-cultural studies 202; experiences of 199–201; interventions 190; labels 246–247; lack of research 51; Norway 179; service user involvement 276
criminal records 105, 222, 229–234, 241, 261–262, 283; Ireland 59, 61–62; labelling theory 247; Norway 173, 175–176; sealing of 252–256, 261–262, 285, 291; Sheffield Desistance Study 102, 120n8; Spain 68, 77; stigma of 251–252, 253; Stockholm Life-Course Project 29; women 289
criminality 104, 222, 229, 287–288
criminogenic situations 76, 111, 147, 191, 212
criminology 222, 244, 283–284, 292; environmental 286; life-course 1–2, 36, 38, 39–40, 43–44, 46, 144, 170, 222; narrative 38–39
cross-cultural studies 202, 289, 290, 291
cultural beliefs 287
Curran, P. 127

data 94, 164, 202; Criminal Career and Life-Course Study 151–152; criminal records 175–176, 261–262; police records 173; registry 173–174; see also self-reports
de-escalation desistance 87
De Giorgi, A. 269
De Schipper, Niek 144–169
De Unamuno, M. 54
definitions of desistance 1, 3, 87, 145–146
Deleuze, G. 215
delinquency 24, 85–86; building down of delinquent acts 92–93; capacity to offend 95; co-occurrence of different forms 92; data accuracy 94; definition of desistance 87; developmental pathways 93; female 11–12; future research 96; gender differences 95–96; peak periods of desistance 88, 89; peer influences 19; Stockholm Life-Course Project 29, 30; typologies of desisters 89, 90; see also adolescents; young people
Denver, Megan 244–264
Denver Youth Survey 90
depression 197, 198, 249

derailments 25, 205, 212, 218, 249, 259, 260
desirability of criminal behaviour 15–16
'desired self' 106, 109
'desistance by default' 110, 111, 170
desistance paradigm 273–274
deterrence 254, 269
developmental pathways 93, 133–137, 140
developmental theories of desistance 146
deviance 245, 247
diachronic self-control 101, 110, 111, 113, 286
'Discovering Desistance' project 276
discrimination 75, 77, 78
divorce 148, 163, 285; Criminal Career and Life-Course Study 150, 152, 154–162; detrimental effects of 165–166
domino effect 133
doubt 35
drugs: age–crime relationship 148; Australia 205, 213, 215; Criminal Career and Life-Course Study 150; dealing 92; gender differences 288–289; illegal earnings from 224; impact of employment 236–237; Ireland 53, 55, 56–57; marriage impact on marijuana use 179; methadone maintenance programmes 59, 62; Ohio Longitudinal Study 23; Pathways to Desistance study 129, 130–131; probation supervision 197, 198; Sheffield Desistance Study 112, 116, 122n28; Spain 70, 79n10; spatial dynamics 192, 286; Stockholm Life-Course Project 34; support programmes 59–60; Tracking Progress in Probation study 189; U.S. arrests 230; welfare ban policy 238–239
Duncan, G. J. 179

'early desistance' 5, 111–114, 118, 119
earnings, illegal 224, 225–227
economic recession 52, 53–54, 67, 68, 77, 290
education 76, 213, 228, 238
Eggleston-Doherty, E. 148
Elder, G. H. Jr. 28, 35, 43
election outcomes 234, 238
emerging adulthood 121n17, 165
Emirbayer, M. 35
emotions 16, 25; emotional coping strategies 57–59; social experiences 18;

Tracking Progress in Probation study 194, 195
emotive change 249
employment 5, 11, 284, 285; age influence on 181; appeals process 257–260; Australia 213; causal relationship with crime 250–251; cognitive transformations 171; commitment to reform 171; criminal background checks by employers 229–230, 231–232, 254–255, 261–262, 289; criminal labels 231–232, 238, 241; data on 261–262; gender differences 287; 'hooks' for change 249; impact of imprisonment on 214; individual offending patterns 225–227; Ireland 53; job characteristics 182; labour market experiments 176, 182n1; life-course theories 30; loose claims about 181; maintenance of desistance process 180; maturation perspective 171; Norway 176–178, 179, 290; Ohio Longitudinal Study 12; pathways to opening up opportunities for 251–260; probation supervision 61, 197; reintegrative strategies 236–238; sealing of criminal records 252–256; Sheffield Desistance Study 104, 116, 121n16; signaling theory 249; social bonds 248; Spain 67, 68, 72, 76–77; stability of 163, 173–174; Stockholm Life-Course Project 34; structural barriers 50; Tracking Progress in Probation study 189; United Kingdom 66; women 289
England 3, 201, 275, 289, 291; see also United Kingdom
environmental criminology 286
equality 276–277
Esping-Andersen, C. 67
ethical issues 101, 116–118, 122n31
ethnic minorities 78, 278; age–crime curves 165; arrest rates 230–231; imprisonment rates 234; religious beliefs 287; Sheffield Desistance Study 103; Spain 68
Europe 254
evidence-based practices 140, 266, 273–274
excitement 115–116
exclusion 33, 53, 59, 215
expectations 58–59, 165, 290

F.-Dufour, I. 119n3
Fagan, Jeffrey 11, 250, 256
false desistance 93–94, 164
family 5, 19–20, 78, 247; Ireland 52, 53; life-course theories 30; Norway 179; Pathways to Desistance study 130, 131; probation supervision 291; Spain 67–68, 72, 73, 74, 76–77, 290; support from 285; Tracking Progress in Probation study 189; United Kingdom 66; see also marriage; parenthood
Farrall, Stephen 1–7, 127, 269–270, 271, 282–293; agency and structure 119; availability of legitimate identities 76; life history interviews 31; masculinity 74; probation supervision 187–203, 291; socio-structural issues 116; spatial dynamics 286; structural changes 66
Farrington, David P. 88, 94, 96n1, 148
Fast Track Project 90
'feared self' 17, 33, 75, 106, 250, 254, 259, 288
financial issues 115, 132, 197, 198; see also income
Finestone, H. 79n14
France 202, 254
fraud 93, 149
Fréchette, M. 92, 93
friends 57, 284; learning to live a non-criminal life 109; Pathways to Desistance study 130; Sheffield Desistance Study 104, 108, 114–115, 117–118; see also peer influences

gacaca courts 240–241
Gadd, D. 31, 74
Gasanabo, Damas 240
gender 24–25, 95–96, 199, 200, 288–289; 'complete respectability package' 12; employment schemes 287; narratives 164; typologies of desisters 90; see also masculinity; women
Giordano, Peggy C. 11–27, 34–35, 36, 56, 109–110, 111, 171, 249, 261, 288–289
Glueck, Eleanor and Sheldon 2, 22–23, 37, 180, 248, 265
Goffman, Erving 38, 229
Gottfredson, M. R. 110, 121n24, 134, 136, 146

Grasmick, H. G. 149
Groves, A. 206
guilt 194

habitus 199
Halsey, Mark 204–221
harm reduction 236–237, 241
health: prisoners 163–164; spillover effects
  on health care 234–235, 238
Healy, Deirdre 35, 42, 50–65, 79n16, 118,
  122n33, 290, 291
Heidegger, Martin 36
Hirschi, T. 110, 121n24, 134, 136, 146,
  247
Hitlin, S. 28, 35, 43
Hoffman, P. B., 246
Hollway, W. 31
homicide *see* murder
'hooks' for change 14–22, 34, 69, 170,
  171–172, 180, 182, 249
hope 275–276, 277
Horney, J. 127, 248
housing 66, 213, 217, 238
humiliation 206, 216, 217–218

identity 14–15, 16, 17, 267, 287; agentic
  selection of new 250; early stages of
  desistance 111, 113; ethnic 68, 199,
  200; gender differences 288; 'hooks'
  for change 21–22; 'hopeless offenders'
  269; immigrants 75, 78; Ireland 54–55;
  labels 245, 247, 259; 'liminal desisters'
  79n16; masculinity 74; sealing of
  criminal records 253, 254, 256; Sheffield
  Desistance Study 104; supervision
  approaches 275, 276; *see also* self
'imagined desistance' 63n6
immigrants 68, 75, 77, 78, 79n14, 80n18
imprisonment 75–76, 269, 277, 285;
  African Americans 234; Australia
  208–210, 213–214, 216; Criminal
  Career and Life-Course Study 150;
  data accuracy 94; growth in U.S. prison
  population 232, 233, 240; health issues
  163; impact on desistance 265–266;
  jails 242n3; Minnesota Exits and Entries
  Project 229; Pathways to Desistance
  study 138, 139–140; probation
  supervision 197, 198; release from
  prison 69, 204, 208, 216–217; Rwanda

240–241; Spain 69, 71, 72, 73, 78,
  79n10, 80n20
impulse control 107, 130, 134
income 115, 224, 225–227, 283; *see also*
  financial issues
indigenous offenders 219
individualisation 42, 289–290, 292n2
inequality 102, 267, 276, 283
infantalisation 216
intentionality 36
intermittency 43–44
interviews: Australia 205, 206–217;
  complexity of people's lives 132; Ireland
  51–63; life history 29–30, 31, 37–41,
  45; Minnesota Exits and Entries Project
  229; Ohio Longitudinal Study 12;
  Pathways to Desistance study 130, 139;
  retrospective research 100; Sheffield
  Desistance Study 102, 103, 106; Spain
  70–71; Tracking Progress in Probation
  study 187–188, 189
intimate partner violence (IPV) 22, 23–25
Ireland 50–65, 202, 290, 291
Islam 287

Jacques, S. 44
jails 229, 233, 242n3
Järvinen, M. 38, 39
Jefferson, A. 31
journey metaphor 265, 266, 267, 268, 269
juvenile offenders *see* young people

Katz, J. 217–218
Kelling, G. 86
Kennett, Jeanette 110, 111
Kerr, D. C. R. 148
Kierkegaard, Sören 113
King, S. 28, 33, 35, 42
Klingele, Cecilia 269
Kurlychek, Megan C. 244–264
Kyvsgaard, Britta 107

labels 237–238, 245, 250, 287;
  communities 235; 'constructive'
  292; discourses of failure 269; natural
  desistance 246–247; pro-social labelling
  274; stickiness of 222–223, 229, 232,
  241–242; stigma of 247, 248, 259; *see
  also* criminal records
Lacourse, E. 91

Laidlaw, James 116–117, 118
Laub, J. 2, 30, 66, 79n17, 104, 127, 180, 182n3, 222; agency 28; cognitive transformations 109–110; definition of desistance 145; family problems 19; informal social control 11, 12, 13, 136, 173; life-course transitions 20–21; life history interviews 37–38; marriage 114, 147, 179, 247–248, 261; onset of criminal activity 245; parenthood 148; retrospective study 100; social bonds 173–174, 245; turning points 72, 73, 110, 113, 170
Le Blanc, Marc 87, 92, 93, 96n1
learning to live a non-criminal life 101, 109–111, 286
LeBel, Tom P. 32, 34, 272, 273–274
legal rehabilitation 254
Lemert, E. 245
Level of Service Inventory-Revised (LSI-R) 51
Lewis, D. A. 274
life-course criminology 1–2, 36, 38, 39–40, 43–44, 46, 144, 170, 222
life-course theory 30, 146–147, 248
life-course transitions 20–21, 30–32, 144–169, 170–184
life event calendars 39, 46n4, 71, 164, 248
life history interviews 29–30, 31, 37–41, 45; see also interviews
lifestyle 5, 16, 244
'liminal desisters' 79n16
Lindegaard, M. R. 44
Liverpool Desistance Study 100, 272
Lloyd, C. 188
Loeber, Rolf 5, 85–98, 287, 288
longitudinal studies 2, 4, 137–138, 202, 282; Cambridge Study on Delinquent Development 86, 90, 94, 102, 120n10, 120n11, 148; cross-cultural comparisons 289; Ohio Longitudinal Study 12, 14–20, 22, 23; Pathways to Desistance study 127–131, 134–135, 138, 139–140, 149; persistent offenders 284; Pittsburgh Youth Study 86, 88, 94; probation supervision 187–201, 270; purpose of 215; Stockholm Life-Course Project 20, 28–35, 46n2; see also Sheffield Desistance Study
Lösel, Friedrich 268, 272

LSI-R see Level of Service Inventory-Revised
Lyngstad, T. H. 174, 175

maintenance 36, 180, 250
Manza, Jeff 234
marginalisation 14, 24, 33, 50, 207
Markus, H. 17
marriage 11, 147, 149, 163, 173–174, 247–248; age at 165; appeals process 259; cognitive transformations 171; Criminal Career and Life-Course Study 150, 151–152, 154–162; 'good marriage effect' 21; 'hooks' for change 249; Ireland 52, 53; loose claims about 181; maintenance of desistance process 180; maturation perspective 171; Norway 174–176; Ohio Longitudinal Study 12, 19; as predictor of desistance 228; Sheffield Desistance Study 114–115; timing of change 178–179, 261; transition to adulthood 147; as a turning point 285; see also partners; relationships
Martí, Joel 66–82, 290
Maruna, Shadd 57, 122n33, 127, 268, 269–270; active rehabilitation 257; agency 245, 248–249; desistance paradigm 273–274; Liverpool Desistance Study 100, 272; maintenance 36; signaling theory 249; turning points 113
masculinity 73–74, 79n15; immigrants 75, 80n18; life history interviews 40–41; male breadwinner culture 68, 77; Stockholm Life-Course Project 20
Massoglia, Mike 127, 137, 148, 171, 224–229
Matsueda, R. 43
maturation 245, 246, 250, 251, 267, 288; appeals process 258; imprisonment impact on 266; Ireland 63; life-course transitions 162, 170, 171–172, 180; Pathways to Desistance study 129, 130, 134–135; sealing of criminal records 253, 255–256; Sheffield Desistance Study 101, 107–108, 113, 121n20
Matza, David 35, 108, 117, 246
McGloin, J. M. 179
McNeill, Fergus 265–281, 290
Mead, G. H. 13, 15, 18
meaning of criminal behaviour 15–16

Meisenhelder, T. 37
mental health issues 25, 163–164, 209, 210, 277
mentoring 276
methadone maintenance programmes 59, 62
methodological issues: Criminal Career and Life-Course Study 152–153; human agency 44–46; Pathways to Desistance study 129–130; Sheffield Desistance Study 100, 101–103; Tracking Progress in Probation study 188–189; *see also* qualitative research; quantitative research
Minnesota Exits and Entries Project 229
Mische, A. 35
Moffatt, S. 3, 6n1, 6n2
Moffitt, Terrie 89, 105, 134
money: *see also* income
Monitoring the Future study 149
Monsbakken, C. W. 176
mortality 163–164
motivation 62, 248–249, 250, 251, 267; appeals process 258–259, 260; desistance-focused probation practice 271; sealing of criminal records 253, 255–256; Tracking Progress in Probation study 189
Mulvey, Edward P. 23, 107, 121n24, 122n34, 126–143, 288
murder (homicide): age–crime curve 223; Criminal Career and Life-Course Study 150, 151; decline in 99; Rwanda 240; sealing of criminal records 252; U.S. arrests 230

Nagin, D. S. 90–91
narratives 38–39, 40, 41, 70–71, 164, 272
National Supported Work Demonstration Project 224, 236
National Youth Survey 148
Native Americans 230–231
natural desistance 246–247, 251, 253, 255–256, 258–259, 260
nautical metaphor 265, 266, 267, 268, 269
needs 206, 270
neoliberalism 42
Netherlands 149–162, 163, 165, 254
'new penology' 61
New York 252, 254–255, 257–260, 261
Nieuwbeerta, P. 105, 147, 148

non-conformity 21
norms 114–115, 165
Norway 172, 173, 174–180, 290
Nurius, P. 17

obstacles to desistance 5, 289; ethnic minorities 278; Sheffield Desistance Study 101, 104, 115–116, 119, 120n14
offence-focused practice 271–272
Ohio Longitudinal Study (OLS) 12, 14–20, 22, 23
openness to change 14, 15, 16, 21, 34, 75
optimism 58, 63n7, 120n14, 271
organised crime 165
Osgood, D. W. 144–145, 149, 152

Pager, Devah 230, 231
Pardini, Dustin 96n1
parenthood 66, 148, 149, 163, 285; age at 165; appeals process 259; Criminal Career and Life-Course Study 152, 154–162; Norway 176; as predictor of desistance 228; transition to adulthood 147
parentification 206
parents, relationships with 19–20, 122n27
parole 204, 206–207, 210–211, 212, 214, 233; *see also* probation
partners 5, 179, 285; criminal records of 175–176; 'hooks' for change 21, 22; intimate partner violence 22, 23–25; Sheffield Desistance Study 108, 114; Spain 72, 73; women 289; *see also* marriage; relationships
Paternoster, R.: 'desired self' 106, 109; 'feared self' 33, 75, 109, 250; identity change 14, 15, 17, 36; negatives 17, 23
Pathways to Desistance study 127–131, 134–135, 138, 139–140, 149
patterns of offending 131–132
peer influences 5, 18–19, 20, 89, 285; adolescents 134; concentrated disadvantage 133; Ireland 57; Pathways to Desistance study 130, 139; *see also* friends
perceptions of events 138–140
persistent offenders 1, 2, 99, 134, 284; Australia 211; Ireland 51–63; Sheffield Desistance Study 100, 102–103; Tracking Progress in Probation study 196; *see also* recidivism

perspective 134
pessimism 59, 120n14, 246
Peterborough Adolescent Development Study 121n25
Pettersson, L. 29
PICTS *see* Psychological Inventory of Criminal Thinking Styles
'piling on' policies 238
Piquero, A. R. 251
Pirsig, Robert 6
Pittsburgh Youth Study (PYS) 86, 88, 94
places 190–193, 286
police records 173
policy 2, 3–4, 185, 245–246, 250–262, 268–269, 291; appeals process 257–260; individual initiated 256–260; individualisation thesis 42; 'piling on' policies 238; proactive 251–254; reactive 254–256; 'rock bottom' desisters 250; Spain 69; stigmatisation 238; United Kingdom 66; United States 128–129
Porporino, Frank 118, 122n33
poverty 53, 63, 67, 77, 205
Prior, D. 107
prison *see* imprisonment
probation 5–6, 187–203, 218, 247, 285, 291; debate on 272–273; desistance-focused practice 270–271; failure to maintain contact 197–198; individualisation 289–290; Ireland 60–62; research on 266; Sheffield Desistance Study 102, 120n8; *see also* parole; supervision
procedural justice 130
property crime 91–92, 99; Criminal Career and Life-Course Study 150, 151, 153, 154, 158–162; Pathways to Desistance study 129; Rwanda 240; Spain 70; United States 230; *see also* burglary; robbery; theft
prosocial behaviour 95, 291
prosocial labelling 274
prosocial networks 25, 181, 285
prospective methodology 100, 129
psy-complex 217, 218
Psychological Inventory of Criminal Thinking Styles (PICTS) 51, 56
psychosocial development 130, 134–135
psychosocial maturity 63, 288
PYS *see* Pittsburgh Youth Study

qualitative research 42–43, 44, 46, 63, 137, 202; complexity of people's lives 133; narratives 164; purpose of 215; Sheffield Desistance Study 101, 102; Spain 71; timing of change 171; *see also* interviews; longitudinal studies
quantitative research 43, 44, 46, 63, 171, 202; causal effects 180; life-course transitions 182; Sheffield Desistance Study 101, 102, 103–104; Spain 71

rape 151, 223, 230, 252
rational choice theory 41, 75
re-entry policies 78, 215, 272, 290–291
receptivity to catalysts 14, 18, 22
recidivism 224, 244, 246; data on 262; family support 73; fluidity 241; labelling theory 247; research on 248; Spain 70, 71, 80n19; *see also* persistent offenders
regret 35, 57, 194
rehabilitation 3, 272, 277, 278, 291; appeals process 257–260; Australia 210, 214, 216; cognitive distortions 59; imprisonment 76; legal 254; pro-social labelling 274; probation supervision 61, 62; sealing of criminal records 255; self-efficacy 80n19; signaling theory 249, 257; Spain 69; state's role 290
Rehabilitation of Offenders Act (1974) 277
Reich, A. D. 216
reintegration 207, 211, 224, 236–238, 241–242, 276, 278, 290
relapses 5, 95, 112, 180, 218
relationships 19, 132, 199, 200, 247–248, 276; gender differences 287; 'hooks' for change 21, 22; impact of imprisonment on 214; Pathways to Desistance study 130; Sheffield Desistance Study 114–115; *see also* marriage; partners; social bonds
religion 14, 149, 199, 287
repeat offenders *see* persistent offenders
replacement 87, 89
'replacement self' 14
responsibility 107, 113, 134, 289; citizenship 193; responsibilisation 216, 267, 290
retrospective research 100, 171
'returning points' 73, 79n17
Reuter, P. 171
Rex, Sue 270

risk factors 11, 31–32, 105

risk, need and responsivity (RNR) model 266–267

risk-taking 33, 246

robbery: Australia 205; impact of employment on 236–237; peer influences 57; sealing of criminal records 255; U.S. arrests 230; see also property crime

Robins, L. N. 85

'rock bottom' desisters 250, 251, 253–254, 255–256, 258–260

Roger, Keir Irwin 292n1

romantic relationships 19, 21, 22, 130, 132, 149; see also marriage; partners

Rose, N. 215

routines 192

Rwanda 240–241, 242n1

Sampson, R. 2, 30, 66, 79n17, 104, 127, 180, 222; agency 28; cognitive transformations 109–110; definition of desistance 145; family problems 19; informal social control 11, 12, 13, 136, 173; life-course transitions 20–21; life history interviews 37–38; marriage 114, 147, 247–248, 261; onset of criminal activity 245; parenthood 148; retrospective study 100; social bonds 173–174, 245; turning points 72, 73, 110, 113, 170

sanctions 265, 277; see also imprisonment

Sandberg, S. 39

Saner, H. 92

Sarnecki, J. 29

Savolainen, Jukka 148, 170–184, 290

Scandinavia 41, 66, 173

Schnittker, Jason 234–235

Schubert, Carol A. 107, 121n24, 126–143, 288

Scotland 201–202, 275, 278, 290; see also United Kingdom

SDS see Sheffield Desistance Study

Seamon, David 192

secondary desistance processes 18, 19

secondary deviance 247

self 15, 20, 245; agency 54–55, 56; belief in unified 206; change in one's self perspective 249; conventional 50, 51; 'desired' 106, 109; 'feared' 17, 33,

75, 106, 250, 254, 259, 288; ongoing projects of the 201; 'rebuilding' 199; 'replacement' 14; scorned 206; see also identity

self-concept 14, 126–127

self-control 101, 110–111, 113, 119, 121n25, 134, 136, 149, 286

self-efficacy 36, 69, 76; hope 275–276; immigrants 75; rehabilitation 80n19; Sheffield Desistance Study 106

self-esteem 44, 149, 194

self-presentation 38, 40–41

self-reports 94, 164; intimate partner violence 24; Pathways to Desistance study 129, 139; psychosocial maturity 135; Sheffield Desistance Study 103, 104, 115; Tracking Progress in Probation study 189

Sen, Amartya 116

sentencing 247, 252–253

sexual offences 150, 165, 252, 255

shame 58, 194

Shannon, Sarah 232, 236

Shapland, Joanna 1–7, 99–125, 187, 282–293

Shaw, C. R. 38, 45

Sheffield 3, 101–102

Sheffield Desistance Study (SDS) 99–125, 277, 286; early stages of desistance 111–114; ethical issues 116–118; future research 119; key results 103–105; learning to live a non-criminal life 109–111; methodological issues 100, 101–103; obstacles to desistance 115–116; relationships 114–115; theoretical framework 100–101; transition to adulthood 105–108

shoplifting 94, 95

Shover, N. 33

SI see symbolic interactionism

signaling theory 249, 256–257

Silva, Jennifer 121n17

situational action theory 117, 122n29

'situational self-binding' 111, 277

Sivertsson, F. 29, 31

Skardhamar, Torbjørn 170–184, 290

skills 217, 276

SLCP see Stockholm Life-Course Project

social bonds 79n17, 126, 245, 247–248, 249, 251, 267, 277; appeals process 259;

sealing of criminal records 253; Spain 72, 73; *see also* relationships
social capital 276, 277, 284, 285, 289; cognitive transformation 13; Ireland 59, 62, 63n9, 79n16, 290
social control 37, 149, 251; appeals process 258–259; criticism of traditional models 249; early stages of desistance 111, 112; informal 11, 12, 13, 21, 72, 74, 77, 136, 170, 173; marriage effect 181; sealing of criminal records 253, 255–256; social bonds 247; Spain 71
social coping strategies 59–60
social exclusion 33, 53, 59
social influences 17–18
social isolation 277–278
social learning theory 13, 76, 149
social networks 250, 276, 287
social norms 114–115
social reinforcement 22
social structures 33, 36, 289
social support 59, 71, 73, 74, 77–78, 147; *see also* support
Soyer, M. 63n6
Spain 66–82, 254, 290, 291
spatial dynamics 190–193, 199, 286
specialisation 87, 150
Spencer, J. William 30
spillover effects 234–235, 238, 241
spirituality 14, 22, 31
stable desistance 87, 94
Steffensmeier, D. J. 45
stigma 14, 33, 229, 250; criminal records 251–252, 253; labels 247, 248, 259; policy interventions 238; Spain 67; women 24, 289
Stockholm Life-Course Project (SLCP) 20, 28–35, 46n2
Stouthamer-Loeber, Magda 85–98
strain theory 149
street-crimes 192
strengths-based approaches 60, 268, 272, 276, 290, 291
stress 25, 149
structural barriers 25, 50–51, 52, 283
substituting desistance 87
suicide 164, 209
supervision 5–6, 187–203, 241, 285, 291; Australia 212; community 266; desistance-focused probation practice

270–271; desistance paradigm 273, 274; Ireland 60–62; redesigning 275–277; sabotage 269; strengths-based approaches 272; *see also* parole; probation
support 74, 77–78; Australia 206; community 276; Ireland 59; 'returning points' 73; Spain 67–68, 71; transition to adulthood 147
surveillance 212
Sweden 41–42, 46
Sweeten, G. 149
symbolic interactionism (SI) 13, 16, 35, 249
synchronic self-control 101, 111

Tanner, Jennifer 121n22
TARS *see* Toledo Adolescent Relationships Study
Taxman, Faye 276
technology 215
temperance 107, 134, 136
temporary desistance 87, 95
Tham, H. 41–42
theft 22–23, 93, 165; age–crime relationship 148–149; Australia 205; Criminal Career and Life-Course Study 151; desistance rates 92; *see also* property crime
theories of crime 244–250
Thoits, P. A. 36
Thompson, Melissa 224, 225–227, 238
time-space dynamics 192, 193
Tittle, C. R. 149
Toledo Adolescent Relationships Study (TARS) 18, 20, 22, 23, 24–25
Tracking Progress in Probation study 187–201
traffic offences 150, 151, 153, 154, 158–162, 166n4
training 57, 285
trajectory analyses 91, 135–136
treatment journals 46
Treiber, K. 110
Tremblay, Richard 86, 88
trigger points 190
'truth games' 218
turning points 5, 30, 72–73, 79n17, 83, 110, 248–249, 284–285; complexity of people's lives 132; critique of 180, 182; employment 176; imprisonment as a

turning point 265; life-course transitions 170, 171, 172; sealing of criminal records 253; Sheffield Desistance Study 113–114
typologies of desisters 89–91

Uggen, Christopher 127, 137, 148, 171, 222–243, 290
Ulmer, J. T. 30, 45
unemployment: austerity 283; Australia 205–206, 219; immigrants 75; Ireland 52, 53, 54; Sheffield 102; Spain 67, 74, 77, 290; structural disadvantage 25
United Kingdom: Asian minorities 78n8; 'Discovering Desistance' project 276; individual responsibility 289; probation supervision 201–202, 272–273, 275, 291; rational-choice policy models 41; Rehabilitation of Offenders Act 277; RNR model 267; structural changes 66
United States: age–crime curves 223; Center for Advancing Correctional Excellence 276; Certificates of Relief 257–261; criminal records 229–234, 241–242, 252–256, 261–262; immigrant communities 79n14; incarceration 240, 269; jails 242n3; juvenile courts 242n4; Pathways to Desistance study 128–131; probation supervision 291; rational-choice policy models 41; re-entry programmes 290; welfare ban policy 238–239
University of Sheffield 3, 4–5, 187

values 78n8, 117
Van Domburgh, L. 88, 90
Van Dulmen, M. H. 91
vandalism 86, 92, 93
victim counselling 190
victimisation 195–197
violence: age–crime curve 91; Criminal Career and Life-Course Study 151, 153, 154, 158–162; desistance rates 92;

intimate partner 22, 23–25; Ireland 53; probation supervision 198; sealing of criminal records 252; trajectories of 91
virtue ethics 118, 122n31
voting 195, 228, 234

Wacquant, L. 215, 269
Wadsworth, T. 182
Wales 201, 275, 289; see also United Kingdom
Warr, Mark 19, 114, 148–149, 181–182
welfare 67, 179, 238–239, 290
West, D. 148
'what works' approaches 266–267, 268, 270, 273, 274, 275
Wikström, Per-Olof 110, 117, 119n1, 121n25, 192
willpower 56
Wilson, J. Q. 86
women 24, 287, 288–289; age–crime curves 165; delinquency 11–12; employment of 68; imprisonment of 277; parenthood 176; parolees 210–211; typologies of desisters 90; U.S. welfare ban policy 238–239; see also gender
Wright, K. A. 133

young people 5, 83; attraction of crime 33; Australia 204–219; behavioural aspects of desistance 85–98; concentrated disadvantage 133; Criminal Career and Life-Course Study 150–151; employment 163; female delinquency 11–12; juvenile courts 242n4; life-course transitions 145; Pathways to Desistance study 127–131; risk factors 11; sealing of criminal records 252–254; Sheffield Desistance Study 99–119; Stockholm Life-Course Project 29, 30, 31–32; treatment journals 46; see also adolescents; delinquency

Zoutewelle-Terovan, M. 148